# Oilfield Revolutionary

Number Twenty-three

**Kenneth E. Montague Series
in Oil and Business History**

*Joseph A. Pratt, General Editor*

# OILFIELD
## REVOLUTIONARY

The Career of Everette Lee DeGolyer

## HOUSTON FAUST MOUNT II

TEXAS A&M UNIVERSITY PRESS College Station

This paper meets the requirements of ANSI/NISO Z39.48–1992
(Permanence of Paper).
Binding materials have been chosen for durability.
∞

Library of Congress Cataloging-in-Publication Data

Mount, Houston Faust, II, 1974– author.
    Oilfield revolutionary : the career of Everette Lee DeGolyer /
Houston Faust Mount II.—First edition.
        pages cm—(Kenneth E. Montague series in oil and business history ;
number twenty-three)
    Includes bibliographical references and index.
ISBN 978-1-62349-182-6 (cloth : alk. paper)—ISBN 978-1-62349-224-3 (e-book)
1. DeGolyer, E. (Everette), 1886–1956. 2. Petroleum geologists—United States—
Biography. 3. Businessmen—United States—Biography. 4. Petroleum industry
and trade—United States—History—20th century. 5. Philanthropists—Texas—
Biography. 6. Dallas (Tex.)—Biography. I. Title. II. Series: Kenneth E. Montague
series in oil and business history ; no. 23.
    HD9570.D44M68 2014
    553.2'8092—dc23
    [B]
                                                                    2014015262

FRONTISPIECE
Everette Lee DeGolyer seated on Potrero del Llano No. 4, the Mexican oil well
that skyrocketed the young geologist to success. Standing is fellow geologist
Leon Russ. (Everette Lee DeGolyer Collection. Courtesy of DeGolyer Library,
Southern Methodist University.)

# Contents

List of Illustrations *vi*

Preface *ix*

Acknowledgments *xiii*

**Introduction** Prospector *1*

1   **Student** *10*

2   **Geologist** *38*

3   **Executive** *70*

4   **Technologist** *98*

5   **Entrepreneur** *129*

6   **Scholar** *152*

7   **Technocrat** *174*

8   **Geopolitician** *208*

9   **Sage** *243*

**Epilogue** Legend *263*

Notes *269*

Index *319*

# Illustrations

Frontispiece:

   Everette Lee DeGolyer seated on Potrero del Llano No. 4.

*The Prospector* 2

Everette Lee DeGolyer, 1908  *17*

Nell Virginia Goodrich  *21*

USGS camp in morning, 1909  *26*

Topographic map  *29*

Plane table and telescopic alidade  *30*

Stadia rod  *31*

Idealized cross-section of an anticline oilfield  *34*

C. Willard Hayes  *43*

Everette Lee DeGolyer on a Mexican road  *45*

Camp at Potrero del Llano  *54*

Potrero del Llano No. 4 in January 1911  *57*

Everette Lee DeGolyer at desk in Tampico  *71*

Edwin B. Hopkins  *82*

Charles W. Hamilton  *83*

Everette Lee DeGolyer and portrait of Lord Cowdray  *86*

American Association of Petroleum Geologists,

   Annual Meeting, 1926  *91*

Idealized cross section of a salt dome oilfield  *101*

Gravimetric and magnetic survey of the Nash Dome  *109*

Prospecting for a salt dome with refraction seismology  *111*

Fan shooting with refraction seismology  *112*

J. C. Karcher *114*

Reflection seismology *117*

GSI seismic truck somewhere outside Dallas, 1931 *136*

Everette Lee DeGolyer and Lewis MacNaughton *144*

Everette Lee DeGolyer, 1939 *158*

*El Rancho Encinal* *169*

Santa Anna portrait in *El Rancho Encinal* Library *170*

Harold L. Ickes and Ralph K. Davies *201*

Ernest O. Thompson *202*

The Mexican Mission *216*

Everette Lee DeGolyer, Secretary of State Dean Acheson,
    and Charles Francis *244*

Everette Lee DeGolyer at Spindletop Commemoration
    Ceremonies *255*

DeGolyer and statue of himself, 1949 *264*

## Maps

The early years of DeGolyer *18*

DeGolyer's USGS activities *25*

Tampico Oilfields and Transportation System, 1912 *49*

Early geophysical prospecting *120*

Technical Oil Mission to Mexico, August–September 1942 *214*

Technical Oil Mission to the Middle East, December 4–16, 1943 *224*

Technical Oil Mission to the Middle East, December 16–24, 1943 *226*

# Preface

The story of Everette Lee DeGolyer is a dramatic one. Decades after his death, the life of the man Edward R. Murrow referred to as "one of the greatest geologists in this or any other country"[1] continues to attract interest. In his magisterial history of the oil industry, *The Prize*, Daniel Yergin wrote, "No man more singularly embodied the American oil industry and its far-flung development in the first half of the twentieth century than DeGolyer."[2]

In the last several years, DeGolyer has been contrasted with J. R. Ewing as a cultural icon of the oil industry, has been considered as an exemplar of the university-trained geologist, and has been the subject of a biographical "primer." DeGolyer has been cast as the hero of a historical novel and, perhaps more speculatively, has been depicted as a figure enmeshed in a web of intrigue surrounding the assassination of John F. Kennedy.[3]

But all DeGolyer researchers since 1970 have stood in the shadow of Lon Tinkle, DeGolyer's friend, biographer, and a remarkable figure in his own right. In addition to being a talented author, Tinkle was a professor of literature at Southern Methodist University as well as a book critic for *The Dallas Morning News*. Tinkle received his undergraduate education at SMU, from which he was graduated in 1927. He studied French literature at the Sorbonne, then returned to Dallas and his alma mater, where he began his career as a professor in 1932. His most celebrated work includes *Thirteen Days to Glory,* a national bestseller on the siege of the Alamo, which won him an unheeded role as historical advisor on the John Wayne film treating the same topic.

Lon Tinkle encountered Everette Lee DeGolyer following DeGolyer's move to Dallas in the late 1930s. The two men shared much in common. Both were Southwesterners with international connections, and connections with Mexico in particular. For DeGolyer, Mexico was the theater that launched his successful career as a petroleum geologist; Tinkle met his Mexican wife in Mexico City in 1938. Both men were book collectors and literary critics who would write for the *Dallas Morning*

*News,* although only Tinkle professionally so. The friendship that developed between them was easy, if not inevitable.[4]

During his lifetime, Everette Lee DeGolyer had no shortage of admirers, and several authors either began work on full-length biographies or sketched outlines of his life.[5] Tinkle closely followed the plans of others for a biography of the petroleum geologist and took up the project following DeGolyer's death, when it became clear that author Cleveland Amory would not complete his plans for a book. His research on DeGolyer was extensive and took far longer than Tinkle had originally planned. In addition to a significant number of interviews with DeGolyer associates, he spent considerable time with DeGolyer's collection of personal and professional papers, at that point still unorganized beyond DeGolyer's own filing system. The result of this effort was the publication of *Mr. De: A Biography of Everette Lee DeGolyer,* by Little, Brown and Company in 1970.[6] Today *Mr. De* continues to entertain readers with an enjoyable account of DeGolyer's life that reflects not just important points in DeGolyer's professional career but especially his hobbies: book collecting, publication, and literary criticism.

In December 1970, having just published *Mr. De,* Tinkle wrote to Wallace Pratt, a petroleum geologist and former Standard Oil of New Jersey executive who had been one of Everette Lee DeGolyer's longtime correspondents and friends. In this letter, Tinkle expressed his satisfaction with the book's reception and his regret at not including all that was relevant and important in the book. He then offered his own prognosis for future studies of DeGolyer. "There will be," he wrote, "and should be, many more [books] about Mr. De . . ." Continuing, he responded to Pratt's warm review of his book, commenting, "I am happy that you tolerate so generously an upstart in the field, but whose initial general survey may inspire others to more complete and more specialized studies . . ."[7]

This book aspires to fulfill Lon Tinkle's prophecy by offering a fresh assessment of the life of Everette Lee DeGolyer. When I began my own research on DeGolyer in 2006, I was well aware that any contribution I might make to historical scholarship would need to offer something beyond Tinkle's own work. I soon discovered that there was, as Tinkle himself acknowledged, still much to be said about DeGolyer. As have others who have encountered the Everette Lee DeGolyer Collection, I found that its 356 linear feet of documents contained a treasure trove of information, not just about DeGolyer's career but also about the development of the oil industry during the years of his professional activity.

This book does not purport to tell all of the stories about Everette Lee DeGolyer. Instead, it aims to place DeGolyer in the context of a crucial chapter in the history of the petroleum industry and understand his place in that story. What was his role in the remarkable professional, technological, economic, regulatory, and geopolitical transformations that took place in the oil business from the beginning of his career in 1909 until his death in 1956? Answering this question is a primary focus of this book.

Of course, as a biography this is more than a story of historical processes. It is the story of an individual life. Encapsulating and evaluating the life of an individual as versatile as DeGolyer is a difficult task. In the words of his friend and biographer Lon Tinkle, the life of Everette Lee DeGolyer "escapes labels."[8] No sooner does one settle on an interpretation of the man based upon one role that he played than one discovers another that seems incongruous with expectations.

In trying to structure my own reflection on the life of DeGolyer, it occurred to me that DeGolyer's versatility itself might provide a useful tool for understanding his remarkable life. In fact, that versatility was central to his remarkable success. Therefore, this book is organized semi-chronologically, with each chapter considering a facet of DeGolyer's identity. Inevitably, some chapters draw from material scattered throughout his life, as is particularly true in my consideration of DeGolyer as a scholar. However, generally speaking, the story will unfold chronologically, beginning with his birth in a sod house in 1886 and ending with his death in a Dallas office some seventy years later.

I hope that the result is a book that will be as interesting and edifying in its reading as it was for the author in its creation.

# Acknowledgments

This study of the life of Everette Lee DeGolyer has been a thoroughly collaborative project. Its completion would have been impossible but for the patience, support, and contributions of many. For those who have encouraged me along the way, I offer my sincerest gratitude.

The origins of this book lie in work begun during my doctoral studies at Southern Methodist University from 2003 to 2008, and there are many who provided guidance at this crucial stage. I am especially indebted to Hal Williams of Southern Methodist University, who directed my dissertation and first suggested that I consider researching DeGolyer. His faith in the project encouraged me to carry through despite the inevitable moments of doubt. Other members of my dissertation committee, then at SMU, provided important insights, including Peter Bakewell and Benjamin Johnson. I would also like to express my particular appreciation for the assistance of Diana Davids Hinton of the University of Texas of the Permian Basin. Her helpful criticism was invaluable as I revised the book manuscript.

In addition to those SMU instructors who served on my dissertation committee, I also am indebted to instructors there who equipped me with skills and insights necessary to this project. In addition to those professors already mentioned, I thank John Chávez, Edward Countryman, John Lowe, Alexis McCrossen, John Mears, Daniel Orlovsky, and Sherry Smith. I owe a special debt of gratitude to the late David Weber, whose own work remains a personal inspiration.

Throughout my research, the staff of the DeGolyer Library at Southern Methodist University provided support that made archival work a joy. I thank the director of the library, Dr. Russell Martin, as well as Pamalla Anderson, Cynthia Franco, Betty Friedrich, Joan Gosnell, Anne Peterson, Susan Schmidt, Kathy Rome, and Nancy Rubenstein. I would also like to acknowledge the assistance of Andrea Boardman and Ruth Ann Elmore of the Clements Center for Southwest Studies. Assistant Dean of Graduate Studies Barbara Phillips helped move the project along, as did Phyllis Payne and Mildred Pinkston.

I also thank Jeff Hesse, MD, who provided assistance regarding

DeGolyer's medical issues. Michael Keveney, Sean R. Keveney and Christopher A. Smith gave their own valuable perspectives on the project and reviewed sections of the dissertation manuscript.

During the dissertation stage, my colleagues at Southern Methodist University played important roles in shaping my thoughts and interests regarding this project. Clive Siegle provided knowledge of the road ahead. Matt Babcock, Alicia Dewey, and Helen McClure also gave useful perspectives on the process. My colleagues were particularly important in shaping the studies that preceded the dissertation: Anna Banhegyi, John Gram, Gabriel Martinez-Serna, and Eduardo Morales. George Díaz, Paul-Michael Dusek, Richard Ferry, and David Rex-Galindo also deserve credit for their assistance at various stages.

When the dissertation was completed in 2008, there still remained a vast amount of work to be done in terms of research, writing, and revisions. Since beginning my career as a professor at East Central University, I have enjoyed the support and encouragement of both faculty and administration in this project, and I thank East Central University's Provost and Vice President of Academic Affairs Duane Anderson as well as Mark Hollingsworth and Scott Barton, Dean and former Dean of the College of Liberal Arts and Social Sciences, respectively. Bringing this to completion would have been impossible without the support and assistance of my colleagues at East Central University. Scott Barton, Chris Bean, Brad Clampitt, Tom Cowger, Linda Reese, and Greg Sutton all provided support, guidance, and understanding as I navigated the process. Joshua Grasso of the ECU English department also assisted me with feedback on the manuscript and helpful advice.

Among the most important contributors to the research and revision of the book manuscript have been members of the staff at Linscheid Library. Without their assistance, this book could have been little more than a superficial repackaging of the dissertation. I thank the Dean of Linscheid Library and Distance Education, Adrianna Lancaster. I also offer my appreciation to Chelsea Baker, Dana Belcher, Angie Brunk, Jolene Poore, Theda Schwing, and Katherine Sleyko. I am especially indebted to those who helped me with interlibrary loan requests. Barbie Cranford, Barry Hardwick, and Wendy McKibben endured a barrage of document and book requests as I revised the book. This book would have been considerably poorer if not for their diligence.

The maps created for this book have significantly enhanced it, and I thank Gregory Plumb, Professor of Cartography and Geography at East

Central University, and ECU student cartographer Billy Ring. I also express my appreciation to photographer Sasha Garza, whose work with the Solon Borglum bronze, *The Prospector,* provided the perfect visual metaphor for DeGolyer's life.

I also owe thanks to the staff of Texas A&M University Press for their support and good work in the publication process. I particularly thank retired editor in chief Mary Lenn Dixon. I also thank Joseph A. Pratt, general editor of the Kenneth E. Montague Series, and associate editor Pat Clabaugh.

The road that I traveled in researching DeGolyer was easier to traverse thanks to other scholars who preceded me. Lon Tinkle's biography of DeGolyer influenced my own, and my work owes him a great debt, thanks to the wealth of documents regarding DeGolyer's life that he preserved, which are currently housed in the Lon Tinkle Collection at DeGolyer Library. I also owe an important debt to the kind assistance of Herb Robertson, who possesses an encyclopedic knowledge of the DeGolyer papers and whose careful scholarship informed my work. I offer my gratitude to Brian Frehner of Oklahoma State University for several reasons. His own research in *Finding Oil,* including his examination of Everette Lee DeGolyer, was helpful, as was his feedback on DeGolyer's years as a field geologist in Mexico and his insights into the publication process.

My thanks are also due to the docents of the DeGolyer home and the Dallas Arboretum, who kindly assisted me with questions and photographs. In particular, I thank Debbie Henderson and Jeanine Jenniges for their help.

I am greatly indebted to DeGolyer grandson Peter Flagg Maxson. An architectural historian as well as a family member, he provided important information that made the book far better than it would otherwise have been.

Over the years, many have encouraged me to pursue scholarship, and any acknowledgment of gratitude would be incomplete without the inclusion of the following instructors and mentors: Tom Benediktson, William Caferro, Russell Hittinger, Jacob Howland, Jayme Howland, Joyce Jones, Edward L. Penington, James Ronda, Ernest Smith, Victor Udwin, and Alan Weyland.

My deepest gratitude goes to my family. My brother and sister have played important roles in shaping the outlook that I bring to my scholarship. My father and mother have never failed in their patient support.

My wife, Betty, encouraged and supported me throughout the long progress of this work and shared in the joys and frustrations of my labors. My children endured the inevitable absences of their father as the book was written and were a chief inspiration for bringing it to publication.

To all these and any other contributors inadvertently omitted, I offer my heartfelt gratitude. For all errors in this work I claim sole responsibility.

# Oilfield Revolutionary

# Introduction Prospector

In 1916, Everette Lee DeGolyer purchased a two-foot-tall statue of a man and his horse. It was the work of Solon Borglum, brother to Gutzon Borglum, the famed sculptor of Mount Rushmore. Molded in bronze, the weary, bearded figure squatted beside his animal companion. Carefully handling samples of rock, the man peered intently, searching for signs of value in the specimens. Borglum's sculpture invoked the past century's quest for California gold and Nevada silver. Its title was *The Prospector.*

DeGolyer bought it from Tiffany's of New York for the not insubstantial sum of six hundred dollars. For the ambitious geologist, who had risen from humble frontier roots to the management of a major international oil company, the purchase of a work of art like *The Prospector* confirmed his professional success and reflected his sophisticated aspirations. However, DeGolyer's purchase of the Borglum bronze was no mere case of conspicuous consumption. *The Prospector* was more than a pricey display piece for DeGolyer; it was a metaphor for his life.

Just as the prospector of the nineteenth-century West had suffered want and weather in pursuit of his golden visions, even so had DeGolyer wandered the earth in search of black gold. Like the romantic figure of *The Prospector,* DeGolyer was also obsessed with the pursuit of his quarry. But unlike the lonely figure depicted in the sculpture, that quest led him away from the splendid isolation of "the field" to the crowded boardrooms of corporate America, to packed auditoriums of elite universities, and even to the buzzing halls and offices of the nation's capital.

DeGolyer's success was attributable to a mind both shrewd and imaginative. His genius lay in an uncanny ability to identify and embrace practical, potentially lucrative innovations. Combining business sense with scientific insight, he pioneered the use of geophysical technology in oil exploration. It was the wave of the future.

By investigating, advocating, and applying these new techniques in the quest for oil, DeGolyer helped to transform the art of prospecting into something more precise, more sophisticated, and more scientific

*The Prospector.* This bronze by Solon Borglum represented the romance of geology to a young Everette Lee DeGolyer. Today it is housed in the DeGolyer home, *El Rancho Encinal,* at the Dallas Arboretum. (Photo by Sasha Garza. Courtesy of DeGolyer-Maxson Family.)

than Borglum's old-time prospector could have anticipated. The most immediate impact of these changes would fall upon the men who made a living looking for oil, but the repercussions would affect many more. What followed was nothing less than a revolution in the oil industry, which made the lone prospector an increasing anachronism and secured a future for the corporate technologist.

At the very heart of this revolution was the role of chance in petroleum prospecting. For a man of science, DeGolyer had a surprising obsession with luck, reminiscent of the boisterous camps of the forty-niners. As he explained later in his career, "The oil business is a combination of skill and luck. If you are lucky enough, you don't have to be skillful—but no matter how skilled you are you have to be lucky too."[1]

For DeGolyer, the question of luck was part of the attraction of the petroleum business. A dedicated card player, he enjoyed the thrill of gambling in the high-stakes oil business as much as in a friendly hand of poker. Nevertheless, for the executives and investors of the petroleum industry *luck* did not mean excitement. It meant risk. As a geologist, DeGolyer's job was to minimize the role of luck in searching for oil. This, then, would become the impetus for an ongoing quest for more effective methods of prospecting. In this mission, he met with spectacular success. Considered from the broadest vantage, the innovative technology that DeGolyer applied to petroleum prospecting ensured the survival of the oil business and transformed the place of earth scientists in private industry and public service.

From 1909 until his death in 1956, DeGolyer would dedicate his life to the pursuit of oil. During these years, he took on many professional roles—as a businessman, as a public servant, and even, for a brief time, as a university professor. Yet there was never any doubt regarding his true vocation. Above all, he was a petroleum geologist.

DeGolyer's career spanned a transformative era in the profession of petroleum geology. By the year of his death, geologists played an essential role in locating new oil wells. Such had not been the case when DeGolyer took his first real job as a field geologist in 1909. At that time, many oilmen still held these "rock hounds" in contempt. And there was a reason for this dismissive attitude. The geologists of the day were frequently mistaken. Stories abounded of scientists who had made the strongest assurances that oil was or was not at this or that location. Inevitably, such stories ended with said geologists eating crow. And the most famous of these stories was also the story of the most historically significant oilfield of the twentieth-century United States: Spindletop.

In 1901, when DeGolyer was a young lad of fourteen, a Dalmatian mining engineer named Anthony Lucas drilled a well near the Texas town of Beaumont.[2] Located on Spindletop Hill, the well was a gusher, spewing seventy-five thousand barrels per day into the humid Gulf Coast air and firing the imagination of a generation of oilmen. It was not the birth of the American petroleum industry—that had come over forty years before in the hills of western Pennsylvania. However, Spindletop opened a flood of oil unlike anything before it. The well Lucas had drilled produced twice as much oil per day as the entire state of Pennsylvania. More oil would flow from the first six gushers of the Spindletop field than from the rest of the world's oil wells combined.

The discovery of oil near Beaumont opened new vistas to the oil business and helped usher in the motor age. It was a dramatic turning point in the industry—and scientists had little to do with it.

Actually, to say that scientists had little to do with the success of the Lucas well would be an understatement. In fact, three out of four professional geologists that had inspected the site discouraged the effort to drill for oil. This would have represented a significant consensus of opinion at a time when there may have been as few as five professional geologists in the state of Texas.[3] Therefore, the credit for the Spindletop bonanza owed more to the tireless promotion of men with limited experience in the oil business and no geological training whatsoever. Patillo Higgins was a colorful character who was not exactly an expert on oil. He had received four years of formal schooling in Beaumont before he "graduated" one day by climbing out of the schoolhouse window, never to return. As a result of a trip to the oil regions of Ohio, Higgins became convinced that oil abounded at a site near his Texas home. Spindletop showed many of the characteristics of a prolific oil region—oil and gas seepages and mineral springs—and he soon became obsessed with drilling there. With a little effort, Higgins found investors to join him in the venture. In 1895, he hired William Kennedy, a geological consultant, to evaluate the prospective field. After rejecting Higgins's theory to his face, the geologist publicly humiliated him in the Beaumont newspaper. As Kennedy put it, Higgins's effort to drill for oil was "a piece of extravagance only equaled by the foolishness of the advice under which it was undertaken."[4] According to orthodox geological theory, the Gulf Coast formations were too recent in origin to contain oil.

Fortunately for Beaumont, Higgins's faith in the hill was unshakable. As word of Higgins's claims traveled, it attracted the attention of Captain Anthony Lucas, who had already achieved some success as a mechanical and mining engineer. Lucas had significantly more education than Higgins, having studied engineering at the Polytechnic Institute at Graz, Austria. He had come to America in 1879, after an unhappy stint in the Austrian navy. Lucas traveled widely in the United States, working in a Michigan sawmill, a New York sugar refinery, and mines in Colorado, California, and North Carolina. In 1893, the thirty-eight-year-old engineer had turned his attention to the salt mines of Louisiana. Here, Lucas learned firsthand the peculiar characteristics of the salt-bearing hills of the Gulf Coast. Crucially, he noted that these formations often held not just salt but also sulfur, natural gas, and petroleum.

When he heard of Higgins's claims about a low-rising hill in East Texas, Lucas decided that there might be something to it.

Still, Lucas's advice from the professional geologists was discouraging. In 1900, Dr. C. Willard Hayes of the United States Geological Survey visited Spindletop. In later years, he would serve as mentor to a young Everette Lee DeGolyer. Hayes found little to encourage him at the site, remarking that he could see "no precedents for expecting to find oil in the great unconsolidated sands and clays of the Coastal Plain."[5] His colleague from the Survey, Edward W. Parker, concurred. Only Dr. William Battle Phillips, a field geologist with the University of Texas, had any positive remarks to make. Phillips believed that Higgins and Lucas might be right, but the weight of the experts was still against the venture when Lucas contracted with the firm of Guffey and Galey to drill the well.[6] After assembling a drilling team, Lucas proved Higgins right beyond all expectations when the well "blew in" on January 10, 1901.

However much respect the petroleum geologist commands today, the efforts of leading earth scientists did not contribute much to the historic moment at Spindletop—in fact, the achievement was despite them. Patillo Higgins, with no scientific education of which to speak, had made a fool of the experts. Anthony Lucas brought more experience to the task, but he too possessed no formal geological training. After DeGolyer had established a formidable reputation as a geologist, Captain Lucas himself wrote to him, saying, "The plain fact of the matter is that I am not a trained geologist [and] hence do not see my way to give interpretation to my—well—visions."[7]

However, by the middle of the twentieth century, earth scientists had become truly adept at interpreting "visions" of mineral wealth. Gone were the days when men with conviction and a little experience could regularly embarrass the learned scientist by discovering a major field where science had declared one impossible. Petroleum geology had developed rapidly since William Kennedy insulted Patillo Higgins in the *Beaumont Journal.* "Rock hounds" now recognized formations such as Spindletop as salt domes—geological structures that often contained a wealth of oil. In addition to advances in the theory of geology, oil prospectors had new and powerful allies: the petroleum geophysicists. DeGolyer played no small role in the introduction of these scientists to oil exploration. The geophysicists used survey methods unavailable to early geologists that allowed them to map rock formations below the surface of the earth.

The rise of these scientists was a slow process that took several decades. Spindletop was not their last surprise, but the discovery of the largest oilfield in the history of the United States during the 1960s indicated just how far earth science had progressed. In 1964, geophysicists, working together with petroleum geologists, were on the cusp of making this discovery. For decades, the federal government and private industry had been probing the remote reaches of Alaska for potential oilfields. Deep in the interior of the state, the spectacular Brooks Range rose to form an impressive watershed. The lands stretching from those mountains to the frigid Arctic Ocean comprised one of the most inaccessible and undeveloped regions in the United States: the North Slope.

The exploration of northern Alaska was far beyond the capabilities of small operators. The arctic climate and the limited to nonexistent infrastructure required the investment of large sums of money, with no guarantee of even a limited return. In Alaska, transportation of scientific apparatus might require the construction of track-mounted camps or even the deployment of helicopters for transportation of heavy equipment. Despite these challenges, some companies perceived real opportunities in this frigid land. In 1964, Richfield Oil Company of El Paso decided to send a team of scientists to Prudhoe Bay on the Arctic Ocean. Carrying complex devices that few but they themselves understood, the geophysicists working for Richfield detonated explosive charges across the Alaskan coastal plain, recording the sound waves that traveled through the earth with sensitive geophones. When the scientists attempted to extend their survey into the Arctic Ocean, they found that ice complicated their analysis. This problem they overcame by extending the geophones to the ocean floor in order to read the detonations more accurately. The data the team collected provided crucial information about the subsurface geology of the region. The news was good. After analysis and comparison with conventional geological surveys of the region, the recently merged Atlantic Richfield Company felt justified in risking a well.[8]

In January 1967, the company moved a drilling rig northward sixty miles from a disappointing "dry hole" to begin work on a well dubbed "Prudhoe Bay State 1." In January 1968, Atlantic Richfield surprised the world with the announcement of a massive discovery on the site. One of DeGolyer's many corporate legacies to the oil industry, the firm of DeGolyer and MacNaughton, was engaged to evaluate the extent of the newly found reservoir. Their conclusion was that the scientists employed by Richfield had discovered a stunning 5 to 10 billion barrels of oil at Prudhoe Bay. It was the largest oilfield ever discovered in North America.[9]

From the initial analysis of surface geology to the seismic surveys that preceded drilling, to the subsequent evaluation of the field, earth scientists were deeply involved in the Prudhoe Bay discovery. Without their collection of data, without their interpretation of evidence, without their recommendation to drill, no company would have been willing to risk the immense outlays of capital necessary to develop this "elephant" oilfield. The Prudhoe Bay well stood as a monument to the prestige and importance of earth science in the oil business.

DeGolyer's career fell between the two signal events of Spindletop and Prudhoe Bay. He witnessed and participated in the revolution that reshaped the industry during these intervening years. Indeed, he would be one of the minds most responsible for the transformation of the world of Spindletop into the world of Prudhoe Bay. The difference between those worlds was more than a matter of fundamentally different roles for earth scientists. It was not just that geologists and geophysicists had become central to the operation of the oil business. The same economic and technological forces that had transformed their place in the industry had also changed the industry itself and, indeed, global civilization. The oil industry had changed the world.

As DeGolyer entered the last year of his life in 1956, he must have been astounded at that transformation. During his childhood, the petroleum industry had relied on the marketing of a cheap illuminant: kerosene. Its days appeared numbered when Thomas Edison produced a practical, incandescent light bulb in 1879. But by the 1950s, oil companies had attained an unprecedented importance in the global economy, providing an affordable energy source for manufacturing and, especially, transportation. Oil had been an essential element in the Allied victory over Germany and Japan, and it was increasingly important to Cold War diplomacy. Oil had changed the very landscape of the nation. It had fueled the postwar move to the suburbs and was the sine qua non of Eisenhower's newly inaugurated interstate highway program. In 1900, it was still the age of coal. By 1956, it was clear that the world belonged to oil.[10]

The advent of "Hydrocarbon Man" would have been unthinkable without the assistance of the petroleum geologist and the petroleum geophysicist. In 1900, global production of crude stood at a little over

149 million barrels total for the year. By 1930, that figure had risen to over 1.4 billion barrels, although much of the new production was still not attributable to the earth scientist. However, with increasing application of scientific methods by 1950, production had climbed to 3.8 billion barrels. In 1956, total production was at 6.1 billion barrels. These staggering totals helped make possible the postwar economic boom that lasted in most Western nations until the crises of the 1970s.[11]

As the importance of the industry grew, so too did the stature of the new and essential professions of petroleum geology and petroleum geophysics. New technologies pioneered by DeGolyer and like-minded colleagues had transformed geology and geophysics from pure sciences to applied sciences. This was not without precedent. Industrialists and engineers had already begun to employ science in practical affairs on a large scale during the nineteenth century. The transformation of the petroleum industry came later, but its effect on the scientific professions associated with it was similar. As in other industries, the "practical" men of the oil business initially resisted the pretensions of the college-educated geologists and geophysicists. The irrefutable successes of the new technologies helped convince oilmen that the earth scientist was worth the significant expense of his employment.[12]

For some, the enhanced prestige of the earth scientists meant power—especially in the business community. From a subordinate and marginal role in the oil industry, many of these applied scientists entered the ranks of company management.[13] As early as 1920, trade periodicals were noting that geologists were ascending corporate hierarchies.[14] By mid-decade, the *Dallas Morning News* confidently proclaimed that the "Erstwhile Humble 'Rock Hound' Holds High Place in Oil Industry Today," noting that many now served as business executives.[15] As the decades passed, business and earth science only drew closer. Roy L. Lay, who had worked under DeGolyer and later assumed the presidency of the Society of Exploration Geophysicists, declared in 1954, "The geophysicist of today, after more than a quarter century of exploration, is a businessman as well as a scientist."[16] As corporate promotion confirmed, there was greater respect for earth scientists than ever before within the industry. DeGolyer was but one of many applied scientists who made the transition from the field to the boardroom with marked success. Earth science had come a long way since Spindletop.

In addition to their growing influence within the corporations, geologists and geophysicists were increasingly relevant in the public sphere. During the nineteenth century and into the twentieth century, government intervention in the petroleum industry had come primarily at the behest of small operators fearful of competition with larger integrated combinations—most especially John D. Rockefeller's Standard Oil. Concerns about the dangers of monopoly continued, even after the US Supreme Court ordered the breakup of Standard Oil in 1911. But reformers increasingly turned their attention away from the issue of fair competition and toward a new concern: conservation.[17]

Conservationists sought to shield the nation's resources from the ravages of reckless exploitation and to develop them rationally. Many oilmen took up the conservation cause because they believed that limited production would raise the price of crude. Whatever the motives, conservation required the participation of earth scientists in order to succeed. Rational development meant scientific development, and only the geologists and geophysicists, if anyone, understood the oilfields well enough to formulate such a plan. Once more, the technologies that DeGolyer promoted were essential to the process. Geophysical methods and subsurface analysis were crucial tools with which scientists would analyze oilfields and make recommendations for responsible development. Some geologists offered such advice from within the industry; others did so through public service. DeGolyer did so in both the private and the public sector. The advent of the Cold War increased the already significant influence of these scientific advisors on national policy.

In the continuing prosperity of the petroleum industry and in the increasing prominence of the earth scientists in industry and government, DeGolyer was both a catalyst and an exemplar. He was a catalyst because of his eager and prescient promotion of technologies that changed the industry and the role of the scientist within it. He was an exemplar because his career so clearly reflected the growing prestige of scientific professionals—from the academy to the field, to the boardroom, to Washington. The story of his life is also the story of this revolution that transformed the way that the world finds and exploits the most important resource of our day: oil.

# 1 | Student

*If in future life I should turn some bright celestial corner and*
*come upon a patch of dull red earth, my throat would tighten*
*and tears of joy would fill my eyes. I was born in a red land. I*
*was raised in a red land. I live in a red land and it is my land.*
– Everette Lee DeGolyer in an undated reflection[1]

For Everette Lee DeGolyer, the "red earth" of the western plains was in his blood. Born in Kansas in 1886, he spent his childhood in Missouri and his youth in the "red land" of Oklahoma. DeGolyer venerated this soil with all the fervor of a native son. But for DeGolyer, this earth had a special meaning that went beyond the typical, nostalgic associations. It not only colored the experiences of his youth but provoked his intellectual curiosity as well. The red earth of the old Southwest would tantalize his young imagination with visions of buried treasure. It would nurture an adolescent interest in the sciences. It would become an arena of his ambitions as a young man and the origin of his celebrity in adulthood. True, the red mantle that draped the surface of his native land was also only the outer layer of his interest. His curiosity and his aspirations would draw him to the ever deeper recesses of the earth, where he would at last find the buried treasure of which he had dreamed as a child. But however deeply he delved under the land, he remembered where he began. For DeGolyer, this first red earth of his youth was the first love of a scientist in the making—the first love of a geologist.

Geologists are made, not born, and it took years of sustained interest, hard study, and determined work before DeGolyer could count himself a member of that scientific fraternity. During those years, he struggled—both financially and academically—to earn an education. He struggled and he prevailed. DeGolyer would memorize the various categories of rock and grow to understand the forces that created them. He would become adept in the use of the instruments of the science. With experience, he would develop into a competent cartographer. He would obtain the intellectual tools that would allow for the spectacular successes of his later years. He received this education in his "red land."

DeGolyer's dedication to his native soil came in spite of his family's recent arrival on the western plains. That was not so unusual. The vast majority of those who made their homes in the area were relatively recent arrivals—even many of the Indians. They had all been a part of the vaguely westward progress of the United States. The DeGolyer family had also been a part of that national and international migration, tracing back their course across the continent to the eighteenth-century coastal colonies of France and Great Britain.

Everette Lee DeGolyer's father was the descendant of Jacques de Golier, a French soldier who abandoned Canada for the British colony of Massachusetts in the years before the French and Indian War. In Massachusetts, he would marry an English woman and settle down, but his children inherited Jacques's propensity for wandering. The year 1806 found his son, Anthony DeGolyer—now spelled with a "y"—having crossed the Appalachian Mountains, in the newly founded state of Ohio. Anthony's son, Jacob, traveled even further west to Indiana. It was there, in the town of Napoleonville, that Jacob's son, John, was born in 1859.

John DeGolyer, Everette Lee DeGolyer's father, was a dreamer and an optimist. Ever ready to seize an opportunity and willing to take risks, he suffered from bad fortune and a lack of business sense. From his forebears, John inherited a restless spirit, and what began as wandering from job to job soon became wandering from town to town. Continuing the family migration westward, he traveled to Illinois, where he met the woman whom he would marry, Narcissus Kagy Huddle.[2]

Narcissus was born in Marion County, Illinois, in 1863, of Swiss-German descent.[3] In contrast to her more convivial husband, she was a somber figure, thrifty and responsible. As her daughter-in-law remembered, "[S]he was a wonderful woman, but beside her husband she seemed to lack humor."[4] Narcissus wed John in the spring of 1883.[5] Shortly thereafter, the two, in the company of John's family, moved to Oxford, Kansas. John and his brother, Lee, built a two-story house there, and John worked for some time with a mercantile firm in the town.[6] However, in 1886, the family left Oxford for the windswept plains of western Kansas.[7] They settled near the town of Greensburg, a rural community situated just east of the hundredth meridian. The town was but one county removed from the notorious Dodge City, where gun smoke of western legend still lingered in the air. Most of the towns of western Kansas sought to downplay this notoriety and emphasize the economic potential of the region.[8] Undoubtedly, this was what attracted John and Narcissus DeGolyer to the place and encouraged their dreams of success.

Young Everette Lee DeGolyer was born in this wild land of possibility. His father had selected a homestead near the small town of Greensburg in the summer of 1886. On that land, he built a humble sod house for his then pregnant wife.[9]

The young couple gave the name Everette Lee to their son, who was born on October 9, 1886. The child's middle name, Lee, was in honor of his paternal uncle, who had shared the rigors of the family's move to Kansas. Although his first name, Everette, was not uncommon in those days, he seems to have preferred to go by others. Since at least his student days, his friends had called him "De."[10] For most of his professional life, he preferred to abbreviate his name: E. DeGolyer or E. L. DeGolyer. Nevertheless, when the time came, he would pass the name on to his own son.

In 1886, the young DeGolyer family had more to worry about than the possible spelling variants of their son's name. The child's early years would be hard ones for the family. A few weeks after his birth, a tornado struck the DeGolyer homestead, an ill omen that came as they had only begun to farm.[11] The storm ripped the roof off the crude home, and young Everette's story almost ended there.[12] The storm was only the beginning. The winter of 1886–1887 and the following winter of 1887–1888 proved to be remarkably severe. Worse, rainfall in the region fell dramatically even as the DeGolyer family had just started to cultivate the land.[13] Trying to scratch out a living, John and his brother opened a "German Restaurant" in Greensburg, but this also was ill timed. Almost all businesses in western Kansas were dependant on agriculture, and the weather took a harsh toll on the economy. Thousands fled eastward.[14] The DeGolyer family would soon follow.

In August 1888, John DeGolyer traded in his homestead for a covered wagon and a team of horses. After loading their belongings, the family departed for Missouri. At each night's stop, John would unload the rocking chair, and Narcissus would rock their young son to sleep. The family's journey ended in Joplin, where they hoped for better fortune than they had found in Kansas.

Joplin was at the center of a regional zinc and lead mining industry. Ever the optimist, John hoped that he might find riches prospecting for mineral wealth in the surrounding countryside. Wandering the hills of southwestern Missouri, he searched for the next big strike. Soon enough, his young son would accompany him on these expeditions.[15]

John's career as a prospector seems not to have met with much success, but the family again extemporized by starting several small businesses. Soon after moving to Missouri, the DeGolyers began operation of a water-powered mill near town. Grinding wheat for local farmers, the place doubled as a swimming hole for Everette's childhood frolic. And he would soon have playmates within the family. In Missouri, the DeGolyers welcomed two more children. Edith Christine DeGolyer was born in August 1890. Two years later, John and Narcissus's last child, Homer DeGolyer, was born. These were eventful years, with the family moving into town in the mid-1890s. In Joplin, John would open another "German Restaurant." It must have been here that Everette's father began to instruct him in the culinary arts—an apprenticeship that would later play a surprising role in furthering his career path as a geologist.[16]

Everette's childhood in Missouri exercised a powerful influence on the young man's aspirations. Despite the fact that his father had failed to thrive as a prospector, the idea of a mining career fascinated Everette. Although the family did not profit greatly from the zinc and lead boom of southwestern Missouri, there were those in the community who did prosper. Everette was keenly aware of the fortunes promised by prospecting, and he was attracted to the possibility of such a career even at this early age.[17]

Despite high hopes, the DeGolyer family struggled in Missouri, and John set his mind to join in the land runs that were opening Indian Territory for settlement. In 1893, he traveled to the border of the Cherokee Outlet near Wellington, Kansas. The federal government threw its extensive lands open to settlement on September 16 of that year, but John's run of bad luck seems to have continued unabated. He returned to Missouri soon thereafter, apparently having failed to secure an acceptable claim.[18]

As the government continued to open Indian lands to settlement, the more orderly lottery system replaced the chaos of the land run. Always willing to try his luck, John DeGolyer registered for surplus lands distributed in the former Kiowa-Comanche reservation. From July 9 to August 6, 1901, the federal government assigned claims to aspiring settlers. Fate smiled on John DeGolyer at last, and he received a city lot in the newly founded town of Hobart.[19]

It was not entirely clear how the DeGolyers would prosper in this new environment, but move they did. Eventually, John turned to the same sort of venture that he had struggled with in Missouri and Kansas, opening another restaurant: The Blue Point Chop House. An acrostic advertisement for the family diner, promising a modern, convenient meal with an impressive menu selection, follows:

*The Blue Point serves a meal that's O.K.*
*Here cooking is done in an up-to-date way.*
*Excellent viands served clean and nice.*

*Best kind of victuals at a very fair price.*
*Lunches the best, short orders all kinds,*
*Unexcelled goods at the Blue Point you find.*
*Everything fixed in a manner O.K.*

*Pull into The Blue Point any time aday.*
*Oysters, Game and Fish we serve here.*
*In every variety, never too dear.*
*Neat, courteous attention—you don't have to wait.*
*The Blue Point is right up-to-date.*[20]

The handbill suggested the sophistication to which the DeGolyer family and the founders of Hobart aspired. Who would have believed that patrons of a restaurant in Hobart, Oklahoma, would have been able to enjoy oysters, hundreds of miles from the sea? The town had scarcely been put on the map. Yet no matter how stridently the town's boosters professed its respectability and culture, there was still much of the Wild West about the place.

On one occasion, John DeGolyer had an unwelcome experience with the untamed recklessness of frontier life and became an unwilling celebrity in the process. This occurred when John witnessed the first "official" murder in the county, while on duty at The Blue Point. The details of the affair are somewhat murky. The basic story involved a Texas gunslinger by the name of Tom Varnell, who shot another character, known as "Frenchy," somewhere near the restaurant. When Varnell stood trial for the killing, John DeGolyer was the main eyewitness. Varnell's mother, a wealthy Texas ranch owner, spent a fortune trying to save her son and secured his release on bond. Despite her efforts, Varnell himself became a victim of frontier violence when another Texan shot him dead while he awaited the conclusion of the case.[21] It is unclear whether young Everette was also present when the murder occurred, but the excitement must have affected him.

This was the Hobart of Everette Lee DeGolyer's youth. He had less time to enjoy himself here than he had had in Missouri—the more birthdays he celebrated, the more he had to work. In Hobart, he took on a series of jobs to help support the family. DeGolyer probably spent many hours helping with the family business, but it was his job at a local china shop that encouraged him to think about the future.

He began work there soon after the family moved to town. At the time, he was the impressionable age of fifteen. Recalling that job in later years, DeGolyer explained the effect it had on him: "I would look at all those gifts and art objects which I thought then were the height of luxury and I used to wonder if I would ever be able to own any myself. I remember I really studied them, which I suppose was a substituted way of possessing them."[22] In later years, DeGolyer would become an avid collector, satisfying those desires awakened in the Hobart china shop. But to realize his dreams, he knew that he would need more than just a job; he needed a career. He knew that he would need to succeed where his father had failed. Somehow, he would win the wealth and security that had eluded his family throughout his childhood. It was a desperate desire heightened by yet another change of residence.

Neither The Blue Point nor young Everette's wages from the china shop brought in enough money to keep the family in Hobart. Soon, the DeGolyers were on the move again. Leaving Hobart behind, they traveled to Oklahoma City in search of better opportunities. Here, events would turn the young man's attention increasingly away from convenient, if unskilled employment, toward higher education.

DeGolyer's schooling had suffered from frequent interruption caused by his family's migrations. He had only begun high school in Missouri, when the family moved to Oklahoma. In Hobart, he had completed a third year in high school before the next relocation. In Oklahoma City, DeGolyer continued his studies, attending Central High School while waiting on tables at Delmonico's restaurant, where his father worked as a chef.[23]

In Oklahoma City, DeGolyer made the fortunate acquaintance of the Edgar S. Vaught, the superintendent of the city schools, who became something of a mentor for young DeGolyer, encouraging him to continue his education. He presented the young man with his first book, an item that DeGolyer treasured greatly.[24] Learning of Everette's interest in mining, he took the young man to the college town of Norman, where he introduced him to Professor Charles N. Gould of the University of Oklahoma. With the superintendent's recommendation, Gould offered DeGolyer a job dusting off rock samples and performing other maintenance tasks in the geology department. Could he have known that this moment would be a turning point in his life? DeGolyer accepted and his training in the science of geology began.[25]

Although he had spent years in high school, DeGolyer was not quite ready for college. Enrolling in the preparatory school at the University of Oklahoma, he spent two years in preliminary studies before entering as a freshman in the fall of 1905. It was excellent timing. The years that DeGolyer spent in high school, preparatory school, and the university were among the most exciting years yet in Oklahoma. Opportunities abounded for the ambitious and the bold, and DeGolyer's budding interest in minerals would offer a profitable venue for the talented young man.[26]

DeGolyer himself was still too young to enter the fray, but the westward movement of the oil industry affected his education and his aspirations. The giant strike at Spindletop, Texas, may have seemed far afield to the young man who had only recently arrived with his family in Hobart, Oklahoma. Yet the 1905 discovery of a giant oilfield at Glenn Pool in Indian Territory was just next door. The size of the strike and the fortuitous proximity to rail lines passing through nearby Tulsa and Red Fork ensured that the highly productive Glenn Pool wells would provoke great interest. The future of the region would be bound up with the energy and optimism—often to the point of folly—of that time and place, and it certainly exercised a formative influence on the young man.[27]

Despite the excitement over oil, it was a promising career as a mining engineer that DeGolyer first envisioned as he embarked on studies of geology at the University of Oklahoma. The school itself was younger than the petroleum industry; indeed, it was younger even than DeGolyer himself. Opening its doors for its first students in September 1892, the founders of the university bubbled with the ambition and optimism of the newly opened land. From humble beginnings, the school flourished under the presidency of David Ross Boyd, offering education free of charge to residents of the Oklahoma Territory.[28]

The science of geology had an important relationship with the

Everette Lee DeGolyer, 1908. Still a college student, DeGolyer was just two years away from remarkable success as a petroleum geologist when this photo was taken. (Everette Lee DeGolyer Collection. Courtesy of DeGolyer Library, Southern Methodist University.)

school from an early date. An act by the territorial legislature in 1899 established a Department of Geology and Natural History, with the current professor of biology as *ex officio* "Territorial Geologist and Curator of the Museum." Of course, animals are not the same as minerals, and the need for a specialist in geology resulted in the appointment of Charles Newton Gould as an instructor in 1900.[29]

Gould was a remarkable man whose passion for science would inspire a generation of geologists whom he instructed. Gould was born in a log cabin in Ohio in 1868. His family, like the DeGolyers, moved west to Kansas in the 1880s. He vividly remembered the dugouts and sod houses of the day, and the landscape greatly affected him. Beginning studies at a teacher training school in 1888, he started teaching his own classes, taking time off each year to further his studies in zoology, astronomy, physics, chemistry, and especially geology.[30]

Gould was a religious man whose zeal was aroused not only in the Methodist church but also in the classroom. While attending a lecture

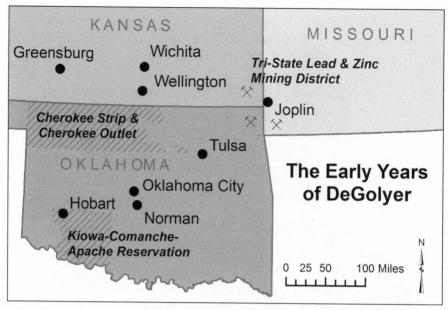

KANSAS
Greensburg ●   Wichita ●
            Wellington ●
Cherokee Strip &
Cherokee Outlet
OKLAHOMA
            ● Oklahoma City
Hobart ● ●
            Norman
Kiowa-Comanche-
Apache Reservation
● Tulsa

MISSOURI
Tri-State Lead & Zinc
Mining District
● Joplin

The Early Years
of DeGolyer

N

0   25  50      100 Miles

The Early Years of DeGolyer. (Map by Gregory Plumb and Billy Ring.)

in 1889 at a teachers' school in Kingman, Kansas, a sense of wonder overcame Gould as Professor L. C. Wooster described the history of two slabs of sandstone that he held before the class. In Gould's own words, "I hung entranced on every word. As Professor Wooster continued his lecture unfolding nature's handiwork, I felt the spinal shiver, which betokens the last word in emotional appeal. This was my conversion."[31]

Despite the discouragement of neighbors and family, Gould was determined to pursue an advanced education. Moving to Winfield, Kansas, he enrolled in Southwestern College, a Methodist institution. Gould's felicitous discovery of a fossil led to contact with Professor S. W. Williston of the University of Kansas. The professor warned Gould that geology was hardly a promising vocation. He advised the young enthusiast, "It's a dog's life, Gould, and there is nothing in it. A geologist never makes any money, he works hard all his days, he is called a fool and a crank by nine-tenths of the people he meets, and he lives and usually dies unappreciated."[32] Not even these sobering words could dissuade Gould. Beginning in 1896, he set out on a variety of well-organized, geological expeditions across Kansas, Nebraska, and Oklahoma. After graduating from Southwestern College and completing a master's degree at the University of Nebraska, the University of Oklahoma offered Gould a position in the newly formed geology department.[33]

When Gould arrived in Norman in 1900, there were no rooms available for the geology department, so he conducted his business at a desk in the office of A. H. Van Vleet. The lack of laboratory equipment, rock specimens, and geology books at the university forced Gould to rely on his own resources. He brought with him his own collection of fossils and a library of two hundred volumes for the benefit of his students. In a blow to the program, these were all lost in a fire that destroyed the university building in 1903. Fortunately, Gould had already begun developing a style of instruction that would use the state itself as one vast geological laboratory. Beginning in December 1901, Gould led students to the mountains, providing them with field experience that went far beyond what they could learn in the classroom.[34]

Although he was already refining his teaching methods, Gould knew that he would need to complete further graduate studies in order to realize his career goals. For this reason, he took a leave of absence during the academic year of 1905–1906 to secure a doctorate. After traveling to a variety of prestigious institutions to confer with authorities in geology, he returned to the University of Nebraska, which awarded him the degree he sought at commencement in 1906. By then, excitement regarding the region's nascent oil industry was growing intense. Although Gould professed greater interest in geology as an abstract science, he began consulting in the oilfields in the summer of 1907. Gould never made much money in the petroleum industry, but many of his students would, Everette Lee DeGolyer among them.[35]

Yet all of this was in the future when DeGolyer began his studies at the University of Oklahoma. In many ways, the university grew up with DeGolyer. In 1903, electricity came to the campus, and sidewalks improved its appearance. No fewer than six buildings were under construction as the still young geology department looked forward to the completion of the new science hall. By the summer of 1904, it was complete, housing Dr. Gould's laboratory and geological collection on the second floor. It was here that DeGolyer began to acquaint himself with the study of rocks.[36]

Classroom instruction included courses on basic principles that promised to educate students in the abstract science of geology. During DeGolyer's college years, he took Elements of Physical Geology, Economic Geology, Historical Geology, Advanced Geology, Lithology, and Physiography. In addition to a class in Advanced Mineralogy, he took two more semesters of further instruction in mineralogy. Crucially, he also took an early course in surveying and would eventually complete a thesis on a geological topic, although that was only after his career as a field geologist had begun. Overall his performance in university classes was good. In general he was a "B" rather than an "A" student but A's predominated in his geology courses, and this in an era before grade inflation. A better testimony to his ability came in 1911, the year that DeGolyer completed his degree. Commenting on DeGolyer's already evident success, his old instructor, Dr. Gould, described him as "an exceptionally bright student, self-reliant, at the same time conservative."[37]

DeGolyer thrived at the university, both academically and socially. Campus life flourished during his years there, as many important aspects of college life took shape. One such development was the football program. A football craze swept the nation at the turn of the century, and the mania took a particularly advanced form at the University of Oklahoma.[38]

Fraternities also arrived on campus, and DeGolyer was among the earliest initiates of Kappa Alpha, the first nationally affiliated fraternity on campus. Soon after its founding, the fraternity moved into a house and began plans for three dances and two "smokers." There was more. Oratorical contests and football games built up the camaraderie among Kappa Alpha's new members. DeGolyer blossomed in this social environment and enjoyed the new friendships that he was making. Indeed, he seems to have won something of a reputation for being a joker. In 1909, he served as the "humorous editor" of the *Mistletoe,* a yearbook produced by the junior class.

Despite, or perhaps because of, his zeal for these various social activities, DeGolyer would eventually grow critical of the role of both football and fraternities in campus life. In 1916, when his brother, Homer, joined the same chapter to which Everette had belonged, Everette was concerned. The older brother feared that the fraternity would distract Homer from his main business: study. Still, he remembered his fraternity brothers and his involvement with Kappa Alpha favorably and certainly was devoted enough to their activities while he was in school.[39]

As his education progressed, DeGolyer's extracurricular interests turned increasingly away from the fraternity toward a certain young woman. The University of Oklahoma would have a special, sentimental

Nell Virginia Goodrich. The young woman who captured Everette Lee DeGolyer's heart at the University of Oklahoma. (Nell Goodrich DeGolyer Collection. Courtesy of DeGolyer Library, Southern Methodist University.)

association for DeGolyer that went far beyond esprit de corps. For it was there that he would meet his future wife, Nell Virginia Goodrich, a woman whose ambitions equaled his own. They met on campus soon after DeGolyer had enrolled in the preparatory school. Called Nellie, she was a month and two days younger than Everette, but already finishing her first degree, a BM in piano, which she received in 1906. In 1907, she received a BA in philosophy. Although the focus of her study was music, she was also an assistant in the German department. In fall 1905, the papers of Everette DeGolyer were among those that she graded. His work was always recognizable—a stick of gum was habitually clipped to the assignment. "Bribery was not in big figures then!" he recalled in later years.[40]

Everette and Nell's acquaintance blossomed into romance, and class-mates soon recognized the two as a couple. *The Mistletoe,* the college yearbook, jibed DeGolyer as "just another spoon-case," acknowledging his warm relationship with Nell. Nell was a petite, fair young woman with blond curls and blue eyes. She was intelligent, talented, and strong willed. DeGolyer grew to appreciate her inner strength and decisiveness. In the twilight of his life, he would remark, "She has always made large decisions without a trace of nervousness or fear."[41]

Nell was the oldest of six children. Like many in the young state, the future of the Goodrich family lay in the emerging oil boom. Both Nell and her sister would marry geologists. Two of her brothers would eventually enter the same profession. Her father was a dentist with a high appreciation for education. Both he and Nell's mother had been teachers earlier in life, and the family had settled in Norman because of the presence of the young University of Oklahoma. At the age of fifteen, Nell enrolled in college and thrived. All of her siblings would receive college degrees, a rarity in a pioneer state.[42]

At first, friends teased Nell for her association with a boy in the preparatory school, despite the fact that he was older than she was. She later recalled, "He suffered at being a 'prep boy' at his age and I looked down on him at first; but only because my friends teased me for having a 'prep boy' as my friend."[43] But he soon won her over; as Nell explained, "He was so full of humor that he could win the friendship of anyone he wanted to. He and my mother were friends from their first meeting."[44] Nell remembered the difficulties that DeGolyer overcame in pursuing his education. "He was a poor boy and had to work his way through college, but my mother always said there was no need to worry about De, that he would manage."[45]

The "prep boy" that won her heart was in fact a young man by the time that Nell was grading his German homework in 1905. At five feet six inches tall, Everette DeGolyer nonetheless towered over most of his classmates in energy and ambition. His biographer and acquaintance Lon Tinkle would later write of his "leonine head . . . which always made him seem to fill more space than he actually did." His round face was ruddy complexioned, brightened by blue-gray eyes, and topped by a thick head of blond hair. A "peasant's face" he liked to call it, but Nell must have disagreed.[46]

In addition to his amorous pursuits, DeGolyer found time for his studies. Professor Gould had been working with the United States Geological Survey (USGS) since 1901.[47] DeGolyer's interest and talent in geology was evident to the instructor, who recommended him for summer work with the USGS in 1906.[48] The position that he took was a humble one, but it was a terrific opportunity for the young man. A letter from the Department of the Interior, dated June 1, 1906, charged him with the position of cook under the direction of N. H. Darton. Continuing, the letter informed him, "[Y]ou are directed to report on July 1, 1906 at Laramie, Wyoming."[49] DeGolyer was not particularly interested in cooking, although experience working in his father's restaurant may have helped to win him the position. Still, this work promised adventure, and his superiors would soon recognize that the young man was talented with more than a skillet. Importantly, DeGolyer would gain invaluable experience with the most prestigious organization devoted to field geology in the United States.

DeGolyer's summer work with the Survey converged with important developments on the national scene. The assassination of President William McKinley in 1901 had ushered in the Presidency of Theodore Roosevelt. An avid hunter and outdoorsman, Roosevelt had a keen appreciation for the natural environment. During his presidency, Roosevelt implemented policies that aimed at the conservation of national resources.[50]

As experts in national geography, the men of the USGS played an important role in providing information used to create conservation policy and meet the engineering challenges posed by Roosevelt's ambitious vision. The appointment of Charles D. Walcott, the director of the Survey, as the concurrent head of a newly founded Reclamation Service indicated the growing prestige of the geologists of the USGS They would become increasingly relevant in shaping public policy as the century progressed. DeGolyer's work on the Survey focused more on mineral resources and probably interested private investors more than federal policymakers at the time. Still, his service with the USGS would mark DeGolyer's earliest contribution as a scientific expert in the service of the public.[51]

Of course, DeGolyer's official position on the Survey in the summer of 1906 was not exactly prestigious. Although his interest in geology led him to the USGS, his supervisors hired him as an expert in the culinary arts. There is no surviving record of what was on the menu in the camps where the young man worked in central and southern Wyoming, but DeGolyer's duties soon extended beyond his official charge. Darton seems to have sensed something of the young man's talent and ambition. In short order, DeGolyer was hard at work, plotting maps of coal beds.[52] That autumn, Darton wrote to the camp cook and novice geologist to express his approval: "I was greatly pleased with our field experience this summer and hope that we may renew our relations in the future."[53] For the next several years, DeGolyer would alternate between school and the Survey. Embracing both of these opportunities, he would develop an impressive mastery of his field that would place him in an excellent position to pursue a career in economic geology.

In the summer of 1907, DeGolyer returned to work on the Survey, this time under E. G. Woodruff, one of DeGolyer's geology professors at the University of Oklahoma. Woodruff was a difficult man, whose austerity grated the nerves of many of his younger assistants. H. B. Fuqua, an associate of DeGolyer later in life, remembered Woodruff as "the most generally disliked man" he ever knew.[54] Woodruff seems to have been particularly concerned with keeping vice in check during Survey work. He banned both drinking and smoking in camp—a regulation that proved inconvenient to Woodruff's colleagues as well as his subordinates. Yet Everette DeGolyer might have thanked Woodruff for his crusading zeal, for he owed his most important friendship to a shared desire to subvert his supervisor's prohibition policy.

That summer, Dr. Woodruff gave DeGolyer the duty of transporting the Survey's chief geologist, C. Willard Hayes, to the camp to conduct an inspection. Driving to the train station, DeGolyer met the mustachioed geologist, who proved to be a convivial fellow. As the two drove to the camp, Dr. Hayes became agitated. He had forgotten his tobacco.

"Don't worry," DeGolyer remarked, "I have plenty of cans back at camp. I can keep you supplied."

Hayes questioned him, "You don't have any on you?"

"No sir. Out of deference to Dr. Woodruff."

"I admire discretion," remarked Hayes, "but don't carry it too far."[55]

Hayes was grateful for DeGolyer's assistance in his hour of need, and it proved the beginning of a long friendship that would be fateful for DeGolyer's career. Hayes was an important figure in the USGS. By 1907, he had been with the Survey for more than twenty years. Serving from 1886 to 1911, he was the first geologist in charge of the nonmetals section established in 1900. Hayes rose to the rank of geologist in charge of the Division of Geology and Paleontology in 1902 and then became chief geologist of the Survey in 1907. Although trained as a chemist, Hayes had developed an interest in geology while a graduate student at Johns Hopkins University. His scientific background put him at the forefront of the study of structural geology, physiography, and economic and engineering geology. He possessed a broad competence in his field and was widely known for the high standards of accuracy that he demanded in his own studies as well as in those of his subordinates.

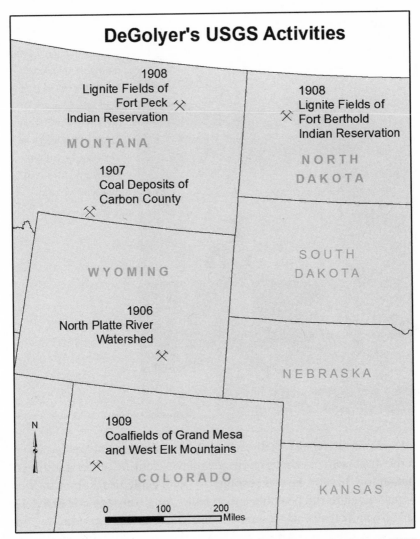

# DeGolyer's USGS Activities

1908
Lignite Fields of
Fort Peck
Indian Reservation

MONTANA

1907
Coal Deposits of
Carbon County

1908
Lignite Fields of
Fort Berthold
Indian Reservation

NORTH
DAKOTA

WYOMING

SOUTH
DAKOTA

1906
North Platte River
Watershed

NEBRASKA

N

1909
Coalfields of Grand Mesa
and West Elk Mountains

COLORADO

KANSAS

0      100      200
                    Miles

DeGolyer's USGS Activities. This map indicates the major focus of DeGolyer's USGS activities, although his travels on behalf of the survey took him beyond those points indicated on the map. (Map by Gregory Plumb and Billy Ring.)

Camp in morning, 1909. DeGolyer as a young man conducting fieldwork on behalf of the United States Geological Survey. (Everette Lee DeGolyer Collection. Courtesy of DeGolyer Library, Southern Methodist University.)

Hayes's experience was diverse. He had conducted a series of surveys in the Appalachians that greatly advanced scientific understanding of that region. In 1897, he was responsible for a geological survey in Nicaragua related to the possible construction of a transoceanic canal. He had also shown an early interest in petroleum geology, conducting one of the first—if ultimately mistaken—evaluations of the future Spindletop oilfield.[56] Hayes was a natural leader who inspired those who worked with him and won the lifelong loyalty of many of his assistants. Through these protégés, he would exercise a far-reaching influence on the development of petroleum geology in the twentieth century.[57]

Everette DeGolyer would become one of the most successful of Hayes's protégés. Yet in 1907, DeGolyer was still only one of many promising students of geology. Hayes made a mental note of the young man. Perhaps he could use his services in the future.

DeGolyer's next expedition came in June 1908. Working under the direction of Carl D. Smith, DeGolyer took the position of foreman of the drill crew with the survey party that would examine lignite fields in Montana and North Dakota.[58] It would prove to be his most interesting summer yet.

The expedition was made all the more enjoyable for DeGolyer by the addition of a real character to the party. After arriving in camp, DeGolyer's supervisor ordered him to ride into Miles City, Montana, and meet with another young geologist who would assist the survey. His name was Edwin B. Hopkins, and the two men were soon to become friends. Born in West Virginia in 1882, Hopkins had originally studied architecture at George Washington University, graduating in 1904. Rather than make a career as an architect, he then entered Cornell University, where he took special courses in geology until 1906. Hopkins worked briefly as a geologist in Louisiana and New York before taking the position with the USGS in 1907. The collegiate relationship that DeGolyer and Hopkins formed in the summer of 1908 would endure, and the two would become frequent collaborators later in life. DeGolyer found the new assistant at the hotel, and the young men introduced themselves, DeGolyer's new associate making a memorable first impression. DeGolyer later recalled, "[He] asked me if I had had breakfast. I said that I had and he said well, if I would excuse him then, he would get breakfast, whereupon he disappeared through a pair of swinging doors and certainly did not go to the dining room." DeGolyer was mildly offended that Hopkins had not ask him to join him at the bar, but he was not one to bear a grudge. Later that day, Hopkins introduced young DeGolyer to chewing tobacco, a habit that he found intriguing but ultimately unappealing.[59]

The two worked together the entire summer, traversing the Yellowstone River and the still wild reaches of Montana. It was a remarkable adventure for the young man, and years later he would recall stories from that year with vivid clarity. There was the time that he and Hopkins met with the United States Reclamation Service, wearing new suits to impress the seasoned engineers with "what the well-dressed young geologist should wear." On that occasion, DeGolyer's horse had bucked him off, throwing him about twenty feet and ripping the buttons off his new uniform. Undeterred, he stubbornly insisted on remounting the animal. DeGolyer recalled later, "He didn't buck again. I guess that was all he had in him." Persistence was a trait that would pay off for DeGolyer in the future.[60]

There were other trials that the young men endured. Among them were the mosquitoes that would "simply boil up there in clouds." There were also the inevitable irritations that went along with spending too much time around the same people. As DeGolyer put it, "[W]hen you put a bunch of men in a camp together [and] they don't have any outside contacts or anything else . . . usually there are all sorts of allergies [that] develop."[61]

One such "allergy" involved another survey assistant named John Allen Davis. DeGolyer later remembered his treatment of the young man with regret when he recalled a discovery made by the party. While working with Davis and Hopkins, DeGolyer chanced upon some broken rock. Examining it closely, he found fossils in the concretion—fossils he immediately recognized to be from the Cretaceous Era. This was an interesting find. Calling Hopkins to the site, he shared the impressive discovery. The two lads decided to keep it to themselves, although Davis was technically in charge of the party. After returning to the camp, their director inquired if they had found anything of interest. After Davis had responded in the negative, Hopkins suggested that DeGolyer had in fact found something. DeGolyer guiltily revealed his cache of fossils.[62]

At the time, the young geologist thought that he had found something of purely scientific interest. In fact, he would later realize that those fossils portended the presence of oil, which held its own charms. The geological formation that those rocks indicated was an anticline—a perfect trap for petroleum. As he recalled, "[W]e knew that the structure was anticlinal, but I didn't pay attention—didn't know anything about oil—didn't pay attention to it in those days." Later someone else did pay attention and drilled there—and found oil.[63]

In September, the adventure ended and DeGolyer returned to Oklahoma for school. After two or three months, he received a wire from back east. Carl D. Smith wanted him to come to Washington to draft maps for the findings from the summer survey. DeGolyer's work with the maps did not promise the excitement of the field, but draftsmanship skills were part of the profession.[64]

Topographical mapping was an essential tool for the geologist and would be particularly relevant for DeGolyer's later work in the oil industry. His onetime mentor, E. G. Woodruff, was particularly interested in the use of such maps by mining engineers. He understood that if properly drafted, these maps could portray a discreet area "better than a personal examination of the area without a map could present it, be-

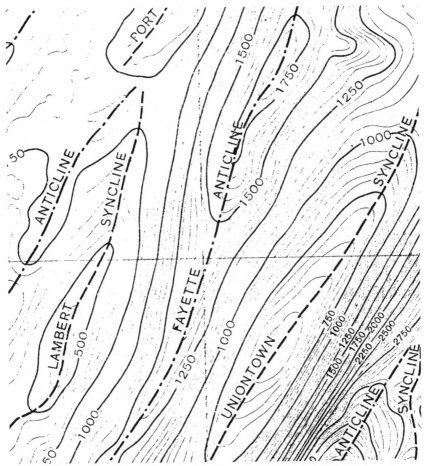

Topographic surveys such as this one could provide important data to early geologists seeking oil. Contour lines labeled with numbers indicate elevation. The hatched and dotted lines indicate the presence of an anticline. Hatched lines show synclines, where rock strata arc downward to form a trough. (Woodruff, "Topographic Maps for the Mining Engineer," *AIME Bulletin*, no. 78 1001.)

cause the person making such examination views only a limited portion of the surface at a time, and estimates distances only roughly with the eye."[65]

The process of creating a topographic map could be conducted by a single surveyor, although a few assistants could help work move quickly. Only a few instruments were required: a plane table, a telescopic alidade, and a stadia rod. The plane table, typically mounted on a tripod,

Plane table and telescopic alidade. Edwin Hopkins demonstrates the use of survey instruments while at work for the United States Geological Survey. (Everette Lee DeGolyer Collection. Courtesy of DeGolyer Library, Southern Methodist University.)

provided a flat surface on which to spread a survey map in progress. Placing the telescopic alidade on top of the map, the geologist would peer through the device, targeting rods held at various locations and taking measurements. Survey information could be marked directly on the map on top of the plane table as the investigation proceeded. The topographic method indicated elevation using contour lines, marking the point at which the land reached a certain height. Hills mapped by this method might vaguely resemble fingerprint patterns, with close spacing of contours indicating a steep rise in the land. Broader spacing specified a gentler slope.[66]

Of course, topographic maps, strictly speaking, indicated no more than the rise and fall of the land. They did not necessarily convey information regarding the geology of an area. However, Woodruff described the essential connection between topographic work and the mapping of geological strata in "structure-contour maps."[67] These structure-contour maps diagrammed the location of a particular stratum, such as a coal bed or oil sand. Because the rise and fall of the land on the surface could replicate the rise and fall of strata below, geologists could use topographic maps to map subsoil formations. Of course, underground features did not always mirror the surface exactly, and inter-

Stadia rod. Everette DeGolyer holds stadia rod for the camera while working for the USGS. (Everette Lee DeGolyer Collection. Courtesy of DeGolyer Library, Southern Methodist University.)

pretations would have to be open to revision. Nevertheless, Woodruff emphasized the value and surprising accuracy of topographical and structure-contour maps.[68]

Under Woodruff and his other supervisors on the USGS, DeGolyer had learned how to employ these methods in the field. Now he turned his attention to the essential, but less exciting, task of organizing the information. DeGolyer was reluctant—he wanted to focus on school—but he feared that declining the "invitation" to work on the maps would blacklist him when it came to future government employment. After all, the government was one of the major employers of geologists, and the young man was, if anything, practical. Therefore, in January he struck out for Washington. Lodged at the Ebbitt House at 14th and F, DeGolyer spent the winter working on the map. In the evenings, he dined with Hopkins, who was also in town.[69]

DeGolyer's hard work for the Survey in 1908 paid off in the form of recognition from his supervisor. Smith was quite pleased with the performance of his team, crediting DeGolyer, Hopkins, and Allen in the *Bulletin of the United States Geological Survey* with efficient and "able assistance" with the project. Of the three, Smith singled out DeGolyer for recognition of the hours of office work that he had contributed.[70]

The summer of 1909 brought another opportunity to travel west with the Survey. Working under the direction of Willis T. Lee, DeGolyer traveled to the Crested Butte area on the western slope of the Rockies in Colorado. The camp was never below an altitude of 8,000 feet, and DeGolyer's assignment was to climb mountains, revising old maps along the way. Drafting detailed topographical maps of the region, DeGolyer identified coal prospects as he traversed the rugged terrain. The work was physically taxing, but DeGolyer rose to the occasion admirably. Ascending the slopes of snow-capped mountains, he discovered that the canvas cover of his plane table could double as a toboggan on the descent, furthering the excitement of an already exhilarating expedition. After completing a short season in the field, DeGolyer returned with Lee to Washington, where he again turned his efforts to drafting a map for publication, with the geological analysis of the party's work.[71]

It would be a fateful summer for DeGolyer, though he would not have guessed it. For in that year, DeGolyer's scientific education at the University of Oklahoma and his field work with the USGS would come together in an opportunity to begin a career in a new, somewhat untested, but promising field: petroleum geology.

The notion that geologists were helpful in the location of oilfields was almost as old as the industry, but it was not widely accepted until well into the twentieth century. As early as 1865, reputable geologists had served as casual consultants for some oil companies. As DeGolyer was hard at work drafting maps for the USGS in the summer of 1909, there were perhaps several scores of geologists working with oil companies throughout the world. Considering the formidable scale of the global oil industry, this was a small number indeed. Geology may have been theoretically relevant to oil production, but many "practical" oilmen still viewed the geologist with skepticism.[72]

It was not that oilmen had ignored geology in the past. Particularly when pioneering a new field with a "wildcat" well, they used their knowledge of analogous, oil-bearing formations to guide their decision for a new site. Hills, valleys, creeks, springs, and most obviously, oil seeps, all played a role in determining where to construct the next derrick. Almost all of the elements that the oilmen took into account were also the subject of study by the geologist. Nevertheless, the oilmen doubted that the abstract "book learning" of the geologists would give them an edge in the search for oil. For this reason, the acceptance of the geologist in the oil business was a slow process that took almost half a century.[73]

During these early years, geologists relied primarily upon surface evidence of petroleum deposits. The most favorable sign was the presence of an oil seep, a location where the oil literally seeped from the ground. Geologists supplemented this evidence with structural, stratigraphic, and topographic analyses that attempted to discern the form of underlying rock layers and the probable location of the "reservoir rock."[74]

Most importantly, by the time DeGolyer was about to enter the field of petroleum geology, geologists had developed accurate methods to map the surface of the land. Woodruff had written of these methods. The plane table and the telescopic alidade allowed them to measure even low-grade changes in elevation that provided essential information about an area's topography. As geologists turned their attention to petroleum, this method would prove invaluable in the effort to locate new oilfields.[75]

The mapping of surface topography was particularly crucial to these early evaluations because there was little else, aside from the oil seeps themselves, to guide the geologists. Rock outcrops, where rock strata broke into open air allowing geologists to examine them, did offer some hints as to what lay below the soil. Still, for the most part, geologists could be certain only of the surface of the earth. Happily, they discovered that the analysis of these surface landforms could sometimes predict the presence of oil. As early as 1861, Canadian geologist T. Sterry Hunt theorized that anticlines—geological structures occasionally recognizable through topographical analysis—could hold petroleum.[76] This remained only theory until Dr. I. C. White "rediscovered" the anticline theory and applied it in search of new pools for the Standard Oil Company of New Jersey in 1882.[77] Essentially, an anticline was a geological formation where rock strata arched upward. If one layer of rock in an anticline was impermeable, then this arch could "trap" oil migrating upward toward the surface, creating a reservoir waiting to be tapped by an oil well. Anticlines were not the only formations that held oil, but they were sometimes identifiable from the surface. As geologists were able to pinpoint these oil-bearing structures, oilmen began to show an interest in the opinions of the once-berated "rock hounds."

This was particularly true in the case of California, where the prevalence of anticlinal structures allowed geologists to apply their knowledge with frequent success. Beginning in the 1890s, geologists serving in the State Mining Bureau, the Union Oil Company, and the Southern Pacific Railroad, conducted studies aimed at the location and analysis

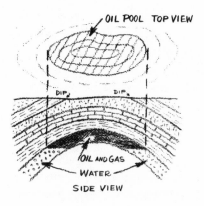

Idealized cross-section of an anticline oilfield. In an anticline oilfield, an arched, impermeable rock stratum creates a trap containing crude oil and sometimes a natural gas cap. In some cases, an observer may perceive the rise and fall of the strata from the surface. In other cases, there may be less evidence or no evidence at all on the surface. (Drawing by Everette Lee DeGolyer, "How Men Find Oil," *Fortune*, August 1949, 98. Courtesy of Everette and Nell DeGolyer descendants.)

of California oilfields. Other companies followed suit and soon California was the cutting edge of petroleum geology in the United States.[78]

Outside of California, the acceptance of geology by the industry was more hesitant. Yet there were some opportunities—DeGolyer was fortunate enough to find one at just the right time. The man who would open the door for DeGolyer to a career in petroleum geology was none other than his cordial superior on the USGS, Dr. C. Willard Hayes.

Now chief geologist of the Survey, Hayes was responsible for directing the field geologists in developing their analyses of the oilfields and potential oilfields of the nation. Hayes's interest in the oilfields dated back at least to the Spindletop gusher. Called in to evaluate that property in 1900, Hayes had found little sign for encouragement. Indeed, he had remarked that he could see "no precedents for expecting to find oil in the great unconsolidated sands and clays of the Coastal Plain."[79] Yet Hayes was not stubborn once the Lucas gusher had proved him wrong. Instead, his interest in oil only grew deeper. Joining with William Kennedy, another geologist whose pessimism about Spindletop had proven misplaced, he published an analysis of the bonanza field.[80] Their study of Spindletop was an exemplar of the challenges and limitations that geologists confronted in oil prospecting. Even with a multitude of wells drilled on the site, and after a thorough reconnaissance of the area, neither man felt comfortable in identifying the geological structure of the field with any degree of certainty.[81]

As Hayes developed a clearer sense of what adequate petroleum analysis entailed, he drafted guidelines for the geologists of the USGS. In 1908, he published his *Handbook for Field Geologists* that detailed the observations that were required to provide adequate information for petroleum prospecting.[82] Hayes's charge to the geologists was a daunting one, considering the difficulty of obtaining accurate information on the structure of many oilfields. According to the *Handbook,* complete knowledge of the general geology was essential to analysis of oil reservoirs. Specifically, he enjoined geologists that "[t]he stratigraphy must be known in order to interpret well logs correctly and to determine (a) the character of the oil or gas bearing stratum and its capacity for holding and yielding the hydrocarbons and (b) the character of the overlying beds and their adaptability for retaining these compounds."[83]

However, mapping the stratigraphy—the layers of subsurface rock—was a difficult task. Among other details, geologists needed a sense of the thickness and the angles of these strata. The search for signs of what lay below the surface could lead the geologist far away from the location that he studied. Hayes warned that rock outcrops "may be a considerable distance from the oil or gas pool, and the beds should be traced from the outcrop to the pool under investigation by the collection of as many logs of wells in the intervening region as possible."[84]

These "logs" were the records kept by drillers on a well, indicating the type of rock that they had cut through at different depths. However, not all drillers kept logs, and those who did were not always particularly accurate or detailed in their observations. Even the most scrupulous driller might have difficulty in determining the depths from which he took well samples. Some saved these "cuttings," which could be analyzed by geologists, but many did not, leaving only written descriptions of the formations through which the drill passed.[85]

Even when the geologist was fortunate enough to work in a location where well logs existed, there remained the problem of obtaining those logs from suspicious oilmen. If oilmen could be convinced to share these logs, a geologist might be able to develop a plausibly accurate analysis of an oilfield. However, even with logs in hand, success was far from assured.

Hayes enjoined the field geologist to exercise a heightened scrutiny when dealing with a petroleum survey. He warned, "The importance of structure is such that it must be determined with a much greater degree of accuracy than is generally necessary for other purposes."[86] The method of observation would inevitably vary with the location, for in some areas geologists could identify promising oil-bearing structures from the surface, whereas in other areas local geology could obscure such structures. In the absence of well logs or revealing surface geology, there was little advice that the geologist could offer regarding the presence of oil at any one location.[87]

Hayes's underlying assumption revealed in the *Handbook* was that accurate analysis of petroleum reservoirs required a great deal of information. First, meticulous observation of the surface geology was necessary. This was within the grasp of a competent field geologist, but other elements were not. For instance, there were the inevitable variations of local geology, which could complicate analysis. Also, the need for well logs presumed not only that the field under analysis was at least partially developed but also that the private companies that had brought the field into production had kept logs and would be willing to share them.

As the oil industry in the Gulf Coast sprang to life, Hayes became increasingly interested in the possibility of working directly with oilmen to locate new fields. In mid-1908, he visited Mexico with his colleague on the Survey, Dr. David T. Day. While there, he met with Sir Weetman Pearson, the British engineer and industrialist who had launched a company that aimed to make Mexico a major producer of petroleum. This was the Mexican Eagle Oil Company. There was only one problem: Mexican Eagle had failed to locate a major pool by which it might realize its ambitious goals. Pearson offered Hayes a position with the company, directing geological exploration for petroleum. Intrigued at the possibility of searching for new oilfields, Hayes accepted. He would retain his position with the Survey, but increasingly his attention would turn south of the border.[88]

Hayes realized that the magnitude of the task that faced the Mexican Eagle Oil Company would require more than a single geologist. What was needed was a team of willing and adventuresome young men who would be willing to trek into the remote reaches of Mexico's balmy coastal plain, searching for signs of oil. They would need to be educated enough to understand how to interpret the unfamiliar geology of the region, to locate petroleum deposits. They would also need to be experienced enough to operate without the immediate oversight of Hayes himself. As he jogged his memory for geologists who might fit the bill, two names, among others, came to mind: Everette Lee DeGolyer and Edwin Hopkins.

DeGolyer vividly remembered the fateful day when Hayes called him into his office. The young man was nervous and more than a little irritated by the request. Mistakenly believing that the conference related to a bureaucratic dispute over $3.50 that DeGolyer supposedly owed the Survey, he entered Hayes's office in a bad mood. He was pleasantly surprised when instead of haranguing him, the chief geologist offered him an intriguing opportunity. As DeGolyer remembered:[89]

> I was mistaken. Hayes had called me in to his office to offer me a job as an oil geologist in Mexico. He had remembered pleasantly our meeting two years previously in Meetetsee, Wyoming, and had remembered favorably certain of my field work which he had reviewed at that time . . . I asked for a few days to consider the offer, spent them miserably fearing that it would be withdrawn and then accepted.[90]

# 2 | Geologist

*We had very good fortune . . .*
Everette Lee DeGolyer to Leonard M. Fanning, July 12, 1945[1]

It happened on a mild winter's night on the Potrero del Llano hacienda. It was well after midnight and two days after Christmas, but the American employees of the Mexican Eagle Oil Company were hard at work. They had just drilled past a depth of 1,911 feet when the well began showing signs of natural gas. Lou LeBarron had just arrived at the derrick and was beginning to investigate when the tools that had been removing debris from deep inside the earth went shooting out of the mouth of the well, smashing into the top of the derrick. The men scurried away like mad. LeBarron rushed to extinguish the boiler, lying some distance from the well itself. The surrounding area would soon be drenched in oil, and any fire threatened catastrophe. He put the boiler out in time, but LeBarron feared that he had been "gassed."[2] When he later met with the young geologist who had located the well, he could only describe the experience with an appeal to profanity. DeGolyer, much amused, passed on a bowdlerized description to his supervisor, Dr. C. Willard Hayes: "I'll tell you, it's the blanked . . . biggest well I ever worked on and the gas is so bad that I wish I hadn't ever seen the blanked . . . thing."[3]

LeBarron was right about the magnitude of Potrero del Llano No. 4. Not only was it the largest well that he had ever worked on, it was the largest well that anyone had ever worked on in the history of the oil industry worldwide. An estimated 110,000 barrels of oil spewed out of the well every day while the men of Pearson's company attempted to bring it under control. In later years, DeGolyer computed that Potrero del Llano No. 4 had produced approximately 130,000,000 barrels in its lifetime.[4] The massive Potrero well, coupled with Juan Casiano No. 7, brought in by Edward L. Doheny's Mexican Petroleum Company, made 1910 the year that the Mexican petroleum boom was born. Potrero del Llano was also a defining moment for DeGolyer. Although he had no ownership interest in the well, his reputation was ensured. Modifying a placement scheme laid out by Hayes, DeGolyer was the responsible party who had approved the final location of the well. For this, his employer would richly reward him.

Six months before, DeGolyer had agonized as he struggled to identify the next location to drill. He was a geologist whose employer had retained him for his expertise in identifying geological structures that promised to hold oil. However, that task was easier said than done. "There is no place in the immediate vicinity of Potrero del Llano where any sort of geologic section can be compiled," he had complained.[5] The work that the drillers had already carried out on the first three wells was not helpful. Their primitive logs that recorded the clays, gravels, marls, and shales through which the drill passed were far too inaccurate to form an idea of the geological structure below.[6] Limited information forced DeGolyer to make educated guesses at geological structure based on what he could see on the surface of the land.[7] Although DeGolyer offered the Mexican Eagle Oil Company expert advice based on the best information available, that information was limited indeed. The technology and methods available to geologists were simply unable to yield more than hints at what lay below the scientists' feet. In the event, Potrero del Llano No. 4 proved to be the well that secured a dominant position in Mexican oil for his employer. But geological analysis provided only a limited contribution to the success. DeGolyer's modesty was genuine when he later claimed that in Mexico, "We had very good fortune . . ."[8] In 1910, Mexico had been ruled for almost a quarter of a century by the same man—General Porfirio Díaz. The Díaz years had meant political stability and economic development at the cost of democratic ideals. One result of the dictatorship had been the emergence of a domestic oil industry. As with much of the development during the Díaz years, foreigners had been prominent leaders in this process. And the first oilman to succeed in oil production on a large scale in Mexico was an American, Edward L. Doheny.

Doheny, who would later achieve infamy for his role in the Teapot Dome scandal, had already made a name as a pioneer in California oil. His business relationships with railroad men drew his attention south of the border, where American dollars were laying tracks across Mexico. Railroads needed fuel, and Doheny thought that he could find it.

Accompanied by associates, Doheny traveled south in 1900 to search for Mexican oil. When residents showed him the bubbling pools that they called *chapapotes,* he was sure that he smelled money. Returning to Los Angeles, he gathered investors and founded the Mexican Petroleum

Company. In less than a year, Doheny's company had a team working at El Ébano, west of Tampico. In 1901, they struck oil. The quality of El Ébano oil proved disappointingly poor, more suitable for producing asphalt than kerosene. Nevertheless, the El Ébano field was the foundation for the Mexican Petroleum Company's eventual expansion into becoming the leading oil producer in Mexico.[9]

In the quest for Mexican oil, Doheny soon had a powerful competitor: Sir Weetman Pearson. Pearson would become, in turn, DeGolyer's employer, patron, and friend. He would be as responsible as any man for DeGolyer's later successes as an oilman, save for DeGolyer himself. But at the time that Pearson made his first steps toward drilling wells in Mexico, he had absolutely no experience in the oil business whatsoever.

Pearson had inherited the public engineering firm of S. Pearson and Son from his grandfather, but he hardly fit the stereotype of the silver-spoon heir. For one, he was intensely interested in the engineering feats of the modern world. As a young man, he marveled at Roebling's Brooklyn Bridge and Eads Mississippi Bridge in Saint Louis. Like John D. Rockefeller, Pearson had an uncanny knack for numbers. His success as an entrepreneur was to no small extent a function of his ability to calculate the costs of any given project and plan its progress in detail. British Prime Minister Lloyd George described him as a man "with an organizing brain of the first order." To his employees, he was simply "the Chief."[10]

During Pearson's early career, his firm focused on drainage and harbor projects in England, but he remained open to opportunities abroad. In 1889, he took on the daunting task of completing the failed Hudson River tunnel connecting Jersey City with Manhattan. While Pearson was in New York on the tunnel project, agents of President Díaz contacted him to see if he might be available for another project. The Spanish colonial regime constructed Mexico City over the ruins of Tenochtitlán, the old Aztec capital built on an island in the midst of a series of interconnected lakes. Although subsequent construction projects gradually drained the lakes over the course of the colonial period, frequent flooding plagued the capital. Construction of a drainage canal began in the seventeenth century, but its completion two centuries later did not entirely solve the problem. Since independence, various governments in Mexico had unsuccessfully attempted to resolve the flooding issue. Now, President Díaz was determined to put an end to this perennial problem. After an initial attempt by American and British contractors failed, Díaz hoped that Sir Weetman might have more luck.[11]

When Pearson agreed to complete the Grand Canal, he was beginning a lifelong relationship with President Díaz that would make him a wealthy man indeed. Pearson got on well with the old soldier. In Mexico, where government rhetoric chronically outpaced accomplishment, Díaz must have found Pearson's dependability refreshing. S. Pearson and Son completed the Grand Canal in 1896, two years ahead of schedule. By that time, Díaz had already rewarded him with another major project: the harbor works at Veracruz.[12]

However, it was a railroad that turned Pearson's attention to oil. The Isthmus of Tehuantepec offered unique possibilities for rail development in Mexico. Visionaries in the government recognized the potential of the region to become a major Atlantic–Pacific artery for trade. Unfortunately, the jungle stood as a significant obstacle to any planned construction. Even this had not stopped a group of British investors from throwing down a railway through the tropical terrain in 1897. But this pioneer railway was unequal to the task. With an average of one train derailment per day, the isthmus failed to develop the kind of traffic that its promoters envisioned. Eager to improve matters, Díaz handed the isthmus railroad over to Pearson. After rebuilding the line and upgrading port facilities, it proved to be a smashing success, drawing substantial trade in the days before the construction of the Panama Canal.[13]

While rebuilding the railroad, one of Pearson's trusted lieutenants, J. B. Body, noted the presence of oil seeping from the ground near the Gulf of Mexico. Pearson made a mental note of the report but did nothing at the time. Then, starting on a trip to New York, Pearson found himself delayed in Laredo, Texas, due to a missed train. It was January 1901, and the town was abuzz with talk of oil. The Lucas gusher at Spindletop had just blown in, and Pearson immediately thought of the oil seep in the isthmus. He dashed off a telegram to Body: "Secure options not only on oil land but on all land for miles around."[14] Pearson had no experience in the oil business, but he could not resist an opportunity.[15]

As in his past projects, Pearson took a systematic approach to the development of oil in Mexico. He arranged for the construction of a refinery in Minatitlán and bought options on land throughout the Isthmus of Tehuantepec and beyond. He hired Anthony Lucas of Spindletop fame to evaluate his properties for petroleum prospects. In 1906, Pearson arranged for special petroleum concessions from the Mexican government to prospect for oil in the states of Veracruz, Campeche, and Tabasco. He took all the steps possible in order to ensure success for his new venture: the Mexican Eagle Oil Company, known in Mexico as "El Águila."

However, the oil business was unlike Pearson's previous venture. He could not "plan" an oilfield with the same precision as a construction project. True, there were some predictable elements of the business. For instance, he knew that he would need a refinery to process any oil produced. Pearson had invested substantial sums of money in constructing one such plant at Minatitlán. But it was useless without oil, and the properties that Pearson had secured for development remained a significant question mark.

When wells drilled in the isthmus failed to generate the volume of crude that Pearson had hoped for, poor production threatened Mexican Eagle with ruin. Matters took a turn for the worse in 1908. In that year, a well soon to be notorious as "Dos Bocas" blew in as a gusher and might have been the company's salvation. Instead, disaster struck when the boilers that powered the drilling equipment ignited the stream of oil, creating an immense conflagration that raged for months, lighting the night sky for miles around. Clueless as to how the flames might be contained, the company allowed Dos Bocas to burn until it was exhausted.

Thus, the fate of the hard-won Pearson fortune was uncertain when Dr. C. Willard Hayes engaged DeGolyer as a geologist in the employ of the Mexican Eagle Oil Company. From Washington, DeGolyer returned to Norman and said his good-byes before embarking on this new adventure. Journeying south by train, he stopped in San Antonio, where he saw the Alamo for the first time. Moved by this monument linking the history of two nations, it may well have marked the beginning of his lifetime fascination with the United States Southwest and Mexico.[16]

He traveled on through Laredo, where his new employer had first caught the oil bug. Crossing the river south, government officials examined his credentials and, satisfied that he was no anarchist, welcomed him to Mexico. Then, passing Monterrey he skirted the eastern foothills of the Sierra Madre Oriental. The train paused in Victoria, capital of the state of Tamaulipas, before continuing onward across a great semiarid plain, then finally downward to the coast. On November 19, 1909, DeGolyer stepped off the train and into the streets of Tampico. He

C. Willard
Hayes. Young
DeGolyer's
learned mentor
on the USGS
and in Mexico.
(Everette
Lee DeGolyer
Collection.
Courtesy of
DeGolyer Library,
Southern
Methodist
University.)

would ever after remember this as the day that sealed his decision to "become an oil man."[17]

Many years later, Tampico remained a vivid memory for DeGolyer, from its crowded plaza to its colorful market, to its quaint restaurants. At the time, Tampico hosted but a small foreign "colony" that frequented the best cafés and celebrated their own national holidays in exile. Amenities were simple and few: strolls on the plaza, open-air concerts, a cup of tea at the tennis club. The town was still poorly lit by night, and the streets mostly unpaved.[18]

DeGolyer was not the first geologist to arrive in Tampico. He was met there by his old friend Edwin B. Hopkins and Chester W. Washburne.[19] Mexican Eagle was still a small operation in Tampico. That was before the construction of the great five-story office building that would house the Pearson operation. DeGolyer could remember only three European employees managing the operation at that time. They were an odd bunch: William Calder, an Aberdeen Scot; Julius Hess, a Dutchman later killed in a payroll robbery; and an Englishman named Burnet, who managed water transportation for the company.[20]

After a few days acclimation in Tampico, DeGolyer set out with Hopkins for the company camps almost a hundred miles to the south, near the small town of Tuxpan. Because roads were inadequate and railroad access was nonexistent, the young geologists traveled the first leg of the journey by water, through Tamiahua lagoon, which stretched along the Gulf Coast near Tampico, shielded by coastal islands. Superintendent Calder saw them off, reassuring the novices that groceries were on board the launch in case of a breakdown. In the event, their transport did fail them, although DeGolyer and Hopkins were close enough to shore that they were able to land without assistance. Fortunately, a local family welcomed the two and treated them to tortillas, beans, and coffee. This meal far surpassed the emergency "groceries," which later investigation proved to be comprised of ketchup, Worcestershire sauce, and vinegar.[21]

The next morning, Hopkins took DeGolyer to view the site of the disastrous Dos Bocas well. There, a scene worthy of Dante greeted the two. Salt water bubbled from the crater, and an overpowering stench of sulfur pervaded the location. Fumes were so strong that DeGolyer found his pocket change blackened. The scene could not fail to impress the observer with a sense of the powerful forces with which oilmen in Mexico contended.[22]

Traveling on to the south end of the lagoon, DeGolyer and Hopkins arrived at the village of Tamiahua. The colorful rusticity of the town made a powerful impression on the recent arrival:

Gaily-plumaged fighting cocks, each tethered by one leg, were staked out in front of almost every door. A few scattered coconut palms curving from the sand and carrying their plumes of dark-gray fronds high into the sky and the white and pastel-colored houses stamped the scene with the mark of the tropics. An old barn of a church in front of which a great bronze bell rested on the ground gave the whole an appearance of great antiquity. Away from cities, bright lights, hotels and restaurants similar to those at home, I began to get acquainted with Mexico.[23]

Everette Lee DeGolyer on a Mexican Road, 1909. Tropical growth in Veracruz made machetes required equipment for field geologists. (Everette Lee DeGolyer Collection. Courtesy of DeGolyer Library, Southern Methodist University.)

In Tamiahua, DeGolyer and Hopkins rested at the establishment of one Luis Kenyon, an American immigrant who made a living in this remote locale as a merchant. After riding over some of the local terrain to see what it looked like, DeGolyer prepared to begin geological evaluations for the company.

In 1910, outfitting for geological exploration in Mexico required careful preparation. The geologist needed a good horse for riding, a dependable pack animal, and above all a trustworthy saddle-boy, or *mozo*, who often doubled as a guide. At Tamiahua, DeGolyer engaged a *mozo* named Hippolyto who took him about twenty miles to the hacienda Tierra Amarilla, where his first assignment awaited.[24]

Don Alfredo Peláez welcomed DeGolyer to the hacienda and offered him the hospitality of the estate during his work there. The Peláez family was one of the most respected and important families in the Huasteca region of Veracruz state. A Spanish family that had immigrated after Díaz took power, the Peláez family became a significant force in the nascent petroleum industry through their landholdings. When Pearson's company first began prospecting in the area, it found the Peláez family both helpful and receptive to business proposals. The alliance deepened when Alfredo's older brother Ignacio Peláez joined Mexican Eagle as legal counsel. In later years, Ignacio Peláez would become one of DeGolyer's close friends. The third brother, Manuel, would later rise to the rank of a general and figure as a local strongman during the Mexican Revolution. However, in 1909, the Peláez family's greatest importance to the oil industry was through its extensive real estate. Mexican Eagle desperately needed oil, and Pearson hoped that the Peláez patrimony might be the balm for his company's woes.[25]

The first step was to reconnoiter the hacienda. From December 13, 1909, to January 2, 1910, DeGolyer traversed the extent of the property.[26] Accompanied by his *mozo,* DeGolyer packed light for this sort of work, bringing only "a clean shirt or two and a clean pair of socks and some underwear rolled up in a slicker and tied up on the back of [his] own horse."[27] Carrying no instrument other than a pocket compass, the object of this first pass was to get a general sense of the task. In 1912, after rising to the rank of chief geologist, DeGolyer would instruct company geologists: "[T]he geologist should first make a thorough reconnaissance of a considerable area, familiarizing himself with its topography and general geology: with locations of land controlled by the company, and with any surface indications of oil which may be accessible."[28] After achieving an overview of the property in question, the geologist proceeded to more specific matters of interest.

Interestingly, much of the information that DeGolyer and other geologists compiled had nothing to do with geology but was nonetheless essential if the company was to develop the property. Road conditions, timber, agricultural development, flood plains, and other basic economic and natural features were important factors in any decision to drill. If good roads did not exist, then the transportation of essential equipment would hamper the process and run up costs. The presence of trees suitable for construction was a desirable feature, especially if transportation to the site was difficult. These important aspects of the business did not escape DeGolyer, who noted in his report on Tierra Amarilla that forest covered the land. "The principal trees are the zapote, chico, pepper and cedar," he reported.[29] He also recorded the primary economic use of the land: agriculture and livestock.[30] All these facts would be irrelevant, of course, if oil were not under the land.

Describing the vegetative and economic conditions on the surface was one thing, but locating prospective wells was a trickier matter.

DeGolyer's survey of the Tierra Amarilla hacienda reflected the limitations of geological prospecting in the early years of the oil industry. As in later years, the geologist's greatest challenge was interpreting the clues that nature offered. In 1909, there were often very few clues for the geologist to consider.

One of the most valuable pieces of evidence was also one that required relatively little sophistication to interpret: surface indication of petroleum. In the early days of the industry, oilmen identified many fields because locals noted the presence of oil seeping from the ground. In some cases, the oil was not immediately evident from the surface, but might appear as an unwelcome intruder in water wells. DeGolyer later stressed the importance of this basic information, noting, "All oil springs and chapapote seepages, both active and extinct, should be carefully examined, located on the map and described: also sulfur and other mineral springs or spring deposits and asphalt veins. Samples of hard asphalt veins should be forwarded to [the] chief Geologist."[31] As he composed his first reports for the company in 1909 and 1910, DeGolyer was carefully attentive to this basic concern.[32]

Once DeGolyer turned his attention below the surface, the real detective work began. Geologists had relatively few tools at their disposal when it came to mapping the subterranean structure of rock formations. This process always involved a fair degree of guesswork because it was impossible to confirm any hypothesis conclusively without drilling, and even this at times was inadequate to prove the geologist right.

Basic subterranean analysis usually required the examination of rock outcrops near the property in question, and the closer, the better. Outcrops were locations where geologists could view subterranean rock strata at the surface. Typically, they existed where some force had thrust the layers upward and where erosion had worn away a cross section of the earth underneath. By examining the thickness, the composition, and the angle of descent of these rocks, geologists could make projections about the structures—the stratigraphy—underlying adjacent properties. DeGolyer's reconnaissance for outcrops at Tierra Amarilla was disappointing: "There are not sufficient exposures at any place in this region to construct a satisfactory stratigraphic section."[33]

Even if rock outcrops were scarce, topography could provide clues to the underlying geology of an area. Although worn by the weather, the rise and fall of the land above might indicate similar patterns in the rock structures below. Combined with information from rock outcrops, surface topography could give a fair picture of what the earth was like below the surface. However, this was not the case at Tierra Amarilla. There, the absence of rock outcrops made interpretation difficult. Worse, deposits of alluvial soil, carried by waterways for many thousands of years, had obscured the underlying geology.[34] But there was one feature that showed promise. A volcanic formation that the locals called Cerro Pelón, "bald hill," rose from the land. Since volcanic structures such as this one disrupted and pushed rock formations upward, DeGolyer believed that there might be a chance for oil around its perimeter. Because oil tended to migrate upward through rock until stopped by some impermeable layer, he hoped that the upward push of the volcanic "plug" might have created a trap that could hold petroleum.[35]

This formed the basis for DeGolyer's recommendation to drill on the hacienda. A drilling team began work on Tierra Amarilla No. 1 in August 1910 on the location that DeGolyer made. They completed the well on April 9, 1911, as six hundred barrels a day flowed forth—all salt water. The drilling of subsequent wells on the hacienda would ultimately yield modest oil production, but this first well located by DeGolyer was hardly an auspicious beginning to his career as a petroleum geologist. Even with the later wells, Mexican Eagle was unable to make a profit on the property. Pearson would have to look elsewhere for the company's salvation. In the meantime, DeGolyer's mind was elsewhere. After half a year away from home, he had concluded that he must act soon regarding a certain personal matter.[36]

In the summer of 1910, DeGolyer suddenly left his work in Mexico and returned to the United States. He had only begun his fieldwork for Mexican Eagle, but he felt compelled to risk the displeasure of his superiors. His decision to leave was decisive, momentous, and intensely personal. DeGolyer had discovered the truth behind the old adage that absence makes the heart grow fonder. Arriving in Norman in early June, Nell Goodrich was surprised at his impulsiveness. As she later recalled, "I don't think he even troubled to get formal permission, he just announced he was coming to get me and left. It was perhaps the only reckless thing De ever did in his life. He got me."[37]

On June 10, 1910, Everette and Nell were married before a small gathering of family members. The pastor of the Methodist church where Nell had served as the organist performed the simple ceremony. The wedding took place at about eight o'clock in the morning. A few hours later, the two boarded a train south for Mexico.[38]

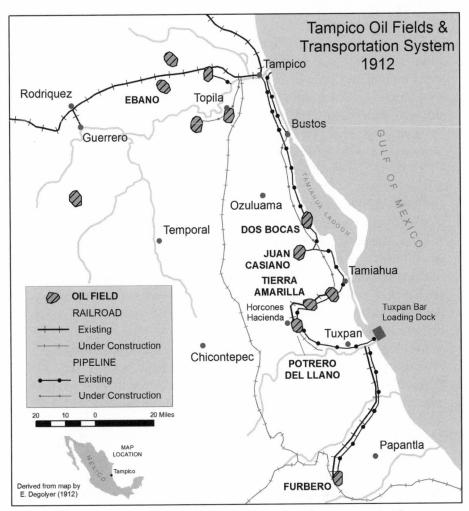

Tampico Oilfields and Transportation System, 1912. (Map by Gregory Plumb.)

There was to be no honeymoon for the young couple. DeGolyer's presence was required immediately in Tuxpan. The sudden changes in lifestyle occasioned by their whirlwind marriage and new life in Mexico tested the young Mrs. DeGolyer's strength of character. For a young woman accustomed to living in a familiar town close to family and friends, the abrupt change of culture and climate was both exciting and slightly disconcerting. Their arrival in Tuxpan gave her an early indication of the changes in her life that lay in store. Among their initial experiences, the accommodations that the young couple shared made a memorable impression on Mrs. DeGolyer. As she later recalled, "He had made . . . no arrangements at all, so we went to the village hotel, I suppose you'd call it . . . There were cots, like army cots, in the room and every kind of bug known to man and all the mosquitoes of the tropics that Mexico had came into the room."[39] Suffering that first night from disappointment and discomfort, she cried.[40]

After a few days, the couple managed to procure a large room in a house that overlooked the river. Making the most of the space that they had, they used different corners of the room as office, bedroom, kitchen, dining room, and parlor.[41] It was a marked improvement over the hotel, and Mrs. DeGolyer began to settle in a little.[42]

While Nell was adjusting to her new surroundings, Everette returned to work. The presence of his young bride did complicate matters somewhat. It was now necessary for him to commute regularly between the oilfields and their new home. During the week, he would explore potential fields, scouting out the presence of oil seeps and carefully recording details. On the weekends, he would return to town and the pleasures of domestic life.[43]

Although Mrs. DeGolyer was growing to enjoy the exotic atmosphere of Tuxpan, she still had a lingering unease with her new surroundings. Everette never carried a gun in Mexico, but he purchased a pistol for his wife. She worried, particularly when he was away in the field, and slept with it under her pillow. Occasionally, she would carry the gun with her in a handkerchief while on outings. Although she never checked to see whether it was loaded, she felt that it might serve some deterrent effect—even if empty. Later she explained, "I didn't even look to see. I was afraid of it, I just carried it; it was some comfort to think others might be afraid of it too."[44]

While Nell did her best not to worry and to enjoy her life in rustic Tuxpan, Everette led the life of a roving geologist. Searching out hacienda after hacienda for signs of oil, not all of his concerns were geological. An important, if nonscientific, aspect of his work involved maintaining company secrets. To be sure, there was something of a brotherhood between all geologists in Mexico, regardless of employer. But in practice, companies employed geologists in order to make money, and information was money. DeGolyer knew this intuitively and attempted to serve Mexican Eagle as best he could in this geological intelligence war. Years later, he remembered one experience when his efforts backfired.

While performing one survey in 1910, DeGolyer made a point of regularly visiting a local telegraph station, where he would make periodic reports to the home office. On one trip, he inquired whether there were any new telegrams for him, and the operator simply passed him the record book. There were no messages for him, but there were a series of suspicious communications between a local recipient named Gates and an office in Mexico City identified as Texaco. Delighted with this unintended discovery DeGolyer fired off copies of the communiqués to Mexican Eagle headquarters that detailed Gates's scouting of local properties. Periodically returning to the telegraph office, DeGolyer made a habit of passing on copies of all correspondence between Gates and Texaco to his supervisor, T. J. Ryder.

Some time later, Ryder contacted him, calling him to Mexico City for a conference. Expecting congratulation for his initiative, DeGolyer was shocked when Ryder confronted him: "By God, if you don't quit sending those telegrams you're going to break the company." A chagrined DeGolyer responded, "Well, they looked like they were worth calling to your attention." "Well," Ryder said, "I wasn't going to tell you this, but I am Gates and Texaco is a private agent I've got down there named Ralph Cullinan and when you wire me and recommend lands, then I wire to Texaco and recommend lands and this business is just getting a little bit too heavy, with your repeating all the telegrams."[45]

Although DeGolyer was primarily concerned with geological information, his duties also included leasing lands for the company. The practices that the company employed to obtain a favorable price on oil land were legal, but not always entirely ethical. DeGolyer recalled one ruse where the company sent him out with Ignacio Peláez to bid on properties. The two would negotiate with the landowners, arranging for a price and formulating a contract. At the last minute, a telegram from Ryder would arrive, saying that the company was no longer interested. DeGolyer later learned that Ralph Cullinan—of the "Gates" and "Texaco" debacle—would follow up a week or two later with a lower offer that the beleaguered owners typically accepted with relief.[46]

Another trick was to offer landowners specific goods instead of an agreed-upon price in currency. As DeGolyer put it,

These fellows didn't know what [was the value of] a hundred times 600 pesos—60,000 pesos—which was $30,000 in those days . . . [T]hey had lost all sense of reality. When we recognized this then we began to offer additional things. We'd ask the people that we were dealing with what they wanted and one man wanted a revolver and some woman wanted a sewing machine, another man wanted a saddle. And so finally we got a trade made and by that time the money involved was [perhaps] three or four hundred pesos.[47]

In addition to the challenges of conducting surveys in a tropical landscape, DeGolyer at times had to contend with the resistance of these local residents. The sudden interest of oil companies in coastal Mexico caught many in the region off guard. The Mexican legal system put less stress on clearly defined property rights and more emphasis on custom and equity. As a result, oil companies found it difficult in many cases to secure unclouded title to properties. While surveying the disputed Horcones hacienda, adjoining Potrero del Llano, DeGolyer encountered an *administrador* named Felicitos who was less than enthusiastic about the young geologist's plan to investigate for oil. Years later, DeGolyer still remembered the encounter vividly.

The *administrador* had warned him to stay away from the property, but the geologist was determined to conduct his investigation. As DeGolyer set up his survey equipment at the front gate of the hacienda, Felicitos arrived to disrupt the work. The *administrador* planted his feet firmly between the geologist and the stadia rod, blocking DeGolyer's view. But DeGolyer was not alone. As he later recalled, "I had a *mozo*, whose name I have forgotten, but who was a rough customer, so since Don Felicitos didn't move the *mozo* came over and gave him a slap across his buttocks with the flat of the machete and said '*Dice mi jefe que se mueva*' ['My boss says move over']."[48] As DeGolyer later put it, the "battle" was won. DeGolyer and his "helpful" assistant went on to finish this survey without further molestation, but uncertain land titles continued to plague the company and its geologists for years to come.

DeGolyer surveyed a number of properties during his first year in Mexico. Dutifully compiling information and drafting reports for the company directors, he passed on his own analysis regarding suitable locations for drilling sites. Dr. Hayes sifted through DeGolyer's reports and those of other geologists, trying to discern the location of an oil strike that would improve Mexican Eagle's position as a producer of petroleum. That position was precarious indeed by 1910. Pearson had constructed a refinery at Minatitlán in anticipation of drilling success, but that success had eluded the company so far. In order to keep the refinery in operation, Pearson imported oil from the United States. It was starting to look as if Pearson had erred in his faith in Mexico's petroleum potential.[49]

Fortunately, deliverance was now at hand. For much of 1910, surveys of the Potrero del Llano hacienda and adjoining properties occupied DeGolyer. Conditions at Potrero del Llano were primitive but adequate for company purposes. Mexican Eagle men had built a camp there consisting of a few canvas-walled structures with palm-thatched roofs and wooden floors. A screen strip about a yard wide ran horizontally around the walls of the cabins serving for light and ventilation. DeGolyer recalled the bungalows as "pleasant places to live" where the residents enjoyed the service of "Chinese cooks and house-boys."[50]

As at Tierra Amarilla, DeGolyer addressed a number of questions in his reports at Potrero del Llano. Again, transportation was a key concern in developing the property. Like most of the properties that Mexican Eagle developed near Tuxpan, access to Potrero del Llano was limited. Supplies traveled by boat from Tampico through the Tamiahua lagoon to a landing over forty kilometers distant from the Potrero camp. From the landing, wagons carried supplies through tropical surroundings to the geologists, drillers, and other Mexican Eagle employees. As might be imagined, trying to ship oil from such a remote location would be commercially impossible without improvements to the transportation infrastructure. This was soon in the works as company men laid out plans for a railroad, a pipeline, and telephone service.[51]

Drillers were hard at work at Potrero del Llano even before DeGolyer arrived in Mexico. Geoffrey Jeffries, an Englishman in Pearson's employ, made the location of the first well on the property.[52] As the drilling progressed, hopes mounted for the success that had thus far eluded Mexican Eagle. DeGolyer was in the camp in February 1910, when Potrero del Llano No. 1 came in.[53] It may well have been the first "gusher" that he had witnessed, and it made quite an impression. He was having dinner when there was a "terrific roar" that sent everyone racing outside to see what had happened. The well had "come in and there was a stream of black oil flowing up through the derrick and hitting the crown block and making two great ears of oil on each side."[54] However, initial excitement faded as the flood of oil from the well slowed. Although a gusher, Potrero del Llano No. 1 soon subsided to a moderate level of oil production.[55]

After the discovery well at Potrero del Llano came in, it became necessary to build a pipeline to the hacienda, where Mexican Eagle still

Camp at Potrero del Llano. Mexican workers rest in the shade of a palm near the narrow gauge rail line. (Everette Lee DeGolyer Collection. Courtesy of DeGolyer Library, Southern Methodist University.)

had hopes for a large and productive field.[56] In the meantime, Hayes visited the camp to lay out the principles for locating the next wells on the property. His proposal was to create a system of rectangular coordinates that would space the wells with geometric precision. Topography and the presence of oil seepages would determine the coordinates chosen for the location of the next drilling sites.[57]

Work on the second and third wells began in the spring of 1910, based on Hayes's plan. DeGolyer was responsible for putting Hayes's scheme into action. In May 1910, Potrero del Llano No. 2 struck oil, but again, production was only moderate.[58] While waiting for the completion of the third well, DeGolyer prepared a report for Hayes regarding the selection of the next drilling location. In it, he openly confessed his frustration in appraising the geological structure of the oilfield, noting, "The wells which have been drilled . . . have thrown but little light on the structure of the field. The dips are very low, and with the present crude method of measurement, the logs can easily be twenty feet in error by the time the bottom of the hole is reached."[59] The lack of precision particularly troubled him, leading him to remark, "Twenty feet in this field makes all of the difference in the world in the interpretation of geologic structures from well logs."[60]

These were the inauspicious conditions under which DeGolyer

would locate the well that would secure his success. DeGolyer seemed to have little sense that his hour of destiny was at hand. Although he hoped that the Potrero del Llano field would prove to be a large one, the drilling recommendations that he offered to Hayes focused on draining the field efficiently. DeGolyer offered two different patterns of geometric coordinates—squares and hexagons—that would ensure an adequate number of wells to cover the property. What he lacked was any clear sense that the next well might be a prodigious producer. Indeed, the drilling scheme that he developed assumed that all the wells would drain oil at approximately the same rate.[61]

Whatever the logic behind DeGolyer's analysis, Sir Weetman Pearson had instructed Hayes that the young geologist should choose the next location.[62] It was a fateful decision. On June 4, 1910, the company suspended work on the third well without success.[63] Work began on Potrero del Llano No. 4 on June 11, 1910, but the company suspended this project as well in July.[64]

In the meantime, construction continued on the pipeline that would link the remote hacienda with Tuxpan. The pipeline was approaching completion when the company recommenced drilling on the well on December 23, 1910. Success was not long in waiting. The well erupted violently at about two o'clock in the morning on December 27.[65]

Potrero del Llano No. 4. was nothing short of astounding. Obliterating the derrick in seconds, oil spewed skyward in a fountain that towered over four hundred feet into the air.[66] Everything within a mile of the well was soon coated by the crude being expelled from the well at the awesome rate of 110,000 barrels a day.[67] Drillers working the well at the time it blew, scrambled for cover.[68] The gusher promised to ensure Mexican Eagle's success if only the company could bring the well under control.

DeGolyer was not at Potrero del Llano when well No. 4 struck oil. He was on a trip with his boss and benefactor, C. Willard Hayes, making a general inspection of the company's oil properties. They had been in the Potrero del Llano camp a couple of days before but had moved on to examine the Furbero oilfield fifty miles southward. Before arriving at Furbero, word arrived of the well's success. Unaware of the chaos that was now unfolding back at the Potrero camp, the party continued on with their inspection, pleased that the well was apparently successful.[69]

DeGolyer had anticipated the success of the well, but nobody had anticipated the scale of the success. When word reached DeGolyer and

Hayes that the well was flowing wild at 60,000 barrels per day—an underestimate—they realized that their tour of inspection would have to wait. As the significance of the moment sunk in, the two departed for Mexico City to confer with the Chief, who seemed to have hit a run of good luck. The preceding summer, Pearson had been raised to the peerage and was now to be addressed as Lord Cowdray.[70]

DeGolyer's time in Mexico City brought his first real experience of celebrity. Cowdray met with him briefly before shuffling off to the Potrero field to manage the battle to control the well. The young geologist remained to attend a luncheon with Cowdray's wife; the British minister to Mexico; and the governor of the Federal District, Guillermo de Landa y Escandón. In addition to his role in the Mexican government, Landa y Escandón also served as a director for El Águila and was responsible for domestic sales. DeGolyer was, as he would only realize later, the "fair-haired boy."[71] Wearing a newly purchased suit, DeGolyer toured Mexico City by car with the governor before making his way to Potrero del Llano via Tampico. In later years, DeGolyer associate H. B. Fuqua mused that DeGolyer's meticulous attention to dress must have come from these days, learning from the British example that "clothes and appearance could open a lot of business doors."[72]

Mexico City must have seemed another world to DeGolyer after his return to Potrero del Llano. Conditions in the camp had gone from comfortable to wretched in very short order. Crude petroleum coated everything. The spray from the well continued to shoot over four hundred feet in the air, raining down on the surrounding area in an oily mist. Anyone who came near the site was automatically soaked, and DeGolyer recalled the futile efforts made by the company to keep the men stocked with clean, comfortable attire: "Everyone's clothes were ruined; they had brought thousands of the cheapest type of Mexican clothes down there and you could get a new suit by applying for one but they usually didn't fit very well."[73] If the suits were uncomfortable, they at least had the virtue of a short lifespan. According to DeGolyer, "[I]f you walked out of doors for ten yards a big mist of oil would be blowing over half the time and ruin your clothes again."[74]

The company men scrambled to dig earthen reservoirs that might temporarily hold the valuable liquid in open air until workers could bring the well under control and connect it to a pipeline. Although they saved some of it, most ran into a nearby creek, which in turn fed the

Potrero del Llano No. 4 in January 1911. The well sprayed over 100,000 barrels of oil daily over the Mexican landscape until workers successfully capped it. Simultaneously, the well saved the Mexican Eagle Oil Company and launched Everette Lee DeGolyer to success. (Everette Lee DeGolyer Collection. Courtesy of DeGolyer Library, Southern Methodist University.)

Tuxpan River, covering its surface six inches deep as it traversed the coastal lowlands and flowed into the Gulf of Mexico. Not many days afterward it had coated the beach at Tampico, traveling more than 125 miles by water.[75]

Downstream, the oil was set on fire in an effort to prevent it from spreading onto cropland. DeGolyer took a hand in constructing flumes to speed the flow of crude so that the flames would not be able to work their way back to the well site. In the meanwhile, Pearson's political connections proved invaluable as local political bosses ordered the conscription of men to battle the well. Among those pressed into service was DeGolyer's old nemesis, Don Felicitos of the Horcones hacienda, and his arrival with fifteen to twenty men was more than welcome.[76]

After extemporizing the flume system, DeGolyer turned his attention to surveying for a pipeline that would handle the company's increased flow of crude. Although not trained as an engineer, DeGolyer felt far more certain in his judgments regarding pipeline location than in his recommendations for drilling sites. The topographical surveys that the young geologist had used in analyzing properties for oil potential proved invaluable in charting the most efficient and cost-effective routes for pipeline construction.[77]

Back at the well, engineers brought a large valve called a "bell nipple" to the wellhead, with hopes of bringing the wild flow of crude under control. Texas oilmen had used a similar device on much smaller gushers. When a smaller valve proved unable to stem the flow of oil, the company sent for a larger bell nipple, which the men winched over the well in March 1911. After tightening the valve, they finally brought the well under control, and the company rushed to construct a pipeline to transport the petroleum to Mexican Eagle's refinery. Over the next few years, workers constructed and reconstructed a mammoth concrete cap over the well, giving it an uncanny resemblance to the pre-Columbian pyramids of Mexico. Even as blood had flowed freely from veins of sacrificial victims in the old temples, the lifeblood of industrial civilization flowed in copious volume from the pipes that emerged from the new well. The future of Cowdray's company looked bright at last.[78]

Potrero del Llano No. 4 promised to secure a future for DeGolyer as well, but by the time the company brought the well under control, DeGolyer was no longer in Mexico. After completing the survey for the pipeline to the bonanza well, he had returned to Mexico City, where he met with the Chief. DeGolyer proceeded to surprise his employer by announcing his intent to resign. The reason he presented for his planned departure was his incomplete education. Although DeGolyer had found the Mexican oilfields most stimulating, he had left his studies at the University of Oklahoma before taking a degree, and he was now determined to finish it. But the Chief was not going to let the young geologist escape so easily. DeGolyer had located the well that had saved Mexican Eagle Oil and the Cowdray fortune. Although Cowdray was a man who made it a habit to leave nothing to chance, he now regarded DeGolyer as his lucky charm, an indispensable part of his staff with whom he was unwilling to part. Cowdray granted him a leave of absence in order to finish his degree but encouraged him to return to Mexico.[79]

DeGolyer's decision to return to the University of Oklahoma for the spring semester in 1911 revealed much about his character. A more cautious young man, if presented with the prospect of sure, steady, and lucrative employment, might have remained in Mexico. However, DeGolyer was a man driven by more than mere lucre. He possessed the persistent curiosity and analytical mind that characterizes the scientific outlook. Both DeGolyer and his wife also shared a respect for education that would inspire philanthropic activities later in their lives.

DeGolyer's Oklahoma homecoming was a triumph. The success of the Potrero del Llano well and the esteem in which his employer held him gave DeGolyer a sense of achievement that few of his classmates could match. Nell's mother, Emma Hatton Goodrich, felt confirmed in her confidence in the young man. As Nell remembered, "[W]hen he returned to Norman to complete his degree after eighteen months in Mexico, he was the richest student in school. Even mother hadn't expected anything like that but she took pride in seeing her judgment proved."[80]

DeGolyer returned to the University of Oklahoma campus as a wiser and worldlier student. Now listing Veracruz, Mexico, as his residence, he turned his efforts to the composition of an erudite thesis titled "Metamorphosis of the Coals of a Portion of the Anthracite and Crested Butte Quadrangles, Colorado."[81] The thesis built upon work that DeGolyer had done with the USGS in 1909.[82] Contacting his old supervisor on the Survey, W. T. Lee, DeGolyer requested information related to his research and asserted his plans to return to Mexico in June. There were aspects of his work in industry that he found quite stimulating, but he also bemoaned the lack of opportunity to contribute to scholarly conversations about geology. He wrote, "I am very much interested in the commercial work. Its only drawback is that one sees so many things that he wants to publish and cannot."[83]

Perhaps aware of the young geologist's scholarly temptation, Lord Cowdray continued to cultivate DeGolyer, sending him a bonus of $345 intended to defray the cost of his education.[84] Although appreciated, the gesture was probably not necessary to lure DeGolyer back to Mexico. In addition to the spectacular success that he had achieved south of the border, he had also fallen in love with the landscape, the culture, and the history of Mexico. After a little over a year of experience, he was already passably proficient in Spanish.[85] He never lost a sense of respect and appreciation for the Mexican people, even after political developments in later years caused bad blood between Americans and Mexicans.

Despite his sometimes traumatic experience of the Mexican Revolution, DeGolyer returned to the United States an eloquent advocate of intercultural understanding. In a fascinating speech that he delivered at the University of Oklahoma YMCA in 1915, he described his own intellectual transformation as he encountered Mexican culture:

> Before I went into Mexico . . . I had thought of the Mexican people as being dressed in flowing garments and large sombreros, eating chille and other foods composed mostly of red pepper, spending their days smoking and their evenings singing and making continual love to their raven-haired senoritas. When I arrived in Mexico, I received the surprise of my life.[86]

Continuing, he speculated about the roots of his own misconceptions as well as the distrust of Americans that he observed among some Mexicans:

> Most of the Mexicans we see here are the laborers that . . . [have been] imported by the railroads to do manual work. Most of the Americans that have gone into Mexico have been railroad men, miners, and oil men. As a rule these men have not tried to adapt themselves to their new surroundings, either by learning the language or familiarizing themselves with the people they work among.
>
> Because of this we get the wrong idea of the Mexican and the Mexican gets the wrong impression of the American.[87]

He made this point strongly enough that one reporter present thought it appropriate to summarize his talk as an appeal for "race sympathy and the abolition of race prejudice."[88] As he would happily assert in later years, he always found the Mexicans to be "very fine, friendly people."[89]

DeGolyer graduated from the University of Oklahoma on June 8, 1911. The scientific education that he had received there coupled with his field experience with the USGS and the Mexican Eagle Oil Company to give the young man a formidable reputation. Now he was eager to return to work south of the border. DeGolyer and his wife returned to Mexico in summer 1911. At first, it seemed that their life there would continue much as before, although improved somewhat by DeGolyer's new prestige within the company.

Rather than return to accommodations in isolated Tuxpan, the couple settled in Tampico, living in a comfortable, single-story house just a block from the Mexican Eagle offices. DeGolyer decorated the walls with maps of the oilfields, an obsession that he could not abandon even in domestic life. Nell DeGolyer found that Tampico was more amenable than Tuxpan. There were a number of foreign ladies there—many wives of oilmen. There were also opportunities to relax at the Colonial Club, and horse racing provided welcome distraction at the Sporting Club. She found fellowship at the Methodist mission, where she often played piano for services. Nell also gave lessons at her home on a rosewood piano ordered by Everette from Mexico City.[90]

The DeGolyers' life in Mexico after their return was eventful, and sometimes difficult. They lost their first son—stillborn—soon after arriving in Tampico.[91] Two years later, Nell was expecting the birth of another child when she fell ill with malaria. Advised by a doctor that a pregnant woman should not receive quinine treatment, Nell returned to Norman in order to recuperate and await delivery. In May 1913, she was back home, and in December she gave birth to their first surviving child, a daughter whom they named Nell Virginia.[92]

In the meanwhile, Hayes, DeGolyer's mentor and benefactor, relinquished his duties as chief geologist for Mexican Eagle to become vice president. Hayes's former job now fell to DeGolyer, who became responsible for overseeing the work of other geologists, even as he continued his own work as a field geologist.[93] DeGolyer issued reports based on his own reconnaissance work from the time of his return in summer 1911 through 1912.[94] But he also began to draft analyses based on statistics and information compiled by other field geologists.[95] As DeGolyer turned more toward work based upon statistical information and the observations of others, he spent less time in the field. To some extent, this was a result of his new role as chief geologist. Oversight of the company's geological work demanded more time in the office than his earlier work had required. However, DeGolyer's retreat from the field also reflected deteriorating conditions in Mexico. For even before he had left to complete his degree at the University of Oklahoma, events were unfolding that would make the geologists' adventures in Mexico rather more adventurous. The tropical coast of Mexico was about to get even hotter.

DeGolyer's tenure in Mexico, as well as the florescence of the Mexican oil industry, coincided with one of the most turbulent periods in the history of that nation—the Revolution. Almost no one foresaw the scale of the bloodshed that would begin in 1910 and continue for years to come. But trouble had been building for decades. The policies of the Díaz regime had achieved remarkable success in modernizing the economy and infrastructure of Mexico. Unfortunately, modernization as implemented under Díaz had come at a terrible price, especially among the lower classes. Rural laborers suffered under a system of hacienda labor that condemned most to debt peonage. Indian communities had seen their rights eroded by a government set on development by private investors. Workers in the new factories that had sprung into being in the nation's cities suffered miserable living conditions. There was broad resentment against the Mexican business elite and foreign investors.[96]

Even among the middle class, the regime's support was slipping. For decades, Díaz had maintained his grasp on power through personal cultivation of local political bosses—the *jefes políticos.* By rewarding these local strongmen and their allies, he was able to secure both their support and that of their cronies. Díaz's patronage extended not only to present office holders but to other longtime supporters and their families as well. The system promoted stability, but it also left many permanently outside of the circles of power. The success of Porifirian economic policies promoted the growth of the middle class, but it also increased the number of people who felt excluded by cronyism.[97]

As the presidential election of 1910 approached, opposition to the reelection of Díaz began to form around Francisco I. Madero, an idealistic liberal and member of one of the wealthiest families in the state of Coahuila. Madero called for a more democratic Mexico and seemed to be gaining support as the election loomed. The regime, unwilling to countenance possible defeat, jailed Madero and proclaimed Díaz the victor. Escaping from prison, Madero fled to the United States, where he began to agitate against the regime. In October 1910, Madero met with supporters in San Antonio, Texas, and proclaimed a revolution. He called on the people of Mexico to rise up on November 20, 1910, and assumed the provisional presidency of the nation.[98]

The uprising began two days early in the state of Puebla. The movement began to pick up steam as rebels rallied to the cause, especially in the north. After an abortive return on November 19, Madero crossed the border for good in February 1911. Federal troops found it difficult to suppress an insurrection that generally enjoyed the support of the local population. On May 10, 1911, Ciudad Juárez fell to the rebels. Defeats elsewhere began to take a toll on Federal forces in the form of desertions. Even Díaz knew that his hold on power was slipping. On May 25, 1911, he submitted his resignation to the Congress. Six days later, he and his family boarded the German ship *Ypiranga* in Veracruz and steamed off into exile in France.[99]

Sadly, the bloodshed had only begun. In June, Madero arrived in triumph in the capital, where crowds greeted him exuberantly. The moment did not last long. Already, the diverse coalition of malcontents that had driven Díaz from power was starting to come apart. In the north, rebel leaders Pascual Orozco Jr. and Pancho Villa expressed their discontent with Madero's leadership soon after the fall of Ciudad Juárez. In the south, the fiery Emiliano Zapata readied for conflict with the government as Madero insisted that his followers disband. Among Madero's generals, the ambitious Victoriano Huerta waited for an opportune moment to realize his own plans for power. As Porfirio Díaz departed for France, he reportedly remarked, "Madero has unleashed a tiger. Now let's see if he can control it."[100]

Madero proved unequal to the challenge that he confronted. Interested in democratic reform but cautious when it came to social issues, many of his more radical supporters abandoned him when it became clear that he would not lead a social revolution. As rebellions sprang up in the north and the south, Madero increasingly relied on the military leadership of General Victoriano Huerta to keep the government afloat. His misjudgment of Huerta proved costly. In February 1913, Huerta betrayed Madero, seizing power for himself. In the aftermath of the coup, Huerta supporters placed Madero under arrest and then murdered him. Far from reestablishing order, this turn of events only deepened what was evolving into a full-scale civil war. While Huerta had the command of the Federal army, the opposition formed around the leadership of Venustiano Carranza, the governor of Coahuila state and a former Madero supporter. Styling themselves "Constitutionalists," Carranza and his supporters enjoyed the sympathy and support of the new American president, Woodrow Wilson. Wilson's determination to shape the outcome of the Mexican Revolution would be fraught with consequences for the foreign-owned petroleum industry and American oilmen like DeGolyer.[101]

As the Revolution devolved into a violent power struggle among factions, the oil industry in Mexico stood in a particularly vulnerable position. Staffed largely by non-Mexicans, the companies were understandably concerned about revolutionaries who indicted the Díaz regime as a puppet of foreign capitalists. The Mexican Eagle Oil Company was especially sensitive to this rhetoric. Cowdray was a particularly close friend of the exiled president, and his staff had assisted in the flight of the Díaz family from Mexico.[102]

In addition to the xenophobic mood of the moment, the companies were also in the uncomfortable position of having something that every faction desired: oil. One of the most remarkable feats of the Díaz regime was the construction of railroads across Mexico. These railroads had been perhaps the most essential contribution toward the modernization of the national economy. Now, they were the focus of military strategy as revolutionary generals used rail connections to move troops deftly from front to front in an effort to control Mexico. However, railroads were useless without fuel, and that fuel was oil. The companies quickly found themselves the target of every aspiring general. Claiming to represent the "legitimate" government, they would demand the payment of taxes, require commissions for well permits, and forbid the sale of oil to the opposition. Because the fortunes of the struggle were constantly shifting, most companies found themselves dealing with different, antagonistic camps, often at the same time.[103]

Soon, the oilmen who had taken refuge in Tampico found that even there they faced the threat of violence. DeGolyer was there when thing began to go to pieces in 1913. Federal forces there held the city on behalf of General Huerta, but in November an army led by General Cándido Águilar arrived in order to assert control for the Constitutionalists and Carranza.

For six months the two armies nervously faced one another, with neither able to drive away their opponent. The siege of Tampico was a tense but exciting experience for DeGolyer and his colleagues. Charles Hamilton, one of DeGolyer's geologists, recorded the details of one battle that took place on December 10, in a letter to his parents: "About 11 o'clock . . . the first skirmish began and a rapid fire was continued all day long. From the top of our building through my telescope, I could plainly see the trenches of the National [Federalist] troops and could hear the sharp putt of the Mauser rifles."[104] Then the Federalist cruiser *Bravo* began lobbing shots over the city and into the hills where the

Constitutionalist army lay. Hamilton remarked with naïveté, "Altogether, it was a grand sight and sound."[105]

DeGolyer was apparently a witness to this skirmish and almost paid for the experience with his life. Standing behind a cement parapet on top of one of Tampico's tallest buildings, he was observing the action when his hat flew from his head. Retrieving the headgear, he found it freshly ventilated just inches above where his skull had been moments before. DeGolyer later asserted that this brush with death was "[m]y only claim to heroism in the revolution."[106]

DeGolyer continued to work through the siege, dashing off messages to Nell in the United States, assuring her that all was well. "Rebel attack on Tampico and everybody alright," he wrote just days after his near miss on the rooftop.[107] The stress was mounting, and in another message he revealed both sentimentality and frustration with his work: "The building is full of refugees and there is not one chance in a thousand of any one being hurt. I am sick and tired of the whole business . . . Sweetheart, I am absolutely heartsore and weary."[108] DeGolyer knew that he could not continue for long if these conditions endured, assuring Nell, "I should be with you and I know it. Instead, I am loafing around here and can't do a thing unless it is to die of lonesomeness. You are my sweetest heart and we are going to live together if I have to get a job teaching school."[109] By late December, he was growing bored with his captivity in Tampico, writing, "Everything in Tampico is dead as a door nail. In fact, I just have two things to do. One is to worry about you and the other is to work."[110]

Among the projects with which DeGolyer occupied himself was research in the history of oil in Mexico. It would be the first of many scholarly projects that would win him respect for his detailed analysis of highly technical topics. DeGolyer investigated the use of oil in Mexico, beginning with the Aztecs, and followed the development of its exploitation down to the present day. Putting his findings to paper, DeGolyer's account of the industry was replete with figures—numbers of wells, feet drilled, barrels produced.[111]

In contrast to his frustrated telegrams home, he painted a rosy picture of oil in Mexico. The figures did not lie. From 2.7 million barrels of oil produced in 1909, the year of his arrival in Tampico, production had ballooned to 24 million barrels.[112] He predicted that 1914 would be the biggest year for the industry yet, producing from 30 to 40 million barrels of crude.[113] On March 11, 1914, DeGolyer read his paper, titled "History of the Petroleum Industry in Mexico," before the Mexican Oil Association in Tampico, an organization headed by Hayes.[114] As the oilmen and geologists listened in the audience, they might have wondered how the battle raging over Mexico would affect the future of the industry. DeGolyer had not even mentioned the Revolution. Events would soon intervene that would call that future into question.

In April 1914, as Federalist and Constitutionalist armies confronted one another outside Tampico, the diplomatic situation with the United States had become a volatile one. President Woodrow Wilson refused to recognize the aspirations of Victoriano Huerta and determined to pursue a policy aimed at isolating the Federalist regime from international support. An incident that occurred in Tampico provided Wilson with the justification for armed intervention—a decision that would be fateful for American oilmen in Mexico.

Off the Mexican Gulf Coast, the USS *Dolphin* was running low on fuel. Captain Ralph T. Earle dispatched a paymaster and crew to reprovision on a Tampico wharf operated by a German merchant. The decision to land so close to a militarily significant railway bridge prompted Federal soldiers to place the Americans under arrest. After holding them at gunpoint for an hour, the Federalist commander promptly released the sailors when he learned what had happened.[115]

It might have all ended at that had not Rear Admiral Henry T. Mayo demanded that the Mexicans make amends. Mayo insisted that Federalist General Zaragoza raise the American flag at some prominent location on shore and offer a twenty-one-gun salute. The general agreed to comply, but only if the Americans returned a salute to the Mexican flag. Apprised of the situation, President Wilson proved unwilling to authorize such a concession because he feared the interpretation of any sign of deference as recognition of Huerta's regime.

Despite the absurd terms of the dispute, the Tampico flag incident provided Wilson with the justification to take a more active hand in Mexican events. With the matter still unresolved, the American president received word from the American consul in Veracruz that the German ship *Ypiranga* was soon to arrive with a shipment of arms for the Federalists. Remarkably, this was the same ship that had steamed President Díaz to his French exile in 1911.

Wilson reacted to this development by dispatching an expeditionary force to Veracruz. The primary motive in so doing was to deny Huerta the supplies needed to continue his struggle with the Constitutionalists. It was a disastrous decision for Americans in Mexico. A wave of anti-American indignation swept the country. In Mexico City, angry locals looted American-owned businesses and destroyed a statue of George Washington, and newspapers called for retaliation against the "Pigs of Yanquilandia."[116]

President Wilson made no provision for Americans in Tampico—among whom DeGolyer numbered. They were now in an awkward situation that threatened to become deadly. It was about this time that the company dispatched DeGolyer to Cuba in order to evaluate oil prospects there.[117] It was good timing. Tension was high even before the landing at Veracruz. As DeGolyer described it, "[F]riendliness toward Americans was very conspicuous by its marked absence."[118] Hayes was also in town, and in a conference on April 19, the two determined that any resistance against the Mexican authorities was unthinkable. That evening, DeGolyer dined nervously with Ed Hopkins and his wife. It would be his last dinner in Tampico for some time to come.[119]

The next morning DeGolyer boarded the *Antillian,* bound for the United States, with plans to proceed from there to Cuba.[120] As wild rumors flew that the United States had declared war on Mexico, American gunboats near Tampico received orders to withdraw to Veracruz. American citizens in Tampico were bewildered. Fear swept the foreign population that a bloodbath was imminent. Many Americans dreaded the events they foresaw. As one of them described the scene as he perceived it: "Brown howling mobs, armed with clubs, stones and pistols, immediately congregated all over the city, parading the streets and howling for 'Gringo' blood. To a Mexican everything with a white face is a hated 'Gringo.'"[121]

Many of the passengers aboard the *Antillian* shared these concerns. They were a diverse lot—Americans, Englishmen, Spaniards, Mexicans, and a Japanese naval mission. As the ship steamed away from Mexico, it passed the USS *Des Moines,* where sacks of coal stood piled to provide cover for its crew. "The marines were grinning," DeGolyer noted in his diary.[122] A little more than a day later, the *Antillian* arrived in Galveston Bay. Authorities ordered the ship quarantined, and the refugees anxiously waited for news from Mexico. They soon learned that American forces had indeed occupied Veracruz.

The American occupation was a catastrophe from the perspective of US–Mexico relations. Nevertheless, it did ultimately contribute to Wilson's objective of undermining Huerta's presidency. As the Constitutionalist armies closed in on Mexico City in summer 1914, Huerta would blame the American president for the outcome of the struggle. Tragically, even the fall of Huerta did not put an end to the shedding of blood in Mexico. The Revolution would rage on for years to come.[123]

But all this lay in the future as the passengers of the *Antillian* awaited their release from quarantine. For most on board, there was little to do aside from worrying. But at least one passenger found plenty to do during the wait: Commander Mori of the Imperial Japanese Navy dispatched numerous wireless messages to his superiors when not taking copious notes. After two days in quarantine, the sight of American reinforcements steaming out of the bay moved DeGolyer and his fellow detainees. As he later remembered, "[The] transports convoyed by the destroyers carried the reinforced fifth brigade to Vera Cruz [sic]. There were tears in my eyes but the feeling was one of patriotism and exultation. There were also tears in the eyes of many of the Mexicans but the reason was probably different."[124]

The occupation of Veracruz did not put a stop to the involvement of Americans in the Mexican oil industry, but it did effectively bring DeGolyer's work there as a field geologist to an end. On April 25, 1914, DeGolyer disembarked from the *Antillian* and once more set foot on US soil. A day later Nell and his young daughter, Virginia, would join him. His international travel had only begun, but he was entering a new stage in his career.[125]

DeGolyer's life in Mexico from 1909 to 1914 was a grand adventure for the young geologist. More so than any other chapter of his life, his memories of those days remained vivid, even as he approached his twilight years. DeGolyer's career led him in a new direction after 1914, but he maintained an interest in Mexico and a relationship with the Mexican oil industry for the rest of his life. It was there that he had made a name for himself, and he seems to have always borne a sense of gratitude to the nation and the people that had treated him so well.

DeGolyer's tenure as a field geologist revealed much about the state of geologists and their profession in the early twentieth century. Lord Cowdray's rival in the Mexican oilfields, Edward L. Doheny, openly expressed his contempt for geologists and their potential contributions to the location and development of petroleum resources. "Geology profs don't find oil," he famously remarked.[126] Everette DeGolyer's fieldwork in Mexico called Doheny's skepticism, and that of many "practical" oilmen, into question. His reports and recommendations contributed to a more rational and efficient development of the oilfields and helped ensure his employer's success.

However, there were significant restrictions to what geologists could do during these years. In report after report, DeGolyer expressed frustration with the limits of the information available to him. What geologists needed was some method of penetrating the shroud of soil, clay, and rock that made the mapping of subsurface geology at best an imprecise science and at worst a guessing game. At the time, geologists were able to make only limited contributions to drilling decisions that were in many ways still a question of chance. As he entered the twilight of his life, DeGolyer confessed that he believed the oil companies might have done just as well without the geologists in those early days. "With the crude methods then available to us, structure could not be mapped in Mexico with much degree of precision," he asserted. "I suspect that the companies would have done as well if they had drilled on oil seepages alone."[127]

# 3 | Executive

*Geology is the kit of tools with which the commercial geologist works
rather than the mistress whom he serves.*
—Everette Lee DeGolyer in Economic Geology, August 1924[1]

When DeGolyer departed Mexico in April 1914, under the cloud
of US military intervention, he reconsidered his future with Cowdray's
Mexican Eagle Company. Hired in 1909 as a field geologist, DeGolyer
had offered his employer technical skills related to fact gathering and
analysis of the landscape. His good fortune in locating the bonanza
well at Potrero del Llano secured him the gratitude of his employer and
the promise of promotion within the company hierarchy. Despite these
changes, he essentially remained a geologist until 1914, passing judgment on the probability of finding oil in diverse locations. But as the
Mexican Revolution raged on, it became increasingly apparent that geological surveys were becoming dangerous ventures. With the hazards
of the battlefield compounded by the anti-American hostility stirred up
by Woodrow Wilson's occupation of Veracruz, it was hard to see how
DeGolyer could continue to work in the same capacity.

Back in the United States, DeGolyer faced an important career decision. When he had accepted work with Mexican Eagle, he had been a
bachelor. Now, he was married and the father of a young daughter. The
situation in Mexico was too risky to chance continued work as a geologist. The question, then, was whether to seek geological employment
closer to home or to continue to work under Cowdray in some other capacity. Ultimately, DeGolyer opted to stay with the company. However,
over the course of the next decade the nature of his work transformed.
He would spend less time in geological fact gathering and analysis.
Managerial duties claimed an increasing share of his time.

Within ten years, DeGolyer would become an officer in a half-dozen
companies, for the most part underwritten by Lord Cowdray. As general
manager, vice president, and president of a variety of oil businesses,
DeGolyer would be challenged to think about the relationship between
his former, primarily scientific work, and his new, commercially ori-
ented responsibilities. As a newly hired geologist, DeGolyer had

Everette Lee DeGolyer at his desk in Tampico, 1911. One aspect of DeGolyer's transition to managerial duties was more time spent in the office. (Everette Lee DeGolyer Collection. Courtesy of DeGolyer Library, Southern Methodist University.)

accepted the necessity of following an agenda set by company management. Now, working within management, he was forced to reconcile a professional commitment to the interest of science with duties to company investors. He found the task a difficult one.

For the rest of his life, DeGolyer continued to weigh scientific and commercial commitments. Initially, he seems to have given greater priority to science. Yet by the mid-1920s, he increasingly found business opportunity to be as compelling as scientific advancement. Science was a "kit of tools" rather than the "mistress" he served, and his true goal was commercial success.[2] In an age of business, DeGolyer embraced his new role as a business executive.

But was it necessary to choose between the lofty ideals of science and the less altruistic promise of profit? As he settled into his career as a company executive, DeGolyer paradoxically increased his efforts to promote the science of geology, particularly through his efforts on behalf of professional societies. These organizations, especially the American Institute of Mining and Metallurgical Engineers (AIME) and the American Association of Petroleum Geologists (AAPG), were full of young geologists like DeGolyer, whose stars were also rising in the business world. Blessed with financial success and possessing an extraordinary eye for innovation, DeGolyer would become a natural leader in this generation of scientifically trained executives.

DeGolyer's transformation from a young field geologist into a company executive was a gradual one. Although the most abrupt change in his duties took place after his departure from Mexico in April 1914, he had been moving toward management for some time. As he gradually earned the respect of his superiors, they increasingly gave DeGolyer managerial responsibilities.

This was particularly true following DeGolyer's promotion to the position of chief geologist in 1912.[3] Soon, DeGolyer was giving direction to others on a whole host of nongeological matters. One such area involved the tangled legal questions with which the company struggled, usually involving conflicting titles to oil properties. DeGolyer did not shy away from legal issues. On the contrary, he happily waded into these murky waters. In at least one instance, he felt confident enough to offer direction regarding questions of Mexican legal procedure to one of the company's Mexican attorneys.[4] In matters regarding oilfield leasing, DeGolyer would soon take on an intermediary position between the company's top executives and its Mexican lawyers.[5]

He also started to offer his superiors advice regarding company organization and labor–management relations. Evaluating an oil reservoir acquired through the purchase of a competing company, DeGolyer could not resist commenting on the poor management of the field. He asserted that the drilling operations boasted "a record of inefficiency without equal," faulting a "lack of understanding between [general management] and workmen."[6] Better direction and better pay was the solution that he advocated.

DeGolyer did not restrict himself to commentary on the practices inherited through acquisition of other companies. Mexican Eagle had problems of its own. By 1914, DeGolyer was taking an active hand in resolving interdepartmental disputes within the company, most pointedly in an ongoing squabble between the Legal Department and the Land Department. The Legal Department was to blame, he thought.[7]

Two days after he passed that judgment on to Dr. Hayes, DeGolyer's role within the company transformed significantly. This was April 1914, and DeGolyer was soon to leave Mexico and return to the United States. But before his departure, it was evident that his position was in question. Because of revolutionary violence, the situation in Mexico was inauspicious for field geologists in general and for American geologists in particular. DeGolyer's future with the company was uncertain as he embarked on his return voyage to Galveston, Texas.

Reflecting on the situation in quarantine, DeGolyer considered his next step. Among the many displaced Americans who were in Galveston was his old friend Edwin Hopkins. The two had been through much together: the USGS, Mexican Eagle, and now the evacuation and an undetermined future. Discussing their predicament DeGolyer and Hopkins explored the possibility of going into business together. If they did not have enough capital to start their own oil company, they did at least have the intellectual capital to start a geological consulting firm. The two agreed to hold out against any unfavorable propositions that their employers might offer and instead put this plan into action. Hopkins left the meeting with a sense that their course was determined. DeGolyer was less committed, taking a more pragmatic, wait-and-see attitude.[8]

DeGolyer did not need to wait for long before word came from his patron in London. A cable from Lord Cowdray suggested his responsibility for paying employees evacuated from Tampico to New Orleans, so five days after his arrival he set out by train for Louisiana.[9] Arriving on May 1, he proceeded to the United States immigration office to meet company evacuees and disburse their wages. Catching his breath, DeGolyer spent the next four days touring the French Quarter and taking in vaudeville shows. His employment was still in question as Cowdray attempted to get a handle on the turbulent situation in Mexico.

In the meantime, DeGolyer would travel to Cuba and rendezvous with Dr. Hayes and his old associate Ben Belt. Their official business would be a geological evaluation of prospective oil properties, but DeGolyer had his own agenda. Hopefully, Hayes would be able to clarify the company's plans for him. Cuba captivated DeGolyer, but the geology was disappointing. Hayes also proved unable to answer questions that DeGolyer had about his future with Mexican Eagle. Only the Chief himself could make those decisions. Hayes promised to see that the company paid DeGolyer his worth, but it would be necessary to travel to London and negotiate with Cowdray. Would DeGolyer be willing to accompany him on this errand? Hayes had to know that the lure of such an adventure would be irresistible. DeGolyer accepted, and the two planned to cross the Atlantic in late summer.[10]

Leaving Cuba, DeGolyer returned to the United States to consider his options. His first stop was Washington, DC, where he visited with friends working with the USGS. After a tumultuous five years in the private sector, perhaps steady government work was just what the doctor ordered. On the other hand, private work in the United States also offered tempting opportunities. The Gulf Coast and Mid-Continent oilfields of Texas and Oklahoma were booming and conveniently located close to his family. Then, there was also the discussion that he had with Hopkins in Galveston and the possibility of going into business for himself with his old friend.[11]

At the same time that these possibilities lured him homeward, developments in Mexican Eagle's Tampico office were pushing him away from the company. In the aftermath of Wilson's intervention at Veracruz, Mexican Eagle's Tampico officers moved to purge Americans from employment. They hoped thereby to remove cause of offense to the Mexican government, but this justification gave little comfort to the company's exiled American workers like DeGolyer. It was enough to prompt DeGolyer to consider resignation. Nevertheless, he would wait—better to see what Cowdray might offer first.[12]

In June 1914, DeGolyer embarked on the journey to England with the hope of settling the question of his employment. It was his first trans-Atlantic voyage. With him traveled Nell and six-month-old Virginia. Embarking on the *Imperator,* the DeGolyers were amazed at the modern amenities of the liner. Nell recorded the voyage in detail, meticulously noting the "marble tiled swimming pool," the "half-dozen elevators," and the elaborate "Grand Salon." With tongue in cheek, she remarked, "J. Pierpont Morgan's daughter Anne is on board . . . but hasn't called on us yet." She could still joke about their anonymity. In later years, the DeGolyers would become celebrities in their own right.[13]

Arriving in England on June 12, the family boarded a special train for London, where work awaited DeGolyer. In the aftermath of revolutionary disruptions, Cowdray wanted detailed analyses of company operations. Although DeGolyer must have been impatient to define his new role in the company, these matters required immediate attention. As with his work in Mexico, the company called upon DeGolyer to go beyond geological analysis, to offer his thoughts on management, legal matters, and financial practices. In a series of memoranda, he competently and concisely summarized these issues, again demonstrating to his superiors at Mexican Eagle that his talents went far beyond technical brilliance in geology.[14]

Cowdray recognized this and looked about for some place for De-

Golyer in Mexican Eagle. In the meantime, he would entertain his young protégé, hosting him during "polo week." As the summer wore on, DeGolyer and Hayes began to make suggestions of their own. A geological expedition to China would be an interesting possibility—the company had one planned already. But further negotiations would be necessary before the realization of any such project. Closer at hand was Spain, an inviting proposition to Hispanophile DeGolyer. He planned his departure for that country at the end of July.[15]

Before DeGolyer left, Hayes submitted a memorandum to Lord Cowdray recommending terms for DeGolyer's continued employment. Following DeGolyer's mission to Spain, Hayes envisioned DeGolyer taking over the management of geological work for Cowdray both in Mexico and in the greater Caribbean region. Hayes had only just delivered the proposal when DeGolyer crossed the English Channel.

The timing of DeGolyer's Spanish mission was inauspicious from a business perspective, but it made him witness to one of the most remarkable moments in the history of the twentieth century. On June 28, 1914, a Serbian nationalist assassinated Archduke Franz Ferdinand, the heir to the hodge-podge Hapsburg state of Austria-Hungary. Supported by German Kaiser Wilhelm II, the outraged Habsburg monarchy issued an ultimatum to the neighboring kingdom of Serbia, whom they blamed for the killing. Russia, asserting her role as patron and protector of all Slavic people, backed the Serbs. As heightened tensions led to military mobilization, an alliance system that had divided the powerful states of Europe into two camps came into play. On one side were Austria-Hungary and Germany; on the other were Russia and France. The exigencies of German military planning, which called for an attack on France through Belgium, ensured that even Great Britain would enter the conflict. The continent was poised on the brink of the unimaginable, self-destructive folly that would be known first as the Great War, and then later, after an even more unspeakable tragedy, as the First World War.

Even as DeGolyer made his final travel arrangements, Austria-Hungary declared war on Serbia. Two days later, on July 31, Russia mobilized for war. As DeGolyer boarded the train in Charing Cross station on August 1, French and German officials were already determined to put their nations on footing for war. After a "delightful" journey to Dover, he boarded the ferry for France. In Calais, he noted, "Everything was quiet and peaceful."[16]

His arrival in Paris was another matter. Gare du Nord station, one of the largest railway stations DeGolyer had ever seen, was overflowing with people. The place was in "a fever of excitement." DeGolyer had difficulty securing a cab but managed to make it to Quai d'Orsay, where he hoped to secure transportation to Madrid. Here too "the utmost confusion prevailed," and he found that the Madrid express was already booked. Giving up on the prospect of leaving for Spain that day, he first tried to find a hotel.[17] He reconsidered this decision as he passed "numerous bodies of troops and a mob of 1,500–2,000 Frenchmen with French, British and Russian flags singing the Marseillaise."[18] In his words, "The gravity of the situation began to dawn on me."[19]

Changing his destination, he returned to Gare du Nord, hoping that he could still get back across the Channel to England. By now matters had worsened. The scene was bedlam as "[t]housands of people were fighting for tickets, and women who were being crushed and trampled on were screaming."[20] Despite the circumstances, DeGolyer managed to obtain a ticket and made his way toward the platform, where a crowd awaited the next train. While he anticipated departure, a French officer approached DeGolyer, apparently believing him to be a German spy. Fortunately, he had not lost his passport. Just before he boarded the train for Calais, another left for the frontier, carrying German and Austro-Hungarian nationals. French soldiers guarded them.[21]

DeGolyer's train did not reach Calais until early the next morning. There he found what he reckoned to be a thousand Americans and Britons, scrambling to board ferries for Dover. By six in the morning, he was back in England. Tensions were high in London. Walking with Nell in Trafalgar Square later that afternoon, they witnessed "a great peace demonstration" where a large number of Englishmen gathered to oppose involvement in the conflict that was unfolding. More belligerent voices would soon drown theirs out. In three days, Britain would be at war.[22]

The DeGolyers reconsidered their plans in light of these dramatic developments. It was an unhappy situation. Nell and baby Virginia would return to the United States, traveling to Canada on a ship with portholes blackened for the sake of caution. German submarines were prowling the Atlantic.[23] However, Everette DeGolyer felt compelled to stay on the job in Britain until Cowdray settled on the terms of his future employment. It was a frustrating experience. Writing to Nell, he shared his irritation: "The Chief sits tight and says and does nothing." Despite all this, he knew that his relationship with Cowdray offered career possibilities that he would not find elsewhere. "I think it would be foolish to resign," he wrote and, exaggerating a little, remarked, "I don't want us to starve."[24]

It took almost a month for DeGolyer, in conference with Hayes and Cowdray, to iron out the details of his employment with the firm. Even then, there was little determined beyond one short-term project: a comprehensive report on Mexican geology. On September 1, Hayes drafted a memorandum authorizing DeGolyer to travel to Mexico, gather relevant maps and materials from the Mexican Eagle offices, and return to the United States to compose the report. Hayes estimated that six to eight months would be necessary to complete the work. Then they would revisit the scope of his duties within the company. DeGolyer might have hoped for a more definitive resolution of the matter, but he was ready to accept these terms. At least he would be able to return home, albeit with a detour through Mexico.[25]

DeGolyer's report would be a much larger enterprise than anyone anticipated. On September 4, he departed Liverpool, beginning a week-long voyage for Quebec. After a brief hiatus in the United States, he was off to Mexico by train. By early October, he was back in Tampico, compiling materials for his comprehensive report on Mexican geology. If he had doubts about the impracticality of returning to work in Mexico, the situation there laid them to rest. Writing to Hayes, he grimly reported, "It looks like the country would go over to Villa. The oil business is absolutely dead . . . Everything is at a dead standstill."[26] Two days in Mexico were enough for DeGolyer. Returning to the "homeburg" in Oklahoma, he was happy to settle down at last with wife and child to compose his report free of the menace of revolutionary violence.[27]

The six to eight months that Hayes anticipated for DeGolyer's report soon proved to be unduly optimistic. It was not that the time was insufficient for the task that Hayes envisioned, but DeGolyer did not share Hayes's vision of the project. The doctor seemed to have in mind a compilation of geographical and topographical reports put into "the best possible shape" within the available time.[28] DeGolyer, on the other hand, put the matter differently. The company commissioned him to compose "[a] complete report about everything that ever happened (geologically speaking) in the Republic of Mexico."[29] By February 1915, he was referring to the project as "the Encyclopedia Britannica of the Mexican oil fields."[30] At that point, he still seemed optimistic about completing the report, but by April he was asking Hayes for more time.[31]

Although his supervisors indulged him, they also began adding tasks to his agenda. The company needed DeGolyer for another geological survey in Cuba. He would spend his summer there, conducting evaluations of petroleum resources.[32] Was this the sort of work to which he would turn after finishing the report? Although DeGolyer was excited at the prospect of pioneering oilfields in a new country, he was ultimately disappointed by the island's prospects—there was no future for him in Cuba.[33]

Looking beyond the ultimate completion of the Mexican report, DeGolyer still felt torn about his career path. He considered the desirability of returning to the university and pursuing graduate research in geology. As he put it, it might be worthwhile to investigate "some ideas that I have with regards to oil, and carrying on some experiments with them."[34] His scientific interests contended with the tangible benefits of commercial work.

First, he had to finish his geological report on Mexico. Delayed by his Cuban work, DeGolyer redoubled his effort to make up for lost time. He had the final edition of the Mexican report bound and issued on July 1, 1916. Titled *The Oil Fields of Mexico,* it was more than a report; it was a book that filled 858 pages.[35] Included were many color maps and diagrams demonstrating everything from the location of oil wells to hypothetical cross sections of Mexican geology. In his analysis, DeGolyer not only related the course of recent oilfield operations but also traced back the history of oil in Mexico to the Aztecs. Even today, *The Oil Fields of Mexico* remains a truly magisterial work on the history of oil in that country for the extensive period that it covers.

*The Oil Fields of Mexico* marked something of a transition for DeGolyer. He began to recognize that his future career might not mean a return to the sort of work that he had done in Mexico. Writing to Hayes, he acknowledged the importance of field geology but revealed his excitement at the analytical work in which he was engaged, remarking, "I believe that more can be done in the field than in the office, but there is no question that the office work has its place."[36]

As the completion of the Mexican report had loomed, DeGolyer realized that his place in the company—whether in the field or in the office—needed final resolution. Writing to J. B. Body, he was somewhat apologetic but firm, noting, "I should like more than anything else to continue with the Firm, but I feel that I shall be doing both the Firm and myself an injustice unless the matter is settled at the present time for some years to come."[37]

DeGolyer's sense of urgency intensified when Dr. Hayes fell ill, effectively ending his direction of DeGolyer's work. But Cowdray and Body delayed. Following the completion of the Mexican report, they ordered DeGolyer to Mexico to confer with company officials regarding recent geological and legal developments. It was there that he learned of Hayes's death. It was a hard blow to DeGolyer; to his diary he confessed his sorrow. In a letter to Mrs. Hayes, he went further, remarking, "I feel as one who has lost a father."[38]

With Hayes gone, Body realized that it would be imperative to conclude some sort of satisfactory arrangement with DeGolyer. He knew that the talented geologist could certainly obtain employment elsewhere in the United States, where the oil industry was entering a boom period. However, Body determined to offer him something more: the prestige and compensation of oil company management. He would place DeGolyer in the financial capital of the United States and give him authority over the array of geologists employed by Mexican Eagle. Would that be enough to secure DeGolyer?

DeGolyer accepted the terms that Body offered. Although his official title was to be that of a "consulting geologist," the position was managerial. His new office would be in New York—on Broadway to be exact—not so far from the former headquarters of Rockefeller's Standard Oil, which the courts had recently broken up for monopolistic practices. While DeGolyer was to occupy himself with "Mexican work," his friend and associate in Tampico, Paul Weaver, would conduct the close supervision of field geology. His superiors charged DeGolyer only to "outline work for Mexico" and freed him from the burden of detail. Most remarkably, the company tasked him with developing a plan to organize the geological department, calling on DeGolyer to "investigate the forms of organization of the large geological staffs of such oil companies in the United States as can be conveniently visited with an idea to arranging our own work most conveniently and for the greatest efficiency."[39]

Therefore, in May 1916, Everette and Nell DeGolyer found themselves combing suburban neighborhoods in New York and New Jersey, in search of a home suitable for the family of an oil company manager.

Despite DeGolyer's good fortune in securing the position, it was a somewhat difficult situation. Having shipped all their furniture from Oklahoma, they found it difficult to find a place to store it. With the European war threatening to draw in the United States, the army was requisitioning available warehouse space. Because there was little time to arrive at a solution, DeGolyer hired movers before he had concluded a contract on a home. Having loaded the family's possessions into the truck, he proceeded to Montclair, New Jersey, where he had found a suitable prospect. The truck followed him there, where he managed to finalize a contract on the property while keeping the realtor in the dark about his desperate situation. Having closed the deal, the agent was surprised when the moving truck pulled up. "My furniture," DeGolyer said, grinning, "I couldn't wait another day to find a place to store it. Forgot to tell you that."[40]

For the next twenty years, DeGolyer's official residence would be New Jersey, with his primary office in New York. These were in many ways the most crucial years in his career, years that he began as a prominent employee in a British-controlled oil company and ended as a wealthy American oilman, a figure of national significance in the petroleum industry. They were also remarkably eventful years for his family, which expanded substantially while in Montclair. In 1916, Everette and Nell welcomed their second daughter, Dorothy Margaret DeGolyer. In 1919, they were joined by another baby girl, Cecilia Jeanne DeGolyer, and then finally a son, in 1923, Everett Lee DeGolyer Jr., soon to be dubbed "Ev" or "Eff." The children would compete for attention with their father's demanding business commitments.[41]

Considering all these remarkable events, it is a little surprising that DeGolyer's experiences in the New York area did not make the powerful impression that his years in Oklahoma, Mexico, or his later years in Texas did. DeGolyer loved to reminisce about his youth in Norman, the tropical landscape of Veracruz, and later became a patron of all things Texan. He had less to say of the Big Apple. To be sure, he moved in the circles of the cosmopolitan elite that comprised the corporate world of New York. He joined exclusive clubs, rubbing elbows with bankers, lawyers, and other executives.[42] Yet he never thought of himself as a New Yorker.

One reason that New York never really stuck to DeGolyer was his constant motion. He rarely sat still long enough for the city to stick to him. Some of this motion filled the space between his office in New York and his home in New Jersey, and he found the commute to be punishing.[43] However, bridging the gap between Montclair and Manhattan was only one aspect of DeGolyer's manic activity during these years. The fact is that he was frequently away from home on trips to Mexico, trips to London, and increasingly, trips to Oklahoma and Texas.[44]

DeGolyer's travels in the Southwest reflected more than a desire to visit family and friends. They were part of a conscious initiative on his part to change the nature of his work on behalf of Lord Cowdray. Rather than serve as caretaker to Mexican Eagle's operations, DeGolyer hoped to seize opportunities in the vast Mid-Continent and Gulf Coast oilfields of the United States. The course that he suggested was not without controversy, and it took several years for Cowdray to warm to DeGolyer's proposal. DeGolyer's goal was to put Cowdray's money and business acumen to work in the booming American oilfields. And who would be better to oversee the project than DeGolyer himself?

As early as 1914, DeGolyer had recommended that Cowdray's company expand its operations north of the Rio Grande.[45] The Chief was apparently reluctant to enter the highly competitive American market. Yet whether or not Cowdray was willing to chance investment in the United States, DeGolyer was determined to seize the opportunities he discerned. As early as January 1915, he was risking his own money in drilling oil wells in the Southwest. He joined his old friends Edwin Hopkins and Charles Hamilton in some of these schemes, although they lacked funds for large-scale operations.[46] In early 1916, he secretly commissioned A. W. McCoy as an investigator to gather data on drilling costs, transportation costs, crude prices, and leasing practices in Texas and Oklahoma.[47] J. B. Body and T. J. Ryder, also of Mexican Eagle, were both aware of the mission, which was ostensibly on behalf of the firm. The two later joined with DeGolyer and Herbert Carr, the head of Mexican Eagle's New York office, to form the Alabama Exploration Syndicate, a company that would independently seek oil leases in the same area investigated by McCoy.[48] His interest in exploring for petroleum in the United States was shared by his associates. Still, official company policy backed by the Chief was to stay out.

In June 1916, DeGolyer wrote his friend Paul Weaver, "The whole United States is in a fever of excitement regarding oil."[49] The same day he wrote his supervisor, J. B. Body, urging the company to look into oil prospects in Texas.[50] Following the final "publication" of *The Oil Fields of Mexico* report, DeGolyer wrote Body again, pleading for action.[51] In his

response, Body conceded a reconnaissance of the Rio Grande Valley, but emphasized that the focus must be on the Mexican side of the border.[52]

Over the course of the next year, DeGolyer became more anxious and insistent about pursuing American prospects.[53] In July 1917, he secured support within the firm to dispatch a scout to Oklahoma who would gather information on oilfields in the Osage Reservation.[54] This move provoked resistance from within Mexican Eagle's Foreign Department, which balked at the expense.[55] Worse, support from his superiors was not forthcoming. To his frustration, Cowdray continued to resist entry into United States oilfields. In August 1917, DeGolyer received a conclusive statement on the matter from London. Unfortunately, the firm was not interested in entering oil production in the United States. But there was a silver lining to the cloud: DeGolyer was free to investigate and to enter the oil business in the United States as long as he continued to give ultimate priority to his Mexican work. This concession allowed DeGolyer to continue looking into American oilfields in his spare time and to argue in favor of bringing the firm into the United States.[56]

While DeGolyer stubbornly repeated his attempts to change his em-

Edwin B. Hopkins (left) and Charles W. Hamilton (right). Hopkins and Hamilton joined DeGolyer in some drilling investments, following his return to the United States. After leaving Mexico, Hopkins pursued a career as a consulting geologist and served as an officer in a number of oil production companies. Hamilton, who had been DeGolyer's protégé in Mexico, went on to a remarkably successful career as an executive with Gulf Oil. (Everette Lee DeGolyer Collection. Courtesy of DeGolyer Library, Southern Methodist University.)

ployer's mind, he moved ahead to drill a number of small wells together with Edwin Hopkins. Investing money in Texas and Alabama, DeGolyer hoped the two could look into drilling in Louisiana also.[57] He and Hopkins also brought into their association Earle Porter, DeGolyer's brother-in-law. Porter scouted oil prospects in Kansas, in Texas, and in Louisiana.[58] However, the spectacular success that DeGolyer had enjoyed in locating Mexican wells eluded him for the present. Without Cowdray's backing he and his geologist friends lacked the resources to take on more than small projects. Nor was freelance geological consulting providing the lucrative opportunities for which he was looking.[59] In despair, he wrote, "I have not done anything which is even worth while mentioning since I left Mexico."[60]

To realize his ambitions, DeGolyer knew that he would have to win over the Chief. It took a global change of circumstances before he had any luck. On November 11, 1918, DeGolyer made a laconic entry in his personal diary: "Peace has come and so the Great War ends."[61] The conclusion of World War I meant significant changes for DeGolyer's career. Cowdray had been reluctant to enter the oil business in the United States while the guns were still blazing. He had been further distracted from new ventures by his own participation in the war itself. In 1917, Cowdray had served as president of the Air Board, managing the battle in the skies for Britain. In the aftermath of the armistice, Cowdray was at last ready to set aside the caution that had tempered his wartime business and chart a new course for his investments. One such move was already in motion—the sale of Mexican Eagle. The deal was sealed with Royal Dutch Shell, more commonly known as Shell Oil, in early 1919. Cowdray retained a minority interest in the firm, but management passed to Shell. With his involvement in Mexico waning, Cowdray found DeGolyer's suggestion of a gamble in the United States attractive. In January 1919, the Chief summoned him to London.[62]

There, he found Cowdray eager to define more ambitious roles for DeGolyer and for A. C. Veatch, the company's other chief geologist. DeGolyer felt that matters were finally going his way. His excitement continued to grow when he learned that Cowdray envisioned the creation of a new company. Moreover, DeGolyer was not just to be a manager and a consultant; he was to be an executive officer in the business.[63]

Aware that he was taking on something new, DeGolyer reflected on the challenges that would face him. In one meeting with Cowdray, he seized on a quip that he thought providential. He wrote to Nell, "The Chief unintentionally gave me a motto. I don't know whether he read it out of a book or whether it was original but it fits my case: 'The essence of this business is self control and its success will depend very largely upon your ability to say no.'"[64] The remark so impressed DeGolyer that he later wrote the Chief, requesting that he send a photograph of himself endorsed with Cowdray's autograph and the epigram.[65] It is ironic that DeGolyer singled out this piece of wisdom for special honor, for in some ways it represented the exact opposite of the approach that he would take in the oil business. It was DeGolyer's willingness to say yes that would make him a pioneer in innovation and propel him to ever greater heights when a more cautious man might have said no. However, perhaps it was for this very reason that he latched on to Cowdray's advice. For DeGolyer's propensity to take risks could also be a weakness that required temperance.

Returning to the United States, DeGolyer mulled over the details of the new company. Writing to J. B. Body, he confessed his growing enthusiasm and professed specific plans for the organization of the business.[66] By the summer of 1919, the envisioned company was nearing incorporation. With plans to operate in both the United States and Canada, Cowdray and his collaborators settled on the name Amerada, a combination of the first syllables of America and the last syllables of Canada. On June 4, 1919, the new company was officially "born" with a capital of $1 million subscribed by the Cowdray interests.[67] Amerada would be devoted to exploring and developing oilfields in the United States and Canada—a prospect that DeGolyer relished.

From the start of the new company, DeGolyer played a central role in directing operations. For the first seven years of its existence, he served as vice president and general manager of Amerada.[68] It quickly absorbed the lion's share of his attention. Less than a week after Amerada's incorporation, DeGolyer submitted his formal resignation from the Mexican Eagle Oil Company to J. B. Body.[69] Body delayed acceptance, apparently with the hope that DeGolyer would reconsider.[70] DeGolyer pleaded for permission to leave, convinced that his future was with the new company.[71] But his employer held all the cards. DeGolyer would be required to juggle his managerial responsibilities with both companies, at least for the short term.[72]

Despite the burden of the workload, DeGolyer met with remarkable success in his stewardship of the new company. Having thoroughly investigated prospective oil provinces in the United States, DeGolyer stood ready with the information needed to form an agenda for exploration. Because he had dabbled in drilling as a private investor, he also knew something about the production process. Equally important were the managerial skills that he had developed in the service of the Mexican Eagle Oil Company. The quality of the men whom he hired to staff Amerada was responsible for much of the company's subsequent success.[73]

But matters were uncertain when the company began operation in the summer of 1919. In fact, there was some reason for pessimism. Unlike Mexico, the United States was a highly competitive market for oil producers. Although Cowdray had profited from political connections in Mexico during the infancy of the Mexican Eagle Oil Company, he would not be able to repeat that performance with Amerada in the United States. Yet the Chief, egged on by an optimistic DeGolyer, pushed forward with plans to enter production in America. Within a year, Cowdray

Everette Lee DeGolyer and portrait of Lord Cowdray, 1949. "The Chief" launched DeGolyer's career as an oil executive and was an influential mentor. Here DeGolyer, long after Cowdray's death in 1927, works while his patron looks on with approval. (Everette Lee DeGolyer Collection. Courtesy of DeGolyer Library, Southern Methodist University.)

added $2,500,000 to the $1,000,000 that he had already poured into the business.[74]

It proved to be an excellent investment. The company's progress was swift and spectacular. Its first success came in an area that DeGolyer had investigated years earlier: the Osage Reservation in Oklahoma. When he hired an oil scout to examine the Osage oilfields in 1917, the foreign department in Mexican Eagle had chided him. Now he relished his vindication.[75] Although the first Oklahoma well would be a dry hole, "Hominy No. 1" on the Osage Reservation would produce the first oil sold by the company. That sale took place in July 1920, little more than a year after Amerada's incorporation. Three years later, Amerada would strike a bonanza in the nearby Tonkawa field that would propel the company to outstanding levels of profit.[76]

In the meantime, DeGolyer scurried hither and yon, examining prospective oil properties throughout the Southwest, conferring with company geologists, and when he could find the time, attending to office business in New York.[77] His frantic lifestyle was a reflection of the exponential growth of Amerada's petroleum production. In its first complete year of operation, 1920, Amerada produced 267,000 barrels of oil. In 1921, production grew to 1,726,000 barrels. By mid-decade the figure was about 4 million barrels and rising.[78]

DeGolyer's accession to the rank of vice president and general manager of Amerada completed his gradual transformation from a field geologist, concerned primarily with scientific evaluation of specific properties, to a corporate executive, focused largely upon the management of commercial enterprise. With more and more of his time focused upon questions of corporate organization, investment, and personnel, he might have been excused had he devoted less thought to the place of science in industry. In fact, he did quite the opposite.

DeGolyer was a thoughtful man, who was uncomfortable with contradictions. Where a less rigorous mind might have been tempted to compartmentalize potential conflicts between the interests of science and business, DeGolyer felt compelled to push toward some sort of intellectual resolution. On the one hand was the duty to advance the frontiers of knowledge; on the other hand was the duty to the investor, in this case, his longtime patron, Lord Cowdray. DeGolyer knew that he did not face this conundrum alone. The growing number of geologists employed by the oil industry shared his predicament. DeGolyer determined to address the issue in the forum of the professional societies where his peers congregated. If science and business were to be reconciled anywhere, it would be there.

When DeGolyer joined the executive ranks at Amerada, petroleum geology was still a relatively young science. It was only in the last decade that oil companies in the United States had come to recognize the indispensability of geological analysis.[79] For this reason, when DeGolyer began to search for a forum in which he could address some of the issues that confronted the geological profession, he found his options rather limited. The most prestigious and relevant organization seemed to be the American Institute of Mining and Metallurgical Engineers (AIME). DeGolyer hoped that his participation in the Institute would allow him to contribute to scientific advancement even while he forged ahead in his career as vice president and general manager of Amerada.

AIME was a professional organization that brought together men in a variety of careers, all having to do with mineral extraction. Founded in 1871, AIME aimed to achieve two objectives: "First, the more economical production of the useful minerals and metals; [s]econd, the greater safety and welfare of those employed in these industries."[80] Industrial affiliation rather than professional credentials determined membership, and the organization welcomed anyone "practically engaged in mining, metallurgy, or metallurgical engineering."[81] Reflecting the basis for membership, the agenda of AIME during its early years was not professional, but rather commercial: to serve the needs of the mining industry.[82] The "benevolent despot" of the Institute, Rossiter W. Raymond, viewed engineering as a type of business and only reinforced this tendency. Raymond oversaw AIME publications and refused to print collegial discussion of papers, as other professional societies did.[83] However, Raymond's reign as secretary of the Institute ended in 1912, allowing AIME to move in the direction of greater professionalism about the same time that DeGolyer became active in it.[84] Beginning in 1918, AIME would gradually phase in modest professional standards for new members.[85] DeGolyer would rise to leadership in the Institute as it was grasping toward this new vision of itself, a vision of the "mining engineer" that looked beyond the commercial import of work toward a greater scientific, even social, purpose.

DeGolyer's activities with AIME coincided roughly with the founding of Amerada in 1919. He immediately fell in with the Petroleum Committee, which was at that point still not a professional division of the Institute. But DeGolyer had ambitious plans for his fellow petroleum geologists, plans that would come to fruition three years later. In the meantime, he threw himself into the thankless task of issuing "begging letters," soliciting scholarly articles for publication by AIME.[86]

He also took on another task that others might have thought to be beyond the ability of a geologist with only a few years of business experience. This was to chair a temporary committee formed in 1921 to evaluate the business management of the Institute. If there were any doubts as to his competence in financial affairs, they were soon dispelled. The report issued by DeGolyer was thorough and incisive, denouncing "confusion" in the AIME accounting department and identifying faulty provisions in the bylaws of the Institute as the source of the problem. In all of this, he demonstrated the decisive judgment that also helped to propel his career as a corporate officer.[87]

Perhaps the most consequential aspect of DeGolyer's involvement with AIME was his role in the organization of a professional Petroleum Division. In May 1921, he expressed his concern that the Institute was neglecting the increasingly important bloc of petroleum engineers. At the time, AIME was undergoing a process of decentralization, but on a geographical rather than professional basis. DeGolyer was convinced that this was the wrong path to take. Instead, he argued that decentralization should have proceeded based on professional interest. DeGolyer was convinced that members devoted to work in the petroleum industry would have more in common than members who happened to live in the same city.[88]

The idea was not unprecedented. There was already an Institute of Metals Division of AIME. Why not form a similar body on behalf of the petroleum industry? The reasoning proved persuasive. In 1922, the Institute of Petroleum Technologists Division of AIME was born. In short order, the new division elected DeGolyer as chairman. Later, the group would abridge its name to a less cumbersome title: the Petroleum Division. The founding of the division was a significant step in the professional organization of petroleum engineers. Much of DeGolyer's work in AIME during the mid-1920s focused on building up this fledgling group. His efforts did not go unrecognized. In 1927, the AIME membership elected DeGolyer as president of the Institute.[89]

DeGolyer's leadership in developing the Petroleum Division of AIME was not his only pioneering role in professional development. He also played a vital part in the founding of the most important society for petroleum geologists in the United States: the American Association of

Petroleum Geologists (AAPG). Paralleling his involvement in the AIME, DeGolyer's promotion of AAPG took place about the same time that his career was taking a managerial turn.

Although there is some question as to who was first to suggest the founding of a society of petroleum geologists, DeGolyer may have been its first advocate. At about the same time that he was engrossed with writing his *Oil Fields of Mexico* report, DeGolyer had dined with Professor Charles H. Taylor, the head of the geology department at the University of Oklahoma. Considering the rising number of geologists active in the oilfields of the Southwest, DeGolyer asked if the professor would consider organizing an association for these men. It seemed a good idea.[90]

Taylor called a conference for January 1916 that would meet in Norman. Working together with another geologist, J. Elmer Thomas, Taylor and DeGolyer helped to organize the meeting. A severe case of "la grippe" almost stopped DeGolyer's participation, but he dutifully managed to attend and even gave a presentation on oil production in Mexico, a topic over which he possessed encyclopedic mastery.[91] It was a respectable gathering with about sixty geologists present. And although the assembly did not establish any formal organization, it did lay out a "technical program," issuing plans for another meeting after one year's time. DeGolyer would be attending to duties in Tampico when Taylor's group gathered again in February 1917 and declared themselves the Southwestern Association of Petroleum Geologists.[92] But despite his absence, DeGolyer was "elected" a member of the new organization.[93] One year later, with rising membership and growing enthusiasm, they formally changed the name to the American Association of Petroleum Geologists.[94]

DeGolyer rose through the ranks of the AAPG to a height appropriate for one of the organization's founders. Beginning in 1923, DeGolyer was active on the Research Committee, which aimed to distribute grants to fund research experiments relevant to petroleum geology.[95] In 1925, the Association elected him president.[96]

DeGolyer's involvement in the AAPG seems to have been less of a battle, at least in the 1920s, than his activities with the AIME. To some extent, this reflected the fact that the petroleum geologists in AIME had to struggle for recognition with other "mining engineers." The AAPG was a creature of the petroleum geologists' own making.

Both of these organizations offered a forum for DeGolyer to explore

American Association of Petroleum Geologists (AAPG), Annual Meeting, Dallas, Texas, 1926. Everette Lee DeGolyer, in the dark suit, is seated slightly to the left, behind the podium. DeGolyer played an instrumental role in the founding of the AAPG and served as its president in 1926 when they held their annual meeting at the Baker Hotel in Dallas, Texas. DeGolyer was deeply involved in professional societies like the AAPG and the American Institute of Mining and Metallurgical Engineers, activities that represented an attempt to merge his scientific and business roles. (Everette Lee DeGolyer Collection. Courtesy of DeGolyer Library, Southern Methodist University.)

the relationship between his business and professional obligations. And in no area did his identity as an earth scientist clash more with his role as an executive than in the matter of scholarly publication. This conflict antedated his vice-presidency at Amerada. It antedated even his assumption of managerial duties with Mexican Eagle.

As a young geologist in Mexico, DeGolyer had chafed under the strictures of secrecy that were important to serving the company interest. Writing to an old USGS supervisor in 1911, he bemoaned the limitations of commercial work, noting, "[O]ne sees so many things that he wants to publish and cannot."[97] DeGolyer carried these regrets with him in later years as he ascended the company hierarchy.

Despite occasionally frustrating prohibitions, DeGolyer managed to publish articles with trade periodicals and professional journals. His first article on the Mexican petroleum industry appeared in *Petroleum Review* in August 1912.[98] Titled "Petroleum Industry of the Tampico Region," it was a general overview of the oilfields he knew best, but it certainly provided no information that could be of use to competitors. Other articles followed. His next piece was of the same mold as the first, featuring vague descriptions of operations and production estimates.[99] Over the next decade, DeGolyer would turn to increasingly technical topics as he began publication in the scholarly journals of the geological profession.[100] In all of these essays, he had to balance his genuine commitment to advance the frontiers of science with a realistic appreciation of the value of information to his employers.

As a geologist, DeGolyer understood the value of information. Indeed, his employment in the oil industry presumed that geological information was worth the expense to obtain it. For that reason, he understood that in order to justify publishing scholarly work, its effect needed to be neutral or, even better, beneficial to the company. Therefore, these were the sorts of arguments that he employed when appealing for permission to send an article to a journal. Sometimes he met with success, and sometimes he did not.

Consider an exchange between DeGolyer and J. B. Body that took place in 1916. DeGolyer wrote his superior in support of publishing a scholarly paper on the geology of the Isthmus of Tehuantepec. The isthmus was the first region in Mexico that had drawn the attention of Lord Cowdray, and Mexican Eagle's lease holdings there were extensive. DeGolyer believed that the geologists could serve the company interest by publishing a piece on the petroleum potential of the area. Mexican

Eagle already had a refinery built there at Minatitlán. Encouraging other companies to risk money in developing the isthmus could help supply the refinery with crude.[101] DeGolyer thought that it was a good case for publication. Body disagreed.

Even this apparently compelling argument failed to overcome the presumption in favor of secrecy. Body wrote DeGolyer that the matter was out of the question. He dismissed DeGolyer's proposal, concluding, "After years of time and trouble we have spent in acquiring leases on the isthmus and thus tying it up to prevent the intrusion of outsiders, it would go very much against the grain to now write a paper with the object of inducing them to come in."[102] DeGolyer felt the sting of denial in this exchange with Body, but as an ascendant executive DeGolyer would sting his own scientific subordinates in their own quest for publication.

As DeGolyer's career as an Amerada executive began, he found his position reversed. Now, he was the one who denied publication requests made by the company's scientific staff. One of his frequent partners in these exchanges was Dr. Donald C. Barton, division geologist at Amerada. Many of DeGolyer's communiqués with Barton focused on questions of conflict between the desire to keep company secrets and the importance of scholarly publication. DeGolyer often had to say no to Barton's requests.

Consider his response to one request made by Barton in 1920. Denying Barton permission, he wrote, "I should very much prefer that we did not release any additional maps or information for some time to come."[103] But DeGolyer was also aware of the importance of publication to the professional standing of geologists, so at least in this case, he offered an alternative. "Do you feel that you would care to submit a paper on West Columbia or a sort of general paper covering developments in the Gulf Coast region for the year 1920[?]" he wrote.[104] That would be perfectly fine. However, if Barton did choose to do so, he would need to submit the manuscript to DeGolyer for approval.[105] Barton ultimately agreed.[106]

DeGolyer did not always reject publication requests, but he was guarded about regions where Amerada and its affiliates had active prospects.[107] This was particularly true when it came to the salt domes of the United States Gulf Coast. Here, DeGolyer opposed even the publication of general physiographical papers on the region.[108] As the Gulf Coast attracted more attention from the oil companies, DeGolyer committed to passing on almost no information, even if it could be readily attained elsewhere. As he explained the policy, "[I]t would give us the advantage of a few days or weeks at least over some of our competitors."[109] In the oil business, time was of the essence. A few days could mean the difference between signing a favorable oil lease and losing it to another company.

Not all of DeGolyer's concerns regarding scholarly publication were about keeping Amerada's secrets. He could also display a selfish streak when faced with a request to publish or not. In some cases, DeGolyer denied permission to publish because he himself wished to publish related material.[110] On at least one occasion in 1923, he granted permission to Donald Barton to send out an article on salt domes, and then requested Barton withdraw it so that he himself could publish an article on the same topic.[111]

A variety of factors, then, encouraged DeGolyer to prohibit the publication of scholarly studies on geological questions. What of DeGolyer's commitment to science? Had he cast aside all interest in advancing the frontiers of knowledge? Should not the cause of science trump any crass commercial concerns that he might have? It bothered him, but DeGolyer was no longer a mere scientist; he had become a businessman, and he knew that he would not last long in business if he operated Amerada or its affiliates without keeping an eye on the bottom line. Responding to criticism from one colleague that he was too stingy in sharing company information with the geological profession, DeGolyer became defensive. He wrote to Barton about the discussion, concluding, "I had always thought that I was quite liberal until recently, but I really do not feel that we can give prompt publication of detailed material which has cost us thousands of dollars and several months time to collect, even when the material would be available to anyone else who cared to spend the time in collecting it."[112]

The relationship between the scientific and business aspects of his work continued to trouble DeGolyer. Although others might have been able to ignore the cognitive dissonance and continue work unperturbed, DeGolyer was unwilling or unable to do so. In the years following the letter to Barton, he carefully probed the relationship between these apparently conflicting interests. Even more remarkably, he did so in the public fora provided by scholarly journals.

In spring 1921, DeGolyer published an essay in the *Bulletin of the American Association of Petroleum Geologists* that explored the relationship between the business and science of geology. Titled "The Debt of

Geology to the Petroleum Industry," DeGolyer defended the work of his colleagues in the business from "holier-than-thou" geologists who were dedicated to pure science.[113] According to DeGolyer, envy was the motivation of some of the attacks on commercial geologists. Whereas geologists who worked for universities or the government struggled to make ends meet, some geologists in the petroleum industry were making a fortune—men like DeGolyer. It was wrong to attack these geologists because of their remarkable success, or at least DeGolyer thought so.[114]

Not only were the motives of these critics impure, they were also unfair. Commercial geologists were engaged in business, and their scientific contributions were only incidental to their work. It was not reasonable to expect the same level of scholarly contribution from men who were essentially engaged in entrepreneurial activity.[115]

DeGolyer stressed the scientific contributions that petroleum geologists had made despite the limitations of a commercial context. They had demonstrated the relevance of geology and had encouraged schools and universities to develop geology programs. They had pioneered new methods in structural mapping. Most of all, they had conducted extensive geological surveys throughout the globe, adding a wealth of raw data upon which academic geologists could draw.[116]

Thanks to all of these important contributions, DeGolyer thought that commercial geologists could hold their heads high. But he was no triumphalist. The attacks on commercial geology were unfair, but that did not mean that there was no room for significant improvement. DeGolyer concluded:

> [T]he writer has but one plea to make—that is for greater attention by petroleum geologists to the scientific by-products of their work and for freer publication of such results as they have obtained as soon as publication may safely be made without detriment to the economic advantages resulting from exclusive ownership of the information. Publication should be regarded as an obligation, which we petroleum geologists owe to the science of geology upon which our profession rests.[117]

DeGolyer believed that it was an obligation that the commercial geologists were not meeting. Interestingly, he argued that the blame for this failure was not the fault of company executives, who were "generally blamed," but rather the result of "procrastination or laziness on the part of the geologist."[118] Presumably, DeGolyer would have preferred that more of his geologists at Amerada had approached him with requests to approve geological studies. Lest anyone confuse his position, DeGolyer closed his argument with the concise maxim "Publication is the best policy."[119] However, DeGolyer always qualified his support for scholarly contributions with consideration of the importance of protecting the "economic advantages" that companies gained from geological information. If he was never able to cleanly resolve these conflicts between the scientific and economic impulses in petroleum geology, he did at least strive to establish a reasonable balance between the two that was in part idealistic and in part realistic.

DeGolyer expanded on the ideas of his "Debt of Geology" article in an essay titled "Cooperation in Geology" that he published two years later.[120] Appearing in *Economic Geology*, he retraced many of his old arguments, calling for more publication by commercial geologists, or as he now referred to them, "economic geologists." Again, he stressed the obligation of geologists to publish, and again he blamed the laziness of geologists for the dearth of scholarly contributions.[121] Yet DeGolyer refined and elaborated these ideas as well. What was needed was not just more publication but more interaction between the economic geologists and geologists dedicated to noncommercial work. Cooperation with government geologists would benefit the science because only government surveys stood in a position to coordinate the diverse geological information that a multitude of company investigations offered.[122] Economic geologists also needed to interact with academic geologists, to allow for the cross-pollination that he believed would spur innovative approaches to the object of their study.[123]

In contrast to his vision, DeGolyer decried the increasing isolation of the various geological fields. "Unfortunately," he wrote, "from the general viewpoint, the present tendency in economic work is toward greater specialization and too little is done by geologists to break through the water-tight compartments which such specialization tends to build."[124] Ironically, DeGolyer would benefit greatly from the tunnel vision of his colleagues. Whereas others would remain restricted by the narrow confines of their specialization, DeGolyer would cultivate the perspective of a generalist and make connections with work in other scientific fields, profiting immensely from his insight. This impulse for broader cooperation and interaction between scientists offers another reason for his increasing involvement in professional societies during the 1920s.

DeGolyer's angst over the issue of scientific publications and his involvement in professional societies all reflected the transformation of his career that took place from 1912 until roughly the mid-1920s. In the space of a few years, DeGolyer had gone from field geologist with technical emphasis, to chief geologist with managerial duties, to vice president and general manager of Amerada with distinctly executive status. He had not found the transition to be a completely smooth one. Indeed, DeGolyer became ever more aware of potential conflicts between the interests of science, broadly understood, and the interests of the shareholders, to whom he was also obliged. Through professional organizations and scholarly publications, he tried to search out a balance between geology and business, but decided that while he should assist the geological community when possible, his first duty was to win a return on company investment.

Beginning in the mid-1920s, that investment increasingly took the form of experimental technologies. DeGolyer's interest in new, sophisticated prospecting tools—most based upon geophysical principles—would pay off handsomely both for the shareholders and for DeGolyer himself in future years. When it did, DeGolyer was able to juggle his business interests with his professional duties so well that by the end of the decade he emerged with a national reputation as both a capable businessman and a committed scientist.

Perhaps his associate, A. Rodger Denison, described DeGolyer's evolving "dual identity" best, when in later years he wrote:

He is a man who never let executive duties interfere with his geological curiosity. He is likewise a man who never let geological theory blind him to economic reality. He is, in short, a man who can be equally enthusiastic over a fresh, new exploration concept as in initiating a new billion-dollar corporation.[125]

# 4 | Technologist

*[T]he development of a fairly reliable divining rod . . . seems to have been fairly realized by modern science . . .*
– Everette Lee DeGolyer in *Economic Geology*, May 1926[1]

In September 1924, Everette Lee DeGolyer wrote to Dr. David White of the United States Geological Survey to share exciting news. For the past several years, DeGolyer had been directing efforts to bring new technology to bear in oil prospecting. Geologists knew that geological formations of the Gulf Coast, called salt domes, were probable locations for oilfields. However, they could not always easily identify these structures from the surface.

A decade earlier, DeGolyer had learned of an instrument developed by a prominent Hungarian scientist that measured variations in the earth's gravitational field. DeGolyer believed that this instrument might be useful in identifying elusive salt domes. For years, he worked to acquire the device and to employ it in the field. Finally, DeGolyer's efforts were bearing fruit.

He was reluctant to talk about it. The new technology would give his companies a competitive edge in the search for oil. Discretion was the order of the day. Nevertheless, DeGolyer could hardly contain his enthusiasm. Certain that White could be trusted, he confessed his recent successes and expressed his concern, writing, "For your own information, we have found a new salt dome in Texas by use of gravity survey."[2] DeGolyer had toyed with the idea of announcing the discovery at the next meeting of the Geological Society of America. But as he remarked to White, "The difficulty is this: I have no objection to giving the results obtained, with perhaps the results obtained on one other dome for comparative purposes, but I cannot enter into a free discussion of the work, which we have been doing."[3] DeGolyer's company had invested more than $75,000 in experimenting with the new technology. And so, he sadly concluded, "I do not feel that it would be fair for me to open up this material to general discussion at the present time. Perhaps, under the circumstances, it would be better to say nothing at all."[4]

DeGolyer was aware that geophysical methods of exploration—such as the gravity survey—held the potential to revolutionize the industry. He also knew that information about the new approach was a valuable trade secret. Then again, publicity—if done the right way—could also be valuable. A company known to be on the leading edge could attract investors, and a businessman who earned a reputation for innovation might find opportunities for advancement forthcoming. "Build a better mousetrap . . ." as the old adage said. Then there was the cause of science, whose advancement depended upon information sharing among the community of researchers.

DeGolyer was torn—but not indecisive. He decided to reveal just enough about his work to attract the attention of the industry, but chose to leave out details that might benefit his competitors. In addition, he carefully regulated the publications of men who were working on these innovative projects for the company. In December 1924, he announced the discovery of the new salt dome by geophysical methods to the Geological Society of America.[5] Then in May 1926, DeGolyer published an article in *Economic Geology* describing his companies' research in geophysical prospecting.

In this article, titled "Geophysical Methods in Economic Geology," DeGolyer heralded the advent of a revolution in oil prospecting. He began by considering the limitations in geological knowledge up to that point in history. According to DeGolyer, "Progress in geology, since it first emerged as a science from the broad field of natural philosophy, has been due almost wholly to increased ability to interpret and to advances in knowledge resulting from accumulating observations."[6] In contrast, there had been only slight progress in the geologists' ability to observe. As he put it, "The geologist today goes into the field with his hammer, compass-clinometer, collecting bag, and notebook, as did the Adam of all geologists, whoever he may have been."[7]

In undeveloped regions, the tools on which the "Adam of all geologists" depended limited his horizon to the surface of the land. He might have made educated guesses regarding subsurface structure, but a strong element of uncertainty pervaded early geological analyses. Yet geologists and the oil industry they served stood on the brink of a new era. DeGolyer asserted, "We have now found new tools and it may well be that they will make possible such an extension of our powers of observation as to mark a new era in the science."[8] These were the geophysical instruments.

Geophysics would bring together science and profit, opening the earth to the searching eyes of geologists who would advance scientific knowledge even as they would make millions for shareholders. The wonderful devices that geophysicists employed promised nothing less than "a fairly reliable divining rod" and called to mind "the alchemist's dream of transmuting baser metals into gold."[9] Geologists would soon possess greater knowledge than ever before about what lay beneath the surface of the land, and knowledge was power. As a pioneer in the application of these new methods, DeGolyer won the respect of the industry as an expert on the lifeblood of twentieth-century civilization—oil.

The early advances in geophysical technology involved not only a relatively small set of scientists, technicians, and businessmen, but also a relatively specific type of geological phenomenon, the salt dome. Found in a variety of regions throughout the globe, salt domes lie beneath the surface in both Mexico and the United States. The Isthmus of Tehuantepec is the location of many of these formations in Mexico. In the United States, they are generally limited to the Gulf Coast of Texas and Louisiana.

Because the oil industry in the United States began in the Appalachian regions of the East, salt domes were generally unknown to American oilmen and petroleum geologists until the twentieth century. The discovery of oil at Spindletop changed that. Along the Gulf Coast, oil companies were soon eager to identify salt domes where they hoped to find petroleum.

The salt dome is a geological formation that occurs when an intrusive body of rock salt deep in the earth penetrates overlying layers of sedimentary rock. Generally a fourth of a mile to one mile in diameter, the rising salt disrupts and warps the rock above creating "traps" that can obstruct the natural, upward journey of petroleum through the rock formation that contains it. These traps were the treasure troves of the Gulf Coast during the first half of the twentieth century, containing vast reservoirs of oil-bearing rock.[10]

DeGolyer's first encounter with salt domes took place within Mexico, while he was a geologist with the Mexican Eagle Oil Company. In later years, when prospecting for salt domes became the primary focus of his work, he jotted down an account of his early experiences with this peculiar geological formation. He recalled, "I first became actively interested in the salt dome structures of the Isthmus of Tehuantepec during the early part of 1913, at which time I visited the Ixhuatlán field, in company with the late Dr. C. W. Hayes and there met Paul Weaver."[11] DeGolyer was

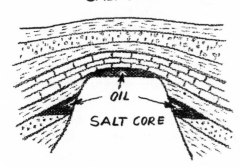

SALT DOME

Idealized cross section of a salt dome oilfield. The upward force exerted by salt pushing toward the surface can warp and disrupt rock strata, creating traps that hold oil. Note the prominence of the protrusion of the salt body. (Drawing by Everette Lee DeGolyer, "How Men Find Oil," *Fortune*, August 1949, 98. Courtesy of Everette and Nell DeGolyer descendants.)

impressed with the unusual geology of the field, but other duties precluded detailed investigation until several years later. In 1916, DeGolyer and Weaver reviewed the Concepción oilfield in detail. Its wealth was the result of an underlying salt dome.[12]

DeGolyer's interest was more than casual. In 1918, he published scholarly articles discussing the origin of salt domes.[13] By this point he was, for the most part, living in the United States, and his research into the Mexican salt domes naturally drew his attention to the United States Gulf Coast, where these formations abounded.

DeGolyer discovered that the geological literature about American salt domes was distinctly inadequate. As he noted later, "No real detailed study of even a single American dome was available and the more general descriptions ran high in theory and speculation but low in detailed description."[14] In the absence of adequate studies of the formations in the United States, DeGolyer conducted his own investigations. Personally visiting the salt domes of Texas and Louisiana, the geological—and economic—significance began to dawn on him.[15] Although DeGolyer might not have guessed so at the time, his interest in salt domes, an "obsession," would have momentous consequences for his career.[16]

The significance of the salt dome is that while the geologist may not always find it easy to identify one from the surface, it is a dramatic, even conspicuous formation beneath the surface. If one could somehow penetrate the shroud of overlaying earth and "see" the structure of the underlying geology, then the geologist would find them easily recognizable. Indeed, if the geologist could overcome this challenge, then the salt dome would be even more obvious than most anticline structures—formations that geologists had already met some success in identifying.

Geologists could sometimes identify anticlines that were close to the surface by topographical mapping. Those that were deeper in the earth were often too subtle to discern by the tried and true method of surface analysis. True, there had been great strides in analysis of well "cuttings." Sometimes the presence of microscopic fossils in rock strata could suggest the presence of oil. However, this method required the drilling of a well, ideally multiple wells, to gain a more complete idea of the contours of a potential oilfield. In other words, deep structures offered limited opportunities for prospecting using existing technology.[17]

Salt domes, on the other hand, invited technical innovation in petroleum exploration. In this regard, there were several significant characteristics of salt domes. First, the rock salt that comprised the bulk of the formation was relatively light, although overlying cap rock might be quite heavy. Second, the domes were relatively dense when compared to surrounding rock. Although most anticlines that could not be seen from the surface were too subtle to be detected by other means, by the 1920s, technology existed that could identify salt domes based upon the gravity and density of the formations—if only it occurred to some open-mined individual to try. Everette Lee DeGolyer, geologist and businessman, was one such man.

DeGolyer's fascination with prospecting technology went back at least as far as his association with the Mexican Eagle Oil Company. His curiosity was probably even older than this and may date to his father's involvement in prospecting in Missouri. Whatever the origins of his interest, DeGolyer maintained a remarkably open mind when it came to the application of new methods and instruments in geology. To some extent, this reflected an ideology of scientific progress that prized innovation. However, DeGolyer's fascination with prospecting methods also seems to have had something romantic, or perhaps childlike, about it—as if he were in search of buried treasure. In a review of a book on divining rods, he confessed that he had looked into the rather unscientific method himself, although he had not met with much success. DeGolyer seemed to take as much pleasure in the hunt for riches as in the enjoyment of riches.[18]

Despite his open mind, DeGolyer was no fool when money was involved. He was, after all, a scientist, and he would risk his money, and the money of fellow investors, only if a scientifically plausible method promised success. In 1914, while in the employ of the Mexican Eagle Oil Company, DeGolyer had come across one such innovation that seemed to fit the bill. It involved a device known as a torsion balance. The torsion balance was not a recent invention; it had been refined and promoted for some years by the prominent Hungarian scientist, Baron Roland Eötvös.[19]

Eötvös was a giant in the field of physics. Born in 1848, the son of a prominent Hungarian author and politician, Eötvös had begun his studies at the University of Budapest with plans for a career in law. His interest in the natural sciences soon drew him to physics instead. Leaving Austria-Hungary for Germany in 1867, Eötvös studied under some of the most learned physicists of the day. In 1871, he returned to Budapest, where he joined the faculty of the University of Science.[20]

Eötvös's work focused on the measurement of the earth's gravitational and magnetic fields. In April 1896, he presented a paper before the Royal Hungarian Academy of Sciences in which he reviewed his theoretical studies and described the revolutionary instruments that he had developed to measure gravitational fields. The idea of using a device to measure the relative gravity of different locations was not a new one. As early as 1833, Sir John Herschel had suggested a design for such an instrument, but early attempts to develop a workable model failed. Eötvös improved upon existing designs by placing the sensitive equipment in a relatively small, closed metal case with double (later triple) walls. These aspects of Eötvös's approach helped to stabilize the instruments so that the operator could measure minute differences in gravitational fields.[21]

DeGolyer first learned of the possibility of prospecting for oil with the torsion balance as early as 1914, hearing about the instrument in a conversation with P. C. A. Stewart, a geologist colleague with the Mexican Eagle Oil Company. In later years, DeGolyer recalled that Stewart, in a "general" conversation, "mentioned that some Hungarian physicist was said to have succeeded in locating a [salt] bearing . . . dome in Transylvania by gravity anomalies."[22]

The innovative method intrigued DeGolyer when he learned of it. Variations in the gravitational field of the earth depended upon underlying geology. Could a device that measured these changes in gravitational fields indicate a certain type of geological structure not observable at the surface? More important from DeGolyer's perspective, could it indicate a geological structure known to hold petroleum?

It seemed plausible, and he began to look into the possibility of obtaining one of these torsion balances.

After learning of the device, DeGolyer arranged a visit with an uncle of P. C. A. Stewart in order to further investigate the method. This uncle was a professor of geodesy emeritus at the University of Cambridge. A personal acquaintance of Roland Eötvös, he volunteered to write the scientist on DeGolyer's behalf. Eötvös replied promptly, offering to sell an instrument, and DeGolyer eagerly accepted, but in the meantime, war had broken out in Europe. DeGolyer offered to pay more in order to compensate for the difficulties of wartime shipping, but it was no use. The First World War proved more than an inconvenience. Gravitational prospecting would have to wait.[23]

Five years later, DeGolyer found himself in London, again conversing with P. C. A. Stewart regarding the possibility of prospecting with the torsion balance. Following the eruption of war, others had considered the possibility of using the instrument to search for petroleum. In this regard, an article published in *Science* in 1917, titled "The Possibility of Using Gravity Anomalies in the Search for Salt Dome Oil and Gas Pools," drew DeGolyer's attention.[24] He asked Stewart to look into the matter further. Following encouragement from a physics professor and from the chief geologist of the Royal Dutch Company, DeGolyer began to search for a scientist with adequate knowledge of geology and physics to look into the matter.[25]

Although the war had ended by then, circumstances continued to frustrate DeGolyer's efforts to obtain a torsion balance. For one, Baron Eötvös died on April 8, 1919, considerably complicating the process. Until the spring of 1921, there were apparently only two of the instruments in existence, and neither of these was available for purchase. Then, in May 1921, DeGolyer learned that the firm of Ferdinand Suss had obtained the rights to manufacture the balance. A flurry of dispatches passed between companies, and DeGolyer made arrangements for the purchase of two balances.[26]

Of course, there was still the matter of finding someone to operate the balance in the field. One scholar at the newly founded Roland Eötvös Institute in Budapest wrote to P. C. A. Stewart, offering to calibrate the instruments following purchase. Perhaps he would be willing to instruct a qualified scientist in the use of the balance. On July 14, 1921, DeGolyer conferred with J. B. Body and Thomas J. Ryder to plan the matter. The company would send a geologist to Europe to receive training and convey the new instruments to the United States. The man they had in mind was Dr. Donald C. Barton, the division geologist in charge of Gulf Coast work for the Amerada Petroleum Corporation.[27]

Barton, or "Doc" as his colleagues knew him, was three years younger than DeGolyer, but had benefited from a formidable education. Born in Massachusetts, the talented Barton pursued advanced studies in geology at Harvard, receiving a PhD in 1914. For the next two years, he served as an instructor in geology at Washington University in St. Louis. However, the private sector soon tempted Barton. He had only begun to work for the Empire Gas and Fuel Company when the United States declared war on Germany in 1917. Barton left his job to join the army, serving with the American Expeditionary Force in France. In 1919, he returned to industry, accepting a position as division geologist with Amerada. Barton shared with DeGolyer an intense interest in the salt dome geology of the Gulf Coast.[28]

Thus, it was Barton to whom DeGolyer, Ryder, and Body turned in the late spring of 1922. Traveling to Budapest, he studied the devices carefully, sending detailed weekly reports to DeGolyer. Barton traveled about the continent, most importantly to Germany, where he would examine another geophysical method under development: seismography. In due time, seismic prospecting would overshadow the gravimetric approach employed by the torsion balance, but for the time being, the focus remained on the Eötvös instruments. After a fair degree of wrangling over the details of the transaction, the Suss firm delivered the balances in New York on September 5, 1922. By November, they were in Houston, Texas, where plans were underway for a field test in December.[29]

The site of the first survey with the torsion balance was none other than Spindletop. Years before, Dr. Hayes had doubted the presence of petroleum at Spindletop. After the discovery of oil there, he had worked with William Kennedy in 1903 to piece together the geology of the field by examining the logs of multiple oil wells.[30] Now, DeGolyer and Barton hoped to examine the field without appealing to information from existing wells, as if it were a new, untested prospect. Would they be able to identify the salt dome formation with the torsion balance? Positive results would confirm the new instrument as a revolutionary tool in prospecting.

On April 19, 1923, DeGolyer received a summary report of Barton's findings. Having drafted the report a week before, "Doc" Barton concluded that the results were "in part, very favorable and in part unfa-vorable."[31] It was not exactly the ringing endorsement of the method for which DeGolyer had hoped. On the one hand, the survey with the torsion balance did find that "very high anomalous gradients prevail at the edge of the salt core."[32] Relative to the surrounding area, the gravity readings over Spindletop were rather high. This was due to the presence of a dense "cap rock" thrust upward by the underlying salt formation. For DeGolyer and Barton, this was the good news.

Barton drafted a map to demonstrate what he had found. It was, to be sure, less pleasing to the eye than the closed contours of the topo-graphical survey. A series of points indicated the location of the "sta-tions" where Barton's team had made their readings. Pointing from these locations were vector arrows, determined through mathematical analysis, which indicated the direction of greatest relative gravity. In the case of Spindletop, those vectors pointed as surely as on a treasure map to the black gold that DeGolyer sought.

Barton and DeGolyer's investigation of gravimetric prospecting was indeed revolutionary—probably the first survey of an oilfield in the United States using a geophysical technique.[33] If the torsion balance could identify gravity anomalies, then the instrument could indicate the existence of a salt dome. Through the Eötvös device, DeGolyer and Barton were opening the underworld to view, giving geologists new in-formation that had been beyond their grasp.

Why then did Barton view the method as "in part unfavorable"? There were also significant drawbacks. The process involved in the grav-ity survey was highly cumbersome. The Spindletop survey required a total of sixteen days, of which four were lost because of rain. Work pro-ceeded at a pace of one "reading" a day.[34] This meant that the gravity could be measured at only one site a day, making it necessary for the team to spend weeks in the field in order to garner sufficient data to make an evaluation. Barton described a typical schedule for DeGolyer in the report:

| | |
|---|---|
| 8:00 a.m. | Start to tear up the old station. |
| [where the previous day's reading was taken] | |
| 9:15 a.m. | All loaded on the truck. |
| 10:00 a.m. | Start to set up new station. |
| 1:00 p.m. | Station set up completed. |

| 2:00 p.m. | First reading taken. |
| 3:00 to 10:00 p.m. | [Hourly] readings taken . . . [35] |

Considering the slow progress of the survey, Barton concluded that the torsion balance could really only be effective when used in combination with other geological information. It would not do simply to send out teams across the nation, taking readings here and there. Instead, the company would need to have a site in mind.

Barton suggested that company geologists should identify potential salt dome locations. Then, the company could dispatch a torsion balance team to confirm the presence of a salt dome at the location. Notwithstanding these limitations, the 1923 Spindletop survey was a significant event in the history of the oil industry. For the first time, a company had employed geophysical methods to analyze an American oilfield.[36]

Despite the drawbacks of the torsion balance that Barton described, the new method promised to be a useful tool in locating prospective oilfields. The only question now was where to look. One site came to the attention of the company and demonstrated the practicality of the new instrument. Southwest of the city of Houston, in Fort Bend county, there was a well-forested tract of land where several water wells proved high in sulfur content. Although there was a slight swell in the ground, the topography of the area had been difficult to ascertain because the terrain was broken with trees and tall weeds. But it was the sulfur in the wells that had attracted attention. Sulfur had abounded in other salt dome formations, along with petroleum. Perhaps the barely discernable rise of the land indicated the presence of a salt dome—and oil. DeGolyer and Barton thought the location to be worthy of further investigation.[37]

As at Spindletop, Barton supervised the survey. Working in early 1924, the team transported the cumbersome equipment to the so-called "Nash Prospect" and began taking readings. Ultimately, they would measure the gravitational fields at thirty "stations" in the area. As the early results came in, Barton became excited. It seemed clear to him that they were indeed working over a salt dome. Even before the work was finished, he dashed off a preliminary report to DeGolyer. Barton believed that he could identify the location of the salt dome with precision. He confidently asserted, "I recommend this dome as the most favorable, completely wild wildcat prospect that we have had. If there is no dome here, we may as well abandon the use of the [torsion] balance on salt domes."[38]

DeGolyer felt confident enough with the findings to set in motion a drilling plan for the site. A test well proved Barton right when it drilled into salt late in the year, confirming the presence of the salt dome that the survey had detected. Of course, this was still no guarantee of oil, but by 1926, the company completed a successful oil well on the Nash Dome. The time and money invested in the torsion balance was paying off at last.[39]

The gravimetric method employed by the torsion balances was not the only prospecting technology that interested DeGolyer in the 1920s. The magnetometer, which measured the magnetic field produced by underlying geology, was another device that DeGolyer's companies began to employ at about the same time as the Nash Dome discovery.[40] But the impact of the magnetometer paled in comparison to other technologies that DeGolyer would investigate.

Even as Donald Barton worked to secure the Eötvös instruments in Europe, he passed on information regarding other innovations to his superiors. One such method that proved interesting was a development of the First World War. Up until 1914, the science of seismology was largely limited to the study of earthquakes. This was a matter of practical concern, but not obviously related to military matters. However, with the advent of the Great War and the grim realities of trench warfare, scientists on both sides turned their attention to the battlefield. Geophysicists who considered the importance of artillery barrages on the Western Front believed that they might have something to offer to the war effort. Treating cannon discharge as seismic "events," scientists on both sides of the conflict developed methods for locating enemy batteries by deploying seismic recording stations along the front.[41]

Following the war, Allied and German physicists who had developed the military application for seismology began to think in terms of its possibilities in industry. The seismographs might reveal more than just the location of an explosion; they might reveal something about the earth that seismic waves passed through as well. It was not an entirely new idea. As early as 1846, Irishman Robert Mallet had conceived the possibility of using seismology to investigate geological formations, but he had never succeeded in developing a practical method for putting his vision into action. Later scientists had tried experiments similar

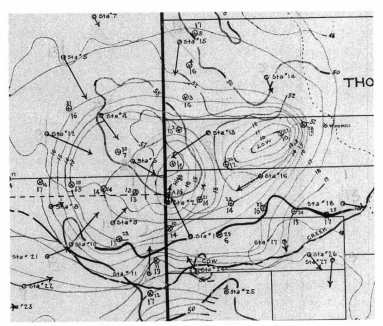

Gravimetric and magnetic survey of the Nash Dome. This map suggests both the degree of information that geophysical methods made available and the level of sophistication required in analysis of that information. (Everette Lee DeGolyer Collection. Courtesy of DeGolyer Library, Southern Methodist University.)

to those of Mallet although little had come of them. But the men who created the artillery-ranging technology of World War I had developed equipment sensitive enough to allow precise analysis of seismic events. Perhaps they could also use these devices to map subsurface geology. The idea was plausible, and it occurred at about the same time to several men who had fought on different sides in the war. Although former Allied scientists would ultimately play an important role in the development of seismic prospecting, a cigar-chomping German named Ludger Mintrop would make the first successful efforts.[42]

Mintrop was a remarkable figure whose education and experience prepared him well to be a pioneer in geophysics. He was born in 1880 on the family estate near Essen-Werden, the fifth son of fifteen children. Mintrop received thorough training in mining methods in the Ruhr region. Studying in the Mining Academy in Berlin, then the Technical University in Aachen, Mintrop attained a remarkable mastery of geological knowledge. In 1905, he became a mining surveyor while continuing his studies in Aachen. Two years later, he began studies in seismology at the University of Göttingen. Working under the eminent professor Emil Wiechert, he began to experiment in geophysics, setting up seismic stations and working to develop more easily portable seismographs. Even before the war, Mintrop was convinced that seismology had significant practical applications.[43]

With the outbreak of World War I, Mintrop served as a physicist with the Imperial German Airship Division, then with the Artillery Control Commission. He long fought with the conservative general staff of the army, which remained skeptical of his assertion that seismographs could locate artillery emplacements. Finally, after the bloody battle of the Somme, he was able to persuade General Ludendorff that the method could work. After a convincing demonstration of seismic ranging of artillery, Ludendorff ordered the creation of one hundred seismic teams for deployment to the front in 1917. However, with suitable personnel and materials scarce, the Germans failed to mass-produce the seismographs in time for the war.[44]

When the war ended, Mintrop considered the peacetime applications of the seismograph. Thanks to his extensive experience with both geophysics and geology, he had come to an advanced understanding of what seismographic data might mean in terms of local geology. With the war over, Mintrop used controlled explosions of dynamite in place of artillery fire to create the small earthquakes that analog readouts recorded as a series of waves. The first wave noted by a seismograph— a head wave, or "indirect wave," as Mintrop referred to it—varied in its arrival time based upon the density of the material through which the sound refracted. Through analysis of the timing of these waves, Mintrop knew that he could draw certain conclusions about the underlying geology. Importantly, he believed that this knowledge was sufficient foundation on which to build a business. On April 4, 1921, he founded the Seismos Institute and began work in Europe, serving the continent's mining industry. That same year, Mintrop successfully used refraction seismography to discover a salt dome in Germany. It was the first salt dome found by seismic prospecting in history.[45]

DeGolyer had become aware of the seismic approach by the time that Barton was in Europe, training to use the Eötvös balance. Directing Barton to Germany, he was interested in learning more about the new technique. The application that DeGolyer had in mind was the same as that of the torsion balances: salt dome prospecting. The seismic approach

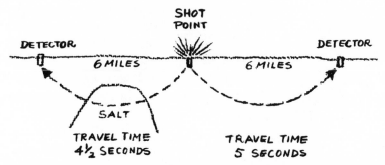

REFRACTION SHOOTING

SHOT
POINT

DETECTOR    DETECTOR

6 MILES    6 MILES

SALT

TRAVEL TIME
4½ SECONDS

TRAVEL TIME
5 SECONDS

Prospecting for a salt dome with refraction seismology. By timing the arrival of the head wave or "indirect wave," Mintrop was able to deduce the presence of a salt dome. The principle would soon be applied in the United States Gulf Coast on a large scale. (Drawing by Everette Lee DeGolyer, "How Men Find Oil," *Fortune*, August 1949, 99. Courtesy of Everette and Nell DeGolyer descendants.)

offered certain important advantages over gravimetric prospecting, including a more complete understanding of the underlying geology. Barton was apparently impressed with the potential of seismology and plans went ahead to acquire the appropriate equipment for Amerada. The great obstacle to the company's plan was the Seismos Institute, which was reluctant to sell equipment to independent operators. Instead, Seismos hoped to use its own people to operate the equipment, maintaining secrecy regarding the details of its operation.[46]

Mintrop's determination to maintain control over seismic technology worked, but only in the short run. Intrigued by Barton's reports on the new method, DeGolyer recommended that the Mexican Eagle Oil Company hire a Seismos team as a trial. Mintrop's men worked for the company from March 1923 until the spring of 1924. DeGolyer later recalled the results of their work as "not extremely successful" and confessed, "I consequently did not have much confidence in [the method] when competing oil companies engaged crews for work in the United States."[47]

DeGolyer would soon change his mind regarding seismic prospecting. Although the Mexican Eagle Oil Company did not have much luck with their seismic crew, other clients fared better. The Gulf Oil Company of Texas hired Seismos to prospect for salt domes in the spring

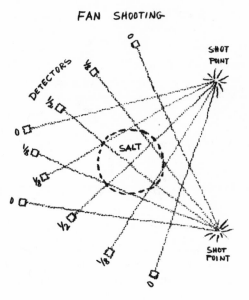

FAN SHOOTING

"Fan shooting" with refraction seismology. The use of multiple sensors and multiple detonations (not simultaneous) could map a salt dome with precision. (Drawing by Everette Lee DeGolyer, "How Men Find Oil," *Fortune*, August, 1949, 99. Courtesy of Everette and Nell DeGolyer descendants.)

of 1924. Their investment paid off when the seismic team discovered the Orchard Dome on the Texas Gulf Coast. It was the first seismic discovery of an American salt dome, and the significance of the find was not lost on DeGolyer. He later admitted, "I was inclined to be skeptical with regard to the possible value of the seismic method. Repeated successes of the Seismos crews for the Gulf [Oil Company], however, soon convinced me that the method was one to be reckoned with."[48]

The introduction of seismic prospecting by Mintrop meant competition for the gravimetric method already deployed by the Amerada companies. Both approaches possessed certain advantages that kept each in play for some time. On the balance, seismography was generally superior. Seismic teams could conduct surveys on any type of terrain, while the torsion balance was unmanageable in regions where lakes, swamps, or marshes were present. Seismic results were also initially more definite and conclusive than gravimetric records. In addition, seismic work proceeded at a much faster pace than its competitor did.[49]

On the other hand, the cost of a seismic survey was much greater than that of torsion balance analysis. There was another advantage of the gravimetric approach that became apparent with the passage of time. Seismic refraction was highly effective at identifying shallow salt domes, but its accuracy declined when searching for deeper structures.

As seismic refraction surveys rapidly identified the shallow domes of the Gulf Coast, companies began to discover that the torsion balance was comparatively better at finding the deeper domes. Because of these differing advantages, both seismic refraction parties and torsion balance teams remained active through the close of the 1920s.[50]

Although the gravimetric approach would continue to be relevant in petroleum prospecting for some time, DeGolyer believed that developments in seismology were too important to ignore. In formulating a plan for Amerada and her affiliates, DeGolyer might have chosen to rely on outside consultants like the Seismos Institute to carry out seismic surveys. Instead, he envisioned a new company that would compete with Mintrop in the race to identify new oilfields. This was the origin of the Geophysical Research Corporation. But DeGolyer knew that he was beyond his expertise when it came to seismology. He was, after all, a geologist and not a geophysicist. Where would he find a scientist who could realize his ambitious vision?

Early in 1925, DeGolyer requested that Barton compose a list of capable geophysicists. At the same time, DeGolyer drew up his own roster of professionals. After comparing the two lists, DeGolyer discovered one name in common to both: John Clarence Karcher. Karcher was a remarkable figure whose biography shared much with DeGolyer's own. Born in Indiana in 1894, Karcher's family moved to Oklahoma when he was a toddler. Settling in a farming community in northern Oklahoma, he spent his childhood on the plains not so far from DeGolyer's first home in Greensburg, Kansas. After graduating from high school in 1912, Karcher attended the University of Oklahoma, where he studied physics and mathematics. Completing college in 1916 with an excellent record, Karcher continued to pursue graduate study at the University of Pennsylvania. Still in school, he worked briefly as an assistant at Thomas Edison Laboratory, occasionally chatting with the famous inventor, who counseled him, "Without perseverance and persistence, little can be accomplished in any endeavor." Karcher would put this advice to work in his geophysical experiments.[51]

When the United States declared war on Germany in April 1917, Karcher had completed only one year of studies. Nevertheless, he was determined to contribute to the war effort as a scientist. Going to work for the Bureau of Standards as an assistant physicist, he joined a project, already in development, to interpret acoustic waves from gunfire in order to locate enemy artillery batteries. The American sci-

J. C. Karcher. The pioneer geophysicist and DeGolyer collaborator whose work with reflection seismology transformed the nature of oil prospecting. (Everette Lee DeGolyer Collection. Courtesy of DeGolyer Library, Southern Methodist University.)

entists were working along lines similar to those that Ludger Mintrop was exploring at roughly the same time on behalf of the German army. Where Mintrop began with the notion of using seismic waves to locate gun emplacements, Karcher and his colleagues started with interpretation of sound waves carried through the air. The Americans soon found that sound waves—essentially the same as seismic waves—that traveled through the earth were less susceptible to distortion due to atmospheric conditions.

Shifting their emphasis from the air to the earth, they monitored these waves through "geophones" that fed the information to a recording station where the waves would be logged on a uniformly moving "smoked chart," or on photographic paper or film. Karcher and his associates noted that a single gun blast created a series of seismic "events"—an initial wave followed by later-arriving impulses. Interpreting the information, they identified the first event as a sound wave that refracted through the uppermost stratum of the earth. This refracted wave was the focus of Mintrop's analysis. However, it was the seismic waves that arrived after the initial refracted wave that intrigued Karcher. He understood these events as reflections that bounced back from deeper levels where one layer of rock met with another underlying layer. It was an important insight that would later prove to be of significant consequence to the oil industry. Like Mintrop, the American scientists had fine-tuned their system with military use in mind, but Karcher was already thinking about broader applications.[52]

The Americans put the ranging project into action, and Karcher traveled to France, where he served as a technical attaché to the United States Embassy. He was in Paris when the Armistice ended the war on November 11, 1918. Now he could complete his education. Returning to the University of Pennsylvania, Karcher continued his studies, all the while considering what he had learned about sound ranging. Remembering his education at the University of Oklahoma, he recalled how his classmates who studied geology had described the relationship between oilfields and geological structures.

Some time soon after he returned from France, he made a connection between this rudimentary geological knowledge and his wartime work. It was something of a breakthrough. He later remembered, "[I]t began to become apparent that one might be able to map these limestone capped domes or anticlines and thus be able to locate such traps for oil and gas."[53] Discussing the possibility with Dr. Anton Udden, a geology professor at the University of Texas, and Dr. D. W. Ohern, former professor of geology at the University of Oklahoma, Karcher became increasingly convinced that it could work. Additional consultation with Dr. W. P. Haseman, a physicist at the University of Oklahoma, encouraged Karcher to give his idea a trial run. In June 1920, Karcher was graduated from the University of Pennsylvania, receiving a PhD in physics. He took a job with the Bureau of Standards but continued to develop his plans for seismic prospecting. After finding some willing investors in the oil industry, Karcher joined with Haseman and Ohern to form the Geological Engineering Company.[54]

In May 1921, Karcher took a six-month leave of absence from the Bureau of Standards to see if the system he had in mind could work. In the late spring and early summer of that year, he tramped out into the field, together with Haseman and a few other associates. The first site that the group chose was a farm about three miles north of Oklahoma City. Detonating dynamite charges that disturbed the otherwise peaceful and rustic scene, Karcher and his team fine-tuned their geophones and analyzed the records they produced. It seemed to be working.[55]

In order to confirm the success of the system, Karcher and company planned another expedition, this time to the Arbuckle Mountains of southern Oklahoma. There, the surface exposure of rock strata revealed more information about geological structure than could be determined on the farm where they had conducted the first fieldwork. By correlating this ready information with the results of the fieldwork, Karcher hoped to confirm that the new seismic method worked. The team began shooting on July 4, 1921. Their effort proved a resounding success.[56] Karcher later described the process: "The records were of good quality and easily read. I timed out all the records and calculated the dip slope of the Viola Lime beneath the Sylvan Shale. These calculations were found to be in good agreement with the dip slope as determined by the geologists with alidade and plane table."[57] In other words, the results suggested that analysis of seismic reflections could map the rock strata below without resorting to simplistic projections based on rock outcrops or topography. This was a departure from the method of seismic refraction that Mintrop and the Seismos Institute were using in Germany. It was a revolutionary advance.

Karcher soon found an oil company that was interested in the new technology. Marland Oil signed an agreement with Geological Engineering Company, and fieldwork began in September 1921. Until November, Karcher cooperated with Marland staff geologists to map structures near Ponca City, Oklahoma. Yet the timing of the venture proved unfortunate. The same year marked the discovery of major oilfields in Oklahoma. The price of oil plummeted. With lower profit margins, Karcher and his company became too expensive for Marland or any other oil company. In December 1921, the Geological Engineering Company closed down and put its equipment in storage. Karcher returned briefly to Washington and the Bureau of Standards before accepting a new position with AT&T.[58]

Had the price of oil not recovered, it might have ended with that. However, by March 1925, the cost of a barrel of oil, which had fallen as low as 15¢, had recovered to a healthy price of $3. Marland Oil and a company based out of Chicago that had learned of the seismic work both contacted Karcher to see if he would consider returning to seismic prospecting. He was certainly willing, but another fierce competitor would soon edge out these two companies—Everette Lee DeGolyer.[59]

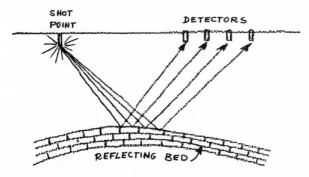

REFLECTION SHOOTING

SHOT POINT

DETECTORS

REFLECTING BED

Reflection seismology required the interpretation of a multitude of reflected waves in order to chart the depth and angle of a variety of rock strata. (Drawing by Everette Lee DeGolyer, "How Men Find Oil," *Fortune*, August, 1949, 99. Courtesy of Everette and Nell DeGolyer descendants.)

DeGolyer's consultation with Barton regarding promising geophysicists had highlighted Karcher's brilliance and potential. As a result, he determined to meet with Karcher and discuss the innovative methods of mapping that he had developed. DeGolyer contacted professor Harold Bozell, who knew Karcher and had taught at the University of Oklahoma and Yale University. Now the editor of *Electrical World,* Bozell arranged a meeting with Karcher at DeGolyer's behest. In March 1925, DeGolyer, Barton, and Karcher gathered at the Bankers' Club in New York. Karcher later recalled how, over lunch, they "discussed the seismic reflection method of measuring the depth of rock layers at various points below the surface and the procedure to convert this information into a contour map of an anticlinal structure capable of entrapping oil and gas." DeGolyer was impressed.[60]

After conferring with the board of directors of Amerada and its affiliates, DeGolyer contacted Karcher again, requesting a meeting on April 10, 1925. He wondered whether it might be possible to rendezvous with Karcher in St. Louis, a stop on a trip that DeGolyer was making to Tulsa; Karcher agreed. Both arrived at the train station at about the same hour, so the two gathered in the second-floor waiting room of St. Louis's Union Station. DeGolyer proposed that Karcher accept a position as vice president with a company not yet formed, named Geophysical Research Corporation (GRC). Karcher drove a hard bargain, demanding 15 percent of the stock of the new corporation. Amerada, and one of its subsidiaries, Rycade, would own the remainder. After shaking hands on the deal, Karcher returned to Chicago. On June 1, 1925, he resigned from his position and embarked upon a new career in association with DeGolyer.[61]

The decision to form an independent company for the development of seismic prospecting was a departure from the approach earlier taken by the companies with which DeGolyer was affiliated. Amerada had pioneered geophysical prospecting methods with gravimetrics. But it had done so as a corporation engaged in the business of producing oil. The creation of GRC, an entity devoted exclusively to geophysical prospecting, was in some ways a throwback to an earlier stage of professional development in the realm of petroleum geology.

Until the early twentieth century, most earth scientists with professional ties to the oil industry served companies as consultants. Skepticism within the oil industry impeded the application of geology during this period, but the earth scientist became progressively more prominent in years to come, in part because the number of easily identifiable oilfields declined. California oil companies were pioneers in hiring geologists and the establishment of a "geological department" by the Union Oil Company in 1907 seemed to bode the future of the profession. After all, other industries were drawing scientists within the corporate hierarchy through the formation of research laboratories.[62]

In contrast, the formation of GRC as a separate entity suggested a more autonomous role for the scientist in the petroleum industry. At least it left open the possibility that a corporation devoted to scientific analysis of oilfields could stand as an independent player among oil production companies. If DeGolyer did not already envision such a role for the new company, he would soon do so. Nevertheless, there were significant restrictions on the freedom of GRC to operate independently. The most notable of these limitations was the matter of stock ownership. Aside from Karcher's 15 percent share, Amerada and its subsidiary, Rycade, controlled GRC. This meant that GRC remained beholden to the interests of these oil companies. Of course, many of the same men were involved in running all three. DeGolyer himself was vice president of Amerada and president of Rycade. Robert Nock, the secretary of the newly formed GRC, was also the secretary of Amerada. Still, neither DeGolyer nor his fellow officers absolutely controlled the companies that they managed. In future years, DeGolyer's inability to maintain control over the direction of GRC would imperil its potential to serve the industry as a quasi-independent consultant.[63]

Nevertheless, for the next five years, GRC would preserve its somewhat autonomous role in the oil business. During those years, DeGolyer, Karcher, and the team of talented geophysicists that they assembled would take a leading role in the application of seismography in oil prospecting. The scientists hired by DeGolyer represented a remarkable array of talent in the field of geophysics. In addition to Karcher, this group included E. E. Rosaire and Eugene McDermott. It is difficult to overstate the impact of the team of men that DeGolyer assembled to the development of geophysical prospecting. Of the first twenty-six presidents of the Society of Exploration Geophysicists, fifteen worked under DeGolyer, including eight of the first ten presidents. At least at the beginning, the stage for their work would be the Gulf Coast. Here, GRC would enter the business of petroleum prospecting in competition with Mintrop's Seismos Institute.[64]

Despite Karcher's promising experiments with reflection seismography, most of GRC's initial work focused on the same sort of refraction work carried out by Mintrop's teams. Introduced in 1924 and generally accepted within the industry by 1926, refraction seismography rapidly became the focus of an intense prospecting campaign to locate coastal salt domes. Karcher worked to improve the refraction method, which proved increasingly effective. From 1924 to 1930, oilmen shelled out approximately $20 million for refraction surveys, resulting in the discovery of forty new salt domes. Despite the considerable cost, refraction seismography was a smashing success, and GRC benefited enormously. Gradually, the company overtook Mintrop's Seismos Institute in its share of seismic work.[65]

Even with its effective management and devotion to technical innovation, the success of GRC was uncertain. Ludger Mintrop's Seismos Institute enjoyed a significant head start in seismic prospecting and dominated the field from 1923 to 1925. But GRC possessed certain advantages in its struggle for market share. One was home field advantage. DeGolyer, Karcher, and their associates were Americans who benefited from connections within the business and from greater familiarity with the national industry. Equally important, they also had less distance to travel. Seismos teams and their equipment had to journey by ship from

# Early Geophysical Prospecting

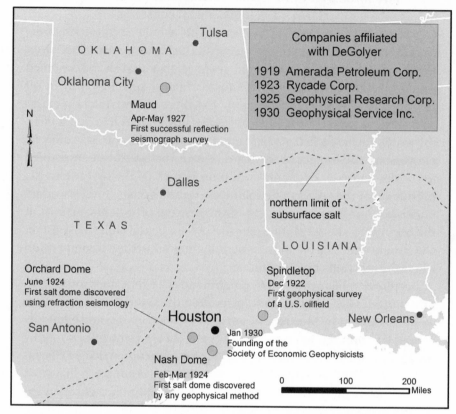

Early Geophysical Prospecting. Of the geophysical firsts indicated on the map, all were conducted by companies associated with DeGolyer except Orchard Dome (conducted by Seismos on behalf of Gulf Oil). The Society of Economic Geophysicists, later renamed the Society of Exploration Geophysicists, inducted DeGolyer and Mintrop as its first honorary members in the year of its founding. (Map by Gregory Plumb.)

Germany to arrive at the oilfields of the Americas. Lost time and travel expenses were not irrelevant considerations when it came to profitable operation.

GRC also enjoyed a superior financial climate in the United States. In the years following the First World War, the German economy suffered from rampant inflation. Seismos was unable to fund expensive but necessary research projects that were essential to maintaining their technological lead. Finally, Mintrop himself became something of a liability. His devotion to refraction seismography caused him to discount the value of the reflection methods that GRC was developing. It was, in the words of one biographer, "the most fatal misconception of his career." In March and April 1927, a GRC team successfully mapped the geological structure near Maud, Oklahoma, proving the value of the new method.[66] More successes would follow for reflection seismography. By 1930, the industry had dismissed the last Seismos party in the United States. In contrast, GRC's future looked bright.[67]

At that time, few would have guessed the fall that lay in store for GRC. Ironically, the figures most responsible for its impending decline were none other than Karcher and DeGolyer. GRC's bad fortune began with a new company founded by these men in 1930, Geophysical Service Incorporated (GSI). It was the first in a series of personnel defections and corporate fractures as numerous companies broke away under the leadership of former GRC employees. Eventually, some in the business would refer to the various spin-offs as the "Amerada Tree," with Amerada representing the trunk of a growing industry that was branching off into a variety of competing companies. The Amerada Tree owed much to the work of DeGolyer, whose vision and advocacy of the then innovative methods of prospecting were among the vital "roots" of the new industry of geophysical exploration.[68]

DeGolyer's importance to the development of geophysical exploration was his role as a visionary who recognized the potential of these new prospecting methods. But his power of persuasion as a respected scientist who knew the oil business well was at least as significant as this initial insight. Although DeGolyer was no geophysicist, he was a crucial figure who connected the scientific world with the entrepreneurial world and helped call into being an industry. Of course, had DeGolyer not been there to seize the opportunities of the day, someone else eventually would have been. Nevertheless, his keen insight into the relationship between geophysical technology and the oil business made an important contribution to that industry's development.

On the other hand, DeGolyer was not an infallible prophet. His admirers have rightly celebrated his successes in the oil business, but a more complete picture of his role investigating and promoting technologies reveals a man who was accustomed to failure as well. It could hardly have been otherwise. In grasping for innovative approaches to the old problems of prospecting, DeGolyer was taking risks. To

DeGolyer, those risks were necessary, and the occasional failure was perhaps inevitable.

DeGolyer was convinced that the oil business required companies to stay abreast of the most recent technological innovations in order to profit, and perhaps even to survive. The manager of such an operation of necessity would be a "technologist" rather than a mere technician or, even worse, simply an investor. In charting the course for his own companies, DeGolyer showed sustained interest in the application of new techniques to oil prospecting. This certainly reflected a conscious decision to always stay ahead of the game and ensure the prosperity of his enterprises. On a deeper level, it was a function of his intellectual curiosity and the characteristic of a mind that was objective and calculating, but also intensely passionate. For DeGolyer was at heart, a committed scientist.

As a scientist, he was well aware of the limitations of his own special area of training as a geologist. DeGolyer had succeeded in exploring the application of certain geophysical technologies in the field of petroleum prospecting. In his investigations of the torsion balance and seismography, he crossed beyond the boundaries of geological practice and was required to rely on conjecture, common sense, and especially imagination to discern how new techniques might be applicable. Communicating with specialists in the field of geophysics, DeGolyer wanted to understand how the new technology might work in the context of his own business. Over the years, he learned quite a bit about how geophysical instruments worked, but he was no geophysicist. To a fair degree, he remained dependent on the experts he consulted.

In the case of the torsion balance, refraction seismology, and reflection seismology, DeGolyer's risks were rewarded. Not all of his investigations of innovative technology were so fortunate. Even DeGolyer seems to have occasionally fallen prey to the scourge of the oilfield— the "doodlebug" operator.

The pedigree of the doodlebug was old, if not venerable. After the discovery of oil in Pennsylvania in 1859, a variety of charlatans descended upon the region, claiming the power to identify undiscovered oilfields. Divining rod practitioners, "oil smellers," and spiritualists all promised riches at a reasonable commission. The doodlebug soon joined these colorful characters in the search for oil. "Doodlebug" could refer to a special oil-detecting gadget or to the man who operated it. The devices ranged in sophistication from modified divining rods to more elaborate electrical instruments for which the operator offered some scientific justification.[69]

DeGolyer was not a fool. As an increasingly prominent oilman, bold hucksters and aspiring inventors regularly approached him with suggestions for investment. As early as 1926, he referred to a "freak" file to which he dedicated letters regarding these devices that he found amusing.[70] One gentleman, years after DeGolyer had become an acknowledged scientific authority in oil prospecting, was still trying to sell him a divining rod. The confident promoter promised, "My six years of experiment have convinced me absolutely that a divining rod when *made out of the right material* will locate almost any mineral. A few of the things it will respond to are gold, water, glass, aluminum oxide, bentonite drilling mud and the steel of pipe lines."[71] After years of dealing with characters like this one, DeGolyer still took the time to issue this terse response: "The job of going into a new method of oil finding is too big for me to take up at the present time."[72]

Yet he also maintained an open mind. The success of geophysical prospecting methods had taught him that new approaches to the old problem of finding oil could work. Writing to a colleague in 1930, he remarked, "As a matter of policy we are continually giving attention to anyone who comes to us with any scheme for geophysical work."[73]

One such "scheme" that proved a dead end was the Carmody-Calvert radiograph. DeGolyer's involvement with this project began in 1935, after years of experience with geophysics and prospecting technology. In May of that year, W. R. Calvert, an apparently persuasive promoter, met with Chester Washburne, a friend of DeGolyer's since his days in Tampico, who was then working with the Cowdray companies in the United States.[74] Washburne must have heard the story before. Calvert told him of a remarkable new invention that could locate oil in the field, even to the point of being able to identify its depth. In contrast to some "doodlebug" men, Calvert offered a complex, perhaps even plausible, explanation of how the device worked. Washburne took down detailed notes, forwarding them to DeGolyer. He reported:

A carrier wave of 1.5 meter (wave length) is shot into the earth from a generator and also a longer radio wave, the wave length of which is kept secret, but which is a "short wave." These waves are reflected from an oil sand, just as radio waves are reflected from the ionized zones of the upper air . . . because live oil carries an electrostatic charge, which is being regenerated in some unknown way . . . The inventor has solved the secret of obtaining deep penetration for the waves, and has made successful tests as deep as 8,666 feet.[75]

Or so Calvert claimed. There were other qualifications offered by the wily promoter. Washburne dutifully passed these on to DeGolyer, noting, "Very thin oil sands are said to show only faintly. Dead oil and dry gas will not show. The oil must be 'live,' i.e. containing gas in solution. Gas heavily charged with distillate will give returns similar to oil . . ."[76] These caveats only added to the credibility of the story. This was no snake oil that Calvert was peddling. The method had limitations, just like any other realistic, scientific approach would have had.

On the other hand, there were warning signs that Calvert and Carmody were less than legitimate operators. Washburne noted, "[T]hey have no office" and reported the temporary address for the two—the Sam Houston Hotel.[77] So there was certainly cause for suspicion.

But Washburne, aware of DeGolyer's interest in any plausible innovations, recommended further investigation. Perhaps Karcher would be a better judge of the efficacy of the method?[78] DeGolyer agreed. By the early summer, he was in contact with Calvert, who was confidently predicting the success of the new method. In June 1935, Calvert wrote DeGolyer:

> I am convinced beyond a shadow of a doubt that Carmody *can* determine the presence or absence of oil, and *can* give its depth. A friend of mine here—a geophysicist—tells me that his confreres hold the opinion that Carmody *can't* get a reflection back. Personally, I don't care *what* they say; I *know* he *can* and *does* and eventually they will need to revise their theories to fit the facts.[79]

In retrospect, DeGolyer might have sensed the "hard sell" in all those desperately stressed words. Calvert shouted at DeGolyer through the ink. Yet DeGolyer remained open minded. His interest was provoked, and he considered Calvert's device important enough to trouble the work of his chief geophysicist, J. C. Karcher. In July, as Calvert planned to go ahead with more tests, DeGolyer wired Karcher, requesting his presence in Houston. The matter was, according to DeGolyer, "extremely important."[80]

Karcher was not amused. He had little faith in Calvert's assertion that radio waves, even ultrashort radio waves, would give "reflections" of oil.[81] DeGolyer insisted. His dogged optimism reflected an unbounded faith in the power of science. However, it was more than faith that moved him to distract the best men under his direction with Carmody and Calvert's device. It was hope—the hope of a gambler that a big win awaited a man willing to take risks. Writing to Karcher, he remarked, "While common sense forces me to share your skepticism to some degree. I still can't help feeling that there might be something to the Carmody proposition and it would seem to me to merit a most exhaustive test."[82] Stressing the importance of the investigation, DeGolyer assured his associate, "While you probably don't like wild goose chases, this thing has a better background than most and is a gamble for an empire."[83] There was no "sure thing" in the oil business. DeGolyer knew that every oil well drilled was to some degree a gamble. His investigation of the radiograph was another such wager. Unfortunately, it proved a poor one.

Problems abounded after Calvert promised DeGolyer and Karcher to demonstrate the instrument in the field. Sometime in the early summer of 1935, Carmody "tore up" the apparatus for reasons that are obscure. It may have had something to do with a falling out with Calvert, who now took charge of reconstructing, operating, and promoting the device. In August 1935, he loaned the radiograph to Karcher, who drafted a scathing report for DeGolyer. Karcher was now convinced that the machine was a fraud. He reported, "[T]here is not a single meter that is sufficiently sensitive by at least a factor of one hundred for taking observations to the precision to which he gives his results."[84] Not only that, but Karcher believed that Carmody had destroyed the device because the circuits were "faked."[85]

Despite repeated promises, Calvert never successfully demonstrated the radiograph in action. This makes DeGolyer's persistent interest in the device even more astounding. In March 1936, long after Karcher had condemned the project, DeGolyer wrote to Calvert expressing some doubt, but continuing interest in the radiograph. Responding to Calvert's reports of some progress with the technology, he wrote that he was "still a little skeptical," asserting that the most convincing evidence that Calvert had offered was "the conviction which you have in yourself."[86] These reservations notwithstanding, DeGolyer surprisingly asserted, "If there is room for me, I should like to work with you on it at some stage. To be of any value in your set up, however, I would have to be as convinced as you are yourself."[87] Despite DeGolyer's continued interest, nothing would come of Calvert's radiograph. In the end, the episode amounted to nothing more than an example of DeGolyer's open-mindedness when it came to new technology.

DeGolyer's faith in scientific advancement, his intellectual curiosity, and his willingness to take risks all made his approach to innovation possible. However, he also found motivation in insecurity and even fear—fear that the days of easy money in the oil industry were coming to an end. In the early days of the industry, the presence of oil seeps had been common and the oilfields were often quite shallow in depth. Fields like these were becoming scarce. Oilmen would have to look deeper, perhaps so deep that surface geology would offer few clues as to the presence of oil.[88]

Over the next two decades, DeGolyer's meditation on these changes in the industry would evolve into a complete theory of prospecting technology. As he would come to explain it, there were identifiable cycles of development in oil exploration technology. In the early days, there was little to guide the prospector, but gradually, through experience, they came to recognize certain signs indicating the presence of oil. Initially, these were basic observations that needed no special training or technology to discern—the presence of an oil seepage for instance. Gradually, as the more obvious oilfields were developed, new techniques, and new technology became necessary in order to detect the presence of an oilfield. The application of new technology or new technique—for instance, topographical analysis—inevitably led to the discovery of new oilfields in areas to which the new approach was well suited. But soon, a decline in the utility of a new method would make new technological innovation necessary.[89]

The constantly changing landscape of prospecting technology required something special of oilmen. They could not simply be investors or managers, but they needed to possess a level of understanding of the industry that would allow them to recognize these technological cycles and identify opportunities to exploit the latest advances in method. In later years DeGolyer would single out a term for this special individual: "technologist." DeGolyer drew a distinction between the skilled workers who operated sophisticated equipment in the oilfields and those who could see the technical side of the industry from a broader vantage. The former were mere technicians: "the driller, the tool dresser, the pumper, and the still man."[90] The latter were technologists. DeGolyer explained: "To my mind, the technologist is concerned with the whole group of techniques in a given field and thus is several cuts above the technician who may be skilled only in a single technique."[91] In contrast to the technician, "[t]he technologist is an applied scientist and as such is concerned with the application of scientific knowledge to any practical art. He may even be an inventor of techniques."[92] DeGolyer concluded, "The metallurgist, the chemist, the petroleum engineer, and the geologist are technologists."[93]

The technologist could see beyond the tried and true practices of the industry and imagine new models for business, new methods of gathering information, new ways of finding oil. For DeGolyer, the technologist was a man who could see the "big picture." He was, perhaps not surprisingly, a man much like DeGolyer himself.

In later years, DeGolyer would be hailed by colleagues and associates as the "father of applied geophysics," the "father of geophysical exploration," or even, simply, the "father of geophysics."[94] A number of men might have challenged these claims to paternity and three in particular had a much stronger case: Roland Eötvös, Ludger Mintrop, and J. C. Karcher. DeGolyer himself would have been the first to concede that he was, after all, no geophysicist. Nevertheless, the accolades that he received were not without justification. DeGolyer's role in the emergence of applied geophysics was not unlike that which he ascribed to the ideal technologist. Eötvös, Mintrop, and Karcher certainly provided the scientific expertise that pioneered the development of geophysical techniques. But DeGolyer played an important part in the process, in recognizing the plausibility of the new technologies, in discerning their potential for profit, and, most of all, in being willing to risk the capital necessary to put the new methods in action.

By putting geophysical prospecting into action on a large scale, DeGolyer proved the practicality of the new technology to the industry. This helped to open the door for application of geophysics by other companies, and ensured further investment in the development of the new technologies. With the industry increasingly willing to risk money on geophysical technologies, the refinement of the instruments and techniques involved accelerated. The role of earth scientists in the industry—geologists and geophysicists alike—would become increasingly prominent. Their analyses would grow ever more sophisticated. The business of oil exploration, and the petroleum industry as a whole, was changed.

Was DeGolyer an indispensable man in the progress of the industry?

The answer is almost certainly, no. The market pressures created by the world's unquenchable thirst for oil in the twentieth century would have been irresistible in any event. Nevertheless, the fact remains that he was one of the first and most avid advocates of geophysical exploration. The consequence of his open-mindedness and dedication was that the industry employed the new technologies earlier than it otherwise would have accepted them. In this sense DeGolyer was a true herald of the technological revolution that would transform the oil industry in the years to come.

# 5 | Entrepreneur

*. . . the question of substantial success is still upon the knees of the gods.*
— Everette Lee DeGolyer to Arthur H. Bunker[1]

In April 1939, Everette Lee DeGolyer wrote to Henry Johnston to offer an explanation of failure. Johnston represented Case, Pomeroy, and Company, an investment house that had helped to finance De-Golyer's Felmont Corporation.[2] Felmont, which was primarily an oil exploration and lease-trading company, had not fared well. Three years after its organization in 1934, the company was spending well over $1 million a year, with less than $100,000 in income to show for it.[3] By 1939, DeGolyer had given up hope on Felmont. In his letter to Johnston, he conceded, "It has been apparent for a long time that Felmont was not likely to do much if anything more than pay its debts and preferred stock."[4] Continuing, he expressed his embarrassment: "I deeply regret that Felmont has not been more successful . . . Much of it is my fault."[5] But DeGolyer was unwilling to accept all of the blame, asserting that in addition to bad decisions, "Much of this is a matter of luck."[6]

Questions of "luck" or, at the very least, circumstances beyond DeGolyer's control, had played a major role in the failures—and successes—that he and his associates experienced during the 1930s. The close of the 1920s not only ended the bull market on Wall Street, but it also brought hard times to the petroleum industry in the United States. The price of oil plummeted, and profits shrank.

Yet in these years, DeGolyer came into his own as an entrepreneur. To this point, he had focused most of his attention on projects closely associated with Lord Cowdray and his successors. For most of the 1920s, he remained a protégé of the Chief, with whom he had developed bonds of loyalty that were personal as well as professional. Cowdray's death in 1927 loosed these bonds, but it was not until the 1930s that he cut himself fully free from old associations and began to act with greater independence from his British friends.

As DeGolyer's letter to Henry Johnston suggests, not all of DeGolyer's ventures were successful. Considering the business climate of the era, it is surprising that his failures were not more numerous. In fact, the Depression years saw DeGolyer launch some of his most successful companies.

The stories of many of these ventures are worthy of their own books. Geophysical Service Incorporated (GSI), which DeGolyer founded in the inauspicious year of 1930, was one such success. Core Laboratories, organized in 1936, represented another remarkable accomplishment. However, no company that he formed in these years was more personally relevant to its founder than the consulting firm of DeGolyer and MacNaughton, officially established in 1939. Until his death in 1956, DeGolyer took an active hand in the direction of this company, which exemplified the growing importance of geological analysis to the industry and indeed to national life.

DeGolyer's arrival as an entrepreneur had special significance to the geological profession. Despite occasional failures like the Felmont Corporation, investment bankers, who could make and unmake businesses, respected DeGolyer's name. And the confidence of the banking community in DeGolyer spoke volumes about the rising prestige of all geologists. No longer could oilmen dismiss these "rock hounds" with derision. DeGolyer had become an independent force in the industry, and so had geology.

At the start of the 1920s, and not for the first time, oilmen were fretting at the possibility that domestic petroleum reserves were nearing exhaustion. By the 1930s, their concerns had proved misplaced. In fact, the industry now suffered from a surfeit of oil. Many were worried, DeGolyer among them.[7] As early as 1929, he was apprehensive that "[t]he oil business appears to be headed for a nose dive." Events would confirm those fears.[8]

In fall 1930, a lease trader and small-time operator known as "Dad" Joiner brought in an oil well in Rusk County, Texas. Daisy Bradford No. 3 proved to be a gusher and the discovery well in the vast East Texas field that some would refer to as the "Black Giant."[9] Oilmen rushed to the scene with all the frenzy and excitement of previous oil booms. Yet the scale of the East Texas field made this boom exceptional. Within a year, the field Joiner had discovered was producing over 350,000 barrels of oil per day, causing a drop in oil prices of 78 percent from the preceding year. The national oil industry, already producing too much oil for the market, tottered toward a catastrophe.[10]

The collapse in prices caused significant hardship in oil-producing states, already suffering the effects of a general economic depression. In Oklahoma and Texas, state governors used their powers as head of the National Guard to shut down production at gunpoint. As matters grew desperate, oilmen began to talk with sincerity about the desirability of effective government regulation. This was a question that DeGolyer would wrestle with in years to come as he turned greater attention to public service.[11]

Combined with the collapse of the financial markets that began in 1929, the crisis in the petroleum industry ensured that the 1930s would be relatively lean years for DeGolyer. Following the panic stricken days of Wall Street in October 1929, he was at first hopeful that the market had suffered only a temporary adjustment. Writing in December 1929 to his brother-in-law, Robert Goodrich, he remarked, "[N]ow seems about as good a time to go into the market as any. I don't think that you have to be precipitate about it, but it is as good a one as I can see."[12]

Despite this optimistic advice, DeGolyer found it expedient to sell off much of his stock over the next few years. He concluded most of these sales on unfavorable terms. His personal income tax return for 1929 reported a staggering capital loss of $166,615.89 from sale of investments.[13] Losses were comparable, although lower, in 1930 and 1931.[14] In 1931, the capital loss from these sales resulted in a negative gross income. Of course, the financial pains that DeGolyer and his family suffered during these years were negligible compared to the fate of many during the Depression. Although selling stock at a loss meant that DeGolyer's assets were worth less than during the boom years of the 1920s, he still received a fortune from the sales. And he was still drawing six-figure compensation in the form of dividends, salaries, and other sources.

So, although the onset of the Depression and rampant overproduction in the domestic oil industry may have forced DeGolyer to scale back his wildest ambitions, it did not stop him from proceeding with plans for new businesses, and even taking some risks. One of the first of these risks that DeGolyer would hazard was his secret encouragement and financial support for J. C. Karcher's defection from Geophysical Research Corporation (GRC) to found Geophysical Service Incorporated (GSI) in 1930.

The story of the founding of GSI is one that dovetails with the technological revolution in oil prospecting that was taking place at this time. It was a revolution in which DeGolyer took an active part. However, the creation of GSI was also a story of boardroom intrigue, and it was one of the more controversial episodes in DeGolyer's career. It began with an honest difference of opinion about the future of that revolutionary Amerada affiliate—GRC.

Despite ominous developments in the oil industry, the future of GRC looked bright in 1930. With some of the most talented geophysicists in the industry on board, GRC was at the forefront of geophysical prospecting. But behind the façade of corporate confidence, GRC was in trouble. It was not that the company was not successful. Rather, it was a clash of visions that imperiled the venture, and at the center of the struggle was DeGolyer. His opponent was the current president of Amerada Corporation, Alfred Jacobsen.

Jacobsen had made his name in Mexico about the same time that DeGolyer was working there as a field geologist. Born in Denmark, he started his career as an employee in a hardware store and then took a job as a legal secretary. In 1906, he traveled to Mexico, where he found a job with the Mexico City branch of the Bank of Montreal. As manager of the slow-loan department, he became an expert in Mexican land law. In 1917, the Mexican Eagle Oil Company hired Jacobsen as a legal expert, and he rapidly rose through the company ranks. Within five years, he was managing director of the company. To the employees of Mexican Eagle, he proved to be amiable but shy, a man of "almost frightening industry and efficiency."[15] During conferences, the thin, blond Jacobsen would pace the room in circles, giving visitors stiff necks. Working late after dinner with special night-shift stenographers, Jacobsen developed a reputation for competence and dedication that won him respect within the oil industry.[16]

Jacobsen remained content at Mexican Eagle until its sale to Shell in 1921. By 1925, he was ready for a change and tendered his resignation, to move to New York and take over as vice president of Amerada. Over the next several years, Jacobsen and DeGolyer frequently traveled together from New York to Tulsa, discussing the company and developing plans for its future. They were friends, but the two did not always see eye to eye.[17]

From 1919 to 1926, DeGolyer dominated Amerada and its subsidiaries through the force of his personality and his service in various official positions. However, from 1926 to the close of the decade, his influence gradually waned. Some of this decline was due to the sale of the Cowdray interests to Dillon, Read & Co., an investment bank whose representatives were less responsive to DeGolyer than his old friends had been. In part, the change also reflected the increasing influence of Jacobsen, who was a very persuasive man.[18]

Reflecting on the transition decades later, J. C. Karcher described Jacobsen's aggressive displacement of DeGolyer's leadership:

> Whenever Jacobsen took hold of anything he moved in, and in a very short time [he] had taken over the entire active management of Amerada Corporation. In a year or so Jacobsen was elected President of Amerada and DeGolyer was made Chairman of the Board. The result of the change was that Jacobsen took complete charge of the management of Amerada Corporation and DeGolyer was moved upstairs to a box office seat (Chairman of the Board) to watch the show.[19]

This was not a role with which DeGolyer could be content. And the emerging struggle between DeGolyer and Jacobsen was about more than mere power; it involved basic questions about the direction that Amerada and its subsidiaries should take.

The issue that would divide these two powerful personalities and ultimately drive DeGolyer from the companies that he had helped to found was geophysical technology. At the time, GRC employed roughly 70 percent of all the seismic exploration scientists in the world. The company had the potential to reap tremendous profits if managed properly. DeGolyer and Jacobsen had differing ideas of how to go about this.[20]

Jacobsen saw GRC's dominance of the new prospecting methods in terms of the benefits that it offered to the mother Amerada companies. He believed that GRC should perform surveys for Amerada and its affiliates alone, giving the companies significant advantages over competing production companies. Profits for Amerada would soar, as would its stock value.[21]

DeGolyer saw matters differently. Although he acknowledged the strong points of Jacobsen's plan, he envisioned GRC as far more than a mere adjunct to Amerada. DeGolyer believed that with GRC's significant lead in seismography, the company could dominate the exploration stage of the petroleum industry. Yet the company would only realize these ambitions if it served the entire industry, and not just the handful of ventures associated with Amerada. In effect, DeGolyer was betting on the future of geophysical prospecting as a major component of the petroleum industry. His position reflected his faith in science and technology, as well as a gambling spirit.[22]

DeGolyer was ultimately unable to win over key members of the board, and Jacobsen's position prevailed. It had to have been a bitter experience for the man who had been responsible for so much of the company's success. Some of this frustration seems to have boiled over in 1929 at a banquet where a number of his Amerada associates were sharing testimonials. Despite the official rigors of Prohibition, the drinks prior to the performance had flowed freely. Normally a moderate drinker, DeGolyer enjoyed more cocktails than usual, then rose to offer his contribution to the occasion.[23] Despite his relative inebriation, DeGolyer was, if anything, wittier than usual. He was also more frank. Summarizing the shortcomings of the executives, one after another, DeGolyer offended his colleagues. It was a sign of things to come. That year, he tendered his resignation as chairman of the board at Amerada. It was not accepted—this time.[24]

As he came to understand that the shareholders would not back his plans for GRC, DeGolyer weighed his options. Rather than accept defeat, he refused to abandon his vision for a geophysical exploration company that would serve the industry independently. By 1930, he had come to a decision. It would be a controversial one but, typically, daring.

In December 1929, DeGolyer met with J. C. Karcher to discuss the plan forming in his mind. He realized that one of GRC's greatest assets was its expertise in geophysical prospecting and its familiarity with the oil business. These qualities were not the fixed property of Amerada, but lay in the excellent team than ran the company—particularly DeGolyer and Karcher.[25]

Why not strike out on their own and form an independent, geophysical exploration company? Karcher was interested. But would this not create a conflict of interest with GRC? Would Amerada accept such a flagrant act of defiance? DeGolyer thought of a way around that. Of course, Karcher would have to leave Amerada to form the new company. But DeGolyer wanted his involvement kept secret. He was prepared to spend $100,000 to start the new company, and his interest in the venture would be 50 percent. To maintain DeGolyer's anonymity, Karcher held the shares in his own name, but kept them in trust for DeGolyer. They agreed to divide the other 50 percent among others with Karcher getting the larger share. Karcher would be president and Eugene McDermott, a seismic party chief at GRC would join as vice president. Another GRC veteran, E. E. Rosaire, would also come aboard the venture.

And for a name, they christened the new company Geophysical Service Incorporated (GSI).[26]

Karcher and McDermott soon resigned from Amerada to form the new company. DeGolyer lingered for a while longer. He resubmitted his resignation to the company in 1930, to no avail. Again, on October 3, 1932, he asked to leave.[27] This time the company granted his request.[28] Clive Pearson, one of the Chief's sons, had hoped that DeGolyer would stay on as a consultant. Explaining his decision against this proposal, DeGolyer wrote in a telegram, "In view of [the] fact that I intend [to] engage generally in oil prospecting [I] believe the consultant proposal [to be] impracticable because it would give the other interests in Amerada justifiable reason for objecting."[29] He did not mention that he had effectively been engaged in oil prospecting through his interest in GSI for several years.

The corporate schism that resulted in the formation of GSI was a significant blow to GRC's dominance of geophysical prospecting. Yet even in the absence of DeGolyer's surreptitious action, GRC's decline in market share was probably inevitable. Seismic surveys were the future in petroleum exploration, and the world's thirst for oil was growing. United States demand for oil would continue to rise, with only a brief decline for several years during the Great Depression. With many of the more obvious petroleum fields already located and developed, the future was bright for companies that could offer affordable analysis of less evident oil prospects.

From a long-term perspective, GSI proved to be the most successful and revolutionary business that DeGolyer would found during these years. The company was innovative on a number of counts. First, it was something new, even in its conception. Although Ludger Mintrop's Seismos company had been the first to apply refraction seismography in the field, GSI would be the first independent exploration company to use reflection seismography in its surveys.[30]

Beyond its founding, DeGolyer's involvement in the direction of the company was somewhat limited, especially in comparison with the hands-on approach he took in other ventures. Perhaps that is part of why he willingly divested himself of his interest in the GSI venture in 1941. Of course, the proceeds handsomely compensated him for his investment. His stock in GSI's "parent," the Coronado Corporation, yielded $3,500,000. Ownership of Coronado went to Stanolind Oil and

GSI seismic truck somewhere outside Dallas, 1931. On the ground are three geophones designed by J. C. Karcher and Eugene McDermott. The box on the running board is a photographic developing compartment. On the tailgate, a dynamite plunger is visible. (Texas Instruments Records, Southern Methodist University.)

Gas Company, a successor company to the Rockefeller empire.[31] At the same time that Coronado went to Stanolind, Eugene McDermott and three associates—Cecil Green, H. B. Peacock, and J. Erik Jonsson—purchased GSI's assets, and therefore its independence, for $300,000.[32]

Had DeGolyer been able to see the future more clearly, he might not have sold all of his stock, even on these most favorable terms. Under inspired leadership, GSI would go on to become a major force in the rise of the twentieth-century electronics industry, albeit under the new name it took in 1951—Texas Instruments. Texas Instruments would pioneer the commercial development of the transistor, then the integrated circuit in the 1950s and 1960s. As the company entered the third millennium, it stood as one of the largest semiconductor manufacturers in the world. However, all of this would be a story in which DeGolyer played no significant part aside from his role as a revered founder.[33]

The founding of GSI was a key moment in DeGolyer's transformation from executive to entrepreneur, as he began to use his own substantial wealth to launch ventures. He was not, however, so wealthy that he did not seek support from other investors in his business initiatives. A number of these corporate creations would owe their genesis to DeGolyer's association with banker Walter Case. Case and DeGolyer first met in the New Jersey suburbs; Case's mansion in Essex Fells stood just a few miles away from DeGolyer's Montclair home. The two liked one another, and as DeGolyer planned new projects, he turned increasingly to Case's investment bank of Case, Pomeroy and Company for backing. The first such venture was the founding of the Felmont Corporation in 1934, about which DeGolyer would later pen his apologetic letter to Henry Johnston. The name of the business combined syllables from the Case and DeGolyer homes in Essex Fells and Montclair. Felmont never succeeded in finding the "elephant" oilfields that DeGolyer hoped, and in 1939 he let the company go.[34]

A more significant venture, Core Laboratories, arose out of DeGolyer's interaction with another Case, Pomeroy business, the Petroleum Reclamation Corporation, or "Pete Rec" for short. It was during a visit to Pete Rec wells in Pennsylvania's Bradford oilfield that DeGolyer first considered the formation of a company devoted to the analysis of oil well "cores." These cores are cylinders of rock that are carefully removed during drilling to provide a cross section of the rock material through which a well has passed.[35]

Visiting Pete Rec's Bradford lab, DeGolyer encountered James Lewis and William "Jack" Horner's work and, being impressed, questioned them about their method. Among other details that fascinated DeGolyer may well have been the use of the term *millidarcy,* a measure of porosity that is an important statistical unit in core analysis. In later years it was said that his curiosity about the millidarcy led him to plan a new business that would apply the analysis techniques that he witnessed.[36] Whatever the case, DeGolyer's visit to the lab was decisive. According to Hadley Case, Walter Case's son, DeGolyer reacted to what he had seen with the remark: "We don't do analysis like that down in Texas. We look at the core, smell it, suck it to see if any oil comes out—that's all. You fellows are way ahead of us."[37]

For DeGolyer, this was a state of affairs that was ripe with opportunity. In addition to his admiration of Lewis and Horner's analysis, DeGolyer apparently added an insight of his own—the value of creating portable laboratory facilities that could analyze core samples in the field,[38] a significant innovation. The value of mobile labs lay in the fact that shipment often degraded the quality of cores. On-site analysis meant more accurate information.[39] Conferring with Walter Case, DeGolyer secured backing for the new company, Core Laboratories, Inc.[40]

Founded in 1936, Core Laboratories proved to be so successful that some reckoned it to be worthy of mention alongside DeGolyer's pioneering advocacy of geophysical exploration.[41] As in the case of GSI, the work done by the company was beyond his own area of expertise. Instead, DeGolyer relied on Lewis and Horner to organize and manage the venture.[42] Nonetheless, he continued to be highly interested in the company's activities. In 1939, DeGolyer approached Hadley Case about the possibility of selling an interest in Core Laboratories to his new consulting firm of DeGolyer and MacNaughton. It was an offer that Hadley rebuffed.[43] With DeGolyer's own contributions in managing Core Laboratories thus limited, he opted to sell his private interest in the company, noting with regret, "I have not been able to give as much attention to Core Laboratories as I had hoped in the beginning."[44]

As the stories of GSI and Core Laboratories suggest, DeGolyer had a weakness for ventures that planned to capitalize on technological innovation. In the cases of GSI and Core Laboratories, the profits would come from service fees. But DeGolyer also hoped to use the information that these new technologies made available to profit directly from oil production. This was the rationale behind the various royalty companies in which DeGolyer took a hand during the 1920s and 1930s.

The possibility of parlaying their geological information into easy profit had occurred to DeGolyer and his associates as early as the mid-1920s. About that time, DeGolyer began pushing for the creation of a corporation that would trade exclusively in royalties. Using information acquired through the oil exploration program of Amerada and her affiliates, the new company would purchase royalty rights in promising locations and then let other production companies do the heavy lifting in drilling and marketing.[45]

J. B. Body, T. J. Ryder, Herbert Carr, Adrian Moore, and others joined DeGolyer in financing the venture. Dubbed Alamo Royalties Corporation, the company was, as its name suggests, focused upon trading in royalties in the state of Texas. DeGolyer viewed the Alamo Corporation as highly speculative, warning others that it was not a safe investment.[46]

Indeed, the new company almost immediately ran into trouble. By 1926, DeGolyer bemoaned the company's poor prospects, noting, "After we got started it was found that the opportunity did not seem to be as great as we had previously thought."[47] Nevertheless, DeGolyer held on to the Alamo stock throughout the 1930s, selling it in 1941 at a loss of $6,356.80.[48] Alamo was, by DeGolyer's reckoning, only a small company, and its failure to earn the sort of return for which its founders hoped hardly commended the "royalty corporation" model.[49] But DeGolyer remained convinced that such a venture, with good management and a little luck, held the potential to reap significant profits.

Federal Royalties Company was another one of these businesses, organized in 1927. DeGolyer was an early investor in the company, but he does not seem to have taken a particularly active role in the business. This one proved to be a better gamble than Alamo. DeGolyer would hold on to his stock in Federal Royalties for twenty-three years, realizing a capital gain of $164,316 when he sold it in 1950.[50]

From DeGolyer's perspective, the most important company of this mold was the Atlatl Royalty Corporation. DeGolyer founded Atlatl in 1933, soon after his resignation from Amerada and her affiliates. It was a Texas corporation and aimed to profit by acquiring interests in potential oil-producing properties. Although occasionally characterized as an "independent petroleum producing" company, Atlatl in fact did not do any drilling on its own. Indeed, the company employed a bare dozen individuals after more than a decade of operation. Atlatl delegated the development of its property to others.[51]

DeGolyer directed the company toward a policy of exploration and judicious purchase of mineral interests. Deploying geological and geophysical teams to evaluate promising locations, Atlatl did well for its investors.[52] Moreover, this was in spite of the fact that the company was "frozen" for several years following the organization of the Felmont Corporation in 1934.[53] The lack of success by Felmont, mentioned earlier, focused DeGolyer's attention anew upon Atlatl. By 1950, he was ready to cash in on the company. The sale of DeGolyer's 100 percent interest in Atlatl brought him $7,500,000—not bad considering his initial investment in the company was a mere $20,000.[54]

GSI, Atlatl Royalty Corporation, and Core Laboratories all represented DeGolyer's willingness to take sometimes-daring business risks in the midst of the Great Depression. And there were other examples. DeGolyer dabbled a little with international ventures, becoming involved with exploration for oil in Brazil.[55] He also invested in a company dedicated to developing oil properties in the St. Lawrence River Valley in Canada.[56] Neither of these investments would occupy DeGolyer's attention as much as his American businesses, but they did reflect his commitment to seize opportunities as he discerned them, however distant.

The greater significance of DeGolyer's involvement in all of these companies lay in the rising importance of petroleum geology. All of his major domestic ventures involved the extensive deployment of either geological or geophysical teams. DeGolyer's various royalty companies used scientific information to make smart purchases that would have eluded the uninformed appraiser. Some of these businesses, such as GSI and Core Laboratories, aimed to carve out a niche where earth scientists could play an independent role in evaluating petroleum properties. These ventures were far larger in terms of capital investment than were the independent geological consultants of the 1910s and earlier. Whether they involved seismic teams armed with dynamite, trucks, and sensors, or mobile core analysis laboratories, DeGolyer's exploration companies were highly sophisticated and comparatively expensive operations. Yet increasingly, the oil industry judged these scientific consultants to be worth the cost.[57]

In addition to founding and in some cases managing these companies, DeGolyer also found these years to be busy ones thanks to his official relocation to the Southwest. This came in 1936, when the family moved out of their Montclair, New Jersey, home and into a house on exclusive Turtle Creek in Dallas, Texas.[58] The move made sense from a practical standpoint: for years, DeGolyer had been spending months in travel to and from Texas, Oklahoma, and Louisiana. Relocating to Dallas should have made such a punishing itinerary less necessary. In fact, the growing success of his business ventures meant that travel would be more important to his career than ever.

This professional lifestyle placed significant strain upon his personal relationships and obviously weighed heavily on Nell. In January 1937, she wrote him in despair, noting that he had spent a bare forty-one days with his family in 1936. Suffering from pneumonia, she was clearly emotional about being left alone so much and complained, "I had thought my widowhood was over when we left Montclair."[59] Heartsick, she wrote, "I am convinced there is something sadly wrong with our way of living and I should like for us to be together long enough and quietly enough to see if there isn't some other way of life than the monastic one we lead now."[60]

If DeGolyer's move to Texas did not offer a respite from travel, it did offer something else of value—a sense of cultural connection. In moving to Dallas, he found a home in a place more in tune with his own Southwestern roots. This made the move more than a mere change of residence. It represented a shift in career orientation and even in identity. His resignation in 1932 from Amerada, with its New York headquarters, marked the beginning of this process. At the same time, the major new companies that DeGolyer organized chose to locate in Texas: GSI, Atlatl, Felmont, and Core Laboratories. When DeGolyer purchased his Turtle Creek home in 1936, the local press labeled him a wealthy buyer from "Jersey."[61] By the 1940s, DeGolyer, who for the first fifty years of his life had lived in Kansas, Missouri, Oklahoma, Mexico, and New Jersey, was being identified as a Dallasite and one of a newly iconic breed—a Texas oilman.[62]

DeGolyer's embrace of Southwestern culture would be most evident in his book-collecting activities and amateur scholarship. But perhaps the most amusing evidence of his regional enthusiasm took the form of a "hobby horse" business—the Anahuac Piquant Pepper Company. DeGolyer organized Anahuac in conjunction with B. P. Manning, an old associate from his Tampico days. It was one of the earlier instances where DeGolyer allowed his personal interests—in this case, spicy Mexican cuisine—to intrude on his business affairs. In later years, it would be his experiments in publishing that siphoned off capital into unprofitable ventures. The Atlatl Royalty Corporation financed Anahuac, and it proved to be a poor investment.[63]

Yet with such a "business," DeGolyer's primary aim was less profit than personal diversion. During the brief period when the company was profitable in 1938, DeGolyer dispatched complimentary shipments of peppers. Despite consistent losses, Anahuac Piquant Peppers limped on for more than a decade before DeGolyer, perhaps finally bored with the project, ordered it liquidated in 1948.[64]

Although DeGolyer eventually tired of his jalapeño business, his move to Texas was lasting. DeGolyer confirmed his long-term commitment to the city, to the state, and indeed the greater Southwestern region as he and Nell planned the construction of a home on White Rock Lake, on the outskirts of Dallas. Tellingly, the new house would be built in a striking Spanish Colonial style. It was ambitious enough to attract the interest of the *Dallas Morning News,* which reported plans for the estate in detail. Described as "large, rambling, and impressive," the plans called for a badminton court, three fountains, and a swimming pool.[65] A large recreation room, called the "Indian room," would house DeGolyer's collection of "Southwestern relics." A "Hall of Maps" would lead to the jewel of the home, the library, where bookcases would line all the walls. Two concealed closets, hidden behind bookshelves would be a playful feature of the room.[66]

Completed in 1940, *El Rancho Encinal* ("Oak Ranch") cost $150,000 for its construction alone. In addition, the DeGolyers spent $66,000 to purchase its forty acres of land on White Rock Lake and another $30,000 to $40,000 on landscaping and additional furnishings.[67] It was the perfect home for this oilman, geologist, and amateur scholar of Southwestern history.

These early years in Dallas were busy ones. In addition to DeGolyer's career and the planning and construction of a new home, his children were growing up. The eldest daughters, Virginia and Dorothy, were already in their early twenties at the time of the move to Texas. The two had active social lives that were regularly reported in the newspapers. Both sisters married in 1937 in weddings performed in the garden of the family's Turtle Creek home. Virginia's husband, John "Jack" Maxson, was a University of Texas football and track star, and the match proved a good one. Dorothy wedded David Perry Stephenson but was not as fortunate; the marriage ended in divorce in 1940.[68]

The youngest daughter, Cecilia, followed suit in 1938, marrying George Crews McGhee. McGhee, a Rhodes scholar and a highly ambitious man, would participate in the formation of DeGolyer's geological consulting firm in Dallas before embarking on a career in the diplomatic service. McGhee would play a significant role in shaping United States foreign policy in oil, and eventually rise to serve as undersecretary of state in the Kennedy Administration. His influence on government petroleum policy and connections with DeGolyer would raise the eyebrows of some in Congress, suspicious of the involvement of the oil industry in shaping United States relations abroad.[69]

Weddings were not the only familial transitions that took place about this time. Two sad events, the death of DeGolyer's father in 1937 followed by the death of his mother in 1938, mark these years as the beginning of a new chapter in his life. When DeGolyer's career took him to New York, his parents had followed him to live on a farm that he purchased for them in Pompton Plains, New Jersey. The years in the Northeast had therefore been a time of close connection among three generations of DeGolyers. With the death of his parents and the marriage of his three daughters, the character of life would change. Only young Ev remained at home and DeGolyer was now the elder patriarch of the family.[70]

At the same time that DeGolyer's family life was being redefined, his professional life was undergoing a significant evolution. Probably the most significant professional consequence of the move to Dallas was the development of a close working relationship between DeGolyer and Lewis MacNaughton, a young and talented geologist with Amerada. Born in 1902, Lewis Winslow MacNaughton's father was a businessman and veteran of the Spanish-American War. The family was in Cuba at the time of Lewis's birth and led a nomadic lifestyle for much of the boy's childhood. After brief residences in California, New Jersey, and Connecticut, the MacNaughtons finally settled down in Saugerties, New York, where Lewis received his early education.[71]

Having developed an early interest in geology, MacNaughton entered Cornell University. Like DeGolyer, he built an impressive résumé of work experience while enrolled in college. He spent his summer vacations in the employ of Standard Oil of Venezuela, mapping the Orinoco Delta. MacNaughton received an AB from Cornell in 1925, working as an assistant geologist with the American Museum of Natural History in New York following graduation. Finding the career opportunities in the oil industry irresistible, he took a job as a field geologist with the Humble Oil and Refining Company of Houston, Texas, in 1926. There, he worked under DeGolyer's friend and geological colleague, Wallace Pratt.

When MacNaughton's work for Humble came to DeGolyer's attention, DeGolyer arranged a position for him with Rycade, which MacNaughton duly accepted in 1928. Two years later, MacNaughton transferred to Amerada, where he worked until 1936. Over fifteen years junior to DeGolyer, MacNaughton would become both his protégé and collaborator. The professional relationship between the two that developed during MacNaughton's years with Rycade and Amerada laid the groundwork for what would follow. The ultimate result of this association would be a new and innovative company that would take the name of the two men most responsible for its direction and success—DeGolyer and MacNaughton, Inc.[72]

DeGolyer's move to Dallas in 1936 provoked him to think anew about business opportunities in the oil industry. His work with GRC, his

Everette Lee DeGolyer (r.) and Lewis MacNaughton (l.). Collaborators in the consulting firm that bore the names of both men. (Everette Lee DeGolyer Collection. Courtesy of DeGolyer Library, Southern Methodist University.)

founding of GSI and Core Laboratories, and his organization of various royalty companies involved ventures that would use cutting-edge technology to turn a profit. DeGolyer's next venture would also put technology to work, but in a different context.

As his thoughts took form, DeGolyer realized that what he contemplated would require a competent geological collaborator. Searching through the catalog of possible names, he settled upon MacNaughton, whose work he knew from Amerada. On October 10, 1936, one day following his fiftieth birthday, DeGolyer drew up a business proposal. This was the seed from which the future firm of DeGolyer and MacNaughton would sprout. "It has occurred to me," DeGolyer wrote, "that you might be willing, from time to time, to associate yourself with me in doing . . . geological and other work."[73] If MacNaughton agreed to the plan, he should move his office, then in Houston, to Dallas, where DeGolyer would guarantee a minimum salary of $350 a month, with the prospect of greater remuneration as the business developed.[74] Eight days later MacNaughton signed the proposal, and the "informal" association that would grow into one of the most prestigious geological consulting firms in the world was formally established.[75]

In some ways, the association between DeGolyer and MacNaughton was a throwback to an earlier era, a time when independent geological consultants dominated the profession. That was the situation when De-Golyer began his career in 1909. In that sense, the Mexican Eagle Company was ahead of the curve in hiring permanent staff geologists. As geology proved its worth during the 1910s, production companies hired increasing numbers of geologists in the United States. Although geological consultants had never disappeared, the trend within the industry had largely been one away from independent consultants and toward company geologists. Why then did DeGolyer decide that the time was now propitious to found an independent consulting firm? The answer lay in the crisis of the oil industry that had coincided with the Great Depression.[76]

The rampant overproduction that had resulted from the discovery of the East Texas field as well as others had forced the hands of governors and legislators alike. Everyone recognized that the first desperate measures, such as deploying state militias to the oilfields, could not be the long-term answer to the problem. And so, during the 1930s, the petroleum industry and the state and federal governments searched out alternative options. Almost all agreed that the nation required a new policy to manage oil production. This provoked fierce political battles over who should implement such a policy—the industry, the state governments, or perhaps the federal government. Despite these controversies, most agreed that the problem was overproduction, and the obvious remedy was limiting the rate at which oil was taken out of the ground.[77]

The policy imposed during the 1930s was prorationing. Prorationing involved setting levels of allowable production from the nation's oil wells. Because far more Americans were consumers of oil than producers of oil, the industry and sympathetic government officials realized that this policy needed justification beyond simply raising prices, which was, after all, a major reason for the exercise. That justification was conservation.[78]

Oilmen promoted conservation policies aimed at maximum ultimate recovery. By the 1930s, earth scientists had concluded that flush production of oil could actually reduce the total amount of oil ultimately recovered from a reservoir. A slower rate of production, known as the maximum efficient rate (MER), or optimum rate of production, could increase the number of barrels of oil that a field could produce. For an industry hobbled by cheap oil, producing at the MER would secure the added benefit of reducing the amount of crude on the market and hence raise the price per barrel. In this case, conservation and the interest of the oil companies went hand in hand.[79]

Prorationing wells at the MER helped to prop up the price of petroleum at a time when the oil business threatened to destroy itself. Yet the policy raised a whole host of problems for the industry. And DeGolyer understood that there would be a reward for the company that could solve those problems.

Above all, the challenge that prorationing thrust upon the industry involved the issue of financing. Even before the overproduction crisis of the late 1920s and early 1930s, it was clear to thoughtful observers that the business was changing. The first oilfields exploited in the United States were naturally among the easiest to develop. Shallow fields presented greater evidence of their existence at the surface. Wells in such fields were also cheaper to drill and operate.[80]

As oilmen progressively plucked the low hanging fruits, finding and developing new reservoirs was sure to become a more expensive venture. Increasing exploration costs, reflecting the price of the technologically sophisticated geophysical surveys that DeGolyer pioneered, were part of the problem. The expense of drilling at deeper depths also required increasing outlays of cash. In many cases, costs associated with pumping oil from the ground also added to the financial burden of production companies. As these expenses grew, the need for a rapid return on investment became more pressing.

Yet prorationing made quick profits in the oil industry more difficult than ever. True, the prospect of higher oil prices promised greater revenue in the long run, but in the meantime, there were bills to pay and impatient investors to satisfy. The obvious answer lay in financing. Banks could exercise patience for the long-term profits of oil production that many companies could not afford. The proposition of loans on "oil in the ground" promised to be a winning one for both bankers and oilmen. Oilmen could pay their expenses and cash in on their good fortune, and bankers would take a cut of the long-term revenue stream that petroleum production promised.

As with all secured loans, it was necessary to place a value on the collateral. Banks were certainly in no position to determine the worth of any one oil property. Companies, on the other hand, might call upon their staff geologists to make an estimate of just how much oil they had found. But what was to stop the company geologist from exaggerating the worth of the find? Even scrupulous employees might be inclined to see more oil than an impartial observer would discern. It was a situation that called for the expertise of an independent geologist.[81]

This was the role into which DeGolyer and MacNaughton stepped, first as individuals and then later through their various corporate personae. The first of these was DeGolyer, MacNaughton, and McGhee, organized in 1939 with DeGolyer's son-in-law the third partner in the firm. But McGhee left the company soon thereafter to join the diplomatic service. Shortly afterward, the firm took the simpler name it bears to this day: DeGolyer and MacNaughton.[82]

The challenge that the firm faced was a daunting one: to develop a consistent and accurate system of valuation for oil properties. The task was not unfamiliar to DeGolyer. Beginning in 1918, DeGolyer had taken on a number of projects that required him to estimate the amount of oil in various oilfields and predict their productivity. These efforts had not always obtained favorable results.

DeGolyer's least successful attempt was his first. The assignment was the result of the federal government's increasing interest in taxing petroleum companies. This took place before the era of prorationing, before his pioneering advocacy of geophysics, before even the founding of Amerada. In the autumn of 1918, as the First World War in Europe was grinding to its grim end, DeGolyer was contacted by Ralph Arnold, a petroleum geologist of international reputation, on behalf of the government. Arnold was working within the Internal Revenue Bureau (IRB) in the Oil and Gas Section. The IRB was a branch of the United States Treasury, which was increasingly interested in the nation's oilfields. Arnold's primary concern was developing a method of computing a "depletion allowance" for use in taxing oil properties. This depletion allowance would give oil companies the opportunity to take into account the gradual exhaustion of their oil wells in determining tax liability. However, determining just how far a property had been "exhausted" was a task that required advanced technical knowledge, the sort of knowledge that the IRB and Arnold hoped that DeGolyer could provide them.[83]

DeGolyer proved willing to assist Arnold on the project, but he was not particularly enthusiastic about it—or at least so it seemed to his colleagues at the Mexican Eagle Oil Company. T. J. Ryder claimed that "Washington has virtually commandeered DeGolyer" for the depletion allowance work.[84] Whether excited at the work or not, DeGolyer was given the responsibility for analysis of oilfields in Louisiana and Texas. In order to give the government a scientific basis for the depletion allowance, he was to develop mathematical curves that would predict the rate by which any given oilfield would decline in productivity. Given the limited information available to the geologist in 1918, it proved to be an impossible errand.[85]

DeGolyer ran into trouble from the beginning of the project, and not all of it was attributable to the unrealistic expectations of the IRB. First, he fell victim to the Spanish influenza pandemic that would kill hundreds of thousands of Americans and millions of persons worldwide.[86] Following a slow recovery, he turned his attention to the "immense task" of compiling the oilfield information for the Texas and Louisiana Gulf Coast.[87] What DeGolyer must have known before was just how complicated this sort of analysis would be. Multiple variables influenced the rate at which a field was exhausted, including the unique geology of each field and the activities of other companies active in the area. Coming up with a single curve that could fit more than one oilfield was unrealistic. Above all, the lack of information available to the geologist foiled DeGolyer. In one letter to Arnold, he confessed his frustration with the work:

> I spent seven whole days on the voyage over in working on this information and the more I worked the more trouble I seem to have. The difficulty lies in the almost impossibility of deriving any formula for general application in the salt dome region . . . If I were forced to report at the present time, I should say that no formula can be given, but I intend to continue to struggle with this matter in hopes of ultimately arriving at something that will be a little better than nothing at all.
>
> To be done properly, we should be able to outline clearly the geology of the fields as it now exists, and as you know we are still deficient in information of this sort.[88]

DeGolyer's attempt to provide something "a little better than nothing at all" proved elusive. As his work dragged on without satisfactory conclusion, Arnold became impatient, claiming that the delay was "embarrassing" and demanding that DeGolyer wrap up the project. DeGolyer responded angrily and continued on his fool's errand. In February 1919, he gave up, concluding that "a formula for depreciation, is not possible."[89]

DeGolyer's work for the IRB established in him a firm tendency toward skepticism when it came to making estimations of oil in the ground. For instance, when geologists contended in the mid-1920s to estimate the size of the nation's remaining petroleum reserves, DeGolyer declared himself to be "one of the anti-estimators."[90] His objection to this sort of work was twofold: "the impossibility of measuring undiscovered reserves and the probability of general misinterpretation of results."[91]

The difficulties presented by valuing "undiscovered" oilfields were an obvious hurdle to these broad national projections, but less problematic in analysis of established oilfields. In the years following the IRB debacle, DeGolyer was increasingly impressed with the possibility of estimating these fields with some degree of accuracy. In one "anti-estimator" editorial that he wrote in 1922 for *Economic Geology,* he conceded the progress of the geological profession in making such forecasts, noting, "Geologists and engineers have made great advances during the past few years in the development of methods for estimating the petroleum content of developed or proven properties."[92] Indeed, DeGolyer himself would undertake just this sort of work the following year on behalf of Cities Service Oil Company. These estimates proved to be not too far off the mark. As geophysical surveys and independent advances in well logging made more information about the oilfields available, the prospect for reasonably accurate valuation seemed possible.[93]

Therefore, when DeGolyer contemplated the role that he envisioned for his new venture with Lewis MacNaughton, it was with a keen sense of the challenges and obstacles that they faced. As DeGolyer knew, the work for the new firm would be quite different from the sort of geological work involved in exploration. That sort of analysis had involved identifying geological structures favorable to the presence of oil. The question of valuation was trickier. Because there could be no certainty about the total amount of oil that a field would produce until after the fact, only the history of other oilfields could offer clues in advance of actual production. So it was obvious from the start that careful analysis of production statistics—statistics of other oilfields—would play a key role in the new firm's success or failure.

Yet as DeGolyer was well aware, statistics could be treacherous. The problem was that each oilfield was unique. The geological structure that "trapped" the oil, the source of the pressure that propelled the petroleum to the surface, the depth of the field, the viscosity of the oil itself, and a whole host of other factors differentiated one reservoir from another. With so many variables in play, DeGolyer, MacNaughton, and their staff would have to carefully sift all of this information in order to find analogous fields with, hopefully, analogous production. Only then would they be able to predict with any degree of accuracy the value of an oil property.

In order to conduct the careful analysis necessary to identify relevant statistics, DeGolyer understood that extensive, detailed, and accurate information about other oilfields was essential. And so, assembling a catalog of relevant data became a major task for DeGolyer and MacNaughton. Each year more and more such information accumulated. Organized on cards that would eventually number in the millions, the company kept extensive records on individual wells and properties. These included production memoranda, well completion details, and scout reports. Housed in the firm's Dallas office, DeGolyer's future protégé, John Murrell, would hail the library as the "backbone of our firm."[94]

Although appraisal for purposes of financing was one of the more important roles for DeGolyer and MacNaughton, the firm would engage in a host of other activities as well: general geological surveys, oilfield development studies, reservoir engineering projects, and even evaluation of management problems.[95]

In the first decade of its existence, DeGolyer and MacNaughton completed over a thousand separate contracts on behalf of fourteen of the twenty largest integrated oil companies, hundreds of smaller entities, and a number of large natural gas firms. The partnership served as a consultant for government-run oil companies in Mexico, Peru, Uruguay, and Brazil and was active in Ecuador, Colombia, Venezuela, and Trinidad as well. The United States government too would rely on DeGolyer and MacNaughton to evaluate oil in Alaska and the strategically important Middle East. But all of this and more lay in the future in 1939, when the firm was formally organized.[96]

The founding of DeGolyer and MacNaughton closed a decade of remarkable creativity on DeGolyer's part. It had begun with the founding of GSI, which had allowed him to step out from under the shadows of the Cowdray interests and definitively established his independence as an entrepreneur. In the following years, he had capitalized on his reputation as an astute businessman and a learned scientist to found a variety of companies that aimed, in different ways, to cash in on cutting-edge technology.

The performance of these ventures was variable, with some markedly more successful than others. This had only accentuated DeGolyer's penchant for giving credit for his accomplishments to "luck," "fortune," or "the gods." But the geological and geophysical professions of his day shared DeGolyer's good fortune. Scientific and technological advances, some of which DeGolyer himself pioneered, were responsible for creating many of the opportunities that he seized during this decade. Moreover, no venture belied DeGolyer's commendation of luck more than his successful association with Lewis MacNaughton. Although production companies might rise and fall on the good fortune or failure of a few wells, the new consulting firm would thrive only if it could maintain a good reputation. That reputation depended upon consistent, accurate forecasts of petroleum production in existing fields. Perhaps there was a little room here for luck, but not much.

DeGolyer was gratified by the progress of his venture with MacNaughton, but it was not his only interest in the late 1930s. For years, he had been tempted to take a hiatus from business affairs. His professional reputation as a scientist had brought him to the attention of the scholarly community. Acquaintances at the University of Texas had been prodding him to consider a professorship. With corporate ventures promising profits and requiring attention, few of his associates in the industry would have accepted such an offer. But DeGolyer was cut from a different cloth. In 1940, he accepted a position at the University of Texas as a Distinguished Professor of Geology. MacNaughton would have to handle the firm's business in Dallas. DeGolyer was off to Austin.

# 6 | Scholar

*What I have urged upon you this evening is extremely simple: to search for truth and understanding in all fields. This is the end of science and the goal is worthy of the efforts of mankind in all its affairs.*
— Everette Lee DeGolyer, Commencement Address,
  University of Oklahoma, May 31, 1948[1]

*From books would come freedom to visit in time and space. In the pages of the old chroniclers I would discover the Seven Cities and die a gorgeous death with the moor, Estevancito. I would fight my way through the pueblos of the Rio Arriba and wander out across the High Plains in search of the mythical [Quivira] with Coronado. I would visit this new land again with Espejo, colonize it with [Oñate] and reconquer it, after bloody rebellion, with De Vargas. I would ride with the iron clad conquerors and walk with the grey-gowned fathers.*
— Everette Lee DeGolyer, from an undated reflection
  on the history of New Mexico[2]

In the summer of 1938, Hal P. Bybee of the University of Texas wrote to Everette Lee DeGolyer with a suggestion. The university was in the process of establishing a series of distinguished professorships. Would DeGolyer consider taking a position as a distinguished professor of geology? Bybee added the tempting proposition that DeGolyer might play an important role in shaping and strengthening the geological curriculum.[3]

DeGolyer was interested, and the two exchanged a series of letters discussing the possibility. But the plans were premature. The university, like most bureaucracies, moved slowly with its plans. The possibility of teaching in 1939 became less likely as the calendar advanced without a definitive conclusion of the matter. Finally, DeGolyer declined, but not before he communicated his interest in teaching sometime in the future.[4]

Although university officials moved slowly, they did not lose interest in DeGolyer or forget the enthusiasm he had voiced. By the fall of 1939, they were finally ready to move. The board of regents named DeGolyer to a distinguished professorship in geology. The oilman would join the academy after all.[5]

His decision to accept a position at the University of Texas struck some of his colleagues as odd. Reflecting on DeGolyer's interest in teaching a decade after his death, J. C. Karcher still doubted that he could have been serious about it. After all, DeGolyer already enjoyed a high reputation within the industry; he already had earned enough money to enjoy a comfortable lifestyle, even in the midst of the Great Depression. Surely, this was not something that he needed to do on account of any practical necessity.[6]

But DeGolyer's desire to teach realized ambitions that had been evident from almost the beginning of his career. To some extent, it was a hunger for academic acclaim that motivated him to accept the professorship. His early career decision to leave his studies in 1909 and take a job with the Mexican Eagle Oil Company had troubled him in some ways. There was a nagging sense that he had somehow ignored a higher calling—the calling of science. The completion of his undergraduate studies in 1911 only partly alleviated this unsettling thought. His struggle to maintain a scientific commitment as a company executive was a continuing sign of this discomfort. For his entire life, the university laboratory beckoned, a place that seemed somehow sanctified in its devotion to pure science.

Although the university embodied the spirit that DeGolyer yearned to cultivate, it was not the only place where he expressed his scholarly commitment. In fact, his professorship was but the most explicit aspect of a lifelong devotion not only to science but also to knowledge in the broadest sense. In a commencement address at the Colorado School of Mines in 1925, he pleaded that the graduating students seek "truth and understanding in all fields."[7] To some, this might have seemed the boilerplate material of a thousand such addresses. But for DeGolyer, it was a serious matter.

Over a lifetime, DeGolyer made scholarly and quasi-scholarly contributions to a variety of fields. DeGolyer's work reflected his own broad-ranging interests and remarkable versatility—geological analyses, industrial evaluations, histories, and literary critiques. He particularly loved the history of the Southwest and Mexico. It allowed him to indulge his romantic side.

If the many facets of DeGolyer's professional life suggested the outlook of a Renaissance man, these diverse publications offered conclusive confirmation. In some ways, they told more about the man than his remarkably successful career. For DeGolyer's scholarly work as a devoted scientist, an amateur historian, and a literary aficionado offered insights into his character not afforded by his efforts in pursuit of a livelihood. These obsessions were labors of love that revealed much about his own sense of identity.

That DeGolyer, a professionally trained geologist, was such a persistent advocate and exemplar of scholarly research and publication was not really so surprising. His attitude toward scientific scholarship was a natural result of the education he received at the University of Oklahoma. The men there who instructed DeGolyer, like Charles N. Gould and E. G. Woodruff, were steeped in an awareness of the duty of the scientist to publish his findings, add to the collective knowledge of the scholarly community, and advance the frontiers of knowledge. The sense of obligation that these mentors cultivated in their student grew, flowered, and produced fruit in abundance over the course of DeGolyer's career.

The development of his scholarly interests faced significant obstacles. As a company executive and an entrepreneur, DeGolyer was keenly aware of the balance that existed between the pursuit of profit and the pursuit of knowledge. But if he sometimes felt compelled to suppress information regarding research, he also knew that such measures could only be temporary. Therefore, even as a businessman, DeGolyer strived to contribute to scholarly discourse among the nation's geologists.

Throughout his career, DeGolyer produced a steady and mounting body of scientific literature that addressed both theoretical and practical questions raised by his work. The list of DeGolyer's publications begins even before the initiation of his professional career. In 1907, at the age of twenty, he published his first article in a trade periodical on the topic of glass sand.[8] But DeGolyer became truly prolific during his years as a young field geologist in Mexico. While in the employ of Cowdray's Mexican Eagle Company, he published a number of scholarly articles on the geology of the Mexican oilfields. His first article of importance appeared in the *Bulletin of the American Institute of Mining Engineers* in September 1915. The subject was the Furbero oilfield. As best he could, DeGolyer detailed the structure of the field and offered his own hypotheses regarding its formation. It was an impressive first effort.[9]

More works of fine detail and careful analysis followed. There was a broader piece on the Tampico-Tuxpan region and another on the geology of Cuba.[10] The Cuban piece was the first of many that he would publish in the *Bulletin of the American Association of Petroleum Geologists.* DeGolyer soon went beyond descriptive geology to offer his own theories of geological development in a piece on the volcanic origin of salt domes.[11] Then, he speculated on the significance of the temperature of oil in another article that focused upon his work in Mexico.[12] All these scholarly efforts reflected a substantial amount of work, for which DeGolyer had to find time when not engaged in company business.

By 1918, DeGolyer was primarily a company executive. Had he wished, he might have left his scientific aspirations aside and devoted himself unreservedly to business affairs. Yet in that same year, he proposed to write a book that would comprise a geological catalog of oil deposits throughout the world.[13] The prospect of remuneration was not great, but DeGolyer was clearly interested in more than that.

For the remainder of the decade and into the 1920s, he would continue to publish in geological journals, with articles based upon his Mexican work as well as his more recent investigations in the United States.[14] Beginning in the 1930s, DeGolyer also turned his attention to exploration methods, with special emphasis on the geophysical techniques that his companies pioneered.[15] Though DeGolyer was careful not to prematurely reveal company secrets, the body of material that he did eventually publish was impressive.

Even more numerous than his geological articles were pieces that he composed, mostly for trade journals, addressing the state of the petroleum industry. Initially, these works focused on the Mexican oil business and then gradually broadened in the years leading up to his professorship at the University of Texas.[16] However, he also turned his attention to the question of the place of geologists and geological methods in industry.[17] These were questions that "pure" scientists might disdain, but they were of growing interest to more practical minded men, particularly engineers.

In 1927, DeGolyer's work had attracted enough interest that Vannevar Bush, professor of electrical engineering at the Massachusetts Institute of Technology, invited him to offer a lecture at the school.[18] Bush would later achieve fame as a science advisor to the federal government. DeGolyer's busy calendar made it impossible for him to speak at that time, but when the school renewed the invitation for spring 1929, he accepted. He titled his lecture "Our Mineral Virtues" and focused the attention of his audience of engineers on the nation's dwindling energy resources.[19] He concluded by commending the challenge to the "indomitable mind of man."

In 1939, he accepted an invitation to deliver one of the Cyrus Fogg Brackett lectures at Princeton University. His topic would be "The Development of the Art of Prospecting." DeGolyer subsequently published the lecture in book format. In this historical analysis, he developed his cyclical theory of prospecting technology.[20] DeGolyer found these opportunities to play the professor appealing, even if only for an evening or two.

Considering DeGolyer's love affair with science and the academy, it may come as a surprise that he never pursued graduate study. True, he had certainly considered it as the course of the Mexican Revolution called his career plans into question. In April 1915, he wrote to Dr. Hayes, expressing his hope of studying petroleum geology at Yale or the University of Chicago. As he contemplated a future as an oil company manager, he pleaded a genuine interest in the scholarly value of earth science, writing, "I am really interested in the subject of the geology of oil from more than a financial standpoint and I hope some day to be one of the authorities on the subject."[21] One month later, he wrote to his friend and fellow geologist Charles Hamilton, expressing a similar wish that he would be able to devote the next couple of years to graduate study, and his excitement at the prospect of "working up some ideas that I have with regards to oil, and carrying on some experiments with them."[22] There can be little doubt that DeGolyer's interest in advanced research in geology was sincere.

The frenetic lifestyle that he led as a company executive ensured that he never found the time for graduate study. Yet DeGolyer's scholarly publications and his remarkable foresight in the advocacy of geophysical technology earned him a reputation among the scientists of the nation's universities that was unusual for a man of business. Although he was unable to pursue scholarship to the degree he desired, the academy would soon recognize him with a host of honorary degrees.

The first came in May 1925, when the Colorado School of Mines invited DeGolyer to offer the commencement address. In conjunction with the event, he received an honorary doctorate from the school. It would not be the last commencement speech that he delivered. In 1947, he delivered the address at Trinity College of Hartford, Connecticut, and the next year at the University of Oklahoma.[23] Over half a dozen colleges and universities would ultimately bestow honorary degrees upon DeGolyer. These included Southern Methodist University in 1945; Trinity College in 1947; Princeton University in 1949; the Universidad Nacional Autónoma de México in 1951; Washington University of Saint Louis, Missouri, in 1952; and Tulane University in 1954.[24]

These honors gratified DeGolyer, but the greatest evidence of his respect within academic circles came in 1940 when he accepted the position as Distinguished Professor of Geology at the University of Texas.[25] He would teach there beginning in January 1940. The timing was not especially good. Construction projects were still underway at *El Rancho Encinal*.[26] Although most of the work on the home was complete, DeGolyer would be unable to oversee the finishing touches personally.[27] Instead, he moved into a fine Mediterranean villa in Austin, where he would spend the spring semester preparing lectures on petroleum geology. Nell and the children would not join him.[28] It was an inconvenient arrangement, but as he confessed, "For some reason or other, I seem to have gone academic mentally."[29]

DeGolyer taught two classes at the university: one was a survey of petroleum geology, and the other a seminar on the world oil situation.[30] Though he enjoyed the experience of teaching, he also found it to be much more difficult than he anticipated. He assigned so much work that he was almost unable to keep up with the material.[31] Perhaps this explained "the blank expression" on some students' faces that he noted in one letter to a friend.[32] Nevertheless, DeGolyer relished the opportunity to indulge his academic interests.

In addition to classroom instruction, he delivered at least three addresses for scientific organizations on campus. The first, titled "Severinus Brought Up to Date," examined the challenges that faced the young scientists of the 1940s.[33] Increasingly, the needs of the petroleum industry dictated that a geologist spend less time in the field and more time in the less exciting work of number crunching and analysis. It was a speech that concisely summarized the professional trends that had taken place over the course of his career. Two weeks after his "Severinus" lecture, DeGolyer explored the contributions of engineers to conserving the mineral resources of the nation.[34]

The final significant extracurricular lecture that he offered considered "Oil in the Near East."[35] In contrast to his more analytical, almost philosophical address on Severinus, DeGolyer offered little more in this talk than a description of the region's oilfields and an assertion of its emerging importance. Nevertheless, this prophecy would prove to be

Everette Lee DeGolyer, 1939. DeGolyer, the self-assured businessman, was ready to indulge his intellectual and academic aspirations as the 1930s came to a close. (Everette Lee DeGolyer Collection. Courtesy of DeGolyer Library, Southern Methodist University.)

significant in light of his subsequent career in government service and the course of global events.

DeGolyer's tenure at the University of Texas lasted for only one semester. Although he thoroughly enjoyed the opportunity to teach, the strain of living in Austin while his family remained in Dallas made it difficult for him to justify another semester, let alone an academic year. Writing to Professor Walter Stewart of the Princeton Institute for Advanced Study, he confessed that "Nell absolutely refused any favorable consideration to . . . spending another year at Texas and therefore, I have had to resign."[36] It was a step that DeGolyer took with no little regret, noting that "teaching caused me to review and study propositions that I had been accustomed to take for granted."[37] It had also been a good excuse for him to indulge in reading more than a few books.

The end of DeGolyer's professorship at Texas did not put an end to his scholarly activities. He already had plans afoot to deliver more lectures. In 1941, he would return to Princeton for a series of five talks as the Louis Clark Vanuxem lecturer. His topic was again broad and industry focused: "World Petroleum—The Utilization of a Natural Resource." He took a historical approach to the development of the global oil industry.[38] DeGolyer also continued to compose analyses of petroleum geology and the oil industry that he published in professional and trade journals. Some of these examined topics that he had developed in talks while at the University of Texas.[39]

The Japanese attack on Pearl Harbor and subsequent embroilment of the nation in the Second World War put DeGolyer's adventures as a lecturer on hold for a few years, but they hardly slowed his composition of science and industry-related articles. In fact, his published explanations of government petroleum policy would form an important part of his contribution to the war effort.[40] Following victory, he would return to these topics repeatedly, offering his thoughts and opinions on developments in the oil business and the place of earth scientists in the industry.[41]

DeGolyer fostered a lifelong dedication to all these activities loosely associated with the academy—study, teaching, and scholarly publication. All indicated a sincere commitment to the cause of science, both to pure science as an end in itself and to applied science as an engine of industry. It was a conviction that at times he could give almost religious overtones.

Indeed, DeGolyer viewed science as the pursuit of truth, and the scientist as a heroic figure, battling against the forces of ignorance. No evidence better illustrates this point than DeGolyer's love of a book that was more than a decade old when he began his career, Andrew Dickson White's *History of the Warfare of Science with Theology in Christendom.*[42] DeGolyer first read White's book in the winter of 1922.[43] The book made a strong impression on the company executive who was struggling to reconcile his business life with his vocation as an earth scientist. Over the years, his devotion to White only intensified. In 1945, he listed the book in a column he wrote for the *Dallas Times-Herald* as the first of "Ten Unusual Books He Would Have Most Hated to Miss."[44] In the brief summary that he wrote, DeGolyer described the work as "[a]n extremely interesting and rather full account of the age-old struggle between the growth of science and 'dogmatic theology.'"[45] For DeGolyer, White's *Warfare of Science with Theology* was the acme of civilization. Two years after the *Times-Herald* article, he proudly cited popularity of the book in Dallas bookstores as evidence of his claim that the city held a "diamond-studded heavyweight intellectual championship."[46]

What was it about the work that impressed DeGolyer so? No explicit account has survived, but White's approach to the topic offers some possible explanations. First, it was a polemical work that resulted from the author's personal experience as the President of Cornell University. White was a determined opponent of religious control of collegiate education, and he came under fire for his convictions. His *Warfare of Science with Theology* was a reaction against the opposition he met in this struggle, supporting his own position by cataloging the occasions in which theologians had opposed scientific inquiry. The book, published in 1896, had evolved from a series of lectures and magazine articles.[47]

Although White made the obligatory concessions to the value of religion, his account consistently cast churchmen as ignorant conservatives and scientists as heroic champions of truth. As one contemporary and sympathetic reviewer summed it up, "The book is in effect a score of terrible pamphlets, dealing death to the dunce-spirit that endeavors to barricade the roadway of science."[48] Considering the exalted position that White's book accorded the scientist, it is easy to understand DeGolyer's attraction to the work.

By his own admission, DeGolyer had never been a particularly religious man, so there was little to offend him in White's book.[49] As a geologist, he also felt something of the same pressure that had troubled

White years before. After all, the science of geology was a major theological battlefield thanks to the controversy over Darwinian evolution. The notorious Scopes Monkey trial came just three years after DeGolyer's first exposure to White's book in 1922.

Above all, it was the heroic role of the scientist that DeGolyer would have found appealing in *The Warfare of Science with Theology*. He had seen firsthand the ignorant opposition of "practical" oilmen in the infancy of petroleum geology. He aspired to be a heroic pioneer in the introduction of geophysical prospecting. Here was an interpretation of his chosen profession that exalted his work—a scientific religion. Science was indeed the goal "worthy of the efforts of mankind in all its affairs."[50]

If White's book reflected DeGolyer's attitude as a professional scientist, not all of his scholarly pursuits related to his chosen field. In fact, as the years wore on, he increasingly cultivated a love of subjects rather distant from the finer points of petroleum geology—history and literature. As with his scientific and industry-related interests, he felt compelled to express these "hobbies" through public addresses, compositions, and publications.

There were signs early in DeGolyer's career that petroleum geology represented only one facet of his intellectual curiosity. From the beginning of his work as a field geologist for the Mexican Eagle Oil Company, questions of the origin and history of the oil business in Mexico had fascinated him. As the Revolution blazed around Tampico, DeGolyer decided to look into the matter, composing an essay on "The History of the Petroleum Industry in Mexico."[51] He would deliver the piece to an audience of oilmen, glad to let thoughts of their Aztec predecessors distract them from unpleasant contemporary events. Apparently meeting with a positive reception, DeGolyer decided to publish the piece.[52] Although the focus of the article was industry related, DeGolyer already showed signs of an abiding interest in Mexican culture. It would be the first of numerous articles that he would publish on the history of Mexico and the United States Southwest.

It would take some time before DeGolyer fully indulged his historical curiosity. Although he would devour history books, his historical publications were sparse and not particularly substantial for decades after his initial article on oil in Mexico. True, he did manage a brief biographical entry on General Santa Anna for the *Encyclopaedia Britannica* in 1928.[53] But it was not until the 1940s that he really began to produce historical and cultural articles on a scale that rivaled and for a time surpassed his professional publications.

At about the same time that DeGolyer was in Austin, outlining lectures, he entered in the early stages of a career in amateur publishing. After his move to Dallas in 1936, DeGolyer made the acquaintance of Elizabeth Ann McMurray, known in that city for managing the Personal Bookshop. The two soon hit upon the idea of publishing books that suited their own personal interests, with their own press. Lacking any printing equipment of its own, they named the new venture the Peripatetic Press. As its name suggests, this private press would operate in a variety of locations, ranging from Natchez, Mississippi, to Santa Fe, New Mexico. Although the place of publication might vary, Peripatetic Press was consistent in its collaboration with Carl Hertzog, a talented El Paso printer with a deep interest in Southwestern culture. Hertzog, often working in conjunction with noted El Paso artist Tom Lea, produced strikingly beautiful works on behalf of the press.[54]

The first of the new press's projects was *My Adventures in Zuñi* by Frank Hamilton Cushing. First published in the 1890s, Peripatetic Press reprinted the book in 1941 with a new introduction by DeGolyer. Not content to offer context for the piece, DeGolyer carefully edited the original for typographical errors. The outbreak of World War II would temporarily silence Peripatetic Press, but it would be back after victory, when the press would publish a tongue-in-cheek piece by DeGolyer on *The Antiquity of the Oil Industry,* as well as another work of "Southwestiana," *The Journey of Three Englishmen Across Texas in 1568,* which would likewise include an introduction by DeGolyer.[55]

Long before these publications, DeGolyer's amateur interest in publishing had taken a more serious turn. This came in the summer of 1942. Although already stretched to the limit with his work on behalf of the government, he found an offer to obtain a plurality interest in the *Saturday Review of Literature* irresistible. The *Review* was a respected literary magazine that had operated on a "semi-philanthropic" basis since 1934. As with many endowed institutions, the magazine ran habitual deficits. When DeGolyer bought into the *Saturday Review,* the editors hoped that the infusion of private capital would allow it to increase its circulation to a point where it could show a profit. Circulation would in fact increase, but the periodical never managed to live up to its financial expectations. The editors would call upon DeGolyer time and time again to make loans to the *Review.*[56]

No matter—DeGolyer never understood his involvement with the publication to be strictly an investment, as the editor of the *Review,* Norman Cousins, would soon discover. In later years, one of DeGolyer's close associates would claim that the venture had been intended to set up a career for De's son, "Ev."[57] And indeed, DeGolyer would write to Cousins in 1946, asking the editor to let Ev "get acquainted with your crowd." DeGolyer noted that his son was "practically an expert on railroads and seems to have built himself into almost an authority on symphonic recordings."[58] In September 1947, the *Review* would find a place for Ev, publishing in a new affiliated publication, the *Saturday Review of Recordings,* where he could showcase his mastery of the record business.[59]

However, Ev DeGolyer was not the only beneficiary of his father's proprietary interest in the *Saturday Review.* The elder DeGolyer used his influence to draw attention to his favorite authors, some of whom were personal associates. His old friend Wallace Pratt was one of the first to enjoy sunshine from the publication in a review of his book *Oil in the Earth,* which DeGolyer composed himself.[60] Carl Hertzog also benefited from the association. The *Review* published a positive review of his *Twelve Travelers,* following a note from DeGolyer.[61] At the time, DeGolyer was in the midst of another capital infusion for the *Saturday Review.*[62] The following year, the *Review* honored DeGolyer's friend Sumner Pike with an article detailing his reading list.[63] Later that month, DeGolyer would approve a $40,000 loan to the magazine.[64]

Dillon Anderson, a lawyer who worked closely with DeGolyer during the war, would enjoy special solicitude. In spring 1948, DeGolyer suggested that Cousins allow Anderson to publish a book review in the magazine. Anderson's review of *Summer on the Water* appeared in the May 29 issue that year.[65] But this was not all. When not engaged in lawyerly activities, Anderson was also an aspiring writer. Two years later Anderson published his own book, *I and Claudie.*[66] Understandably, DeGolyer hoped that the *Saturday Review* would give the novel a lift. DeGolyer wrote Cousins about the matter, opining, "I hope you have a good review of Dillon Anderson's *I and Claudie.* I have read it in book form and am delighted with it."[67] There was more; he continued:

While I am on this subject of book reviews, I have a letter from Ralph J. Prior, a co-director of mine in the Republic Natural Gas, hoping that S.R.L. will pay some attention to a novel to be published September 17 entitled *The Big Play.* The novel is by his daughter and, as he says, is an oil story. Life would probably be easier for me if the S.R.L. would give this book the attention it deserves or, since I have not read the book, it may be that what we want is mercy, not justice. How about a little bit more than it deserves.[68]

One can only guess at what Cousins made of all this. Yet he had little choice in the matter. The article on *I and Claudie* appeared in November 1951. Needless to say, the reviewer was, like DeGolyer, also delighted.[69] A review of *The Big Play* followed in short order, though it was on the balance a negative one.[70]

None of this was particularly surprising or especially heinous. It was natural for the primary investor in a magazine to have some say in the content of the publication. This was certainly true in popular media and newspapers. Moreover, DeGolyer did not use his power to influence the editorial content of the *Saturday Review,* as Norman Cousins gratefully acknowledged.[71] Nevertheless, DeGolyer's occasional meddling in the content of the *Saturday Review* did show that he judged himself sufficient authority to rule on matters of literary taste. In fact, there was greater testimony of this conviction than these few odd intercessions on behalf of friends and associates. The greatest evidence included the numerous book reviews that DeGolyer himself published in the *Saturday Review* and elsewhere.

Published discussions of articles in professional journals were a common feature of scientific scholarship. Peer review played an essential role in the advance of scientific knowledge. Some of DeGolyer's earliest publications were contributions to these discussions.[72] In 1928, he published a book review in *Economic Geology* on a topic of curiosity to the journal's readers: *The Divining Rod.*[73] But aside from this foray, he largely limited himself to reviewing the work of other geologists—at least until 1942.

That year marked DeGolyer's deepening involvement in the *Saturday Review,* and he began commenting on books with clockwork regularity. His first review considered *The Golden Flood,* a history of the early oil industry in the United States.[74] If Cousins feared that he would need to institute a new column on oil industry books, he could soon rest easy. DeGolyer's subsequent reviews often dealt with subjects of wider interest. Predictably, books that featured the Southwest made frequent appearances.[75]

Although DeGolyer may have bought a captive editorial board at the *Saturday Review,* his book reviews were, in fact, well-written, quasi-scholarly pieces. DeGolyer was hesitant to critique literature where he did not possess a fair degree of mastery over the subject matter. Indeed, other periodicals attested to the quality of his work by publishing a number of his reviews, which never appeared in the *Saturday Review.*

Consider, for instance, the long list of reviews that DeGolyer wrote for the *Dallas Morning News.* These began in 1943, with an article on the autobiography of his "boss" in the Petroleum Administration for War, Harold Ickes.[76] As with the *Saturday Review,* DeGolyer followed the first publication on an oil-related topic with pieces on literature related to Mexico and the Southwest.[77] His publications with the city's other leading newspaper, the *Dallas Times-Herald,* also included articles focused on Mexico.[78] In addition to his numerous reviews for the *Saturday Review* and the major Dallas papers, DeGolyer also published reviews of petroleum industry books in the *Southwest Review.*[79] By any standard, he was a prolific reviewer. For an oilman, it was an unusually large body of work.

DeGolyer's work on behalf of the *Dallas Morning News* also won him a significant admirer, Lon Tinkle, a writer for the *News* and professor of literature at Southern Methodist University and DeGolyer's future biographer. DeGolyer's interest in the literary world particularly endeared him to Tinkle, who proclaimed that the word *civilized* best encapsulated DeGolyer, a man who otherwise escaped labels.[80] Through informal groups such as the Dallas News Café Society and the Federation, DeGolyer interacted with writers like Tinkle, local figures in the book world like Elizabeth Ann McMurray, and feted associates from the *Saturday Review of Literature* like Bennett Cerf, the publisher and television celebrity best remembered for his many appearances on the popular game show *What's My Line?*[81] It was an important part of his life.

DeGolyer's literary activities demand something of an explanation. After all, he was a man whose primary business was petroleum. Furthermore, at the zenith of his review-publishing record, he was at one of the busiest points in his career. At the time, DeGolyer had immersed himself in public affairs related to the Second World War and its aftermath, while managing his manifold private business ventures. It would not seem to have been the most auspicious moment to begin dabbling in recreational literary journalism. Yet that is precisely what DeGolyer did.

On the other hand, the 1940s marked the highest point yet for

DeGolyer's public profile. People were interested in what he had to say—and not just in his newly adopted hometown. However, it was more than a simple matter of public interest. On subjects that interested him, DeGolyer possessed a passion that he simply could not keep to himself. Combined with a confidence in the worth of his own perspective, his enthusiasm bubbled over in his numerous book reviews. Moreover, it seems fair to say that it was also something of these same qualities that had led him to success in the business world. In that sense, his non-technical publications and his career as a businessman were connected.

Part of DeGolyer's passion for book reviews was simply a reflection of his delight in books themselves. That delight was, on the one hand, the delight of a voracious reader with an appreciation, even a hunger, for the knowledge that books held—for books as repositories of knowledge. On the other hand, it was also the delight of a collector with esteem for the value of books as tangible objects, as items unique in the time and place of their creation—for books as historical relics.

Although DeGolyer had owned books since at least his days as a student in Oklahoma, his activities as a collector did not really begin until his journey to England in 1914.[82] It was during that trip, while visiting Lord Cowdray, that DeGolyer acquired his first book that was truly valuable as a collector's item: a first edition of *David Copperfield,* a gift from Cowdray himself. DeGolyer's vast library would grow from this seed. When a later visit to the Chief yielded a first edition of Shakespeare, Cowdray's gift became a project, then a mania.[83]

DeGolyer's book collecting soon became something of a domestic hazard as his library outgrew the space available to house it. Ten years after his first London trip, increasingly cramped living quarters forced DeGolyer to hire carpenters to line his New Jersey residence with bookshelves. One can only guess at Nell DeGolyer's reaction to such consequences of her husband's "hobby."[84]

The thrill of the hunt seems to have given DeGolyer as much pleasure as the actual possession of his books. Indeed, as with many of his professional pursuits, DeGolyer poured energy into the creation of a library, then passed on its care and management to others after he felt that he had built something valuable. And indeed, DeGolyer created several libraries during the course of his lifetime because of his fascination with book collecting.

The first such library, which DeGolyer handed on to a worthy recipient, was his collection of rare first editions of English and American

literature. For over three decades following Cowdray's gift of *David Copperfield* in 1914, DeGolyer was entranced with these books. To detail the
contents, value, and rarity of the collection would require a chapter of
its own. DeGolyer's collection of Kipling, Whitman, Dickens, Steven-
son, Thoreau, and hundreds of other authors was enough to provoke
the envy of university librarians. DeGolyer was aware of this, and by the
1940s, he was ready to let go of the books.[85]

Sometime soon after his semester as a professor, DeGolyer conceived
of the idea of donating his rare literature library to the University of
Texas. In 1942, he suggested the possibility to university President
Homer P. Rainey. Rainey, of course, was eager to accept. Initially,
DeGolyer planned to send the collection to the school on loan. Although
he claimed that his hesitance to offer the collection as an outright gift
was because of a desire to avoid taxes, he also used the indeterminate
status of the library as leverage to influence the ultimate disposition of
the books within the university library. DeGolyer would later repeat this
strategy in creating a library of the history of science for the University
of Oklahoma.[86]

When DeGolyer finally felt assured that his books would receive
the treatment he desired, and perhaps after he had personally come
to terms with giving them away, he made the transfer official. This
came on December 27, 1946. It was a remarkable gift for the university. Altogether, DeGolyer had amassed a collection of rare literature
that included approximately 1,300 volumes. He reckoned it to be worth
$45,960.[87]

The gift of the rare editions library included a significant number of
DeGolyer's books, but it was only a fraction of the total. In fact, it was
less than a third of his collection. Afterward, DeGolyer continued to
acquire volumes that interested him, although he conceded after the
transfer of the literature section that "I am out of the market for firsts,
[that is, first editions], having given mine away."[88]

The remaining books in his extensive library focused in part upon
topics of professional and scientific interest. These books would become the core of a collection on the history of science that he would
ultimately donate to the University of Oklahoma. Building that library
would be one of the chief projects of the twilight of his life.

The other component of his remaining collection and a major focus
of his book collecting activities was the history of the Southwest and
Mexico. Considering the early interest that DeGolyer took in the his-

tory of Mexico, it is a little surprising that he did not begin to collect these books in earnest until the mid-1920s.[89] Nevertheless, his library of Southwestern and Mexican history grew steadily, although its growth stalled somewhat during the years of the Great Depression.[90]

These historical books were particularly dear to DeGolyer. Unlike his collection of rare literature and his library on the history of science, he was unable to part with them while alive.[91] It was not the rarity of this library that made it so indispensable, although DeGolyer certainly possessed many valuable and extraordinary books on the Southwest and Mexico. Rather, there was something intensely personal in his love for these volumes that requires special consideration. It was a love reflected in his scholarship and publications as well as in his propensity to collect books.

DeGolyer's interest in the history and culture of the United States Southwest and Mexico was every bit as earnest as his scholarly work in fields directly related to his career. Indeed, these extra-professional pursuits reveal much about his character and self-perception. For while his scholarship as a geologist and a businessman resulted partly from his occupation, these other interests stood independent of such concern. The significance of DeGolyer's fascination with the Southwest and Mexico was more than the result of mere residence. To be sure, he had been raised in, broadly speaking, the American Southwest and had started his professional career in Mexico. Possessing more than the average ration of intellectual curiosity, the lore of the Spanish Empire, the Mexican Republic, and the Wild West all interested him. However, his enthrallment with these subjects in particular is striking when compared to his relative disinterest in other seemingly analogous matters.

Consider the history of New York. DeGolyer spent as many years of official residence in the New York area as he did in Texas. Yet he never displayed the searching interest in that city's rich history that he displayed in the case of the Southwest and Mexico. Commenting in later years on his time in Gotham, DeGolyer was dismissive: "I never wasted a dime's worth of time trying to learn anything about the history of New York. Whatever I learned about New York was what anybody would learn just from the current scene and you can well believe that I didn't even know that too well."[92]

DeGolyer never really became a New Yorker, although he had certainly spent enough time there that he might have. His decision to return to the Southwest in 1936, when the family moved to Dallas, con-

*El Rancho Encinal.* The home the DeGolyers constructed in Dallas embodied Everette Lee DeGolyer's interest in Southwestern culture. (Everette Lee DeGolyer Collection. Courtesy of DeGolyer Library, Southern Methodist University.)

firmed this. That decision said something about the promise of the region, but also about DeGolyer's self-understanding.

When the DeGolyer family moved to the New York area in 1916, they arrived in the financial and cultural capital of the United States. The plains of Kansas, the hills of Missouri, and the bustling new towns of Oklahoma all had their share of economic opportunity, but they obviously paled in comparison to the tremendous financial power of New York. Indeed, the West at the time was in some ways a colonized region, with raw materials flowing eastward, where industrialists made fortunes processing raw goods, manufacturing, and marketing finished products.[93] DeGolyer's very presence in the great city suggested the power of the East as a magnet for talent as well.

But DeGolyer's ultimate conclusion that the oil industry offered greater opportunities in Texas than in New York hinted at possible changes in this relationship. Even before Spindletop, Texas politicians were using state laws to ensure that local merchants and developers

Santa Anna Portrait in *El Rancho Encinal* Library. DeGolyer's fascination with
Mexico was reflected in this portrait of General Santa Anna displayed prominently
over the fireplace in his renowned library—an unusual choice for a Texan, even
an adopted one. (Everette Lee DeGolyer Collection. Courtesy of DeGolyer Library,
Southern Methodist University.)

did not fall prey to Eastern oil interests.[94] The rise of locally based oil
businesses gave Southwesterners greater confidence in the future of
the region. Moreover, for the historical-minded DeGolyer, the promise
of the future naturally suggested the value of the past.

DeGolyer embraced the history of the Southwest with all of its romantic charm. The daring exploits of Coronado, the failed ambitions
of Santa Anna, the reckless adventures of Billy the Kid—all held a special place in DeGolyer's heart. Some of this devotion reflected a chip
on the shoulder, an awareness that many Easterners viewed the land
of his origin as uncultured, unimportant, and unworthy of attention.
DeGolyer reacted against this attitude by glorying in the legendary
West. DeGolyer took pleasure in bringing the Spanish and Mexican
heritage of the region to the attention of the public. In his nontech-
nical, nonscientific scholarship, DeGolyer embraced a Southwestern
identity. He did his best to promote an appreciation of the culture and

history of the region, even pioneering scholarship in one of his favorite dishes, chili.[95]

DeGolyer's fascination with the Spanish-Mexican origins of the Southwest and his high regard for Mexican culture was remarkable and deserves comment. His years in Mexico from 1909 to 1914 seem to have captured his imagination for a lifetime. Few Texans proudly displayed portraits of General Santa Anna over their mantle as DeGolyer did, which must have provoked many remarks, bemused and otherwise.

DeGolyer's admiration for Mexico was not private view, but a public position that he actively promoted. As early as 1915, he was publicly pleading for greater cultural understanding and engagement between the United States and Mexico. Acknowledging the social challenges faced by Mexico during the Revolution, he nonetheless asserted, "Many Mexicans, however, are highly educated and have traveled . . . [W]hen the first settlement was made in the colonies, Mexico City was a progressive capital with beautiful churches, a well organized university, and other developments that go toward making a city. We Americans here in the States often do not realize this when we think of Mexico as a country just becoming civilized."[96] He went on to argue that Americans would do well to study Spanish in school, rather than German or French.[97]

As these early words suggest, his attitude toward Mexico was shaped as much by historical past as by present reality. The age of the conquistadores, of early Spanish settlement and missions—all were central to this interest. It would take concrete form time and time again in publications on Mexico, in related book reviews, and in his book-collecting proclivities.

The diversity of DeGolyer's scholarly interests may have seemed to some observers to be the disconnected and unrelated fascinations of a curious mind. DeGolyer himself did not see the matter quite this way. Generally, he understood all knowledge to be a part of a seamless web of human experience. As he put it, science demanded "the search for truth and understanding in all fields."[98]

How did his interests in geological science and Southwestern lore relate to one another? What was it about both of these fields that drew his reverent devotion? Certainly, they reflected the intellectual development of different aspects of his identity. Part of his interest in geology was the result of his professional self-conception. His profession was a scientist. His interest in the history of the Southwest addressed questions about his cultural identity. His culture was Southwestern.

However, there was a deeper connection between these scholarly pursuits that he discerned. The metaphor that tied them all together was an experience with powerful resonance in America. It was the frontier. Binding together DeGolyer's regional and professional identities was the image of the rugged pioneer, pressing beyond the bounds of the settled and striking out into the undeveloped spaces that lay beyond. It was an interpretation that he explicitly developed in his commencement speech delivered at the Colorado School of Mines in 1925. He began by invoking the mythical pioneers of western legend: "The old frontiers are almost gone, but their influences and traditions are still alive. Many of you, I doubt not, are Westerners and the sons of Westerners, as I am. Our fathers were of the adventurous vanguard of the great army of pioneers—they were the Pilgrims of the West."[99] He praised the "traders, hunters, cattlemen, Indian fighters, steamboatmen, miners, railroad-builders, lumber-jacks, soldiers, farmers, and home-builders." And DeGolyer confessed his own "keen disappointment" that this "golden time" had faded into the past.[100]

Yet though the old West had disappeared, the frontier had not. Rather, the Industrial Revolution had transformed it. Even as the "old frontier" had closed, "new frontiers" opened. To be sure, the challenges of modern industrial life were different from the challenges that faced the nineteenth-century settlers of the West. DeGolyer conceded that "highly organized, co-operative and corporate effort" had replaced the "individualism" of the old frontier. But he also asked himself whether there were still opportunities for "individual effort." The answer, he thought, was yes, and he concluded:

> The prime requisite for the existence of a frontier, new or old, is an unexplored and underdeveloped or not fully explored and not fully developed territory. Such provinces, mental and physical, exist and always will exist until that impossible time when man attains perfection in all of his works, or until the end of the world. As long as there is human progress there will be new frontiers.[101]

A spirit of curiosity and adventure united the frontiers of DeGolyer's beloved Southwest, and the frontiers of science. Both were romantic ventures, beckoning brave individuals to press on beyond the well-worn paths of convention, to strike out and to take risks. In his scholarly research, lectures, and publications, DeGolyer revered the daring exploits of the past, celebrated the adventurous spirit of the present, and worked toward a future in which scholars pushed the frontiers of knowledge ever outward.

# 7 | Technocrat

*Each field is a unique thing and requires special regulation, such as is being given to them by your regulatory bodies.*
– Everette Lee DeGolyer, address before the Interstate Oil Compact Commission, Fort Worth, Texas, October 16, 1941[1]

On a rainy Thursday in April 1943, three professional societies devoted to oil exploration gathered at the Texas Hotel in Fort Worth for a joint wartime conference. That morning, Fritz Aurin of the American Association of Petroleum Geologists delivered a presidential address titled "The Geologist in the War," in which he reflected on the changing nature of his profession.[2]

Noting the recent rise of the earth scientist in industry, Aurin began, "Not so many years ago, geology was studied and used in a purely scientific manner, but later practical applications began to be made in the mining industry and the development of the natural resources."[3] He went on to describe early resistance by practical oilmen to the practice of geology and its "gradual climb to a place of prominence in industries."[4] But the geologist's time had now definitively arrived. Aurin proudly stated:

> [Y]ou have noticed that in many . . . companies, the petroleum geologists have climbed up through the ranks of administrative [sic] to the uppermost and top ranking executive positions in the petroleum industry and in the government agencies. The history of the rise of many company petroleum geologists as well as independent geologists to positions of affluence would read like some of Horatio Alger's books.[5]

Also mentioned in Aurin's speech was one man who fit this description to a tee, Assistant Deputy Petroleum Administrator for War Everette Lee DeGolyer. It is not known what DeGolyer, who also spoke at the conference, thought of Aurin's remarks. But he too must have marveled at the course of a career that began with the study of a scientific field of dubious practical value, skyrocketed him to prominence with a bonanza oil strike in Mexico, transformed him into a corporate executive, and now had established him as a powerful representative of the federal government.

In some ways, he had come full circle. Although DeGolyer made his name through his work on behalf of private companies, his career as a geologist began with government service. His first formal field training had been with the United States Geological Survey, a branch of the Department of the Interior. So when DeGolyer directed more attention toward government affairs during the 1930s and 1940s, he was in some ways returning to his professional roots.

No mere representative of industry, DeGolyer offered himself to regulation advocates as a disinterested master of technical questions, a man who understood the complexity of industry operations and who could identify problems and formulate solutions with scientific precision. True, his objectivity was open to question. After all, he was a participant in, as well as an analyst of, the petroleum industry. Yet his ability to apply statistics and translate complex processes into terms that nonspecialists could understand made him an ideal go-between in the awkward dance between government and industry.

Indeed, men like DeGolyer were essential to the development of the regulatory regime that would govern the oil and gas business. Regulation promised to stabilize the price of oil, but that could also look like price fixing, a practice fraught with political and legal peril. Yet scientists like DeGolyer could offer another compelling and more respectable reason for regulation—conservation. Elimination of waste would be the primary public justification for regulation; if it incidentally stabilized the market for oil, so be it. As one of the foremost petroleum geologists in the nation, DeGolyer made significant contributions to the evolution of petroleum industry regulation. And when World War II finally arrived at America's doorstep, setting into motion a vast bureaucracy to manage the war effort, DeGolyer would transform himself into the consummate technocrat.[6]

Rapidly shifting attitudes toward regulation of the oil industry provided the fundamental context for official interest in DeGolyer as well as for his attitude toward government service. Aside from his early work with the USGS, DeGolyer's cooperation with government planners began with mobilization for World War I. During the war years, federal oversight of the industry reached unprecedented heights with the creation of the United States Fuel Administration. But in the 1920s, the military rationale for federal regulation faded, and industry leaders moved to block plans for government direction promoted by conservationists. In the 1930s, circumstances again changed; overproduction of petroleum resulted in plummeting oil prices. Many within the oil business, though certainly not all, began to warm to government regulation as some businessmen came to believe that it was necessary to rescue the industry from itself. During the Depression years, officials and oilmen would engage in rancorous debates over the nature of state and federal regulation, often with little consensus in government or industry over the direction to take. Pearl Harbor altered this state of affairs. Federal direction reached its high water mark during World War II, when DeGolyer's tenure in government service arrived at its fullest expression in the Petroleum Administration for War.[7]

DeGolyer's transformation into a technocrat was a gradual process that took several decades to complete. Aside from his experience with the USGS, the government's first interest in DeGolyer was connected with the nation's involvement in World War I. On March 30, 1917, George Otis Smith, the director of the USGS, wired DeGolyer, at the time staying at the Rice Hotel in Houston. The message was direct: "How soon could you come to Washington without too great personal sacrifice to render brief but important service for which you are best fitted? [ . . . ] only few days necessary but urgent [ . . . ] survey can reimburse traveling expenses."[8] Though Smith did not specify exactly what "important service" meant, DeGolyer already had some idea of what was involved. Otis had been prodding him to pass on a variety of maps related to his work in Mexico, and DeGolyer had already forwarded plans of the Tehuantepec Railway. On April 3, he wired Otis to let him know that he would soon be in Washington with more maps that the government wanted.[9] On April 5, one day before the United States declared war on Germany, DeGolyer was in the nation's capital, passing on more maps of Mexico to the War College Division.[10]

Under normal circumstances, the USGS would only be interested in maps of foreign countries to the extent that they shed light on the development of resources in the United States. But with the United States' entry in World War I imminent, all branches of the government were turning an eye to questions of national defense. And Mexico had become a nation of particular interest when it came to these matters.

There was more than one reason for the United States government's interest in the geography south of the border. One cause was the Mexican oil boom. Since World War I had begun, petroleum production in

Mexico had doubled and would reach a staggering 63 million barrels of annual crude production by the end of 1918.[11] For ships, industry, land transport, and experimental weapons like the tank, petroleum products were essential. The Mexican oilfields were a matter of great interest to both sides in the war.[12]

And the United States military had other reasons to be concerned about Mexico. For several years, border violence had put a strain on relations between the two countries.[13] Then came a diplomatic incident involving a German attempt to incite war between the United States and its southern neighbor. On February 25, 1917, President Wilson received a message from London that revealed the plot. The British had obtained a communication from German Foreign Secretary Zimmerman to the German Minister in Mexico City. The Zimmerman telegram counseled the Kaiser's representative that should hostilities break out between the United States and Germany, he should offer Mexico an alliance, with promises to restore Texas, New Mexico, and Arizona to that nation in exchange for a declaration of war against the United States. Several days after receiving this sensational communiqué, Wilson released it to the Associated Press, shocking the nation and raising fears that the war in Europe might spread to United States soil.[14]

Under the circumstances, the United States military was very interested in Mexico. Whether planning a limited operation to secure Mexican oilfields or considering the exigencies of all-out war, the United States armed forces wanted as much information as they could obtain regarding the Mexican republic. This was the cause of the initial interest of the USGS in DeGolyer's map collection. Soon, the military would communicate directly with DeGolyer to request information.

One day after the United States declaration of war, DeGolyer was contacted by Major Ralph H. Van Deman. Sometimes referred to as the "father of American military intelligence," Van Deman was at the time attached to the general staff of the US Army.[15] Van Deman acknowledged DeGolyer's "very patriotic assistance to the General Staff of the Army" and offered an inventory of the items that he had provided.[16] Among the information that DeGolyer had passed on were maps of the northern part of the state of Veracruz, plans of oilfields, schematics of the electric power network of Tampico, diagrams of petroleum shipping terminals, and a variety of Mexican railroad surveys. Also included were a number of detailed topographical maps drawn with an eye toward geology, but of equal value from a military standpoint.[17]

Fortunately, the army never needed those maps. Despite fears and strained relations that resulted in part from earlier United States intervention in Mexican affairs, war did not break out between the two nations. However, that did not quash the interest by the United States military in DeGolyer's superb collection of maps. In 1925, intelligence officers contacted him again, asking for more topographical surveys of Mexico. DeGolyer complied, although he expressed some misgivings regarding the confidentiality of the materials he passed on to the government.[18]

One notable point about the military's early interest in DeGolyer was the essentially nongeological nature of their inquiries. They did not seek him out for his knowledge of geological structures, nor even as an expert in the strategically important resource of petroleum. At the time, there was more interest in what geologists could tell military planners about the stability of trenches than what they could tell them about oil.[19] Their interest in what DeGolyer had to offer focused on matters only tangentially related to his work as a scientist. The military did not plan to use his topographical maps for the same purposes that he would. Nor did their desire for oilfield plans have anything to do with drilling for petroleum. Their concerns were limited to the questions of territorial control and the logistics of a potential invasion. DeGolyer was a man who could offer them information useful to these ends, but strategic thinkers were not yet interested in his proficiency in petroleum geology.

Although strategic thinkers were not particularly interested in DeGolyer the geologist, there were some in the government who did covet his technical expertise. It will be remembered that the Internal Revenue Bureau (IRB) retained DeGolyer during the last days of World War I. DeGolyer had labored to develop a method of computing a "depletion allowance" for taxing oil wells. Focusing on the oilfields of the Gulf Coast, he struggled to create dependable, mathematical curves that would predict the rate of declining production over time. It was a task in which he ultimately failed.[20]

During the war, President Wilson had created a United States Fuel Administration to help coordinate industry. With peace and the subsequent election of Warren G. Harding, there came a reversal in the expansion of government direction of the economy. During the 1920s, officials interested in DeGolyer's perspective as a geologist only rarely troubled him. During these years, he was able to devote himself to his business ventures without distraction. Aside from a few map requests from the military, the only occasion on which a matter of public importance intruded on his private work came with an inquiry from the newly established Federal Oil Conservation Board (FOCB). Harding's successor, Calvin Coolidge, had created the FOCB in the aftermath of the Teapot Dome scandal, which brought to light a web of corruption involving the secretary of the interior and powerful oilmen. The FOCB aimed to investigate whether an oil shortage was imminent, as some feared, and whether the petroleum industry was wasting oil, as some conservationists accused.[21]

Spurring the FOCB and encouraging conservationists was the voice of Henry Doherty, a maverick oilman who issued renewed warnings that the nation's oil reserves were running out. Doherty argued in favor of stricter conservation measures and scientific "unit" operation of the oilfields. Unit operation, or unitization, involved the development of an entire oil reservoir under a single plan, regardless of the number of producers engaged in exploiting the field. Instead of allowing the exigencies of the market to dictate development and production, the plan for the unit would guide operations to minimize waste of petroleum. Talk of unitization would figure prominently in the FOCB's investigation of practices in the nation's oilfields.[22]

As a preliminary, the FOCB dispatched a series of questionnaires to oil industry leaders, including Everette DeGolyer. His response to the Board was complex; DeGolyer challenged misleadingly facile questions that seemed to call for straightforward answers. For instance, there was the first question posed by the questionnaire: "Generally, in what directions do you consider that waste in production could be reduced and stabilization effected?"[23] DeGolyer realized this was not a simple question. What did waste mean? Was oil left unproduced in the ground after flush production wasted? Was drilling multiple wells when one might be adequate wasteful? Was spending more money to produce oil than the price it would receive at market wasteful?[24]

DeGolyer began by focusing on the essential matter of defining the problem. Taking his cue from Webster's New International Dictionary, he chose to define waste as "a squandering; needless destruction; useless consumption of expenditure; loss without equivalent gain." Thus, for purposes of his argument, wise use of petroleum resources could not be waste. By DeGolyer's analysis, physical waste of materials was not widespread. Oil left unproduced in the ground due to reduced pressure from overdrilling could be viewed as a "reserve for the future" when improved market prices and newly developed techniques might make production feasible.[25]

DeGolyer argued that other instances of waste in oil production had been blown out of proportion by "editorial overstatements." He did condemn some representatives of the petroleum industry that claimed that the United States would never run out of oil, but he believed that the market would provide corrective incentives so that disaster would be averted. As he described the process: "Decrease in [oil] production will mean increase in price and on a higher price we will be able to use recovery methods such as mining which cannot be used at present. Substitutes [such as other fossil-fuel energy sources] will come in."[26]

As for unitization, DeGolyer's verdict was mixed. DeGolyer liked the idea of rational, scientific management of oilfields and argued that large companies were moving toward unit operation of their oilfields on a voluntary basis. Compelling unitization was a different matter. On the positive side, compulsory unit operation would increase known reserves, keep production on "even keel," deter "over- and under-production," and conserve gas. On the other hand, according to DeGolyer it would "absolutely eliminate the small operator," make "leasing and operation more difficult and speculative," and make the consumer pay more for oil. On the balance, forced unitization was not worth it.[27]

DeGolyer's larger conclusion was that greater regulation of the oil industry would not result in any justifiable reduction of waste, but would simply result in higher prices and the elimination of small oil producers. There was "nothing in the past history" of oil production to suggest that government regulation would conserve more oil.[28] Worse, more pervasive government regulation could kill incentives for oil exploration, the stage of the business in which DeGolyer was most deeply involved. He opined, "Under any condition, the brakes must not be put on . . . We are not expert enough to find new fields as required, but maintain our current supply only by a constant and aggressive search for new pools, and this search should not be interfered with by any artificial restriction."[29]

The stifling federal regulation that DeGolyer feared, a concern shared by many others in the petroleum industry, did not materialize in the 1920s. Although the; FOCB eventually called for voluntary agreement of owners to restrict overdevelopment of oilfields, it did not endorse federal regulation, much less coerce unitization.[30] But this was not the last word for DeGolyer. Like many other oilmen, his perspective shifted significantly over time, and the challenges that the industry faced with rising oil production forced him to take another look at the desirability of some sort of regulatory regime.

As the 1920s came to a close, rising oil production that resulted from the discovery of vast oilfields threatened the profitability of many oil companies. By July 1929, DeGolyer was concerned that the oil business was "headed for a nose dive" and in "for a spell of super overproduction."[31] His words were prophetic. The stock market crash of 1929 and the onset of the Great Depression only worsened the already acute situation in the oil industry. An even greater hazard arose from what otherwise might have been good news for oilmen—the discovery of a vast oilfield in East Texas in 1930.

The problem was the price of oil, which had been falling for years.[32] The development of the East Texas field sent prices tumbling even further. In 1931, the average cost per barrel in the United States fell to 65₵. In East Texas, the price of crude oil fell as low as 2₵ per barrel. Compounding the impact of the Depression, overproduction of oil and the inevitable decline of crude oil prices hit the industry hard. As profits vanished, oilmen became increasingly open to the possibility of regulation. It seemed to many that the oil business needed to be saved from itself. And increasingly, oilmen began to speak of a need for conservation.[33]

Matters became so desperate that the governments of Oklahoma and Texas turned to military force as a remedy. In August 1931, Governor "Alfalfa Bill" Murray of Oklahoma declared martial law and dispatched the state militia to the oilfields to close production until prices recovered. Shortly thereafter, Texas Governor Ross Sterling declared East Texas to be in a "state of rebellion" and ordered the National Guard and the Texas Rangers to the scene. As in Oklahoma, they closed production in order to boost prices.[34]

These extreme tactics succeeded momentarily in preventing a collapse of the industry, but most in the business understood that more action was necessary to ensure long-term stability. Both states had acknowledged this need by granting powers to government agencies that provided for the regulation of petroleum production. North of the Red River, it was the Oklahoma Corporation Commission. In the Lone Star State, it was the Texas Railroad Commission (TRC) that tried to stabilize oil prices by setting limits to allowable production—prorationing in industry terms. Unfortunately for advocates of conservation, litigation by opponents of state regulation in Texas blocked efforts to curtail production in the early 1930s. It was not until 1934 that victory in the courts allowed the Texas Railroad Commission to issue effective prorationing orders. In the meantime, some argued that federal direction would be necessary in order to create a level playing field for producers in all states and to establish stability in the market.[35]

At this point, overproduction in the oilfields coincided with the general economic crisis of the Depression to spur action by the new administration of Franklin D. Roosevelt. Under the presidency of Herbert Hoover, Washington had been reluctant to advocate a federally coerced solution to the oil crisis, employing moral suasion to encourage the industry to reduce wasteful overproduction. Roosevelt had fewer reservations in this matter.[36]

One day after his inauguration, Roosevelt called a special session of Congress in order to address the grim situation that the nation faced. What followed was a whirlwind of legislation that aimed to relieve suffering and revive the economy. They would call it "the hundred days." In diagnosing the malaise, many of Roosevelt's advisors pointed to overproduction—pervasive in many economic sectors—as a central problem.[37]

On the very last day of the hundred days, Roosevelt offered his solution for industrial woes, including those of the oil business, with the creation of the National Recovery Administration (NRA). The NRA aimed to rein in overproduction and stabilize wages. In the context of the petroleum industry, this meant using federal power to enforce state production quotas. The president could prohibit "hot oil," shipped in violation of state regulations, when it entered interstate commerce, according to Section 9(c) of the act. However, the administration envisioned a larger role for the NRA than mere enforcement of state conservation laws. Federal regulation of the industry would also come through enforcement of codes, drafted in consultation with leaders from the various industries.[38]

Designing a code for the petroleum industry proved to be contentious. The question of federal regulation divided oilmen. By 1933, many believed that federal regulation of the oil industry was an evil necessary to avoid catastrophe. Nevertheless, the consensus in the industry was that state regulation was preferable to federal regulation.[39]

Inadvertently encouraging this attitude was Roosevelt's secretary of the interior, Harold Ickes. Ickes was a longtime progressive politician who believed that federal direction was necessary to avoid excessive waste in the oil business. A self-proclaimed curmudgeon, Ickes's outlook and personality was not reassuring to oilmen contemplating the imposition of a federal regulatory regime. His lack of experience and technical expertise in the complex business of finding, producing, transporting, refining, and marketing of petroleum was particularly unsettling for the oil companies. For all these reasons, his appeal for the creation of a new office of federal "oil czar" to directly manage national petroleum policy fell flat.[40]

Nonetheless, oilmen were concerned about a possible nationalization of the industry by Ickes and other advocates of regulation. These concerns, in addition to the chaotic situation in oilfields, brought many to the table in drafting the NRA oil industry code, if only to shape the contemplated regulatory regime.[41]

On June 16, 1933, industry representatives, under the aegis of the American Petroleum Institute, gathered in Chicago to draft a code for submission to the NRA. Some hoped that regulation might be limited to enforcing state production controls through oversight of oil shipped as interstate commerce. However, advocates for federal regulation triumphed, and production and price controls were included in the draft, supported by a large majority of votes at the conference. Dissidents could only hope to alter the arrangement at later government hearings.[42]

The Chicago conference solved nothing. Although NRA Administrator Hugh Johnson received the draft code supported by the majority, he knew that he would have to address the opposition. Hearings would "let everybody blow off steam," but there was still much work to be done before an acceptable settlement could be reached. Because the industry had "dropped apart into over fifty warring groups," Johnson would need his own experts, persons not obviously beholden to the contentious factions.[43]

Among those tapped for service in the summer of 1933 was Everette Lee DeGolyer. *The Tulsa Tribune* was particularly pleased with DeGolyer's selection to advise the formulation of the oil codes. In the paper's view, he represented an "independent" perspective.[44] DeGolyer proved to be an avid opponent of the price controls that the majority at the Chicago conference desired, firmly believing that the key to the problems that confronted the industry was production control.[45] It was a view also shared by NRA Administrator Johnson.[46]

But if DeGolyer proved to be a skeptic when it came to price controls, he had certainly grown more open to regulation than he had been in the 1920s. In July 1933, he collaborated with Joseph Pogue to create "A Suggested Code of Fair Competition for the Petroleum Industry."[47] Pogue, a consulting geologist, was less than a year younger than DeGolyer and had also served briefly with the USGS.[48] DeGolyer and Pogue submitted their suggested code on July 22, 1933.[49] The work demonstrated just how far DeGolyer's views had shifted when it came to federal regulation of the industry.

The Chicago code, submitted to General Johnson by the American Petroleum Institute, had called for production quotas, limitations on imported oil, and price fixing.[50] DeGolyer and Pogue's code included similar provisions, with the exception of price controls. DeGolyer now favored federal regulation of the industry, including federally mandated planning for new oilfields. Of course, such planning would require scientific analysis that men like DeGolyer would be favorably positioned to offer. So although he still opposed compulsory unitization of reservoirs, it is clear that the crisis in the industry had made him more open to government regulation. It is also probable that a growing sense of confidence in the ability of petroleum geologists to plan effectively encouraged him in this direction.[51]

Despite his openness to greater federal direction, DeGolyer sided with the more cautious party when it came to the price-fixing issue. The battle over this issue, initially fought among the oilmen, soon became a struggle within the administration, pitting Johnson against Ickes. Ickes, who favored price controls, also hoped that the president would name him administrator of the code.[52]

DeGolyer was a firsthand witness to this conflict. On August 16, 1933, DeGolyer accompanied Johnson to the White House to present President Roosevelt with his proposed oil code. Shortly after they left, Ickes arrived together with his top expert in petroleum law. Although Johnson enjoyed the support of many prominent oilmen, he was ultimately defeated when President Roosevelt decided to back his opponent. On August 30, 1933, Roosevelt appointed Ickes as administrator of the Oil Code and withdrew jurisdiction from the NRA. In its final form, the code gave Ickes the power to fix prices for a ninety-day period. Opponents of the measure were wary.[53]

As an opponent of federally mandated price controls, DeGolyer watched these events unfold with concern. However, by the time the Oil Code took its final form, DeGolyer was no longer in government service. On July 31, 1933, he had tendered his resignation, which, once effective, ended his official involvement with the project.[54]

DeGolyer's tenure with the NRA had been quite brief, amounting to little more than a few weeks of work during the summer of 1933. But his involvement in the debate about price fixing did not end with his resignation. Instead, he continued to fight against efforts to implement the controversial policy. In August, Assistant NRA Administrator Simpson wrote to General Johnson, conveying a plea from DeGolyer to hold off on price controls.[55] Less than two weeks later, DeGolyer and Pogue sent General Johnson a telegram, reiterating the need to try production controls before setting prices.[56] Because Johnson already agreed that price fixing was inappropriate, he might have intended these communiqués as ammunition for the general in his battle with Ickes.

In addition to his work in shaping the Oil Code and his opposition to price controls, DeGolyer also served as a consultant to major oil companies in their interaction with the federal government. The group of companies for which he worked included, not surprisingly, Amerada, but also Atlantic, Continental, Gulf, Shell, Socony-Vacuum, Standard Oil Company of Indiana, Standard Oil Company of New Jersey, and the Texas Corporation. As a participant in shaping the Oil Code, DeGolyer was the perfect emissary for the industry, providing information on behalf of these oil companies regarding the cost of producing crude oil that would justify their positions on government policy.[57]

Although DeGolyer and his corporate associates had lost the battle to shape the Oil Code, they were successful in staving off the implementation of its price-fixing provisions. Although Ickes pushed hard to impose price controls in late 1933, opposition within the industry forced him to first postpone and then abandon his plans. The code administrator never implemented the price-fixing power.[58]

As eventful as DeGolyer's work with the NRA and the Oil Code was, it proved to be little more than a temporary distraction from his business matters. In a letter to J. B. Body, DeGolyer referred to his service under General Johnson as a mere "interlude."[59] But in many ways, his brief stint with the NRA marked a significant turning point for DeGolyer. For the first time, the government had turned to him not only for the technical knowledge he possessed but also for his ideas regarding questions of public policy. Years later, as the nation confronted the monumental task of coordinating its economy during the Second World War, the government would turn again to DeGolyer.

In the meanwhile, there was still the Depression, and the Oil Code proved not to be the answer to the woes of the industry. In June 1935, the Supreme Court pronounced the National Industrial Recovery Act unconstitutional, thus rendering the Oil Code a dead letter. True, the Connally Hot Oil Act was passed to maintain the federal government's power to help enforce state regulation. But the petroleum industry would not be able to count on federal policy to address the fundamental issues that caused overproduction.[60]

There were many in the industry who did not mourn the passing of the Oil Code. The NRA and the Oil Code had faced opposition from many oilmen since the beginning, many of whom favored state over federal regulation.[61] Here state regulatory agencies and the oil companies were grasping at policies that would stabilize the industry. There were many bumps along the road. In Texas, litigation had blocked the Railroad Commission's attempt to provide effective limits to overproduction through prorationing from 1931 to 1933. But by the summer of 1933, the courts had opened the door for state prorationing. At the same time, a forceful Colonel Ernest O. Thompson of the Railroad Commission, voiced strident opposition to federal regulation. He felt sure that state regulatory bodies like his own could do this job better.[62]

Thompson employed rhetoric that drew heavily on Southern support for "states rights" in his opposition to a federally directed regulatory regime. It was a position that frustrated DeGolyer in his work on behalf of the Oil Code. Although he ultimately warmed to Thompson, DeGolyer viewed him as a "pain in the neck" when he first encountered the colonel in 1933.[63]

Over time, the relationship between the two men evolved to be a fairly close one. By 1936, Thompson was praising DeGolyer privately and publicly, hailing him as an "eminent petroleum engineer" who supported his own efforts to conserve oil in Texas.[64] In 1939, DeGolyer admitted, "Friendship is a strange thing . . . and I have enjoyed more and more knowing you as the years go by." A true Lone Star nationalist, Thompson responded to DeGolyer's friendly letter with his own, congratulating him on his move to Dallas with the handwritten postscript: "I'm glad you are now a *real Texan*."[65] Coming from Thompson, this was a compliment indeed. In later years, DeGolyer came to view the chair of the Railroad Commission as a hero in the struggle for reasonable regulation.[66]

DeGolyer's improved relationship with Thompson, whom he subsequently supported in political campaigns, also suggested his shifting attitude in regulatory matters. Like many other oilmen who had been willing to countenance far-reaching federal direction of the industry in 1933, DeGolyer's views continued to evolve. Reflecting on this period in later years, he noted that the "decreasing effectiveness of the [Oil Code]" prodded the industry to consider other possible solutions. Contributing to this change of heart was the threat of a federal takeover of the oil business. In November 1934, Secretary of the Interior Harold L. Ickes had argued for strong federal control of the industry and for a declaration that the oil business was a public utility.[67] Although most oilmen recognized that regulation was necessary, this was not what they had in mind. In light of these developments, the possibility of governing the industry though state regulation looked more desirable than ever. Considering the shift of the industry in favor of state solutions, DeGolyer credited the "increasing effectiveness of state control, which, after repeated judicial tests and continued legislative revamping, was finally getting hold of its job."[68]

The heart of state attempts to regulate the situation in the oil industry was prorationing—limiting well production—but the industry was not unanimous on the subject. DeGolyer's position, however, was not in question. The Mid-Continent Oil and Gas Association to which DeGolyer belonged favored prorationing in general as "the only means the industry had 'to protect the non-integrated [oil] producer against discrimination and drainage and thus to prevent waste.'"[69] DeGolyer publicly advocated prorationing to his colleagues over more radical measures, likening the limitation of oil production to the time-tested tradition of laws limiting the exploitation of wild game. The natural gas industry would also benefit from state prorationing, he thought. If there were any single state policy that promised relief to the oil industry, it was prorationing, and for DeGolyer, its increasing effectiveness under the Texas Railroad Commission must have looked promising.[70]

But the emergence of the TRC as a major force under the direction of Ernest O. Thompson was only one aspect of the evolution of state regulation during the 1930s. After all, Texas was only one state among many oil producers, albeit an immensely important one. Coordination among all the major oil-producing states would be necessary if state prorationing and other conservation regulation were to offer a plausible alternative to federal direction. Here too, Everette Lee DeGolyer would play a significant role.

The individual most responsible for creating momentum in favor of interstate coordination of oil regulations was Ernest W. Marland, an oilman elected governor of Oklahoma in 1934. Marland believed his election was a mandate to address the problems of the oil industry. Recognizing that any long-term solution would require coordinated policies among the various oil-producing states, he believed that an interstate compact might offer the elusive solution to overproduction. To this end, he arranged a meeting of all the oil state governors in his own home in Ponca City, Oklahoma, for December 3, 1934.[71]

This meeting, although inconclusive, marked the beginning of a series of conferences that would establish the Interstate Oil Compact. Subsequent meetings proved contentious, but eventually the governors of the various oil-producing states came to agree on the terms of an Interstate Compact to Conserve Oil and Gas. The Compact envisioned the establishment of an Interstate Oil Compact Commission (IOCC) that would have power "to recommend the coordination of the exercise of the police powers of the several states within their jurisdictions to promote the maximum ultimate recovery from the petroleum reserves of the said states, and to recommend measures for the maximum ultimate recovery of oil and gas."[72] The hope was that these policies would be able to implement something approaching a national "conservation" policy and, not incidentally, stabilize the price of oil at a level at which the industry could survive.[73]

Still, the Compact required federal permission before it could be established. It could easily be interpreted as an intrusion on the federal government's exclusive power to regulate interstate commerce. Nervousness within the industry at the threat of federal regulation helped to unite the oil business in support of the interstate approach. Reacting to sustained pressure in favor of the Compact, Congress authorized its establishment on August 27, 1935, in a bill swiftly signed by President Roosevelt. The IOCC was born.[74]

DeGolyer's deep involvement with the IOCC began in 1938. In April of that year, he appeared at a meeting of the IOCC in Wichita, Kansas, to offer his thoughts on production controls and government regulation. Like many in the industry, DeGolyer's experience with the NRA and the subsequent posturing by Harold Ickes for federal oversight of the oil business had soured his views on federal regulation. He therefore raised the threat of federal control to encourage more robust action on the part of the IOCC, remarking, "I don't believe that the threat [of federal control] is ever over and gone unless the oil industry and the governing states themselves can make the business work."[75]

DeGolyer encouraged the Commission to move to coordinate state oil production, admitting that it was a "complicated problem," but stressed the necessity of addressing the matter. This was something of an understatement, for the question of production quotas would affect the profits of myriad companies—large and small. It would also involve allocating production among the states that had joined the compact, a delicate task to say the least.

To avoid the stigma of merely choosing one interest over another, the Commission would need a scientific rationale for allocation. What the Commission needed, above all, was the compilation of information that could provide the basis for such a judgment.[76] This would require the expertise of earth scientists like DeGolyer.

The question of allocation among the states was not the only issue before the Commission that required such an expert. Aware that the public would not necessarily view attempts to raise oil prices with pleasure, the industry would need to offer justification for its efforts in terms of conservation. A more rational, sustainable, and limited level of production would slow the exhaustion of the nation's oil reserves, as well as prop up the price of crude. But such a promise could only be credible coming from a knowledgeable petroleum engineer.

Recognizing the value of DeGolyer's expertise on this point, the IOCC appointed him to a committee to consider these issues along with his old associate Joseph Pogue and economist Alexander Sachs. By the summer of 1939, the three were ready to offer their thoughts on the matter.

Gathering in Santa Fe, New Mexico, on July 19, the Commission opened its meeting with an invocation by Archbishop Rudolph Aloysius Gerken that praised the noble purpose of the IOCC.[77] After dispensing with the blessing, the Commission proceeded to consider the question of petroleum production and conservation. Time soon came for DeGolyer to offer the findings of the Committee.

Prompted by his friend Ernest O. Thompson, DeGolyer read the brief report, which argued for production limits that would ensure the maximum recovery of oil from the ground. He assured the Commission,

"[This] principle involves engineering efficiency and has to do with the rate at which each pool is drawn upon . . . The determination of such a standard for each oil reservoir and the establishment of rules for its application will in the aggregate insure [sic] effective and practical conservation."[78] In some ways, this was little more than a reminder of the Compact's aim to promote maximum ultimate recovery from the oilfields. But the report also reiterated the need for "adequate production standards, based on engineering criteria."[79] This was a task that would require a scientific mind, and not surprisingly, the IOCC would give the job to DeGolyer.

One year after the Santa Fe meeting, the Commission met again and created an Engineering Committee, charged "to inquire into the principles and practices of conservation in the production of oil and gas."[80] Placed in charge, DeGolyer immediately called for a meeting on January 3, 1941, and wrote to oil company executives and government officials, inviting them to attend and offer opinions on the question of reservoir engineering.[81]

In the meantime, DeGolyer met with the committee in smaller sessions and drafted a progress report on the engineering issue. The Engineering Committee might have been mistaken for a simple, fact-finding body, an informational clearinghouse within the IOCC. But in light of the fact that the Commission would shape conservation regulations for the major oil-producing states, the questions that DeGolyer addressed would effectively reverberate as national policy, with significant economic, environmental, and even geopolitical consequences.

The meeting of the Engineering Committee on January 3, 1941, proved to be a well-attended success. DeGolyer took the opportunity to remind the gathered oilmen that the issue of conservation was one that affected the well-being of the country as a whole: "[C]onservation is a national affair. It isn't entirely industrial, the question of conservation isn't. The objective must be the greatest amount of assured supply of reasonably priced oil for the longest time."[82] The interests of a relatively small number of businessmen must not trump the interests of the people of the United States. Moreover, DeGolyer believed that the enforcement of "strict engineering principles" in the oilfields was the only way to serve the greater good.[83]

The meeting revealed how DeGolyer's perspective on regulation had changed over the years. In 1925, he had written to the Federal Oil Conservation Board in opposition to Henry Doherty's advocacy of forced unitization. Now DeGolyer argued that Doherty was a visionary.[84] To be sure, he had not made this journey alone. There were more and more oilmen that looked to conservation measures as a solution to the price problem that troubled the industry. And Doherty had already undergone something of a transformation from "industry pariah to industry visionary."[85]

But for all his emphasis on the public interest, DeGolyer remained a businessman, and his approach to regulation demonstrated an awareness of the importance of market forces. Working together with the other members of the Engineering Committee, he submitted reports to the IOCC that acknowledged both the economic needs of the industry and the importance of conservation—needs that were happily in agreement from the committee's perspective.

Consider the approach taken by the committee regarding well spacing. Since the birth of the petroleum industry, the rapid development of newly discovered oilfields had been a target of criticism. Forests of derricks were a frequent feature of oil booms that embodied the folly of unregulated development for industry detractors. Extensive drilling often led to greater supply of oil than the market could bear, accompanied by an inevitable drop in prices. In the eyes of many, overdrilling was an absurdity, and during the early twentieth century, calls for regulation of well spacing gathered support. One justification offered for well-spacing rules was that the ultimate recovery of oil was greater when there were fewer wells drilled—it was good conservation practice. During the 1930s, it also became a convenient argument for an industry plagued by overproduction. But did well spacing make sense from a geological point of view?

In a report offered in April 1941, DeGolyer's committee acknowledged the economic sense of well-spacing measures even as it called into question the scientific rationale. The committee noted that though many oil wells, producing at a slow rate, would not reduce the amount of recoverable oil, operators' desire to make a profit would make it difficult to keep production at a level consistent with conservation. Thus, although oil might not be physically wasted in terms of the amount of oil recovered, it would be economically wasted because it would be produced at a level far beyond market demand.[86]

This pragmatic approach characterized DeGolyer's evolving attitude toward regulation. Although he strived to implement more rational policies that would serve the needs of the nation, he was unwilling to interfere in a way that severely compromised property rights. Thus, his committee's endorsement of unit operation was limited to encouraging "regulatory bodies to do everything in their power to promote *voluntary* unit operation."[87] Despite his public praise of Henry Doherty, DeGolyer's committee still chafed at coerced unitization of oilfields. That would have set up the state as arbiter of property rights that oilmen had long viewed as settled and secure. Put simply, it still went too far for DeGolyer.

Whatever the limits of DeGolyer's support for regulation, he was developing a reputation as an advocate of conservation measures. His success as a businessman and his competence as a geologist won him respect both inside and outside the industry, and his work with the NRA and the IOCC had given him credentials as a man who had an eye to the public interest as well.

Perhaps for this reason, DeGolyer was among a number of oil industry leaders contacted by Harold Ickes to attend an oil parley in 1941.[88] A telegram from Ickes requested his presence at a meeting on June 19, to "discuss the development of plans to best accommodate our petroleum resources to the military and civilian needs of the nation."[89] Surely DeGolyer must have winced just a little, and maybe Ickes did too. After all, DeGolyer and Ickes had been on opposing sides in the battle over price fixing under the Oil Code. DeGolyer was also a lifelong Republican who had recently made news in Texas as the largest donor in the presidential campaign for Wendell Willkie.[90] If DeGolyer's candidate had triumphed, Ickes would have been looking for a job. Moreover, how could a self-professed friend of Ernest O. Thompson, Ickes's determined antagonist, now cooperate with the feisty secretary of the interior and petroleum coordinator?

True, Ickes's position had changed considerably since he contemplated possible elevation as oil czar in 1933. Now Ickes, who wore multiple hats within the Roosevelt administration, wrote DeGolyer in his newly bestowed capacity as petroleum coordinator for national defense. The creation of the Office of the Petroleum Coordinator reflected the growing concerns of many in the Roosevelt administration about the international situation. The nation's continuing abstention from an increasingly widespread and devastating world war seemed less likely with each passing day, and the government turned greater attention to planning for possible involvement.

Although Roosevelt seemed generally content to rely on the Interstate Oil Compact and the Connally Hot Oil Act to stabilize the petroleum industry, planners within the administration wanted more power. Echoing attitudes voiced by planners of the United States war effort in World War I, advocates of federal direction made the case that only the federal government could effectively coordinate the industry in wartime. Secretary Ickes, unsurprisingly, was among those who held this position. But despite storm clouds looming abroad, Roosevelt was reluctant to upset the industry too much.[91]

Instead, the president chose to confer advisory powers on Ickes on May 28, 1941, naming him Petroleum Coordinator for National Defense. The powers of the new agency were vague, but Ickes planned to make an inventory of available oil reserves, facilitate pooling of resources, organize advisory committees of industry representatives, and coordinate federal petroleum policies. Significantly, the new office did not include powers to compel the oil industry in its preparation for possible war. Ickes needed the cooperation of oilmen to effect policy.[92]

This then, was the context of Ickes's telegram to DeGolyer. Despite possible reservations, DeGolyer wired back to confirm his plans to attend the conference.[93] The meeting apparently went well, because within two weeks DeGolyer had moved to Washington in anticipation of his appointment as the Director of Conservation for the Office of the Petroleum Coordinator (OPC).[94] On August 1, 1941, he formally took office.[95]

As head of the Conservation Division, DeGolyer faced a task in some ways analogous to his work on behalf of the IOCC. The Division aimed "[t]o promote cooperation with the States and the industry in the conservation of oil and gas. To study existing standards of production practice, management, and control, and to promote wider acceptance of best practices; to conduct research for further improvement of production practices."[96] This was all very good, but what precisely did "conservation of oil" mean with war looming? In certain contexts, conservation might mean preserving oil reserves. But preserving oil in the ground would be counterproductive if petroleum were desperately needed by the military.

Like the bureaucracy that he served, DeGolyer was not entirely consistent on the matter. More often than not, DeGolyer seemed to understand conservation as wise use of the nation's resources rather than their preservation in place. After Pearl Harbor, it was a position consistent with wartime mobilization. Indeed, much of DeGolyer's work focused on how to go about discovering new national reserves to exploit, rather than how to keep such resources safe for the future.[97] Nonetheless, conservation in varied forms remained the major concern of his work for the government. And depending on the circumstances, his understanding of conservation might take the economic interest of oilmen into account; it might be viewed purely from an engineering perspective of avoiding physical waste of petroleum in production; or it might not mean conservation of oil at all, but of some other material needed by the military, such as steel.

Working on behalf of the IOCC in 1941, DeGolyer had included market analysis in his determination of good conservation practices. Prorationing could be justified by this sort of conservation because it limited oil production to a level where it did not grossly exceed demand and depress prices to a level unsustainable for the industry. It was conservation in this sense that oilmen who supported state regulation wanted.[98]

The management of the petroleum industry in the context of preparations for war meant something different of course. In this context, DeGolyer adopted a different definition for the word. On September 12, 1941, DeGolyer submitted a memorandum to Deputy Petroleum Coordinator Ralph Davies that attempted to define the work of the division. DeGolyer began by discussing the meaning of the term *conservation*. He noted that many industrialists and state regulatory bodies understood the word to mean a balance of supply and demand. This was very close to the sense in which DeGolyer had spoken of conservation before the IOCC just five months earlier. But speaking of conservation in the context of the war effort, DeGolyer chose to embrace a different meaning, writing, "To most engineers and geologists the term is used as meaning the elimination of waste in the production of oil and gas. It is in this sense that I propose to use it."[99] Rather than addressing the financial situation of the industry, the Conservation Division would seek to eliminate waste of petroleum resources and thus make more available in the event of war.

DeGolyer's address to the Interstate Oil Compact Commission meeting on October 16, 1941, was a good indication of his new priorities as a public servant. Where he had sat at previous meetings as a geologist and an oilman, he now spoke to the assembled crowd as a representative of the federal government. Nevertheless, DeGolyer began by disavowing any change of heart in addressing the industry. Rather, he claimed that the aim of his previous work for the IOCC and that of his current job as director of conservation were both to advance the same principles of conservation endorsed by the Interstate Oil Compact.[100]

But the policies DeGolyer advocated at the Fort Worth meeting did have a different emphasis compared to the positions taken in his earlier reports. His earlier work with the IOCC had aimed at codifying general aspects of "good conservation practice, of good engineering practice, and of good production practice."[101] Now, he advocated nothing short of specifically tailored regulation of each oilfield, with rules based on the goal of maximum conservation for each unique reservoir. He concluded, "I should like to urge upon the state regulatory bodies . . . the desirability and necessity of studying each independent pool as an engineering problem from the standpoint of trying to get the most oil out of it."[102]

The vision that DeGolyer offered was that of rational, scientific management of the nation's oilfields through state regulation. It was an approach to conservation that he believed would preserve the property rights that were the foundation of the free market economy, even as it would ensure better stewardship of natural resources. It was a position that was appropriate for a public servant but was also convenient for a man whose business interests included managing DeGolyer and MacNaughton, a firm devoted to petroleum engineering.

One area that DeGolyer's office worked to shape through regulation was the management of oilfield development. Overdrilling had long been a concern voiced by conservationist critics of the oil industry. Now, with war looming, overdrilling threatened to waste materials that defense industries desperately needed—especially steel. But DeGolyer understood that the government would be unwise to put an end to all drilling, because the discovery of new fields was imperative. The nation's military would need oil just as much as it needed steel.[103]

Therefore, in addressing the question of development, DeGolyer advocated a delicate balance between helter-skelter drilling and overcautious inaction. The solution he embraced was well spacing on the "widest feasible" patterns in proven fields to conserve construction materials. He reasoned that "wildcat drilling"—that is, drilling in areas not part of established, recognized oilfields—"must continue at an unabated rate but we can afford to expend material for development drilling only in exchange for substantial additions to our reserves." This became official policy with the issuance of Order M-68 on December 23, 1941, which made 40-acre spacing for oil wells and 640-acre spacing for gas wells mandatory. The order was later amended to require unitization around new oil wells. Interestingly, the blanket requirements of M-68 ran counter to the spirit of his address to the IOCC just a few months earlier, when he had called for specifically tailored regulation of individual oilfields.[104]

In fact, the one-size-fits-all approach taken by M-68 did not serve the nation well in terms of either wise use of steel or direction of oilfield development.[105] DeGolyer realized that M-68 fell short of his goals in the Conservation Division, remarking:

> While I regard M-68 as an able attempt to restrict the use of oil well supplies, it is by no means perfect in satisfying our requirements. Under it equal amounts of steel may be expended in one area to produce 5,000 to 10,000 barrels per acre and in another area to produce 30,000 to 50,000 barrels per acre. Under it, hundreds of wells will be drilled in an area where existing wells are able to produce more than pipeline capacity.[106]

In other words, even setting aside the controversial decision to conserve steel at the expense of increased petroleum production, M-68 did not conserve steel efficiently. Some steel was prioritized for well drilling that might only yield limited production, whereas it was barred from well drilling that might be well worth the investment. Nor was the uniform approach of M-68 the only regulatory obstacle to a rational management of the petroleum industry in wartime.

Other federal agencies presented even greater obstacles to DeGolyer's plans for oilfield exploration. Among the most problematic was the Office of Price Administration (OPA), which imposed price controls on oil for the benefit of consumers. By keeping the price of oil low, the OPA ensured that there would be little incentive for exploratory drilling, even if oil companies were able to obtain steel for their wells. DeGolyer pushed for an increase in the price ceiling on oil, a position that had the unlikely support of both Harold Ickes and TRC chairman Ernest O. Thompson. No matter, the OPA was for the most part intransigent, and for all Ickes influence in the Roosevelt administration, he was not in a position to dictate policy to another agency.[107]

As the struggle over oil prices suggests, even with Ickes support, DeGolyer had at best limited powers to implement any plan that he might develop. In no case was this more apparent than the vast East

Texas oilfield, whose overproduction had done much to undermine stability within the industry during the early 1930s.

DeGolyer was aware of the importance of the field to national security. Geologists estimated that the East Texas field held petroleum reserves figuring in billions of barrels of oil. They also reckoned that one-eighth to one-sixth of the nation's proved reserves lay in this subterranean reservoir. For this reason, conditions in the East Texas field were of special concern to the men working under Ickes. For DeGolyer, conservation of oil in this mammoth reservoir became a major focus of his government service.[108]

Shortly after accepting his position with the OPC, DeGolyer turned his attention to the East Texas field. On August 24, 1941, he submitted a memorandum to Ralph Davies, outlining a situation that he saw as increasingly worrisome. At the root of the problem was pressure. The production of oil in the field was sapping underground pressure at an alarming rate. As a petroleum geologist, DeGolyer understood the grave threat that this presented.[109]

Oilfield conservation was not simply a matter of avoiding waste after the oil reached the surface. It involved understanding the fluid mechanics that produced the oil in the first place. Some force had to be able to push or pull oil from the ground, or it was just as useless to industry as if burned at the wellhead. In all productive oilfields, some sort of force made it possible to extract oil. In some cases, high subterranean pressure could push crude to the surface without assistance. In other cases, it was necessary to pump it up. But even with the aid of pump jacks, certain minimum pressure was necessary to make production economical.

A number of forces at work below the earth could provide this much-needed pressure. Natural gas, pushing down on crude oil from a higher level could help propel it up through a well. Gas might also exist in solution with petroleum and provide necessary lift, much as carbonation in a soda can force liquid out of an agitated bottle. Finally, subterranean water, pressing from below or laterally against the crude oil, could provide the force that would bring oil to the surface—and this was the case in the East Texas field.[110]

That pressure was falling precipitously in 1941, and petroleum engineers had a good idea why this was the case. Throughout the field, oil wells were producing water mixed together with the crude oil. This was a nuisance for many operators but few made any effort to return the water to the reservoir. The result was that pressure continued to fall, and therefore companies would ultimately extract less oil from the field—that is, unless something were done about it.[111]

There was little that oilmen could do to stop the production of water with the oil. Yet once it had made its way to the surface, it was possible to separate the crude from the unwanted water and reinject the water into the reservoir. This involved a complicated process that had not quite been perfected yet. But if properly implemented, reinjection would have the effect of maintaining pressure within the oilfield, thus preventing "underground waste" and ensuring greater ultimate recovery of petroleum. And this is precisely what DeGolyer advocated.[112]

DeGolyer was not alone in his concern regarding the East Texas field. In fact, the Texas Railroad Commission was already considering the matter. The TRC and a number of oilmen agreed that water injection was essential. In order to implement the plan, DeGolyer and these state and local interests supported the formation of the East Texas Salt Water Disposal Company. The name was somewhat misleading. The Company in question would be responsible for "disposing" of water produced by oil wells by reinjecting it into the reservoir.[113]

Despite the national importance of the East Texas field, the OPC had only limited power to implement the plan. DeGolyer followed the matter closely, conferring with prominent oilmen and stressing the urgency of conservation. The plan went forward, but there was resistance, and some major companies refused to participate. Their concern was that injecting water into the oilfield might open them up to litigation from other operators who could claim that injection damaged their oil production. Another issue was the fact that some marginal wells might need to be taken out of production for use as injection wells. DeGolyer himself conceded that for certain marginal wells, this might indeed be the case.[114]

In a memo to Ralph Davies, the most that DeGolyer could advocate was efforts to foster voluntary cooperation.[115] He did suggest that a conservation order from the Office of Production Management, another federal agency, might be issued requiring companies to reinject their water through the newly formed company. Yet even this measure was dependent upon voluntary cooperation of the corporate participants in creating a "disposal company."[116]

In the event, cooperation was forthcoming. On December 7, 1941, the Japanese attacked Pearl Harbor, rousing the nation from a false sense of security and confronting the public with the undeniable fact that war had arrived. The war did not suspend the laws of economics, but it did provide DeGolyer with some additional leverage in encouraging compliance. Speaking to East Texas producers after the attack, DeGolyer warned, "Unless the operators themselves take steps to conserve the field's oil reservoir, the Federal Government will."[117] Whether motivated by patriotism or fear, they took this message to heart. Closing ranks, producers formed the disposal company, and DeGolyer used the resources of the OPC to secure the necessary permits and equipment authorization for the project to go forward.[118]

Although reinjection was implemented in East Texas, the power that the OPC could exercise remained limited, and this made DeGolyer's connections and respect within the oil industry all the more important to his success as a technocrat. Personal solicitation of support for administration policy was essential and required DeGolyer to spend much of his time away from Washington. These trips were frequent enough that within a few months of his appointment, DeGolyer was suggesting that the Conservation Division move its office to Dallas. Despite the convenience that such a move would afford, DeGolyer was required to continue his shuttle diplomacy with the oilfields as long as he served within the agency.[119]

As director of conservation, DeGolyer was committed to wise use of petroleum, but in wartime that meant mobilizing the nation's reserves as well as conserving them. In fact, the apparent conflict between these goals could be troubling. DeGolyer's concerns regarding mobilization focused largely on his assessment of the nation's petroleum reserves.

Since his tax work on behalf of the Treasury Department at the end of the First World War, DeGolyer had dabbled in the uncertain art of reserve estimation—a difficult task at best, and one that had occasionally driven him to despair of genuinely accurate figures. Within a month of starting his tenure with the OPC, DeGolyer was already wrestling with reserve estimations. It was a matter of paramount importance, for how could the government plan if it did not have a sense of how much oil was available for the war effort? But perusing the figures that were available to his office, DeGolyer concluded that even the method of collecting statistics could be misleading. This was because constant revision of figures by the industry could lead to the false conclusion that new oil reserves were being discovered, when, in fact, it only reflected revised estimations of the same fields' productivity.[120]

By 1942, DeGolyer believed that the OPC could no longer rely on informal numbers from the industry, but should conduct its own investigation of national reserves. Writing to Davies, DeGolyer requested the formation of subcommittees to study the question. These subcommittees would compile information on oilfields and would estimate reserves for Texas and several other southern states as a "trial flight." The plan was ultimately to expand the fact gathering to the nation as a whole.

In a memorandum to Ralph Davies, DeGolyer stressed the importance of the work to the agency.[121] He warned, "Some of our most important conclusions, such as number of wells necessary to drill in 1942 and our sustained capacity to produce, rest upon the pretty general evidence and, in my opinion, if attacked would be hard to defend."[122] The obvious remedy was to gather data to back up federal policy. DeGolyer reasoned, "We can get the data and make the necessary studies for sounder and more supportable conclusions than those yet put forward."[123] Precise figures were necessary in order to formulate and justify federal policy. This was particularly true for the OPC, which, hobbled by limited powers and molested by a host of competing bureaucracies, needed to lean heavily upon the "scientific" authority of its recommendations.

However, compiling this data proved to be more difficult than anticipated. For one, a bureaucratic squabble with the Production Division, whose staffers believed that the task was their prerogative, hampered DeGolyer's effort to obtain information. There was also resistance from the industry, where company executives believed that such information was confidential—a claim that DeGolyer dismissed as "fantastic."[124] Despite these objections, the data gathering went forward, with the support of Deputy Coordinator Davies.[125]

DeGolyer's tenure with the Conservation Division had proved him an aggressive and effective administrator. His technical expertise and his cordial relationship with many in the industry made him well suited to promote the policies of the OPC. Considering his record on the job, DeGolyer's promotion to assistant deputy petroleum coordinator was not altogether surprising.

In fact, DeGolyer's promotion was an important part of an effort to heal a new rift that had developed between the OPC and the most

Harold L. Ickes (right) and Ralph K. Davies (left), circa 1942. Serving as petroleum administrator and deputy petroleum administrator, respectively, Ickes and Davies were DeGolyer's immediate superiors in the Petroleum Administration for War. (Ralph K. Davies Papers. Copyright Unknown, Courtesy of Harry S. Truman Library and Museum.)

important of the state regulatory bodies, the Texas Railroad Commission. Beginning in May 1942, the TRC had exceeded production recommendations made by the OPC by more than 100,000 barrels. As the conflict festered into June, Ickes dispatched DeGolyer to negotiate with Chairman Thompson. After Thompson declared the conference to be "satisfactory," it appeared that the crisis was over.[126]

Part of resolving the crisis was DeGolyer's promotion to the new office. The same day that he met with Thompson, Ickes announced DeGolyer's appointment as assistant deputy petroleum coordinator.[127] Thompson was clearly happy about the decision, explaining:

> Mr. DeGolyer's appointment speaks well for the future . . . He has informed me that should discrepancies between the OPC's and the commission's needed production figures develop, he will try to come

Ernest O. Thompson, as a leading figure on the Texas Railroad Commission, promoted state prorationing of oil wells while opposing efforts by Harold Ickes and others to create a federal regulatory regime for the oil industry. Somehow DeGolyer managed to work well with both Thompson and Ickes. (Everette Lee DeGolyer Collection. Courtesy of DeGolyer Library, Southern Methodist University.)

to Austin personally and confer with us to iron them out. This makes for mutual understanding since we don't want to be at variance with the OPC nor produce more or less than is marketable.[128]

Summarizing the state of affairs, the *Dallas Morning News* headline declared "Dove of Peace about to Light on Rail Board."[129]

The new office brought added responsibilities for DeGolyer. It involved coordinating the activities of all of the divisions, as well as representing the OPC in its dealings with other federal agencies. Assistant deputy coordinator was a "top management" position within the OPC that involved shaping national objectives, policies, and programs.[130] DeGolyer's new position promised to be demanding, and he may have not been entirely facetious when he referred to his promotion as a "matter for condolence."[131]

All of DeGolyer's efforts on behalf of the OPC took place under the limited powers granted to the agency by President Roosevelt in May 1941, before the attack on Pearl Harbor. Later, as the nation mobilized for war, Harold Ickes pressed the president for greater authority over the petroleum industry. The result was an executive order issued on December 2, 1942, that rechristened the Office of the Petroleum Coordinator as the Petroleum Administration for War (PAW). Ickes took up his new role as petroleum administrator and enjoyed a slight expansion of his purview. He was now empowered to set rules regarding production, transportation, and distribution of oil. Additionally, the order charged PAW with shaping policies aimed at increasing production through conservation, drilling, and consumption control. But as with the OPC, PAW did not have sole discretion over petroleum policy. The president assigned control over the use of scarce materials used by the industry to the War Production Board (WPB). Further, and to the irritation of Ickes, the Office of Price Administration (OPA) would direct price regulation. This meant that PAW still had to solicit support from these agencies in order to implement its own policies.[132]

So, despite organizational changes, some of the limitations and bureaucratic fragmentation that had troubled the OPC continued to challenge the men who worked in PAW. Still, the tendency over time was a gradual expansion of powers that gave officials like DeGolyer more leeway in directing the industry. Further, as the authority of the office grew, DeGolyer grew more confident and bolder in this advocacy of conservation plans.

One obvious case in point was the question of mandatory unit operation. As early as October 1942, DeGolyer had become convinced that government action was necessary to promote rational unit management of the oilfields. In his words, "[Unit operation] will be brought about only by governmental action . . . On the other hand, a widespread requirement for unitization at the present time would result in pandemonium. The industry hasn't got enough man power, engineers and lawyers to work it out."[133] DeGolyer concluded that the best method to implement unit operation was to give the petroleum coordinator the power to order it "where it is in the public interest."[134]

The conservation record in many states troubled DeGolyer. This was especially the case in states that had not joined the Interstate Oil Compact, such as California. It was also true of some states that had joined the Compact but had failed to live up to their pledge to enact conservation legislation, such as Illinois.[135] As the war dragged on, federal imposition of unit operation of oilfields became plausible policy to address these shortcomings.

The broader powers granted to PAW gave its officials greater leverage in promoting conservation. In December 1942, DeGolyer found himself in agreement with Deputy Administrator Davies in asserting that if voluntary unit operation was not forthcoming, it was appropriate to "force the issue."[136] Despite this surprisingly aggressive stance, he seems to have preferred to use the threat of forced unitization as a tool to promote voluntary action. In another communication to Davies, DeGolyer remarked, "I am hopeful that the existence of the Order [authorizing forced unit operation] will be effective in most cases and that we will not have to use it, but we will not hesitate to use it when necessary."[137]

DeGolyer's reluctant embrace of coercion, or at least the threat of coercion, completed his apparent metamorphosis from industry representative to technocrat. To be sure, DeGolyer remained a businessman who understood the dynamism that entrepreneurial initiative brought to the oil industry. Nor did he approach the radicalism of, say, Harold Ickes, who hoped for legislation that would declare the petroleum industry a public utility. On the other hand, he had come to embrace the view that the long-term interests of the nation and those of the oil industry did not always match. In light of this discrepancy of interests, DeGolyer argued that the good of the nation must take priority over private property concerns, at least during wartime.

Although he had proved himself as a technocrat, DeGolyer was also growing weary of his work at PAW. He had proven to be a highly effective public servant, but he was anxious to return to private affairs. Ickes would be infuriated by this desire to leave, commenting that if all Americans acted this way, "Hitler would soon have us under his heel."[138] On the other hand, DeGolyer may well have felt that he could better serve the country from the private sector than as a government planner. In late 1944, he would enthusiastically embrace economist Friedrich von Hayek's treatise opposing central planning, *The Road to Serfdom,* and he distributed copies to friends as Christmas gifts.[139] Hayek's entire argument ran contrary to DeGolyer's wartime service and suggests an ambivalence on DeGolyer's part about his work directing the industry's war effort. Whatever the case, he was ready to leave PAW by early 1943.

In March 1943, he submitted his resignation to Deputy Administrator Davies. Referring to pressing private business interests, DeGolyer explained, "I regret that this action is necessary but I find that my own oil affairs, which I have chosen to neglect during my stay in Washington, are pressing for attention, which only I can give and the giving of which, in my opinion, would not be compatible with government service."[140]

However, he was not to escape so easily. When Ickes received DeGolyer's letter of resignation, he issued this calculated response: "While I feel justified in refusing to accept your resignation, you, of course, can leave, if that is what you want to do, even though in my judgment, this entails a serious loss to the Nation at the most critical period in its history." It was enough to make DeGolyer hesitate.[141]

Ickes's insistent letter kept DeGolyer at his post with PAW, at least for a while. Nevertheless, DeGolyer proved that he could be just as stubborn as the petroleum administrator could. In July, he resubmitted his resignation, expressing his irritation with Ickes's attitude, writing, "Since I first [attempted to resign], men have continued to leave PAW to meet the requirements of their own businesses . . . All of them, so far as I know, have had their resignations accepted and have carried with them the good wishes of yourself."[142] DeGolyer felt that Ickes had unfairly castigated him, reasoning, "I came here voluntarily and have stayed two years at my own expense and to the neglect of my own affairs. Since I have no reasonable choice and must leave, I feel that if my services have been worthwhile, I am entitled to equal treatment."[143]

Despite these plans, DeGolyer's government service was far from over. His most controversial and arguably his most important work for the nation was still to come. Ironically, it would also come at the behest of Harold Ickes, the man with whom he had expressed no little frustration in the summer of 1943.

By that time, DeGolyer's record of government service was well established. Over the course of a quarter century, his involvement in public affairs had deepened, demanding greater and greater attention. It had also changed qualitatively. Whereas the government's initial requests for assistance during the First World War had only incidentally related to his work as a geologist, the need for technical knowledge of the oil industry meant that DeGolyer's expertise was increasingly valuable to the nation.

However, it was his "dual citizenship" as both scientist and business-man that made DeGolyer invaluable to government planners. As the industry embraced "conservation" in the 1930s as the path to freedom from overproduction, DeGolyer's skill as a petroleum geologist and acumen as an entrepreneur made him an ideal policy advisor. It was a role that he performed well at both the federal level, on behalf of the National Recovery Administration; and at the state level, on behalf of the Interstate Oil Compact Commission. When the challenges of the Second World War required national coordination of the petroleum in-dustry, DeGolyer already possessed the experience, the technical knowl-edge, and the professional acquaintances necessary to achieve success.

The shifting needs of the nation and the industry had opened oppor-tunities for DeGolyer in the public arena, but those challenges had also had an impact on his perspective regarding the government. Although DeGolyer had begun his public career as a skeptic of government plan-ning, he had become a vocal, if moderate, supporter of state and fed-eral regulation by 1942. This shift in perspective would continue as he turned his attention to ever broader questions of national policy.

The nature of DeGolyer's public service underwent a gradual trans-formation beginning in the fall of 1942. Until his resignation from PAW, his focus had remained upon the coordination of the domestic oil in-dustry. The goals of this work were immediate and clear—the mobiliza-tion of petroleum resources for the war effort—and to the extent that it was compatible with mobilization, the conservation of those resources. The geographical dimensions of the task were also fairly clear. Gener-ally, DeGolyer focused upon the domestic oil industry of the United States.

But gradually, issues that called for a broader perspective drew DeGolyer's attention. Geographically, the scope of his work widened after his superiors tapped him to serve as an expert in evaluating the petroleum industry in other nations. Then, as the war progressed and victory seemed inevitable, the government increasingly turned to DeGolyer as a man who not only possessed encyclopedic knowledge about the oil business but who also possessed a talent for strategic thought. The men who had directed and planned the war also hoped to plan the peace. The short-term goals of wartime mobilization and conservation had been obvious to most. The objectives of national pe-troleum policy in the postwar world were not so clear.

One thing was certain: oil had played a major role in World War II and would likely play a major role in the event of another war. The domestic oil industry was successful at providing the Allies with abundant petroleum during the current conflict. But would the nation be able to call on adequate domestic reserves in the future? Among others, Harold Ickes was concerned that the answer might be no. Convinced that the nation must do more to develop foreign reserves, he began to lay the groundwork for a postwar policy that envisioned the government taking an active hand in oilfields beyond the bounds of the United States. The vehicle for this policy would be a government operated entity known as the Petroleum Reserves Corporation (PRC). The aim of this quasi-governmental corporation would be the acquisition and development of foreign reserves, with an eye toward supplying the American armed forces. And the PRC, as conceived, already had a particular location in mind—the remote and largely undeveloped state of Saudi Arabia. Ickes wrote President Roosevelt about the proposed project in early June 1943. By the end of the month, the PRC was a reality.[144]

Although DeGolyer finally made good on his plans to resign from his position as assistant deputy petroleum administrator for war, Ickes succeeded in retaining his services for the PRC. The press announced DeGolyer would serve as a consultant to the new entity, whose purpose was still unknown to the public.[145] If the title "consultant" did not sound that prestigious, the perception of the industry was different. According to *The Oil and Gas Journal,* DeGolyer would serve as the "active head" of the Petroleum Reserves Corporation.[146] The claim was an overstatement, but the fact that the journal of record in the oil industry believed this is a testament to DeGolyer's prestige. And although he would not direct the PRC, his involvement with the organization would be the beginning of DeGolyer's greatest adventure since his work as a young man in Mexico. It was also an important milestone in DeGolyer's transformation from a domestic policy coordinator to an international policy maker, from a technocrat to a geopolitician.[147]

# 8 | Geopolitician

*I hold that the production of every single barrel of exportable oil, wherever*
*it may be in the World, is a matter of definite concern to us as Americans.*
—Everette Lee DeGolyer in a confidential address given to the Brookings
Institution, April 19, 1943[1]

April 1943 was a busy month, even for Everette Lee DeGolyer.
Recently promoted to Assistant Deputy Petroleum Administrator for
War, his responsibilities were demanding to say the least. Congressmen, agency officials, private oilmen, and even the Canadian government clamored for his attention.[2] In addition to assisting his superiors
and managing his subordinates, DeGolyer had to negotiate policy with
competing agencies that shared jurisdiction with the Petroleum Administration for War over the nation's oil industry. He recorded the
variety of projects tackled by his office in weekly reports sent to Deputy
Petroleum Administrator Davies. One of these activity catalogs, Report
No. 39, to be precise, noted an event of some interest. The laconic entry
reads, "Delivered statement at confidential conference on energy mineral power potentials at Brookings Institution."[3]

The Brookings Institution was a nonprofit, nonpartisan organization
whose origins were rooted in the government efficiency movement of
the Progressive Era. It was an organization that aspired to influence
public policy through social science and economic analysis. Although
today known for its liberal leanings, during the 1940s the Brookings
Institution was generally opposed to government intervention in the
economy and national planning. Among others, it had earned the ire
of DeGolyer's old supervisor at the NRA, General Hugh Johnson, who
described it as "one of the most sanctimonious and pontifical rack-
ets in the country."[4] It was, in many ways, an organization with which
DeGolyer the businessman might have felt at ease. DeGolyer the technocrat might have feared a less receptive audience. Happily for him, his
subject had less to do with domestic regulation of industry and more to
do with foreign policy. At the heart of his analysis was the relationship
of petroleum to national security.[5]

The address to the Institution demonstrated the same technical mastery of fact that had earned DeGolyer respect as both businessman and bureaucrat. But it did something more: DeGolyer used the address to voice his own opinions about national security and its relationship to oil. Contemplating victory in the struggle against the Axis nations, he raised concerns about the "next war." In particular, DeGolyer expressed doubt that the United States would be able to continue producing sufficient crude oil to fuel a future global conflict. He also offered his own vision of a domestic petroleum plan for the postwar era. Most importantly, he urged the adoption of an aggressive foreign policy aimed at securing sources of oil abroad.

DeGolyer expressed his position with startling directness, which, as a government official, he could only have voiced with assurance of confidentiality. Describing his viewpoint as "extremely nationalistic," he asserted, "I hold that the production of every single barrel of exportable oil, wherever it may be in the World, is a matter of definite concern to us as Americans."[6] Continuing, he called for the nation to "expand our economic control of the foreign oil industry" through whatever possible means.[7] Above all, he stressed that action was imperative, firmly asserting, "What we need is a strong and determined government policy now."[8]

DeGolyer foresaw objections to his approach, not the least of which was that other nations might view this policy as hypocritical for a country that aspired to liberate Europe and the Far East from German and Japanese imperialism. So he posed the question to the audience: "Is this viewpoint too selfish?" DeGolyer's response: "I think not." Supporting his conclusion, he reasoned that underdeveloped nations that possessed oil, such as Iran, Iraq, Kuwait, Saudi Arabia, Venezuela, and—significantly for DeGolyer—Mexico, would never have exploited their own resources without American and British investment. More importantly, if benign Anglo-American oilmen had not secured oil concessions there, "nationals of governments unfriendly to us" certainly would have. He stressed, "No friendship of nations nor supposed community of interest would have prevented such an occurrence." So the United States government had no choice; involvement in foreign oil was imperative.[9]

DeGolyer's address to the Brookings Institution was breathtaking in its ambition and its frankness. Of course, in some ways it represented a viewpoint that was not so new. As guns blazed in World War I, concern about declining domestic reserves had led the future director of the Oil

Division in United States Fuel Administration to the same conclusions. That the government of the United States would support the aspirations of American businessmen abroad was certainly not a departure from precedent, nor was the assertion of the importance of oil. What was rather remarkable was the scope of DeGolyer's nationalistic aspirations. The question of oil was not a merely a matter of economics, nor even a question of national defense. At stake was nothing less than global domination. He concluded, "[M]ay I say that my viewpoint is that control of oil is the key to world power for the future as far as we can see it." From his view, the United States was as likely as any other nation to use that power "unselfishly and for the maintenance of World peace."[10]

Here was DeGolyer, a homesteader's son, who had studied a science of dubious practicality, and who had navigated the cutthroat business world and the Byzantine labyrinth of the federal bureaucracy, addressing one of the most influential groups of political thinkers in the nation. Here he was charting a course for postwar global domination by the United States. The men and women who gathered in the corridors of power were listening, but would they heed his advice?

DeGolyer's transformation from a technically skilled bureaucratic coordinator to a policymaking visionary was one that took place gradually over the course of his government service. From the beginning of his tenure within the federal petroleum agencies, DeGolyer's contributions to the war effort had gone beyond the narrow purview of his office. Mobilization and conservation were certainly the primary focus of his efforts, but he could not help but think beyond the confines of his charge and consider the wider connections and consequences of his work. Considering his record as an innovative businessman, this was not at all surprising.

DeGolyer the geologist had broken free of the limits of technical work to look for opportunities in business. Then, DeGolyer the businessman had reached beyond the limits of his scientific training to imagine the possibilities of applying the unfamiliar science of geophysics in the context of the oil industry. So, it was completely within character that DeGolyer the technocrat would begin to look beyond coordination of the domestic petroleum industry to consider the wider implications of government oil policy.

Whereas much of DeGolyer's early work on behalf of the government focused on coordination of industry with the exigencies of war, his superiors increasingly tapped him to deal with questions of a broader strategic scope. Starting in the fall of 1942, the federal government dispatched DeGolyer on a series of missions aimed at formulating policy on an international scale. The first of these special assignments took him to familiar ground—Mexico.

DeGolyer had assisted the government regarding Mexico once before, during World War I. At that time, he had passed on maps to the military, presumably for use in the event of an American invasion of that country.[11] During the 1910s, Mexico had suffered immeasurably from violence resulting from the factional struggles of the Revolution. President Wilson had dispatched the military there on two occasions, in 1914 and 1916. This adventurism strained relations with Mexico and made conflict between the two nations more likely than cooperation.

In 1942, the situation was quite different. On taking office in 1933, President Roosevelt had inaugurated a friendlier approach toward Latin America soon referred to as the "Good Neighbor" policy. A major test of Roosevelt's approach came in 1938. In that year, Mexican President Lázaro Cárdenas signed a decree that confiscated the property of seventeen oil companies. This move effectively nationalized the industry in Mexico, provoking outrage among American oilmen who were prominent among the dispossessed. Resisting calls for intervention, Roosevelt limited the role of the federal government to promoting fair compensation for the losses sustained by businessmen. His caution paid off later when the nation faced war in two far-flung theaters.

The policies adopted by Cárdenas's successor, Manuel Avila Camacho, took an increasingly pro-Allied slant as the war progressed. After the Japanese attack on Pearl Harbor, Mexico broke relations with the Axis and urged Latin America to support the Allied cause.[12]

These diplomatic responses might have marked the limits of Mexican involvement in the war, but German provocation on the high seas triggered open hostilities. The sinking of two oil tankers by German submarines in May 1942 resulted in a declaration of war by Mexico. Both of the torpedoed ships had names of special significance to DeGolyer— the *Faja de Oro,* or "Golden Lane," whose oilfields he knew well, and the *Potrero del Llano,* named for the oil well that had made his name as a young geologist.[13]

Now, with Mexico an open ally of the United States, the federal government was eager to make the most of the resources that Mexico could offer to the war effort. But how would it go about doing this? The Mexican petroleum industry had weathered the immediate challenges posed by expropriation, but it was in dire need of rehabilitating its infrastructure—a process that would require both materials and technical aid.

In response to this situation, two conflicting plans emerged within the administration, one advocated by the State Department and another supported by Petroleum Coordinator Ickes. The State Department's oil expert Max Thornburg believed that any aid should be conditioned upon Mexico allowing American oil companies whose properties were expropriated back into the country. Ickes pushed a different plan that was backed by independent oilman and Democratic Party fund-raiser Edwin Pauley. This involved the construction of a 100-octane aviation gasoline refinery by a group of independent oilmen. In order for such a plant to be effective, other aspects of Mexico's infrastructure would need to be improved.[14]

Because the Ickes-backed Pauley initiative would not condition aid on reversing the Mexican expropriation, the State Department viewed this plan, correctly, as undercutting its own approach. But Ickes had the support of President Roosevelt, who believed that a cooperative venture would improve relations with Mexico.[15]

This was the contentious context of the technical mission to Mexico, a study carried out by the Office of the Petroleum Coordinator (OPC) that would examine the needs of the Mexican oil industry. Presumably, Ickes hoped that its findings would help bolster his view that the Pauley project would be a worthy use of resources. But the State Department would also be directly involved, because any mission working with Mexican officials would have an important diplomatic impact.[16]

Despite the dispute in Washington over Pauley's plans for a high-octane refinery, both Ickes and the State Department generally supported greater involvement in the Mexican industry. Therefore, the State Department was quick to accept an invitation from President Avila Camacho to dispatch the mission of oil experts to Mexico. But whom to send? Within the federal bureaucracy, there was one obvious choice to head such an assignment—DeGolyer, of course.[17]

As an able administrator, an accomplished geologist, and an oilman possessing intimate knowledge of the Mexican oil industry, DeGolyer was the perfect man to lead the technical mission. It therefore came as no surprise when Deputy Coordinator Davies appointed DeGolyer to head the mission that would include a variety of industry experts. The five men who accompanied DeGolyer included authorities in refining, construction, and conservation as well as a representative of the War Production Board (WPB).[18]

Despite DeGolyer's association with the OPC, the State Department stressed that the experts exercised an authority independent of the agencies for which they worked. As a telegram to Ambassador George S. Messersmith in Mexico City stressed, "The Mexican authorities should be made to understand clearly that the oil mission has not been sent by nor does it represent any division or department but represents this government as a whole. Every member of the mission is employed by the Government of the United States."[19] The mission would be a departure from DeGolyer's conservation work with the OPC. Whereas before he had been concerned with coordinating domestic industry and public policy within the limited scope of an agency, now he would be a representative at large of the United States, tasked with formulating international policy. It was remarkable testimony to his respect within government circles.

On the other hand, not everyone involved in planning the mission knew him well. Communicating with the American embassy in Mexico, the State Department made the astounding misstatement that De-Golyer "has not been nor is he now, significantly connected with any oil company."[20] A later telegram revealed that despite this apparent unfamiliarity, his reputation alone had secured him an important role in shaping government policy. It urged that DeGolyer be consulted by embassy officials "to make it possible for the Department to understand the [Mexican oil] situation more clearly . . . Furthermore, the Department feels that the Embassy will find consultation with Mr. DeGolyer helpful in its own consideration of these questions."[21] Significantly, the State Department singled out no other expert from the mission for this sort of commendation.

DeGolyer left Washington on August 20, leapfrogging by plane to Dallas; then to Brownsville, Texas, on the border with Mexico; and finally to Mexico City, where he arrived on the August 23. There he rendezvoused with the other members of the American mission. Soon afterward, Efrin Buenrostro greeted the party. Buenrostro served as host to DeGolyer and his colleagues, and was a division chief of Petróleos Mexicanos (PEMEX), the government oil company. One day later, DeGolyer met with Ambassador Messersmith, who advised the party not to contact Mexican officials again until he had made appropriate introductions. It was, after all, a diplomatic mission of some importance.[22]

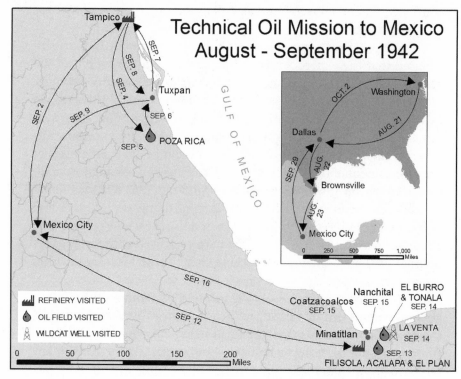

**Technical Oil Mission to Mexico**
**August - September 1942**

Tampico

SEP. 7
SEP. 8
SEP. 4

Tuxpan

SEP. 2
SEP. 9
SEP. 6

POZA RICA
SEP. 5

GULF OF MEXICO

OCT. 2
Washington
AUG. 21
Dallas
SEP. 29
AUG. 22
Brownsville
AUG. 23
Mexico City

0    250    500    750    1,000 Miles

Mexico City

SEP. 16

REFINERY VISITED

SEP. 12

OIL FIELD VISITED

WILDCAT WELL VISITED

0    50    100    150    200 Miles

Nanchital    EL BURRO & TONALA
Coatzacoalcos  SEP. 15   SEP. 14
SEP. 15
LA VENTA
Minatitlan    SEP. 14
SEP. 13
FILISOLA, ACALAPA & EL PLAN

Technical Oil Mission to Mexico, August–September 1942. (Map by Gregory Plumb.)

With Ambassador Messersmith's approval and guidance, DeGolyer and the mission met with officials in the Mexican foreign office and the Mexican treasury department. By August 28, they were ready to begin the challenging task of assessing the Mexican oilfields, refineries and transportation networks. The essential issue that the mission considered was whether American resources earmarked for the maintenance and development of Mexico's oil industry could significantly enhance that nation's contribution to the war effort. And if this were the case, the United States government wanted to know if such an effort would be worthwhile.[23]

DeGolyer covered quite a bit of ground. From Mexico City, he traveled to evaluate the Poza Rica-Mexico pipeline, and then back to the city, then on to Tampico. In Tampico, he observed the operation of the old Mexican Eagle refinery. Then it was on to the Golden Lane, where he had made his name, and the Poza Rica field. Over the next week, the team returned to Mexico City by way of Tuxpan, another of DeGolyer's old haunts. He made a trip to Minatitlán, where his old patron, Lord Cowdray, had built his first oil refinery. Next, he took a whirlwind tour of active Mexican oilfields followed by an inspection of the Isthmus of Tehuantepec. What a sentimental journey it must have been for DeGolyer.[24]

By late September, the fieldwork of the mission was complete, and DeGolyer returned to Mexico City in order to conduct a series of conferences with various officials from PEMEX.[25] After considering what he had seen in the field, and the information that he had obtained from Mexican officials, DeGolyer concluded that the Mexican oil industry was in dire need of attention. The prolific old fields where he had worked on behalf of the Mexican Eagle Oil Company had declined to a low level of production. The entire industry depended upon a single field at Poza Rica. Further, the refining phase of the oil business in Mexico still operated as if there were many competing companies. Many small plants remained open when consolidation into fewer, larger plants made more sense.[26] DeGolyer mulled over the situation as he returned to Washington on October 2 and began to formulate a series of recommendations.

The Report of the Mexican Technical Mission offered a plan for the development of the Mexican petroleum industry that only incidentally addressed the controversy surrounding the planned high-octane refinery.[27] Its construction was endorsed in one brief clause, while the greatest attention was reserved for a proposed exploration program, conservation measures in existing Mexican oilfields, and the consolidation of the refining sector. In this report and in a memorandum to Ralph Davies that accompanied it, DeGolyer offered many recommendations that were similar to those he had made to American oilmen. One departure was the proposed restructuring of the Mexican refining sector to achieve greater economies of scale. This recommendation would have been politically impossible to implement in the United States, where a number of competing companies operated their own plants. But most of his other suggestions would have been familiar to Davies. For instance, he called for a reduction in the level of production at the Poza Rica field in order to ensure maximum ultimate recovery of oil. He also called for the surveying of Mexico "by the most advanced and exact geophysical methods" and the drilling of "as many wildcat wells as possible." According to DeGolyer, "Nothing is more important."[28]

Remarkably, DeGolyer's memo did not offer any explicit rationale for assisting the Mexican industry. Nevertheless, implicit in his evaluation

The Mexican Mission. DeGolyer dines on September 20, 1942, at Manolo's in Mexico City together with members of the mission and Mexican hosts. DeGolyer is seated second from the left, smoking a cigar. John H. Murrell, close DeGolyer collaborator and future DeGolyer and MacNaughton partner is at the head of the table. (Everette Lee DeGolyer Collection. Courtesy of DeGolyer Library, Southern Methodist University.)

was the recognition that maximizing the oil production of an allied nation was almost as important as maximizing production in the United States.[29] Mexican officials, unsurprisingly, shared this outlook, referring to the assistance as "collaboration toward the common victory."[30]

The United States government reaction to the technical mission recommendations was generally supportive, but the plan for aid to promote a vast expansion of exploration and a restructuring of production and refining was not implemented. Indeed, subsequent attempts by the Mexican government to secure a US loan to develop its oil industry were rebuffed in the face of State Department opposition.[31] Instead, activity focused on the controversy surrounding the 100-octane refinery. DeGolyer played an important role in these negotiations, which concluded with the construction of the plant, albeit without the participation of Edwin Pauley in the project. In the end, the high-octane plant was constructed with United States assistance, but the broader reconstruction of the Mexican industry advocated in DeGolyer's report did not come to pass.[32]

Although DeGolyer's analysis of the Mexican oil industry was in some ways comparable to his work regulating domestic petroleum production, the context was different. Earlier, he had worked within the narrow purview of the OPC; now he represented the United States government at large. His work as director of the Conservation Division called on DeGolyer to coordinate private businessmen in the war effort. Now he was engaged in a diplomatic venture, and his opinions would help shape foreign policy. Dealing with officials of the Mexican government was significantly different from dealing with independent oilmen. True, Mexico was not the major oil producer that it had been during the First World War, but its petroleum production was still a significant strategic issue.

The Mexican Technical Mission was not DeGolyer's last international assignment. Indeed, his next essay in globetrotting diplomacy would become the stuff of legend in the oil business and ultimately earn him a reputation as something of a prophet. It would focus on the Middle East.

Although the Middle East is almost synonymous with oil today, the development of the modern petroleum industry in the region is relatively recent. The first major discovery came in Persia in 1908, leading to the rise of the Anglo-Persian Oil Company, today's British Petroleum.[33] The development of oil in the Arabian Peninsula took place even later. In the 1920s, a New Zealander by the name of Frank Holmes became convinced that there was untold oil wealth in Arabia. Geologists scoffed at the prospect, as did Anglo-Persian executives, who were nonetheless irritated at the prospect of competition within the region, however laughable.

Holmes was persistent, promoting ventures to the sheikhs of Bahrain and Kuwait. In 1925, he managed to secure an oil concession in Bahrain, and after searching for financial backers, found Standard Oil of California (Socal) to be interested. As the major European power with interests in the region, Great Britain was naturally interested in these transactions. Although the foreign office, egged on by Anglo-Persian, resisted encroachment by this American company, the deal ultimately went forward. Drilling in Bahrain began in 1931. They found oil in May 1932.[34]

The discovery of oil in Bahrain electrified the region and breathed life into negotiations already underway for oil concessions throughout the Arabian Peninsula. In 1933, Saudi Arabia granted extensive rights to Socal in exchange for sizeable payments made in gold. The kingdom ruled by Ibn Saud was a new one, having taken its official name of Saudi Arabia only a year earlier, but it was vast and, at least Socal thought, promising. To hold the concession, Socal formed a new subsidiary, the California-Arabian Standard Oil Company (Casoc). A year and a half later, the sheikh of Kuwait signed a concession to a company that represented both the Gulf Oil Company, and the Anglo-Persian Oil Company. Discovery of oil in both Kuwait and Saudi Arabia came in 1938. Although infrastructure to support these finds was scarce, it was clear that the Middle East would be a major center of production in the international petroleum industry.[35]

One signal of growing international recognition of the region's potential was the interest provoked among nations desperate to secure oil resources. Prominent among these were the future Axis powers, Germany, Italy, and Japan. The Japanese, in particular, were concerned with securing oil for the Imperial Navy. While American companies eyed the region for potential profits, the Japanese figured these strategic considerations in calculating their concession offers. One such proposition involved a figure of "astronomical proportions" according to a Saudi official.[36]

Yet the outbreak of the Second World War, and its subsequent spread to North Africa, led to the temporary suspension of most oil-related activity within the region. The Italians bombed American installations in Saudi Arabia during October 1940. Industry operations in Kuwait were suspended and wells plugged with cement for fear that the Germans might capture them. In Saudi Arabia, most production halted, and only a skeleton crew of American workers remained behind to maintain minimal production.[37]

The hibernation of the Arabian oil companies was misleading. Although the war had disrupted operations, the importance of oil to the war effort was readily apparent to all of the great powers. In coordinating their struggle for victory, all had achieved a greater understanding of the limits of domestic resources and the desirability of securing oil production. As analysts, generals, and politicians cast their eyes about for reserves abroad, they increasingly fell upon the Persian Gulf as a strategic crossroads.

In the United States government, the Middle East drew the attention of Petroleum Administrator for War Harold Ickes. By 1943, the war was turning decisively in favor of the Allied powers. And though it seemed probable that the oil needed for victory would be forthcoming, he was already looking forward to the postwar order. The decisive impact of oil on the war effort was apparent to almost all. Machines determined the course of the war to an extent that would have been unbelievable in the preceding century. Even the technological developments of World War I had only vaguely foreshadowed the nature of the conflict. All of these machines—tanks, fighters, bombers, trucks, and ships—required petroleum. And Ickes would have been a fool had he not recognized that oil and power would be inseparable in the postwar world. True, the United States produced about 63 percent of the oil in 1940, while the Middle East contributed only about 5 percent. But the production of the United States could not hold at such a high level forever, and Ickes knew it.[38]

He was not alone. The military also understood. Backed by the generals, Ickes began to push President Roosevelt for greater American involvement in Saudi Arabia. The war had disrupted the economy of Ibn Saud's kingdom. Perhaps the United States might be able to offer assistance under the Lend-Lease Act? This would surely gratify the monarch and perhaps make him more receptive to American influence. Roosevelt was reluctant at first, because Lend-Lease aid was supposed to go only to "democratic" nations, and he denied assistance in July 1941. But by February 1943, the President had come around and, encouraged by Ickes, authorized the payments.[39]

This was only the beginning. Ickes had grander ambitions. He hoped to put the United States into the oil business by acquiring concessions for a government-owned corporation. Such ventures may have been unprecedented in America, but they were familiar enough on the international stage. Anglo-Persian was one such entity, with a majority share owned by the British government. In June 1943, Ickes had established a vehicle for this policy—the Petroleum Reserves Corporation—and was swift to put its agenda before the President. In July, he met with Roosevelt to discuss plans to acquire an interest in the Saudi oilfields. This would involve a PRC purchase of a significant share of Casoc stock, perhaps a controlling interest.[40]

In August 1943, Ickes called a conference with the presidents of Socal and Texaco, which had joined the Arabian venture. He proposed nothing less than the outright purchase of Casoc by the United States government. The executives were shocked, but with a war on, they also recognized that their bargaining power was limited. After further negotiations, Ickes agreed to accept a 51 percent share of ownership for the government. The terms of the purchase remained to be determined.[41]

DeGolyer played an important role in these developments, above all in confirming the potential of the Arabian oilfields. On August 6, Ickes and PRC officials determined that a technical mission to the Middle East would be necessary to further the negotiations with Casoc over the stock purchase. DeGolyer seemed the perfect fit for the job.[42] A little over a week later his resignation with the PAW became official and he became a consultant for the PRC.[43]

If DeGolyer's work with PAW had begun to bore him, the PRC venture promised to be much more interesting. As early as 1940, DeGolyer had Arabian oil on his mind. In that year, while at the University of Texas, he had lectured to the Science Club on the history and geology of oilfields in the Middle East. Even before war had come to the United States, he foresaw an increasingly important role for the region, stating, "No such galaxy of fields of the first magnitude over such a wide area has been developed previously in the history of the oil industry. I will be rash enough to prophecy that the area . . . will be the most important oil-producing region in the world within the next score of years."[44] Despite the shutdown of the Middle Eastern oil industry during the war, DeGolyer saw no reason to revise that assessment during his service with the OPC and Petroleum Administration for War (PAW). If anything, the mobilization of the nation's petroleum resources to fight Germany and Japan promised to hasten a realignment in global oil production.

DeGolyer's general familiarity with oil in the Middle East, his technical competence as a petroleum geologist, and his record as an effective public servant commended him to Ickes for involvement in the PRC scheme. DeGolyer's role as an emissary and consultant with the recent Mexican Mission would also have counted in his favor. Perhaps even more important was the high regard that DeGolyer's name commanded. In his diary, Ickes acknowledged DeGolyer as "one of the most respected [men] in the oil industry" and admitted that his support was useful when confronting opposition in the industry. And as Ickes knew, PRC's plans to obtain an interest in Casoc were bound to provoke significant opposition.[45]

Despite the controversial nature of PRC's plans, DeGolyer threw himself into the project with enthusiasm. On August 26, he met with Ickes and other officials to report information he had obtained from the San Francisco office of Casoc. The Saudi fields were fabulously rich, he assured Ickes, and any government initiative in the region should include not only Saudi Arabia but Bahrain as well. Ickes was encouraged to think big about PRC's possibilities.[46]

Although Ickes attempted to keep PRC's plans secret for as long as possible, the potential impact on the oil industry was so significant that this could not continue for long. By October 1943, the *Oil and Gas Journal* noted widespread suspicion of PRC objectives amid rumors that government ownership was set to become a part of US petroleum policy.[47] As the details of the Casoc transaction came to the attention of the public, it provoked outrage in the American petroleum industry. It seemed that no one wanted to face the United States government as a competitor. Companies that envisaged future foreign operations were particularly irritated, including the most powerful successors of Rockefeller's empire, Standard Oil of New Jersey and Socony-Vacuum (Mobil).

It quickly became apparent to Ickes that the Casoc deal would meet with stiff resistance. Despite the powers that he possessed as petroleum administrator, he still required industry cooperation to fuel the war effort. Any disruption of that work was unacceptable. Just as important, there was serious opposition to the plan in some corners of the Roosevelt Administration itself, especially the State Department. By November, Ickes decided to back off and reassess PRC's options. It was not the end of Ickes's effort to shape a foreign policy that secured oil resources abroad, but it was a significant setback.[48]

Despite the suspension of PRC's purchase of Casoc, plans for a technical mission to the Middle East went forward in the fall of 1943. From Ickes's perspective, PRC still promised to have an important role in postwar petroleum policy, although the nature of that role remained to be defined. So on October 11, 1943, as rumors of a government buyout of Casoc were stirring the oil industry into opposition, PRC announced its plans to dispatch a mission to the Middle East to "integrate knowledge of domestic and foreign oil supplies."[49] The mission would include one of DeGolyer's associates from the Mexican mission, conservation engineer John Murrell. Also present would be W. E. Wrather, director of the United States Geological Survey. Wrather was well known to DeGolyer, being a fellow Dallasite and an acquaintance from his work as a young man with the USGS. Because government interest in Middle Eastern oil focused on the issue of military requirements, there would also be representatives from the armed forces: Colonels John H. Leavell and Dillon Anderson. Leavell was detached from the War Department and given the position of "petroleum attaché" with the State Department.[50]

Although DeGolyer had originally been tapped to lead the group, in November he discovered that Undersecretary of the Interior Abe Fortas had been named to serve as head of the mission. Learning of his divestiture, DeGolyer complained to his wife that "Abe doesn't rate any higher technically than I do politically," and confessed that he was "deeply hurt."[51] DeGolyer did not fret for long. When the relevant congressional oversight committee reviewed Fortas's qualifications, they came to the same conclusion that DeGolyer had.[52]

With Fortas out of the picture, the mantle of leadership returned to DeGolyer. He immersed himself in preparations for the trip. In fact, so busy was he that DeGolyer neglected to discuss matters with his wife. When Nell discovered that he had spent one Washington evening in the company of Arabian royalty, she scolded him for forgetting her. In defense, DeGolyer pleaded, "You seem to picture me as one of the international set—a gay butterfly dashing to receptions to Arabian princes . . . There was nothing Arabian Nightish about it except for the three or four men in strange dress."[53]

Despite these protests, DeGolyer's mission undoubtedly held out the prospect of adventure. He conceded enough at the close of the same letter, remarking, "I am still optimistic enough to think that maybe this trip is something I will enjoy having done after it is finished."[54] But he also worried, noting, "It is uncertain—likely to be uncomfortable and a little bit hazardous. I am no Lindbergh."[55]

In referring to Lindbergh, DeGolyer had in mind the extensive air travel involved in the planned trip. His concerns were not misplaced. When the plane carrying the mission on the first leg of its journey touched down in Miami Beach, Florida, the brakes locked, and it blew out a wheel. That waylaid the group for about five days before arrangements were finally back in place to cross the Atlantic. They left Florida on November 17, crossing the Atlantic by way of Puerto Rico, British Guyana, and Brazil. By November 23, they were in Africa, still en route to their destination. It was truly a grueling journey, but it proved to be more than worth the discomfort.[56]

From late November through December 1943, DeGolyer and the mission would tour the Middle East, scouring sites in Egypt, Palestine, Iraq, Iran, Kuwait, Saudi Arabia, Qatar, and the Trucial Coast, now known as the United Arab Emirates.[57] It was a vast undertaking for so small a party to conduct in such a short period. True, the goals of the mission were limited: "[T]he object of the mission's work was solely that of technical review of the reserves and prospects of the area under consideration."[58] However, the itinerary must have been intimidating, even for a well-seasoned traveler such as DeGolyer.

The starting point for the real work of the mission was in Egypt, where DeGolyer arrived during the last days of the Cairo Conference between Chiang Kai-shek, Winston Churchill, and Franklin Roosevelt.[59] By the first day of December, DeGolyer and his party were ready to depart on their first excursion. Their transport would be a twin-motored Lockheed Lodestar, packed with sixty days' rations, "blankets, first-aid equipment, small arms, and sundry other supplies."[60] If the mission members felt reassured by these preparations, they were a little unnerved by one obvious omission. As Colonel Anderson noted, "We carried no parachutes, as the proposition seemed to have been established that in case anything went wrong, the best thing was to go down with the plane."[61] This was even more disturbing because the group planned to fly some tens of thousands of miles.[62]

Parachutes or no parachutes, DeGolyer and his associates were off, first crossing the Sinai Peninsula and the Great Bitter Lakes, with Gaza as their destination. There, they paused to inspect a local sulfur quarry. Returning to the air for the trip to Jerusalem, DeGolyer directed the pilot to fly low over the banks of the Dead Sea, allowing the group to examine the geological formations on the canyon walls abutting the water. With the plane flying so close to the water that it kicked up a wake on the sea, the view was spectacular. When the altimeter marked the plane at minus 1,300 feet, Colonel Anderson could not resist noting that they were flying at an elevation further below sea level than a submarine would go.[63]

Landing in Jerusalem later that night, DeGolyer and his colleagues began playing the first of many poker games that would relieve tension during their assignment. Over the next several weeks, DeGolyer and Anderson would prove their skill at the game. The two would best the others, building a mutual respect that would endure for the rest of their lives.[64]

For the next several days, the mission abandoned the plane for an

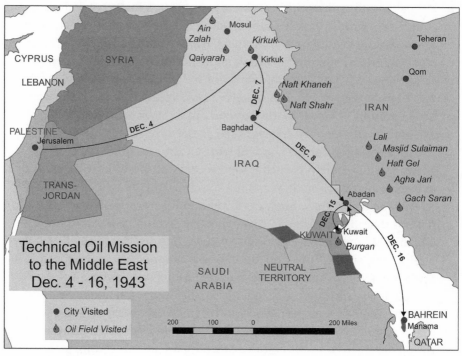

Technical Oil Mission to the Middle East, December 4–16, 1943. (Map by Gregory Plumb.)

automobile, driving to Haifa for an inspection of a refinery dedicated to processing production from oilfields in northern Iraq. Soon, DeGolyer and company had completed their work in Palestine and were ready to carry on and see the really big oilfields of the region. The first of these would be in the area of the Iraqi city of Kirkuk. Returning to the air, the mission arrived in Kirkuk on December 4. From there, they would make a series of forays by plane, examining the producing fields and the geology of the region.[65]

There was little time and much ground to cover, so by December 7, DeGolyer was again on the move, this time to Baghdad, then one day later to Basra. The mission's arrival in Basra placed them firmly in the Persian Gulf region, the area that would impress the party most for its vast petroleum potential. For the next couple of weeks, they would carry out a series of long-distance flights, scanning the geological formations of the land below and examining producing oilfields, often also from the sky.

First was an expedition over coastal Iran, then the Kuwaiti oilfield, where DeGolyer and his colleagues examined highly promising well cores.[66] The Kuwaiti sheik presented the mission with a freshly falconed royal bustard, a bird that was a local delicacy. The Americans graciously accepted the gift, but once out of sight, discarded it with an embarrassing lack of decorum.[67]

The mission spent the final working week on the island of Bahrain and the eastern shores of the Arabian Peninsula. Using the island sheikdom and nearby Dhahran as airbases, DeGolyer and the others flew over vast stretches of often forbidding landscape, impressed with its apparent potential for oil production. By Christmas the assignment was essentially complete, with the main task now to compile statistics, analyze information, and prepare the official report. Although there may have been controversy over a few details, the essential conclusion was never in doubt. DeGolyer knew what must lie beneath the mountains and deserts over which they had flown—billions and billions of barrels of oil.[68]

The mission managed to achieve its basic aims of evaluating the petroleum resources of the region, but it did not go smoothly. For one, a struggle developed between Colonel Leavell and DeGolyer. As representatives of the State Department and the PRC, respectively, this was something of a bureaucratic turf battle. Indeed, the State Department took the matter seriously enough to cable the American legation in Cairo, scolding DeGolyer. From their point of view, DeGolyer was compromising the position of the American government in relation to the British, who were already deeply involved in the region's industry. The message read, "According to the Legation at Baghdad, DeGolyer appears to resent the interest of the Department of State in Middle East oil matters and especially the fact that a representative of the Department is with the mission."[69] The cable alleged that he was actively undermining Colonel Leavell in particular, noting, "It is also stated that DeGolyer has not cooperated with Leavell either in discussion or in exchanging information and has so acted toward Leavell as possibly to injure Leavell's standing with American and British oil companies."[70]

Although the State Department painted a portrait of DeGolyer that might seem embarrassing, his curmudgeonly boss, Harold Ickes, may have been proud of his behavior. Though the military had backed Ickes's plans to promote a larger role for the United States government

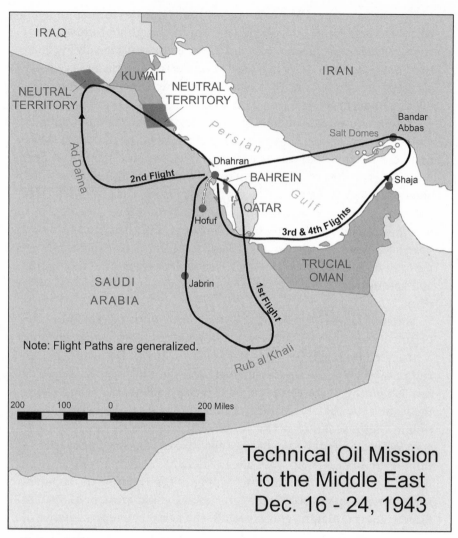

IRAQ

KUWAIT

NEUTRAL
TERRITORY

NEUTRAL
TERRITORY

IRAN

Bandar
Abbas

Salt Domes

Ad Dahna

2nd Flight

Dhahran

Persian

BAHREIN

Shaja

Gulf

QATAR

Hofuf

3rd & 4th Flights

Jabrin

1st Flight

TRUCIAL
OMAN

SAUDI
ARABIA

Note: Flight Paths are generalized.

Rub al Khali

200   100   0                200 Miles

Technical Oil Mission
to the Middle East
Dec. 16 - 24, 1943

Technical Oil Mission to the Middle East, December 16–24, 1943. (Map by Gregory Plumb.)

in foreign oil, the State Department had been reluctant, fearing that such a move would bring about "intense new disputes."[71] Furthermore, Ickes believed Leavell in particular was hostile to the administration and had sought to block his appointment to the mission.[72] Yet there was also a personality conflict at the heart of the dispute between DeGolyer and Leavell. In the last years of the war, DeGolyer wrote to Lieutenant Colonel Dillon Anderson about Leavell. He had heard that "the old boy had aged" since the Middle East mission. DeGolyer remarked, "[I]f the old boy falls to pieces, it's O.K. with me."[73]

Despite the cloud that this dispute inevitably cast over the mission, it was still an undeniable adventure for DeGolyer. Although the primary purpose was geological and industrial evaluation, some of the most memorable moments for DeGolyer were cultural in nature. The food and attire of the region made quite an impression. He later recalled one meal vividly where he and his colleagues enjoyed eating rice and roasted sheep wholly by hand because knives and forks were not customary. The mission also occasionally dressed in local fashion to curry favor with their hosts. When DeGolyer later returned to the United States, he brought one complete set of this "native costume," although he expressed doubt that he would ever wear it again.[74]

But whatever the experience meant to DeGolyer in terms of adventure, it was the conclusions about the region's oil wealth, backed by cold statistics, that made the mission nationally, even internationally, relevant. In 1940, DeGolyer had been willing to wager that the Middle East would become the most important petroleum-producing area within twenty years. His recent travels had confirmed that opinion. In the "Preliminary Report" issued for the PRC, he reiterated this prophecy in more forceful terms: "The center of gravity of world oil production is shifting from the Gulf-Caribbean area to the Middle East—to the Persian Gulf area—and is likely to continue to shift until it is firmly established in that area."[75] This was simply a statement of fact, as far as DeGolyer was concerned, but the implications of that fact would have immediate impact upon the struggle to shape a petroleum policy for the US government.

The "Preliminary Report" presented the facts and figures of Middle Eastern oil. It did not advocate a policy for the government. Nonetheless, the politically charged atmosphere created by Ickes's negotiations to acquire Casoc ensured that partisans of greater government participation, as well as their numerous opponents in the oil industry, would carefully parse DeGolyer's words. DeGolyer sent the "Preliminary Report" to the president and directors of the PRC in February 1944, but five months later, the *Bulletin of the American Association of Petroleum Geologists* published it. Like the battle over Casoc, the issues raised by the Middle East mission had moved rapidly from Washington offices to a larger, national forum.

Although the "Preliminary Report" had been noticeably silent on policy, it was not because DeGolyer and his associates lacked opinions on the issue. Indeed, DeGolyer seemed almost eager to express his thoughts on United States foreign policy in the wake of the mission. It was at this point that the resignation of E. Holly Poe as vice president and general manager of PRC led to an interesting exchange between DeGolyer and Ickes. In mid-March, Ickes called him into his office to ask DeGolyer take the newly vacant position. According to DeGolyer, Ickes stressed that DeGolyer's association with PRC was crucial to its success, imploring, "[W]e need your name."[76] However, DeGolyer was unmoved and, according to Ickes, explained that he "hated an executive job," but agreed to participate in upcoming negotiations with the British over oil policy in the Middle East.[77]

But if DeGolyer was unwilling to serve as the face of PRC, it did not mean that he intended to remain silent on its activities. Just weeks after issuing the "Preliminary Report," he publicly voiced his recommendations regarding oil in the Middle East. From his point of view, the protection and development of the region's petroleum reserves was vitally important to United States interests. To achieve these aims, he backed a new plan that Harold Ickes was promoting that involved the construction of pipelines in the desert.[78]

After Ickes's first attempt at the Saudi honey had stirred up the bees in the oil industry, the secretary decided to try a different approach. Working with the major oil companies active in the Persian Gulf region, Ickes proposed to spend $120 million to construct a pipeline to ship Saudi and Kuwaiti oil to the Mediterranean Sea. In return for the aid, the oil companies would create a one-billion-barrel oil reserve that the United States military could purchase at a 25 percent discount from the market price.[79]

From a strategic view, the plan was logical. Rather than exhausting the oil reserves of the United States in serving European consumers, the Middle East would become a major supplier, slowing the drain on domestic American reserves. In addition, the military reserve would secure foreign oil sources for the United States armed forces in the event of another global war. If it did not solve the problem presented by dwindling American oil reserves, it was at least a step toward a solution—or so its advocates reasoned. Unfortunately, it also conflicted with powerful vested interests.

Aside from the companies already involved in Arabian oil, the industry opposed the move. From their point of view, Ickes's move was merely subsidizing the competition. Their reaction was immediate, vociferous, and exaggerated.[80] Small domestic oil producers denounced the plan as "a move toward fascism."[81] In a prepared statement read in Dallas, J. Edgar Pew of the Sun Oil Company was more measured in his criticism. He denounced the pipeline as a waste of taxpayers' money. Pew warned that a transnational pipeline in the Middle East would inevitably require armed guards to ensure its continued operation because of the region's unstable political situation. As he saw it, the pipeline was a good way to embroil the nation in another war.[82]

Considering the subsequent history of the region, Pew's concerns were not without foundation. On the other hand, his assessment of the United States' ability to supply its own needs in petroleum was almost reckless in its optimism. He confidently asserted, "Given normal conditions, the oil industry believes it can continue to supply plenty of oil for our nation's needs for an indefinite period."[83] Even if this forecast proved misplaced, he was unconcerned. For according to Pew, "If and when there is danger of the failure of reserves, the industry will get supplies from foreign reserves or from synthetics, of which there are practically unlimited supplies."[84]

As far as DeGolyer was concerned, Pew's cavalier attitude toward the limits of domestic oil reserves was not one that the nation could afford. He had already expressed support for Ickes's pipeline, and he proved more than willing to enter the fray as the industry onslaught against the plan unfolded. Drafting a manuscript of "Well Chosen Words," that was ultimately published in *Time*, DeGolyer took aim at Pew's argument, setting national strategic interests over the private interests of oilmen. He argued, "Building the Arabian line is to the advantage of one group and they are for it. It threatens the markets of another group and they are against it. Actually, the problem is not one to be settled by the oil industry."[85] Instead, DeGolyer stressed that the pipeline should be judged on the basis of its benefits to the nation, concluding, "I submit, that whether or not objections to the present enterprise, its initiation, or method of handling are valid, it was conceived, as one supporter put it, 'in the interest of national security and for no other purpose.'"[86]

DeGolyer addressed the objections of the industry one by one, arguing that their concerns were misplaced. For those who claimed that the plan was some sort of fascist conspiracy, DeGolyer offered withering criticism: "The cry of 'Fascist' so commonly raised in objecting to the Government's participation in the Arabian scene is used chiefly to cover a lack of clear thinking which the proposal merits."[87] He was less dismissive regarding Pew's concerns about the need for armed protection, but argued, "It seems fair to assume that the Government is under no greater obligation to go to war to protect its own investment in what is essentially a commercial enterprise than it is to protect the investments of its nationals in similar enterprises."[88] And how could the pipeline be a waste of money when "[t]he oilfields of the Middle East are practically certain to be of paramount importance as a source of the world's oil supplies for a generation to come."[89]

Despite the cogent arguments made on behalf of the pipeline, it was doomed to failure. DeGolyer recognized this within a few months of his "Well Chosen Words" and disengaged from the argument, leaving for Mexico on a "semi-vacation." After his return, he wrote to his mission colleague Dillon Anderson that "I presume that the efforts of the [companies] finally blew the pipeline out of the desert."[90] His assessment was not far from the mark. Although the Joint Chiefs of Staff had earlier backed the plan as "a matter of immediate military necessity," they failed to maintain support for the project as the end of the war in Europe approached.[91] With liberals opposed to corporate subsidies, isolationists opposed to foreign entanglements, and most of the petroleum industry aligned against the pipeline, it died a slow, ignominious death.[92]

Victory over the Axis forces in Europe came on May 7, 1945, following Hitler's suicide. The defeat of Japan, only a matter of time, came on August 14, following the detonation of two atomic bombs at Hiroshima and Nagasaki. Americans relished the moment as waves of elation and relief washed over the nation. The government lifted gasoline rationing, and the United States looked forward to a postwar order where the nation could lay to rest the deprivations of the Depression and war. It was a time to celebrate.

DeGolyer was among those Americans for whom the close of the war brought liberation. True, DeGolyer had not succeeded in implementing his Middle Eastern policy proposals. But in the aftermath of that terrible conflict, DeGolyer must have looked forward to a return to private life, a move that he had tried to make even in the midst of the war. Yet public issues followed DeGolyer, even as he shed the mantle of federal service. For one, there was his involvement in a project that would convert the Big Inch and Little Inch pipelines from federal infrastructure to private property.

This project was the conception of one of DeGolyer's colleagues in the Petroleum Administration for War, E. Holley Poe. Poe had been the head of the Natural Gas Division and had recognized that the vast network of government pipelines, built to transport petroleum during the war, could transport natural gas in peacetime if properly converted. The purpose of the Big Inch and Little Inch lines had been to avoid the hazards of tanker shipment at a time when German submarines threatened shipping. Now that the war was over, the government sought to divest itself of these properties, and prospective buyers contemplated their potential for profit.[93]

Poe believed that using the lines to ship natural gas was not only feasible but also potentially quite lucrative. DeGolyer was the third of Poe's colleagues brought into the scheme. The group, initially operating under the name of E. Holley Poe and Associates, put together a proposed bid on the pipelines. The scale of the purchase brought the matter under searching scrutiny that included congressional hearings.[94]

In the meantime, Poe, DeGolyer and the others organized a business in January 1947 to take over the operation in the event that their bid was successful—the Texas Eastern Transmission Corporation. In fact, the new company outbid its competitors on the purchase, and the government approved its offer of $143,127,000 on Valentine's Day, 1947. The *New York Times* noted that the bid was an "unexpectedly high price" and opposition to the move came largely from the coal and coke industry, which feared the introduction of cheap natural gas into a major market. Texas Eastern went on to tremendous success.[95]

In those first days following victory, DeGolyer seems to have believed that the oil industry could look forward to a return to normality after the regimentation of the business during the war years. In an opinion piece for the *Dallas Times Herald,* he made an explicit comparison with the period that followed World War I, arguing that the industry must "untangle itself from the intimate relationship with Government which was made necessary by war."[96] State regulatory commissions would be sufficient to conduct peacetime oversight of petroleum production, and the federal government could eliminate the variety of price controls and subsidies that regulated and directed the business. Most of all, DeGolyer looked forward to getting on with the business of finding oil, most especially oil in the United States. He urged the industry to begin "the immense job of exploration which lies ahead unless we are content to become increasingly dependent upon foreign oil."[97]

DeGolyer consistently favored exploration for new oilfields, wherever they lay, but his views on imported oil are more complicated than this last quote would suggest. While many in the domestic oil industry sought to limit the scope of imports, he understood that imports could play an important role in conserving United States reserves for a time of crisis. This became a particular concern as the international situation deteriorated in 1946 and 1947. During these years, the emergence of a conflict between the United States and her erstwhile ally the Soviet Union dashed hopes for a postwar order based on international amity and cooperation. By June 1947, DeGolyer had refined his position on petroleum exploration. The search for domestic oil reserves was still necessary, but national security concerns weighed heavily on his assessment of imports. His earlier interest in securing foreign oil for strategic reasons came to the fore once more.

DeGolyer publicly revealed his stance on the matter on June 14, 1947, when he gave the commencement address at Trinity College in Hartford, Connecticut. Titling his speech "The Mines of Laurium," DeGolyer drew parallels between classical Athens, whose prosperity had depended upon local silver deposits, and the United States, whose destiny, he believed, also depended on its mineral resources.[98] DeGolyer's message was ominous. The nation was consuming its resources at far too fast a pace and would face decline if it did not plan better. To help conserve domestic resources, he endorsed a somewhat paradoxical policy of developing foreign minerals. "We should import minerals . . . to the point where further importation would harm our own extractive industries—our first line of defense in time of emergency," he argued.[99] Only by using foreign resources first, could the United States preserve its own "mines of Laurium." DeGolyer did not explicitly identify the nation that played Sparta to the American Athens, but his audience needed no such explanation.

Much of DeGolyer's concern in the Trinity College address was also reflected in consulting work for the military. Less than a year after V-J day, the director of the Naval Petroleum Reserves, Commodore W. G. Greenman, had contacted DeGolyer by telephone regarding an important matter. It involved questions of national security and, of course, oil.[100] In an official letter drafted for the firm of DeGolyer and MacNaughton, Greenman spelled it all out, pausing to warn, "The contents of this letter are to be regarded as a secret matter." Continuing, Greenman described his charge, explaining, "The Army-Navy Petroleum Board has been called upon to make an estimate of the current and probable future supply of oil, that is, or will be, available to the United States under several possible war conditions."[101] Greenman wanted DeGolyer and MacNaughton to assist the Board by offering an estimate of the oil reserves that would be available to the United States in a variety of situations. He presented several grim scenarios, including "(a) Global war with the United States and Canada isolated; (b) Global war with entire North American continent isolated with Panama Canal out of commission; (c) Global war with entire Western Hemisphere isolated"; and most tellingly, "(d) Global war with oil resources in Eastern Europe and Middle East denied to the United States."[102]

DeGolyer played a major role in formulating the firm's response, and once again, he found himself wrestling with the strategic questions of petroleum policy. One month later, he dispatched his first estimates to Greenman.[103] It was the beginning of a relationship with the Department of Defense that would once more place DeGolyer in the public spotlight. Over the next several years, DeGolyer would pass on regular reports to Defense Department officials, offering his prognostications on domestic and foreign oil reserves.

At least initially, DeGolyer's reports were limited to "just the facts" and left the analysis to the military. But increasingly, he felt duty-bound to comment on the situation from a strategic perspective. The Middle East was essential to national security. By 1947, DeGolyer was concerned enough to send a report concluding that the United States would be in "short supply" of petroleum unless the oil industry discovered new American fields at a significantly increased rate and unless the nation could maintain access to Middle Eastern oilfields.[104]

DeGolyer shared this concern with the Navy Secretary, James Forrestal. The Secretary was no stranger to DeGolyer. Forrestal was a former investment banker with Dillon, Read & Co., the same financial house that had bought into Amerada in 1926. As one of the first senior administration officials to foresee a conflict with the Union of Soviet Socialist Republics, he was particularly concerned with national security issues as the postwar era began. About the same time that Greenman dispatched the letter engaging the services of DeGolyer and MacNaughton, Forrestal composed a letter to Secretary of State James Byrnes, in which he expressed his concerns regarding oil. Forrestal's comments included one remark that suggested his closeness with DeGolyer. As he put it, "I am of the opinion that [Secretary of the Interior Ickes] is right about the limitations of American oil reserves—in this I am influenced a good deal by the engineer that I used in private business, E. L. DeGolyer."[105] In 1947, Forrestal became the first secretary of defense of the United States. It was a fateful time for the nation and the world. As the Cold War began, DeGolyer had the ear of the most powerful military official in the world, aside from the president of the United States himself.

Consulting for the government through DeGolyer and MacNaughton was only one aspect of DeGolyer's deepening involvement in strategic affairs. In addition to the military, other government officials soon clamored for his assistance. With the peace, some in the oil industry felt that the bureaucratic apparatus that had coordinated the oil industry in wartime could now be safely dismantled. DeGolyer's old boss at the PAW, Ralph Davies, thought otherwise. He argued that a scaled-down version of the system might give the oil industry a more effective voice in shaping federal petroleum policy. This led to the formation of the Oil and Gas Division in the Department of the Interior and the establishment of a National Petroleum Council composed of industry representatives. In June 1946, Secretary of the Interior J. A. Krug appointed DeGolyer to the National Petroleum Council (NPC), in view of his "extensive knowledge of the petroleum industry and experience in its operations." DeGolyer immediately accepted.[106]

The NPC was the institutional successor to the Petroleum Industry War Council, a body of oil company representatives that advised the government regarding petroleum policy and attempted to coordinate the industry behind the war effort. The NPC had similar cooperative aims for the postwar era.[107] The Council also afforded an opportunity for industry representatives to confer with federal bureaucrats and shape government policy.[108]

DeGolyer's work with the Council was not as demanding as his extensive and time-consuming duties with the wartime petroleum agencies. To be sure, he took care to attend meetings and participated on committees that produced reports targeted at informing government policy. His first service was with the Statistical Advisory Committee of the NPC. Joining the committee in February 1947, he worked with his old collaborator Joseph Pogue. Here, he conferred with other oilmen to study "the improvement and simplification and the methods of assembling (petroleum) statistics" and to "report its findings and recommendations and action as it may deem appropriate."[109] These statistics were in turn employed in Council studies that "provided the only expert basis that Congress, the Interior Department, or defense planners had for making decisions about postwar energy policy."[110]

DeGolyer's involvement in government advisory work deepened in 1947, and the emerging Cold War began to color the nature of the projects assigned to him. Although the NPC had aimed to be a peacetime institution, the agencies and committees that DeGolyer joined in 1947 reflected growing pessimism about the postwar order. Military concerns were paramount.

On May 20, DeGolyer joined the NPC Committee on Military and Government Petroleum Requirements.[111] But this was only the beginning. A little more than a week later, he accepted appointment to the Military Petroleum Advisory Committee (MPAC), later renamed the Military Petroleum Advisory Board.[112] The primary function of this newly established body would be "to provide the Chairman of the Army-Navy Petroleum Board and the Director of the Oil and Gas Division with expert counsel, advice, and information on oil and gas matters relating to national security and defense." DeGolyer's work with the MPAC focused upon crude oil production, and foreign oil production in particular.[113]

If keeping all of these committees sorted out seems a bit confusing, it was confusing for DeGolyer as well.[114] Much of the work overlapped. What, for instance, would distinguish the concerns of the Military Petroleum Advisory Committee from the work of the Military and Government Petroleum Requirements Committee of the National Petroleum Council? The confusion resulted in bureaucratic inefficiencies and redundancies that did not serve the government well. Expressing his own doubts, DeGolyer wrote one federal official, "How many committees are we going to have on military requirements?"[115]

Despite his misgivings, DeGolyer's work with the military committees was important. Representatives of the Army, Navy, and Air Force regularly attended MPAC meetings, and DeGolyer occasionally played a role in advising these officials regarding the logistics of industry operation—both domestic and foreign.[116] On the other hand, his attendance of these meetings was spotty from the start, and he often designated his protégé and business associate John Murrell as an alternate.[117] Most MPAC meetings took place in Washington, DC, hardly convenient since he and his family had moved back to Dallas.

The various petroleum advisory committees were only one aspect of DeGolyer's deepening involvement in Cold War policy. Another intriguing aspect of his government service at this time was his work on behalf of the Atomic Energy Commission (AEC). DeGolyer owed his connection with the AEC to his friendship with Sumner Pike. Beginning in 1928, Pike had served as vice president of Case, Pomeroy, and Company, a financial backer of some of DeGolyer's Depression era ventures. Like DeGolyer, he became deeply involved in government work during the 1930s, serving in the Commerce Department. From 1942 to 1946, he had worked on the Securities and Exchange Commission. During the war, Pike directed the Fuels Price Division under the Office of the Price Administrator, Leon Henderson. Henderson contended with Petroleum Administrator Ickes for control over oil policy. Despite the competition between their bosses, DeGolyer and Pike maintained a strong sense of mutual respect. Following the war, the government appointed Pike as one of five members of the AEC. One of his first tasks was to assemble a body of experts to help formulate the nation's atomic policy. DeGolyer was among those whom he contacted.[118]

In March 1947, Pike asked DeGolyer whether he might be interested in working on the Raw Materials Advisory Committee at the AEC.[119] Pike wrote DeGolyer that he thought uranium was "right down your alley."[120] He explained, "One of the basic questions that we must get some sort of answer to is the quantity and location of the ores of [uranium and thorium]."[121] Would DeGolyer be willing to take on more committee work? "I would be glad to," he responded.[122] DeGolyer thoroughly enjoyed his service with the AEC, but like much of his other postwar government work, it suffered due to his distance from Washington. He missed the first meeting in October 1947.[123]

The advisory committee on which DeGolyer served reported directly to the head of the Raw Materials Section, John K. Gustafson. A mining engineer and business executive, Gustafson confronted the task of developing reliable and adequate sources of uranium for the nation's atomic arsenal. During the war, the government had largely relied on two foreign sources of uranium ore, Canada and the Belgian Congo. Gustafson realized that the limitations of the Canadian mine and the long-term vulnerability of the African mine made the development of domestic uranium imperative.

The advisory committee helped him to formulate a plan addressing this concern. Over the next few years, the AEC moved decisively to exploit uranium ore in the United States, with the major focus for mining on the Colorado Plateau in the Southwest. Using bonuses and guaranteed minimum prices as incentives, Gustafson and his team encouraged private industry to supply the government with the ore it needed. DeGolyer and his associates on the advisory committee made a number of trips to the region in order to gauge the most effective methods to implement this plan.[124] Overall, the incentives proved successful. Although foreign uranium sources remained important, United States production increased greatly, exceeding that of Canada by 1950.[125]

However significant DeGolyer's contributions were to the various advisory committees on which he served, his most remarkable influence on government policy came from his direct counsel of administration officials and congressional representatives. One example concerned the State Department's petroleum policy. In 1947, State Department officials approached DeGolyer to solicit his advice regarding petroleum in Latin America. Robert Eakens, the acting chief of the Petroleum Division, wanted his opinion on a memorandum titled "Principles of Laws Governing Petroleum Development in Latin America."[126] It was a policy directive that the State Department would dispatch to embassy officers throughout the region. DeGolyer's response was swift and thorough. He approved the draft and added his own interpretation of the issues at stake.

DeGolyer's position and that of the Department was a moderately liberal one. He agreed that "it is essential that foreign operations show substantial benefit to the people as well as the governmental units of the country in which the operation is located." To encourage development that was acceptable to all parties, DeGolyer called for support for Latin American oil laws that were "stringent enough to protect the rights and interests of the nation and liberal enough to invite operation."[127] It was a measured, sensible policy that demonstrated DeGolyer's ability to think strategically, transcending the short-term interests of American oilmen and prioritizing the long-term interests of both industry and nation.

DeGolyer's strategic perspective reached its fullest expression in 1948 with his testimony before a Special Subcommittee on Petroleum established by the House Committee on Armed Services. His participation in this investigation of "Petroleum for National Defense" marked the apogee of his involvement in national affairs during the Cold War.[128] The subcommittee aimed to ensure that the nation could meet its immediate and long-term national security needs. Calling dozens of expert witnesses from within the government and the industry, the representatives did not find much that was reassuring.

The first witness was none other than the secretary of defense, and close collaborator of DeGolyer's, James Forrestal. The secretary's testimony revealed just how close DeGolyer had drawn to the reins of power. Before the hearings had taken place, Valentine Deale, an assistant to Forrestal, had sent DeGolyer a copy of the secretary's proposed testimony. Forrestal wanted to be certain that everything looked correct. Two days before Forrestal was to go before the subcommittee, DeGolyer called Deale to offer his approval.[129]

Forrestal would discuss a range of issues related to oil and the interests of the United States. First, he underscored the importance of petroleum to the military. Second, he detailed the bureaucratic structure of the military offices devoted to the oil issue. Third, he explained military policy toward petroleum reserves in the Western Hemisphere, and finally he turned to the question of oil in the Old World, especially the Middle East.[130]

Generally, Forrestal was cautious in his recommendations. Conservation of oil in the United States was imperative. He urged the development of offshore oil reservoirs in the Gulf of Mexico. The government should make a reasonable effort to consume foreign oil before tapping domestic sources. All of these positions had the potential to be controversial, but Forrestal balked at the prospect of offering specific proposals that might have stirred vocal opposition. If DeGolyer was disappointed by Forrestal's caution, he must have at least been gratified by one comment by the secretary during questioning about the volume of United States oil reserves. Pressed to take a position, Forrestal remarked, "I have relied largely upon the men I knew in business, which may make me suspect for having any contact with them. The figures of one man have been the most reliable that I have seen, a man named DeGolyer . . . I have found his estimates to be, broadly speaking, very sound."[131]

DeGolyer's own testimony would come about three weeks after Forrestal's, on February 6, 1948. After Congressman Cole introduced him to the subcommittee as "a recognized geologist," DeGolyer began to speak. He had no prepared statement to read, but only a few notes with which to work. Initially, the representatives wanted to know about the total volume of United States petroleum reserves. They were concerned about how quickly new oil was being discovered, and how fast existing reserves were being consumed. DeGolyer juggled the numbers with an ease that reflected his absolute mastery of the subject, pointing out statistical distortions that would have eluded a more casual observer.[132]

Then the congressmen began to move away from the numbers, asking him about his opinions on various policy matters. Dealing with questions on the support of a synthetic fuel industry and the question of offshore oil development, DeGolyer was rather noncommittal.[133] Then, turning to the issue of petroleum imports, he began to speak with deep conviction.

DeGolyer, like Forrestal, supported the use of foreign oil before domestic oil, in order to support the conservation of a supply in the event of war. Following further testimony, Congressman Lyndon Johnson appeared somewhat confused about DeGolyer's position. Seeking clarification, he asked, "Then, you think that we are safe in assuming that we have sufficient reserves, and also sufficient reserves can be developed in this hemisphere to make us self-sufficient in oil?"[134] DeGolyer was adamant in his denial, stating, "There are two hard facts in the oil business today . . . One of them is that the United States is the greatest consuming area in the world, and the other one is that the Middle East is the area of greatest proved reserves in the world."[135] Thinking through this reasoning, Johnson asked, "And you definitely recommend that the Nation import all the oil possible at the present time?"[136] DeGolyer responded firmly, "My recommendation is that this Nation import all of the oil that it can bring in without damaging its domestic industry, which is fundamental to it."[137]

In making this assertion, DeGolyer had said little more than Secretary Forrestal had three weeks earlier. Yet DeGolyer did not stop there. When questioned about specific policy proposals aimed at increasing imported oil and conserving domestic supply, he happily offered his own opinions.

Here, he wandered into controversy. For one, he advocated the establishment of a new government-operated strategic oil reserve. Strategic reserves had long been a concern of DeGolyer's, going back at least to 1924, when he critiqued management of naval oil reserves.[138] In recent years, Forrestal had called upon DeGolyer to study the operation of the reserve at Elk Hills, California.[139] Now, DeGolyer outlined a plan under which the government would choose a large, developed oilfield in the United States and make a trade arrangement with its owners. Essentially, the private owners of the oilfield would agree to stop producing petroleum in the field, and the government would purchase, for their benefit, a volume of foreign oil equivalent to the daily production that the owners lost. In this way, the government would obtain title to the oil in the reserve at a rate equal to the amount of foreign oil that was purchased. The proposed policy would use foreign oil before domestic supplies and enhance the nation's security in the event of a crisis. Congressman Johnson, anticipating a criticism of the proposal, asked, "You would be putting the Government in business, would you not?" DeGolyer was undisturbed. He did not have the feeling, he remarked, "that everything that the Government does puts it in business." "I don't either," Johnson assured him.[140]

If these were dangerous waters, DeGolyer's position on import tax policy was even more controversial. Again, Johnson raised the first question. "Would you advocate a reduction in the present tariff on the importation of oil?" DeGolyer surprised the congressmen, answering, "I would not charge a tariff on oil." "Take off the whole tariff?" asked Overton Brooks of Louisiana. "Yes, sir. It is crude material. It is an energy resource. It is of tremendous importance to the Nation," DeGolyer responded. His position made perfect sense. If the aim was to increase imports and reduce exhaustion of domestic supplies, any tariff was counterproductive. Brooks, obviously taken aback, queried, "To what extent are your views in that respect supported by the rest of the industry?" DeGolyer conceded, "I doubt if they are supported by the rest of the industry at all."[141]

The reaction to DeGolyer's testimony in the days following his appearance before the subcommittee would remove any doubts he may have had on this point. The Texas Independent Producers and Royalty Owners Association (TIPROA) reacted swiftly with a venomous attack on DeGolyer's policies as well as on DeGolyer himself. H. J. Porter, president of TIPROA, offered his own statement, appended to DeGolyer's testimony, denouncing DeGolyer's ideas as "thoughtless, ill-advised, and contrary to American principles of private enterprise and initiative." Continuing the indictment, Porter asserted, "Dr. DeGolyer apparently has spent so much time with Federal bureaucrats during the past ten years that he has become infected with the deadening virus of regimentation and economic controls."[142]

Worse, DeGolyer had connections with interested parties. As Porter pointed out, "During his entire career in the oil industry Dr. DeGolyer has been closely connected with large oil companies and for a number of years was president of a company owned and controlled by the Lord Cowdray interests of England. He still has close personal connections, and possibly financial connections, with those people."[143] Going further, Porter noted, "He is an unusually wealthy man."[144] In his most-extreme insinuation, Porter claimed that DeGolyer stood to profit from the positions that he took on the matter. This attack was off the mark.

DeGolyer's financial interests were every bit as much tied to the domestic oil industry as they were to any foreign ventures. True, DeGolyer and MacNaughton were international as well as domestic consultants, but DeGolyer's potential gain from promoting imports would have been muddled and uncertain at best. His opponents, on the other hand, generally advocated policies that would have clear benefits for their own financial interests. In retrospect, the arguments of these oilmen, for the most part independent domestic producers, seem obviously wrong. Porter, for instance, asserted that the removal of the petroleum tariff would have no impact on the volume of imports. Porter's fervent opposition to any such move belied this claim.[145]

In the weeks that followed, American oilmen targeted DeGolyer in further attacks. It was something of a compliment. Opponents of the policies that DeGolyer advocated recognized that his national prestige required a coordinated and sustained response to counter DeGolyer's influence. Almost all aspects of his testimony came under fire. Even his assessment of the Middle East's potential was criticized. "Is it not possible that he has over guessed the reserves [in the Middle East]?" asked one oilman, noting that DeGolyer had underestimated the volume of the East Texas field.[146]

Attacking another aspect of DeGolyer's argument, the same oilman pointed out that Middle Eastern oilfields would be vulnerable to Soviet occupation in the event of war. Of course, this was not really DeGolyer's point. His idea was to use as much Middle Eastern oil as possible in peacetime in order to conserve as much domestic oil as possible.[147]

For DeGolyer's ideas about establishing a government stockpile of petroleum, there was, if anything, an even more frigid response. One critic referred to the plan as "a fantastic long stride toward nationalization of the natural petroleum resources."[148] DeGolyer had explicitly denied any such intent. No matter, critics felt free to assail his plan "for taking over oil fields in Texas," noting that "such action would create chaos and ruin."[149]

In the end, these ad hominem attacks and convoluted arguments proved effective at quashing any move toward the policies that DeGolyer advocated. If they convinced few, their vociferous objection to DeGolyer's vision at least made the senators aware that they would meet with strong political opposition if they moved in that direction. True, they could not stop many of DeGolyer's predictions from realization in fact. One came to pass even as DeGolyer's opponents launched their assault. The year 1948 would be the first since the birth of the petroleum industry that the United States would import more petroleum than it exported. His prophecy regarding the incredible potential of the Middle Eastern fields was only just beginning to be fulfilled.[150]

Despite the confirmation of this central assumption in DeGolyer's reasoning, the domestic industry, particularly the smaller producers, effectively mobilized the political force necessary to block these proposed policies. To be sure, DeGolyer had found many within the government to be sympathetic with his concerns. Conservation was certainly in the strategic interest of the nation. But in the end, it was not enough. The final repudiation of the strategic conservation advocated by DeGolyer would not come until after his death. On March 10, 1959, President Eisenhower, whose election DeGolyer had twice supported, reluctantly announced the establishment of mandatory quotas on oil imports into the United States.[151] The goal of the policy was to stem the flood of foreign oil onto the domestic market. The quotas protected United States oil producers, but they also encouraged the use of domestic oil reserves instead of foreign sources. It was precisely the opposite of the position that DeGolyer had advocated and, in retrospect, remarkably shortsighted.

Despite the fact that DeGolyer had failed to win political approval for the policies that he advocated, he remained, in the late 1940s, at the peak of his career. His venture with the Texas Eastern Transmission Corporation had proven a remarkable success. He sat on the board of many lucrative businesses. In Dallas, he was a revered celebrity. DeGolyer had built a national reputation as a scientist, a businessman, and even a scholar. But life was soon to take a turn for the worse. Problems with his health began to interfere with his work and eventually with his hobbies as well. As DeGolyer himself might have put it, his luck was about to run out.

# 9 | Sage

*When you get as old as I am you will find that one of the compensations of old age is that some . . . problems of primary importance are going to have to be left to our children to solve. I hope they can do better than we have done but I doubt it.*

— Everette Lee DeGolyer to Becky Jones, April 2, 1948[1]

As the 1940s ended, Everette Lee DeGolyer could look back on a decade in which he had scaled new heights in fame and fortune. Although policymakers often regarded the political views of other oilmen as tainted by financial interests, there was widespread respect for DeGolyer's opinions. He was, as one college president put it, a "scientific Olympian."[2] A man of wealth with an appreciation for the finer things in life, DeGolyer was comfortable rubbing elbows at cocktail parties with the nation's leading industrialists. Dignitaries visiting Dallas were frequent guests, and the DeGolyers hosted figures as diverse as Secretary of State Dean Acheson, Afghan Prime Minister Sardar Shah Mahmud, and Saudi Prince Mishaal. Acclaimed by bureaucrats and businessmen alike, and possessing more than adequate financial resources, DeGolyer was free to dabble in politics, toy with interesting commercial ventures, and pursue his scholarly hobbies.[3]

Sadly, DeGolyer's remarkable run of good fortune would come to an end in the 1950s. True, many continued to hail him as a scientific and entrepreneurial giant. But beginning in 1949, his health took a turn for the worse. First, he suffered the loss of sight in one eye as a result of a detached retina. Within two years, doctors diagnosed him with a debilitating disease, aplastic anemia, which greatly curtailed the frenetic travel that had characterized his career. For the first time in over three decades, DeGolyer found himself forced to remain home for an extended period of time.

Paradoxically, rising participation in government committees and corporate boardrooms accompanied DeGolyer's declining health. However, his participation was, for the most part, more apparent than actual. He had achieved the status of a scientific and industrial sage whose very name inspired confidence in the ventures to which he nomi-

Everette Lee DeGolyer, Secretary of State Dean Acheson and Charles Francis (from left to right), June 13, 1950. The DeGolyer home frequently hosted dignitaries in Dallas, as in the case of this visit by President Truman's secretary of state. At the time, DeGolyer's son-in-law, George C. McGhee, was serving under Acheson as assistant secretary of state. Charles Francis, together with DeGolyer, was a founder of the Texas Eastern Transmission Corporation. (Everette Lee DeGolyer Collection. Courtesy of DeGolyer Library, Southern Methodist University.)

nally attached himself. A healthy man would have found it impossible to attend to all of the business, professional, and government obligations that theoretically had a claim on his time. Of necessity, DeGolyer increasingly left most of this work to other, younger men and women. He relied heavily on his personal secretary to attend to these matters and to ensure that he met the minimal requirements of his various offices.

The one area where DeGolyer became more active over these years involved his amateur scholarship, book collecting, and philanthropic pursuits. Spending extended time in his formidable library, he indulged his intellectual curiosity with a multitude of subjects. DeGolyer also promoted the publication of books whose themes were close to his heart—the history of science, the oil industry, and the old West. His efforts did not always meet with success, but he pursued his ends with characteristic zeal. One task became particularly engrossing—the creation of a library and a curriculum on the history of science at the University of Oklahoma. This project appealed to DeGolyer as both a scientist and a bibliophile and became a significant aspect of his legacy.

As the 1950s wore on, DeGolyer knew that he had entered the twilight of his life. Although he basked in the glow of professional recognition, these years were in many ways the most challenging yet. Previously, success had come to DeGolyer because he had refused to accept his limitations; he had seized opportunities that had welcomed a risk taker; and he had poured boundless energy into his pursuits. As his age advanced and infirmities worsened, circumstances forced DeGolyer to do just the opposite: to come to terms with his limitations, exercise greater caution, and conserve his energy. He would have to leave "problems of primary importance" to younger men and women in business, government, and even in his own family. DeGolyer would be reluctant, and ultimately unwilling to accept this new reality.

DeGolyer's decline in health began in 1949, when he celebrated his sixty-third birthday. The preceding year had been eventful. He had testified before Congress on matters of national security; he had claimed leadership of the board of the *Saturday Review of Literature;* he had given the commencement address at the University of Oklahoma. These were only the highlights.

In the spring of 1949, Everette Lee and Nell DeGolyer had "married off" their last child, Everett Lee DeGolyer Jr. As the elder Everette put it, this left "two dull old people alone in a big house." He and Nell proposed to "escape" for a while with a European vacation. DeGolyer's concerns about an empty nest were a little overstated. He had never been able to stay in one place for long, and even in his sixties his professional life was more demanding than that of many younger men. Nevertheless, the departure of young Everett Lee was a milestone. Whether or not the motive of the planned trip was to help cope with this change, or just another case of DeGolyer wanderlust, the two looked forward to getting away.[4]

The trip would include visits to Italy, Holland, and Great Britain, with stops along the way to visit with friends and acquaintances that DeGolyer had made over the course of his career. Even before the couple left the United States, there were signs of trouble. DeGolyer had been suffering problems with his eyesight. His right eye in particular would develop "streamers" after extended periods of reading. But it apparently did not occur to either Everette or Nell that his symptoms might make travel inadvisable. The condition might worsen, or it might not. Neither Everette nor Nell was going to slow down because of something that might not happen. Nevertheless, DeGolyer's life was about to slow down, whether he wanted it to or not.[5]

On the surface of things, the trip seemed to go very well, at least at first. The couple arrived in Italy in August. From the beginning, Nell noticed that her husband was out of sorts. His eyesight seemed to be troubling him more than usual, and he was uncharacteristically unsocial. This was bad, but matters took a turn for the worse as the couple traveled from Venice to Rome. Turning to Nell in the car, DeGolyer gasped, "Nell, I can't see. I can't even see you." Turning his head, he realized that he could still see through his left eye, but he was completely blind in the right.[6]

Surely, this would have been the time to call off the trip and seek expert medical attention. But with characteristic determination, DeGolyer insisted on keeping their plans to visit with old friends in Holland and England. Nell was understandably upset, particularly after Everette told her that his good eye was "filled with streamers." In London, American Ambassador Lewis Douglas, a friend of DeGolyer's, insisted he see a specialist. The diagnosis was disturbing. It was a detached retina. Surgery would be necessary.[7]

With the doctor's approval, DeGolyer decided to wait until his return to the United States for the operation. The surgery took place on September 26, 1949.[8] The results were disappointing. Writing to Wallace Pratt, DeGolyer acknowledged, "The operation was not particularly successful. However, I have some hope that the eye may improve with time."[9] DeGolyer's hope was unfounded. He would never regain sight in his right eye.

Still, he managed to put on a brave face, downplaying his disability and even joking about it. Ambassador Douglas, who had lost one eye years before in an accident, welcomed DeGolyer to the "Cyclops Club."[10] DeGolyer, delighting in the idea, wrote to other friends, with tongue in cheek, about his desire to organize a formal chapter.[11]

Above all, DeGolyer refused to allow his ocular ailment to deter him from his scholarly research and book-collecting hobby. In fact, he would spend more and more time in his library at *El Rancho Encinal*.

Unfortunately, this increasing obsession with books was partly a reflection of other health problems that began to trouble him at about the same time.

In January 1951, DeGolyer came down with a case of the flu. At first, there was nothing particularly worrying about it. He was frequently sick in January and rarely let it slow him down. His doctor prescribed an antibiotic, and DeGolyer anticipated recovery.[12] But this time it was different. Instead of bouncing back after a few weeks, he seemed to worsen. Matters became grave. It was not just influenza. The doctor pronounced him to be suffering from a case of "refractory anemia." This was a serious condition. He would need blood transfusions. Writing about the diagnosis and his subsequent hospitalization and treatment, DeGolyer joked about it all in typical fashion:

> The [disease is] what the doctor calls, in his gentler moments, refractory anemia. I think he really invented this term for me. He should probably have called it *Anemia degolyeri.* At any rate, after spending about six weeks at home under the beneficent assurance that nature was the Great Healer, I was finally moved to the hospital last week and a large quantity of other people's blood injected into my system. This may ultimately result in a tremendous improvement in me. I might even get a new idea. The stage in which I now rest is that I was finally moved across the street to a second hospital from which my newly acquired blood had been purchased at what seems to me the rather outrageous cost of $100 a pint, since which I've had busy days.[13]

Humor aside, DeGolyer's illness was very serious. In order to arrive at a more conclusive diagnosis, his doctors ordered multiple blood tests. Dubbing them the "blood snatchers," he complained, "Apparently the hospital is trying to get all of the blood [from earlier transfusions] back in runs of five to ten cubic centimeters per transaction."[14] For over two months, his condition confined him to bed.[15] Once released, he bemoaned the slow pace of his recovery, writing with resignation, "I suppose I will be on and off the sick list for the better part of a year."[16]

Sadly, DeGolyer's illness would keep him "on and off the sick list" for the rest of his life. After extensive testing, his doctors finally settled on a diagnosis of aplastic anemia. The doctor's prescription of the antibiotic Chloromycetin to treat his influenza in January 1951 may have caused the onset.[17] The disease was a serious and usually lethal blood disorder, requiring continued transfusions because of the inability of DeGolyer's body to produce enough of its own blood cells.[18]

It took almost a year before DeGolyer felt well enough to claim recovery. Crediting whiskey for his improved spirits, he looked forward to getting back to a more active life.[19] Nine months later, he wrote with renewed optimism that he was over the worst. However, the respite proved only temporary. Despite periodic improvement in his condition, DeGolyer never shook the disease. He also developed what he saw as a cat-and-mouse relationship with his doctors.[20] They were always trying to pin him down in one place, whereas he desperately wished to travel in pursuit of the social, professional, and business activities that had occupied him in earlier, healthier years.

To make matters worse, he continued to suffer problems with vision. In July 1953, he had a hemorrhage in his good eye that put him under doctor's orders to curtail his reading.[21] The prospect of total blindness loomed, but mercifully he recovered.

DeGolyer's misfortunes continued when his doctors determined that he required further surgery. The decision stemmed from an alternative explanation for his anemia—perhaps the spleen was the cause of it all.[22] He wrote grimly, "My platelets have gone to hell again. I presume that I am being prepared for the knife."[23] He was right; it would be a spleenectomy. DeGolyer underwent the operation in February 1955.[24] It went well, but his health problems continued unabated.

DeGolyer became increasingly and understandably depressed as he contemplated his condition. Following his spleenectomy, he wrote his old friend Wallace Pratt: "Why should a fat man have anemia? At best, it is amusing and at worst, it is ridiculous."[25] More than any other aspect of his declining health, it was the limitation on what had been a remarkably active life that frustrated DeGolyer. Whether or not he was willing to accept it, his illness would increasingly curtail his involvement in business and professional affairs. Yet on the surface, not much had changed as he continued to hold many of the boardroom and committee positions he had taken over the years.

In truth, DeGolyer's activities in the 1950s present something of a paradox. Judging from DeGolyer's formidable résumé of directorships and committee memberships, one would not guess that he was a gravely ill man. Quite the opposite. In 1954, years after the onset of his afflictions, he remained a director on the board of the Southern Pacific Railroad, the First National Bank of Dallas, the Louisiana Land

and Exploration Company, Republic Natural Gas Company, the Texas Eastern Transmission Corporation, the Great Plains Development Company, and the Christiana Oil Corporation. Further, he continued to serve as chairman of the board for the *Saturday Review of Literature* and, of course, DeGolyer and MacNaughton.[26] It was a remarkable portfolio of titles for a man who was constantly in and out of the hospital.

In addition to these posts, DeGolyer accepted appointment to new positions. In July 1954, shareholders elected DeGolyer as a director of Dresser Industries, a leading manufacturer of oil, gas, and chemical equipment.[27] He would hold the position until just weeks before his death.[28]

DeGolyer even participated in founding a few new ventures in these last years. In 1953, he joined with others to form Valdebro, a company that would explore for oil in Spain.[29] Two years later he was a part of founding a new mining corporation.[30]

It is also fair to say that DeGolyer took his various boardroom obligations seriously. Although he was often unable to travel to meetings, he followed developments in all these companies as best he could. He poured over the reams of paper that came in the mail—meeting minutes, financial statements, and geological reports—and wrote to responsible company officers to give his opinion on matters. Well into the last year of his life, he composed analyses of corporate affairs, weighing the advisability of this or that course of action.[31]

DeGolyer's name commanded respect outside the business world as well. His government service over the course of the last two decades had won him a reputation as a thoughtful and public-minded expert in oil affairs. His success as a businessman made him an acceptable representative of the petroleum industry. However, he also had demonstrated a willingness to oppose his fellow oilmen when he felt warranted, as he had during his service with the Petroleum Reserves Corporation and later during congressional petroleum hearings. This earned him the esteem of strategic thinkers and policymakers. And so, despite his declining health, DeGolyer found that there were still many who sought his participation in committees aimed at shaping government petroleum policy.

In many ways, his involvement in public work paralleled his participation in the business world during these years. That is to say, he retained many of his old positions and took on a few new obligations, even as he found his ability to participate in these activities increasingly impaired. He continued to serve on the National Petroleum Council (NPC), where he had been since 1946, and even accepted appointment to the Committee on Productive Petroleum Capacity in 1954.[32] DeGolyer followed the NPC's work closely at least until 1955, offering suggestions and analysis regarding United States oil production.[33] He also retained his membership with the Military Petroleum Advisory Board, on which he had served since 1947. In summer 1951, he accepted reappointment to the Board, but his participation had been no more than nominal since the onset of his anemia in January of that year.[34]

As in his business dealings, DeGolyer also took on a few new obligations, even as his health suffered. Following his unsuccessful eye operation, but before he was stricken with anemia, DeGolyer joined another government commission concerned with national security—the Scientific Manpower Advisory Committee (SMAC).[35] The government formed SMAC in 1950 with the goal of planning the mobilization of scientists for a global struggle with the Soviet Union.[36] Although DeGolyer anticipated an active role on the SMAC, his battle with anemia limited his involvement.

On the other hand, DeGolyer struggled hard to uphold his duties with the Atomic Energy Commission (AEC) well after his ailments had made it difficult for him to do so. DeGolyer seemed to prioritize his activities with the AEC over his other government work, perhaps because his work on the Raw Materials Committee was so close to his lifelong love of prospecting. In spring 1952, as his anemia entered a brief period of remission, he seized a chance to travel with the AEC, touring uranium mines on the Colorado Plateau. DeGolyer thoroughly enjoyed the "work," relishing the opportunity to reconnoiter the canyons of the region by airplane.[37] In 1954, he managed another such trip and wrote to Wallace Pratt about how much he had enjoyed his AEC participation.[38] He would not be able to keep up his involvement for long. The following year, his illness forced him to cancel plans for another AEC trip.[39] His resignation followed in short order.[40] Yet even in the apparent withdrawal from this obligation, DeGolyer found the prospecting that he had conducted on behalf of the AEC irresistible. Within three months, he had joined in a new venture, General Minerals Corporation, with the express purpose of exploring, developing, and processing uranium.[41] Sadly, he had little time left.

In contrast to earlier years, DeGolyer's work on behalf of the government at this time was not controversial. The fact is that up until the last years of his life, DeGolyer was never particularly vocal about his own political views that did not concern his area of expertise—natural resources. It is true that he remained a loyal Republican all his life. He had supported the candidacy of Herbert Hoover twice; canvassed for contributions to Wendell Willkie's presidential campaign; backed Harold Stassen's failed bid for the Republican nomination in 1948; and made sizeable donations to Eisenhower in 1952.[42] But in all of these instances, DeGolyer gave the impression of being more the faithful partisan than the committed ideologue.

It is also true that DeGolyer had been deeply engaged in the political controversies surrounding the oil industry from the 1930s on. However, these issues were technical in nature, and his perspective was closer to that of a technical expert rather than a passionate political commentator transfixed by an ideological vision. And although it is true that his support for Wendell Willkie had attracted the attention of local newspapers, that support too was couched in terms of the consequences for the oil industry.[43] When it came to matters that fell beyond his purview as a scientist and a businessman, he seemed almost reticent.

But in later years, DeGolyer proved somewhat more willing to express his political views. Some of this appears to have been a natural development arising from his status as an icon of industry and a scientific authority. There was more interest in what he thought about the issues of the day than there had been in, say, the 1920s. Another possible cause of this greater expressiveness was his interaction with individuals that were devoted to public political commentary, as was the case with *Saturday Review of Literature* editor Norman Cousins. Whatever the case, DeGolyer became more politically vocal in his last years.

Some of these late pronouncements were public and less controversial in nature. These occasions revealed him to be, unsurprisingly, an anti-communist, but not a particularly polemical one. There was a speech he gave at the semicentennial celebration of Spindletop, which celebrated the virtues of the free market.[44] There was also the publication of a "Declaration of Freedom," to which he contributed along with Norman Cousins, Archibald MacLeish, Reinhold Niebuhr, and others.[45]

His private political remarks were more interesting, if inconsistent, as he occasionally delved into Cold War politics in letters to friends and associates. In his correspondence with Norman Cousins, a liberal public intellectual, he expressed his concern that anti-censorship advocates were hysterical in their response to anti-communist measures.[46]

Yet in a letter to Dallas Public Library staff, he argued the apparent opposite: that censorship could only undermine a reasoned response to communism.[47] And DeGolyer had criticism to offer for both Senator Joseph McCarthy and the senator's opponents as well, identifying himself as "not pro-McCarthy nor anti-McCarthy."[48]

One interesting political association was with William F. Buckley Jr., a founding figure of the twentieth-century conservative movement in the United States. Buckley's father was a Texas lawyer and oilman who had been active in Mexico at the time of DeGolyer's work there in the 1910s. DeGolyer wrote to the elder Buckley, congratulating him on his son's publication of *God and Man at Yale* in 1951, and cosponsored a talk by the younger Buckley, in Dallas, to discuss the book.[49] There were limits to DeGolyer's enthusiasm though, as he turned down an offer by Buckley to invest in his new publication, *National Weekly,* a name soon to be changed to *National Review.*[50]

But if DeGolyer felt comfortable rubbing elbows with Buckley, he had a closer relationship with liberal editor Norman Cousins. The correspondence between the two reveals that if they did not always agree, they still respected one another's views. There is no better evidence of this than a story told by Cousins himself about a speech sponsored by the American Friends' Service Committee that he gave in Dallas in June 1953.[51] Cousins, who was a peace advocate in the midst of the Korean War, had been contacted before the event by a political activist who tried to dissuade him from speaking. Cousins refused and instructed the man to take up the issue with DeGolyer, who was after all, Cousins's boss. The outcome, as related by Cousins, is worth quoting at length:

> He did so. The results were completely predictable. Mr. De told him to jump in the lake. He then telephoned the Quakers, asked if he could join the sponsors of the meeting, and volunteered to introduce me. He telegraphed me saying he expected me to come to Dallas and to be sure to stay at the house.
>
> The moment it was announced that Mr. De would appear on the program, all opposition collapsed. There was no picket line, just an overflow crowd, many of them attracted no doubt by the prestige of Mr. De's name. The entire episode was one that would have made Mr. Oliver W. Holmes sing for joy.
>
> It was the only time Mr. De had introduced me at a meeting, or, for

that matter, had heard me speak publicly. I can't remember a more generous introduction or one that touched me more deeply. On the way home, Mr. De congratulated me on the talk and added he didn't agree with a damned thing I had said. We laughed, then spent the rest of the evening talking about the new publishing program of the University of Oklahoma Press, the need for a new history of science, and the mess the Dodgers had made of the World Series.[52]

The picture of DeGolyer that emerges from statements such as these and from his correspondence is that of an individual who was engaged in the political discussions of his day, but not as an ideological warrior. And generally speaking, he maintained civility in engaging people with whom he disagreed. Although identifying himself as "conservative enough" and maintaining a lifelong affiliation with the Republican Party, there was a lack of consistency, or perhaps a pragmatism, in his political outlook that would have made his views unpalatable to the ideological purist.[53]

In light of his political leanings, a suggested nomination to Dwight Eisenhower's Cabinet in 1952 gratified DeGolyer. The incident reflected his renown as a businessman, public servant, and scientist. In November of that year, following the national election, Carey Croneis, the President of Beloit College in Wisconsin, wrote to the president elect. Croneis was an associate of DeGolyer's on SMAC and the president of the American Geological Institute. His concern was the appointment of the next secretary of the interior. He argued that "the millions of educators, the tens of thousands of scientists, and the more than fifteen thousand geologists in this country would . . . derive a new sense of faith in American democracy" if the secretary of the interior were really qualified for the position.[54] Croneis went on to offer a list of men who he believed fit that description. Among the names was "E. L. DeGolyer . . . One of the world's best known geologists."[55] The letter was in the mail for only a few hours before Eisenhower announced that Governor Douglas MacKay would be his pick for the post. Croneis received a polite reply.[56] Nonetheless, Croneis forwarded the exchange to DeGolyer, who was "pleasantly surprised."[57]

That a respected geologist and educator had suggested DeGolyer for such an exalted office says something about his status as a scientist, public servant, and businessman. That the post ultimately went to a career politician says something about the limitations of scientific and industrial renown. Aside from this, DeGolyer's health was certainly not up to the task.

Croneis' status as a college president also points to something else about DeGolyer's activities during these years. DeGolyer had turned increasingly to his scholarly interests. These involved research, writing, publication, and philanthropic work, of which favored universities were often the beneficiaries. It would be uncharitable to ascribe Croneis' solicitous exchanges with Eisenhower and DeGolyer to a desire to win funds for his school. On the other hand, DeGolyer was a man with money who was building a record for patronage of the academy. The benefits of cultivating such a friend must have been somewhere in the back of his mind. DeGolyer's progressive turn to philanthropy was in part a realization of interests in science and history that he had cultivated over the course of a lifetime. But it was also the result of the unfortunate circumstances caused by his growing list of ailments.

DeGolyer's medical misfortunes were dark clouds that hung over him throughout the 1950s. However, if one could identify a silver lining, it was that he was able to turn his attention to his "hobbies" with an intensity that would have been impossible had doctor's orders not forced him to sit still. Early on, DeGolyer himself recognized that his illness had allowed him to focus on his scholarly interests as never before. He remarked, "If one ever said that an illness is a pleasant thing I might make that remark about mine. There has been no pain and I have got more reading done than during any other period twice as long."[58] He conceded that much of this progress was due to his immobility, noting, "I have been home for a longer period than I have been for many years."[59]

As in earlier years, DeGolyer was not content to enjoy his magnificent library alone. He felt compelled to share his research, to produce book reviews and articles, to begin new book projects that would disseminate the results of his inquiries. So it was that his declining health had surprisingly limited effect on his scholarly output. True, he was not at the peak of his productivity, but he continued to publish his own work well after his health took a turn for the worse. The subjects he picked tended to be those closest to his heart. The oil industry and related topics of geology and science were by far the most consistent objects of his attention.[60] Contending with DeGolyer's publications on these topics were articles on the Southwest and its history.[61] As in past years,

Everette Lee DeGolyer at Spindletop Commemoration Ceremonies. By the 1950s, DeGolyer's renown made him an excellent representative to speak for the petroleum industry at the celebration. (Everette Lee DeGolyer Collection. Courtesy of DeGolyer Library, Southern Methodist University.)

DeGolyer also planned to publish books on topics where he felt that he possessed an expert perspective. As late as 1954, DeGolyer found himself "up to his neck" in a history of the American petroleum industry for Macmillan publishing.[62] As with his other book projects, he would never complete it.

In addition to composing his own pieces, DeGolyer also continued to dabble in publishing works by others that he viewed as worthy. Here, his primary focus was not the oil industry, but the history of the Southwest. Following his eye surgery in the fall of 1949, DeGolyer developed a friendship with Savoie Lottinville of the University of Oklahoma Press.

Lottinville seems to have impressed him with a sense of pessimism regarding the prospects for the press. DeGolyer wrote to G. L. Cross, the president of the university, to plead for its support. By this point, DeGolyer was already deeply involved in philanthropic work on behalf of the university. His voice carried weight. Writing to Cross, he asserted, "I do hope that nothing happens to the University of Oklahoma Press which I regard as one of the great glories of the school."[63] Lottinville must have known that he had won a powerful patron.

Over the next few years, the correspondence between DeGolyer and Lottinville remained friendly and consistent. Then in the fall of 1952, Lottinville raised the possibility of a new series of publications by the press. DeGolyer was excited at the prospect that Lottinville contemplated, writing, "Your letter . . . caused my heart to palpitate. Do you actually intend to start a Western classics [series]? If so, I will be glad to do anything I can to help."[64] DeGolyer went on to suggest *Banditti of the Plains* be given special place in the planned list of books.[65] He would continue to offer suggestions in a hail of correspondence that followed.[66] In the process, he agreed to write an introduction for the first work in the series, *The Vigilantes of Montana.*[67] And DeGolyer helped to solicit introductions for the other works published.[68] In addition to *The Banditti* and *The Vigilantes,* DeGolyer actively assisted in the publication of *The Life of Billy the Kid,* and *Wah-To-Yah.*[69] DeGolyer was particularly proud of his work on these books, referring to himself as the "foster father" of the series.[70]

Despite his commitment and genuine enjoyment of publication, DeGolyer's most significant role as a publisher, as chairman of the board of the *Saturday Review,* ended in 1955.[71] In that year, he sold his interest to Norman Cousins for $25,000. It was a fraction of the amount of money that DeGolyer had poured into the magazine. His "official" reason for selling was that he did not wish to continue investing money to keep the publication afloat.[72] It was more probable that he had found it increasingly difficult to keep up with its business and preferred to leave the venture to others. Over the years, the *Saturday Review* had been a pleasant hobby, but it was hardly a winning investment. It was irresponsible to keep spending money on it after he could no longer enjoy it.

DeGolyer's myriad articles, book reviews, and the various works of others that he brought to publication were serious pursuits, but their significance as a part of his legacy paled in comparison with his book-collecting activities. Since 1914, DeGolyer had built up a remarkable library, with an obsessive zeal. Its contents reflected his own interests: geology and the oil industry, to be sure, but also literature and the history of the Southwest and Mexico. As he came to realize that he was entering the twilight of his life, DeGolyer developed a growing sense of duty about his books. Spending more time in his library, he sought ways to integrate his love of book collecting with a scientific concern to advance the frontiers of knowledge. He wanted his "hobby" to have a greater significance, a larger impact than his own reading pleasure.

The most obvious connection between DeGolyer's books and his commitment to science was, naturally, in his collection of scientific works. Although he had bought scientific works throughout his lifetime, DeGolyer only became a serious collector of scientific "literature" in the 1940s. Purchasing the "classics" of science in their original editions, his historical approach to book collecting eventually resulted in an amazing library of the history of science. Over the course of the decade, he expanded his purchases to include modern critical editions, translations, and modern secondary works. By the close of the 1940s, he was already thinking about a new venue for the collection, someplace where it would reach a greater audience than at *El Rancho Encinal*.[73]

Many knew of the vast extent of DeGolyer's library, and eventually it came to the attention of the president of the University of Oklahoma, G. L. Cross. Writing in the summer of 1949, he suggested, predictably, that DeGolyer's alma mater would be a most fitting repository for the collection. Even better, the library would form a core of documents around which the university could fashion a course in the history of science. Cross's suggestion fit perfectly with DeGolyer's ambitions.[74]

In November 1949, as DeGolyer struggled to adjust to life without sight in one eye, his collection was packed up and shipped to Norman, Oklahoma. Nevertheless, he was still unable to fully part with these prized possessions—they were only on loan. Writing to Savoie Lottinville, DeGolyer expressed pride in the books he had sent, but promised, "You ain't seen nothing yet!"[75] His confidence in this pledge reflected the fact that he had retained many of the rarest items for temporary display at Rice University and at Southern Methodist University. Eventually, DeGolyer would send even these remarkable books to the University of Oklahoma.[76]

However, DeGolyer was most enthusiastic about the prospect of founding a course in the history of science. This was, for him, the most important point. Books on the shelf were useless if they remained unread. A university course would ensure that students would read them. Writing to one of his book dealers, DeGolyer stressed that the library was only on loan. It would go to the University of Oklahoma "if they will institute a course in the history of science; otherwise, it will go to some other school."[77]

To underscore his intent, he wrote to G. L. Cross, reminding him of his interest in developing the course. Lest the president miss his point, he enclosed a catalogue of his exhibit at Southern Methodist University. DeGolyer's willingness to continue his valuable donations was contingent upon the establishment of the course in the history of science. Cross was no fool. Plans for the new class went forward.[78]

Less than two weeks after DeGolyer had written Cross, he received a letter from Savoie Lottinville, detailing progress on development of the curriculum. "The DeGolyer Course in the History of Science and Technology" would be open only to honors-level seniors. Lecturers would speak in the same room that held the magnificent book collection. The university was serious about instituting the course.[79]

It took longer than DeGolyer might have hoped for the realization of those plans. Finally, by the spring semester of 1953, the university was ready to move forward. DeGolyer agreed to pay for a distinguished speaker to give the inaugural lecture. Ultimately, this honor fell to Arthur Holley Compton, a physicist, Nobel Prize laureate, and personal friend of both Cross and DeGolyer. In February 1953, Compton delivered this first lecture on "Science and Its Impact on Society."[80]

Recruiting a professor to teach the course on a permanent basis took longer. Dr. Duane Roller, the technical editor of the Howard Hughes Aircraft Corporation, gave a second lecture three months later. The next year, the university would appoint Roller as an assistant professor of history and the curator of the DeGolyer Collection. The course seemed to be gaining the solid footing that DeGolyer had envisioned.[81]

DeGolyer had not remained an observer as the university struggled to develop the history of science curriculum. Even as he recovered from his first, difficult bout with anemia, he had written President Cross to plan for further acquisitions. DeGolyer was concerned that his library relied too much on original editions often written in medieval Latin and inaccessible to the average student. He proposed a campaign of purchases in modern editions to make the collection more effective in the context of the curriculum. Over the next two years, he would make significant progress toward this goal.[82]

DeGolyer's creation of the library for the University of Oklahoma was tremendously important to him as he struggled to cope with his declining health. Writing to Wallace Pratt, he confessed that the task had afforded many "delightful experiences," particularly his investigation of early works on geology.[83] One year later, he was less positive. In a letter to his old friend Charles Hamilton, he remarked, "I don't do anything worthwhile anymore but manage to keep interested in all sorts of things." He went on to mention his work on behalf of the library. It was the only activity that he felt was significant enough to mention, confessing with resignation, "I am semi-retired."[84] But despite his gloomy outlook, he was also quite proud of his work, boasting that the university now possessed "the finest library in this hemisphere on the early history of geology."[85]

After several years building up the history of science collection, DeGolyer seems to have become a little bored with the project. Perhaps he had simply reached the point where he was satisfied with his handiwork and was ready to move on to something new. Having enjoyed the establishment of this collection so much, he began to suggest other possibilities to President Cross. Perhaps Cross would be interested in building a collection of business histories?[86] Maybe the university would benefit from the establishment of a society of petroleum industry historians?[87] Cross moved swiftly on DeGolyer's latter suggestion. Faculty called meetings. The school made plans for a journal. Responsible parties computed costs.[88]

Yet DeGolyer was ailing and in the hospital again. Responding to Cross's inquiries, he confessed that he did not think the society should go forward. He explained, "[U]ntil more people show greater interest in this subject for its own sake, no historical society can support itself." The key issue was "support." DeGolyer was unwilling to support this venture with his money and increasingly unable to support it with his attention.[89]

Although DeGolyer enjoyed special solicitude from his beneficiaries at the University of Oklahoma, his reputation as a philanthropist and even as a scholar was national. Numerous universities had already recognized him through the bestowal of honorary degrees. In the last year of his life, he would receive genuinely national recognition. In April 1956, the United States Congress passed a joint resolution, subsequently approved by the president, naming DeGolyer a regent in the Smithsonian Institution. The attention pleased him, but he had little chance to make a mark.[90]

In some ways, DeGolyer's renown was at its pinnacle in the 1950s. Although he had been the focus of controversy during the 1940s, when he took sometimes-unpopular positions regarding oil policy, the last years of his life were less turbulent. Despite past differences with businessmen and politicians, he had earned the respect and even reverence of the petroleum industry, the national security establishment, the academy, and his local community in Dallas. So even considering his medical misfortunes, his end was surprising, perhaps even shocking.

In October 1956, DeGolyer celebrated his seventieth birthday. His health was stable, although a number of worrying and apparently chronic conditions troubled him. Despite expert medical attention and a successful spleenectomy, his anemia continued to vex him, making blood transfusions a regular feature of his life. He had recently suffered a succession of small strokes that had not been serious, but were nonetheless a matter of concern. The vision in his good eye had deteriorated over the years, making reading a difficult matter. It also had begun to affect his social activities. He continued to attend parties and receptions, but increasingly leaned upon Nell for help in these situations. He was particularly embarrassed on occasions where his poor eyesight led him to misidentify friends. These moments seem to have become more and more frequent.[91]

DeGolyer was understandably frustrated with his declining health. As his ailments worsened, his attitude itself became a matter of concern. He told his secretary that "the doctors wanted him to simply sit still in a corner, but that he couldn't live like that."[92] His doctor placed him under "psychological treatment."[93] It was not enough.

On December 14, 1956, DeGolyer's chauffeur drove him to his office at DeGolyer and MacNaughton. This was a typical day. He had continued to keep morning hours at work, at least when the doctors allowed him to do so. On the day in question, the only business that demanded his attention was personal. He would have two visitors. Early in the day, DeGolyer's secretary, Dorothy Pitts, noted that a "member of the family" dropped by the office. In light of subsequent events, she would refuse to identify which member this was. Apparently, she believed that the visitor had brought DeGolyer a pistol, an item that he had earlier related a desire for, but for a use apparently unsuspected. The second visitor was less mysterious. The son of an old friend of his was in town and hoped that DeGolyer would be willing to discuss his plans for a career in geology. After this visitor arrived, DeGolyer dispatched his secretary to the bank on an errand. When she returned, the two were still deep in conversation. Finally, DeGolyer wrapped things up, and the aspiring geologist departed.

Pitts peered in the office to see if DeGolyer needed anything. He was sitting immobile in his chair, apparently lost in thought. The behavior seemed odd, but she concluded that he must be thinking about his travel plans. The DeGolyers would shortly be traveling to Washington to spend Christmas with their children and grandchildren. DeGolyer rose from his chair and shut the door.[94]

A sharp crack sounded from the room. Pitts arose, thinking that DeGolyer might have fallen against his desk; it did not occur to her that she had heard a pistol shot. Going for help, she called Phil Porter, who was DeGolyer's nephew, and Lewis MacNaughton. The two men entered the room to see what was afoot. Exiting soon thereafter, MacNaughton informed Pitts of the tragic event—DeGolyer had committed suicide. On the floor lay a smoking pistol. There was no note.[95]

Early dispatches from the office reported that DeGolyer had suffered a heart attack, but this charade could not long endure.[96] Calls went out to summon Nell DeGolyer and Ev. Despite DeGolyer's deteriorating health, the family was unprepared for the shock. As the justice of the peace pronounced an inquest verdict of "death by suicide," they began to cope with the loss and come to terms with its meaning.[97] One day after DeGolyer's suicide, Nell DeGolyer spoke with Dorothy Pitts about the tragedy. At the time, neither could understand why it had happened. However, the family quickly settled on an explanation based on DeGolyer's declining health. Nell DeGolyer explained to the family that "De had taken about all the suffering a man can take."[98] A little over a decade after DeGolyer's death, his son remarked, "I'm not ashamed of it; no one else in the family is."[99]

Even a half-century after DeGolyer's death, the tragic events of that clear December morning call for a measure of sensitivity. Certainty is always elusive when it comes to motive, and even more so when the individual in question has left no testimony on the matter. Still, it seems probable that his declining health played a major role in his last fateful decision. For years, DeGolyer credited his success to a combination of skill and luck, often drawing comparisons with a game of cards. Late in 1956, rather than play with the unfortunate hand that fate had dealt him, DeGolyer folded, and left the table.

# Epilogue Legend

*It seems to me that the dominant characteristic of man, the reasoning animal, is curiosity . . . Further, it seems to me, the natures of men differing as they do, the curiosity of one man may be more tightly focused in a single direction while that of another, equally curious, may be more diffuse. The single tracker is properly endowed to become a great scientist . . . A man of many curiosities is certainly more likely to become the broadly developed man which is the ideal . . .*

— Everette Lee DeGolyer, "More Poetry and Less Physics?" January 1952[1]

Soon after Everette Lee DeGolyer's death in 1956, memorials to his life began to appear in newspapers, professional journals, and magazines. All struggled to grasp the meaning of a life whose diverse achievements defied easy categorization. The *Dallas Morning News* hailed DeGolyer as "a symbol of Texas excellence: a great man of science, a great businessman, [and] a great lover of culture."[2] The *New York Times* stressed his professional renown, remembering him as the "petroleum industry's foremost geologist."[3] Yet the *Times* also pointed out his reputation in literary circles, his efforts on behalf of government, and the importance of his pioneering work in geophysical prospecting. The *Oil and Gas Journal* summed up the consensus of the industry with the words, "DeGolyer: An Oil Legend."[4]

Over the next few months, oil industry observers would weigh in on his significance. Editors of *The Petroleum Engineer* asserted, "The name DeGolyer is almost synonymous with modern petroleum geology, for he contributed not only to the science of 'earth study,' but to its practical application in petroleum exploration."[5] They concluded, "His continued efforts helped in no small measure to elevate the stature of his profession within industry to the position it now holds."[6] Writing in *Oklahoma Geology Notes,* Carl Branson made a broader claim that DeGolyer left the world "vastly better off for his services on earth in geology, in petroleum engineering, in geophysics, in history of science, in southwestern history, and in community, national, and international affairs."[7] DeGolyer's "international" reputation had its deepest roots in Mexico, where his death sent reverberations through the geological

DeGolyer and statue of himself, 1949. By his last years, DeGolyer had attained a level of influence and fame that made immortalization in sculpture seem somehow appropriate, as with this piece created by Dallas sculptor Renato Mazza. (Everette Lee DeGolyer Collection. Courtesy of DeGolyer Library, Southern Methodist University.)

community. Writing in the *Boletín de la Asociación Mexicana de Geólogos Petroleros,* Manuel Álvarez Jr. described DeGolyer as a "great and true friend of Mexico" and "the greatest petroleum geologist."[8]

Some of DeGolyer's friends also tried to sum up his life in a few words. J. C. Karcher concluded, "One of the great men in the history of oil-field exploration has passed away and has left his footprints upon the sands of time. These footprints will be in evidence as long as oil is being produced."[9] DeGolyer's longtime protégé, Lewis MacNaughton focused on his mentor's unique ability to bridge the worlds of science and business, noting, "DeGolyer was *the* scientist-executive, amazingly adept in the field of human relations. Through exceptionally clear thinking and a superb sense of timing, he was able to draw in his associates in the formation of an idea, enabling them to see clearly the same mental image that he himself visualized."[10] MacNaughton hailed him as the "Father of Applied Geophysics," echoing similar claims made by other commentators, years before DeGolyer's death.[11] Yet even the most effusive tributes strained to include all of DeGolyer's passionate interests. The extent and variety of his successes made him a difficult man to describe.

DeGolyer's career was one of remarkable accomplishment. From inauspicious origins on the drought-stricken Kansas plains of the 1880s, DeGolyer pursued and obtained a first-class education in geology. He secured a reputation for technical competence within government and industrial circles while still a young man. By the 1920s, the investors of the nation's financial capital knew him as an efficient and ambitious executive. He managed to prosper as an entrepreneur during the grim years of the Great Depression and served with distinction in the government's attempts to formulate a response to daunting economic challenges. DeGolyer helped to manage the war effort against Nazi Germany and Imperial Japan. He worked to formulate postwar strategy and achieved spectacular success in the petroleum industry. And those were but highlights of his diverse achievements.

To a notable extent, DeGolyer's often dazzling successes were a function of his own exceptional abilities. Yet the critical characteristic that propelled him to his triumphs is somewhat elusive. DeGolyer was a highly competent, even excellent geologist. But there were many men, having similar technical expertise, whose stars failed to shine as brightly as did his star. DeGolyer was also a shrewd businessman. Yet there was in his day an army of executives possessing comparable acumen. There were more efficient bureaucrats. There were more learned scholars. There were more effective policymakers. What, then, accounts for DeGolyer's tremendous accomplishments?

The Greek poet Archilochus wrote, "The fox knows many things, but the hedgehog knows one big thing."[12] The twentieth century was an age of hedgehogs. Industry, government, and academy all became places of increasing specialization. At a time when it was unfashionable,

DeGolyer was undoubtedly a fox. Indeed, he knew many things, and his broad perspective enabled him to make conceptual connections that the hedgehogs of his day were unable to make.

This was the secret to his power of prophecy. Though not a geophysicist, he was able to identify geophysics as the wave of the future in the field that he did know, petroleum exploration. Though uninvolved in Middle Eastern oil, he perceived the rise of that region at a time when many in the domestic oil industry preferred to ignore the writing on the wall. Though he was neither a politician nor a general, he swiftly identified the significance of conservation to national security in the Cold War era.

Of course, there were limits to the significance of his pioneering work. His attempts to shape national policy during the early Cold War were hardly successful. His application of geophysical technology was important, but not unique, and surely others in the petroleum industry would eventually have employed the same methods on a similar scale. To be certain, DeGolyer's career reflected forces far larger than any individual. The eruption of two World Wars and onset of a global Cold War made military concerns more prominent than ever in American society. Scientists—the masters of technology—were bound to enjoy increasing prestige in an era when technology offered decisive military advantages. Although the creation of the atomic bomb was the most obvious example of their ascendancy, scientists in other fields also enjoyed greater regard and power. As a scientist, DeGolyer rode the wave that carried many of his colleagues to greater heights in industry and government.

Yet DeGolyer was more than a mere exemplar of historical trends. His life was consequential. If DeGolyer's leadership was not historically decisive, it was at least highly influential. True, his importance as a leader was not due to success in urging his colleagues to make a choice crucial to his moment in time.

DeGolyer's prophecies proclaimed the inevitable—the changing needs of the industry, the shifting center of global oil, the decline in domestic oil production. A Jeremiah, he urged his contemporaries to embrace what was unavoidable. He believed that only by accepting change could the industry formulate realistic solutions to impending problems. He called on the nation to open its eyes before it was too late.

By drawing the attention of the oil business and the country to these issues—the need for new petroleum exploration methods, the need for new oilfield conservation practices, the need for new strategic thinking regarding petroleum—DeGolyer played the role of a catalyst. He forced others to face these questions earlier than they might have in his absence. It is in this sense that his life was truly consequential to the industry and to the nation.

# Notes

## Abbreviations

ABCD    Herbert Robertson, *The ABCs of De: A Primer on Everette DeGolyer Sr., 1886– 1956* (Dallas: DeGolyer Library, 2007).

BAAPG    *Bulletin of the American Association of Petroleum Geologists*

BAIME    *Bulletin of the American Institute of Mining Engineers*

BAPI    *Bulletin of the American Petroleum Institute*

BUSGS    *Bulletin of the United States Geological Survey*

CMH    Michael C. Meyer, William L. Sherman, and Susan M. Deeds, *The Course of Mexican History,* 6th ed. (New York: Oxford University Press, 1999).

DMN    *Dallas Morning News*

DT    *Daily Transcript* (Norman, Okla.)

DTH    *Dallas Times Herald*

EG    *Economic Geology*

ELD    Everette Lee DeGolyer Sr.

ELDP    Everette Lee DeGolyer Sr. Papers, DeGolyer Library, Southern Methodist University, Dallas, Texas.

EPA    Richard H. K. Vietor, *Energy Policy in America Since 1945: A Study of Business-Government Relations* (London: Cambridge University Press, 1984).

HGP1    George Elliott Sweet, *The History of Geophysical Prospecting,* 1st ed. (Los Angeles: Science Press, 1966).

HGP3    George Elliott Sweet, *The History of Geophysical Prospecting*, 3rd ed. (Los Angeles: Science Press, 1978).

HPAW    John W. Frey and H. Chandler Ide, eds., *A History of the Petroleum Administration for War, 1941–1945* (Washington, DC: United States Government Printing Office, 1946).

JPT    *Journal of Petroleum Technology*

LTP    Lon Tinkle Papers, DeGolyer Library, Southern Methodist University, Dallas, Texas.

MD    Lon Tinkle, *Mr. De: A Biography of Everette Lee DeGolyer* (Boston, Mass.: Little, Brown and Company, 1970).

NDT    *Norman Democrat-Topic*

NGD    Nell Goodrich DeGolyer

NGDP    Nell Goodrich DeGolyer Papers, DeGolyer Library, Southern Methodist University, Dallas, Texas.

NT    *Norman Transcript*

NYT    *New York Times*

| O&GJ | *Oil & Gas Journal* |
| O&I | Roger M. Olien and Diana Davids Olien, *Oil and Ideology: The Cultural Creation of the American Petroleum Industry* (Chapel Hill: University of North Carolina Press, 2000). |
| ORM | Jonathan C. Brown, *Oil and Revolution in Mexico* (Berkeley: University of California Press, 1993). |
| PPPP | David S. Painter, *Private Power and Public Policy: Multinational Oil Companies and U.S. Foreign Policy, 1941–1954* (London: I. B. Tauris & Co., 1986). |
| PR | *Petroleum Review* |
| SR | *Southwest Review* |
| SRL | *The Saturday Review of Literature* |
| TAIME | *Transactions of the American Institute of Mining and Metallurgical Engineers* |
| TOF | Edgar Wesley Owen, *Trek of the Oil Finders: A History of Exploration for Petroleum* (Tulsa: The American Association of Petroleum Geologists, 1975). |
| TP | Daniel Yergin, *The Prize: The Epic Quest for Oil, Money, and Power* (New York: Simon and Schuster, 1992). |
| USFOP | Stephen J. Randall, *United States Foreign Oil Policy Since World War I* (Montreal, Canada: McGill-Queen's University Press, 2005). |
| USOP | Gerald D. Nash, *United States Oil Policy, 1890–1964* (Pittsburgh: University of Pittsburgh Press, 1968). |

## Preface

1. Panel Discussion on Conservation in the Oil Industry, June 10, 1953, Edward R. Murrow Papers, Tufts University, Medford, Mass., 14.

2. Daniel Yergin, *The Prize: The Epic Quest for Oil, Money, and Power* (New York: Simon and Schuster, 1992), 392.

3. Contrasted with J. R. Ewing: Karen R. Merrill, "Texas Metropole: Oil, the American West, and U.S. Power in the Postwar Years," *Journal of American History* 99, no. 1 (2012). Cited as an exemplar of university-trained professional geologists: Brian Frehner, *Finding Oil: The Nature of Petroleum Geology, 1859–1920* (Lincoln: University of Nebraska Press, 2011), 91. The subject of a biographical "primer": Herbert Robertson, *The ABCs of De: A Primer on Everette DeGolyer Sr., 1886–1956* (Dallas: DeGolyer Library, 2007). Cast as hero in historical fiction: Sam L. Pfiester, *The Golden Lane: Faja de Oro* (Georgetown, Texas: Chengalera Press, 2011). Connected with figures surrounding Kennedy assassination: Russ Baker, *Family of Secrets: The Bush Dynasty, America's Invisible Government, and the Hidden History of the Last Fifty Years* (New York: Bloomsbury Press, 2009), 80–81.

4. Kent Biffle, "Lon Tinkle: A Texas Original," *DMN,* April 1, 1979; Frank Tolbert, "Author-Critic Lon Tinkle Lived With Amazing Grace," *DMN,* January 12, 1980.

5. These included George Elliott Sweet, whose biographical sketches were ultimately published in George Elliott Sweet, *The History of Geophysical Prospecting*, 1st ed. (Los Angeles: Science Press, 1966). Cleveland Amory, author of *The Proper Bostonians*, best remembered for his founding role in the animal rights movement, also began work on a biography during DeGolyer's involvement with *The Saturday Review of Literature*, as reported in Lon Tinkle, "Reading and Writing," *DMN*, February 7, 1954. North Bigbee of Dallas sketched DeGolyer's life in a lengthy essay in 1952: North Bigbee, "Underground Explorer," 1952, box 3, folder 26, LTP. Eric Schroeder of the Dallas Morning News and Lon Tinkle both produced biographical articles on DeGolyer for the *Dallas Morning News:* Eric G. Schroeder, "Good Timing, Solid Ability Keyed Local Man's Success," *DMN*, August 20, 1950; Lon Tinkle, "Many-Sided DeGolyer Career Heaped With Diverse Honors," *DMN*, November 20, 1949.

6. Lon Tinkle, *Mr. De: A Biography of Everette Lee DeGolyer* (Boston, Mass.: Little, Brown and Company, 1970).

7. Lon Tinkle to Wallace E. Pratt, December 7, 1970, LTP.

8. Lon Tinkle, "Many-Sided DeGolyer Career Heaped With Diverse Honors," *DMN*, November 20, 1949.

### Introduction

1. Betty Fiala, "Oil: The World and Dr. DeGolyer," December 19, 1945, box 24, folder 2432, ELDP.

2. As with so many other important figures in the oil industry, Lucas would later become friends with DeGolyer. In 1941 and 1951, DeGolyer would be called upon to eulogize Lucas and assess the importance of his achievement in speeches commemorating the landmark discovery of the oilfield in 1901. "Dallasite to Dedicate Shaft," *DMN*, September 28, 1941; ELD, address, "Spindletop: 1901–1951," 1951, box 22, folder 2384, ELDP. In 1945, he examined the importance of Lucas to the industry in ELD, "Anthony F. Lucas and Spindletop," *Southwest Review* 31, no. 1 (1945).

3. "Imagination Needed: Cram Calls on Geologists to Use It to Find More Oil," *O&GJ*, January 18, 1951.

4. Quoted in Judith Walker Linsey, Ellen Walker Rienstra, and Jo Ann Stiles, *Giant Under the Hill: A History of the Spindletop Oil Discovery at Beaumont, Texas, in 1901* (Austin, Texas: Texas State Historical Association, 2002), 49.

5. Spencer W. Robinson, ed., *Spindletop: Where Oil Became an Industry, Official Proceedings of the 50th Anniversary Program Commemorating the Discovery of the Spindletop Oil Field at Beaumont, Texas, January 10, 1901* (Beaumont, Texas: Spindletop 50th Anniversary Commission, 1951), 65.

6. Judith Walker Linsey, Ellen Walker Rienstra, and Jo Ann Stiles, *Giant Under the Hill: A History of the Spindletop Oil Discovery at Beaumont, Texas, in 1901* (Austin, Texas: Texas State Historical Association, 2002), 73–74.

7. Anthony F. Lucas to ELD, May 6, 1920, box 8, folder 1074, ELDP.

8. Michel T. Halbouty, ed., *Giant Oil and Gas Fields of the Decade 1968–1978* (Tulsa, Okla.: American Association of Petroleum Geologists, 1980), 290–97; Robert E. King, ed., *Stratigraphic Oil and Gas Fields—Classification, Exploration Methods, and Case Histories* (Tulsa, Okla.: American Association of Petroleum Geologists and Society of Exploration Geophysicists, 1972), 495; Joseph A. Riendl, "Logistics of Geophysical Operations in Alaska," *World Oil* 160, no. 2 (1965).

9. *TP,* 571–72.

10. Ibid., 543–45, 550–54.

11. *Twentieth Century Petroleum Statistics, 1946* (Dallas, Texas: DeGolyer and MacNaughton, 1946); *Twentieth Century Petroleum Statistics, 1967* (Dallas, Texas: DeGolyer and MacNaughton, 1967).

12. For conflicts between practical oilmen and geologists: Mody C. Boatright, *Folklore of the Oil Industry* (Dallas: Southern Methodist University Press, 1963); Brian Frehner, *Finding Oil: The Nature of Petroleum Geology, 1859–1920* (Lincoln: University of Nebraska Press, 2011), 81–102. For industrial applications of science: David F. Noble, *America by Design: Science, Technology, and the Rise of Corporate Capitalism* (New York: Alfred A. Knopf, 1977), 27.

13. Again, professional development in other business sectors prefigured the relationship between earth scientists and industry. Noble, *America by Design,* 41.

14. "Oklahoma Geology Students Advance to High Positions," *Western Oil Derrick,* April 3, 1920.

15. "Erstwhile 'Rock Hound' Holds High Place in Oil Industry Today," *DMN,* March 25, 1926.

16. Roy L. Lay, "The Geophysicist in Industry," *BAAPG* 38, no. 7 (1954):1383.

17. *O&I,* 185–86.

## Chapter 1

1. Box 3, folder 17, LTP.

2. *MD,* 67–68.

3. Note, n.d., box 24, folder 2432, ELDP; *MD,* 66.

4. NGD quoted in *MD,* 71.

5. Notes, n.d., box 24, folder 2435, ELDP.

6. Ibid.

7. Ibid; *MD,* 68.

8. Craig Miner, *West of Wichita: Settling the High Plains of Kansas, 1856–1890* (Lawrence: University Press of Kansas, 1986), 96.

9. *HGP3,* 52; *MD,* 68.

10. "Local and Personal," *NT,* September 9, 1909.

11. Tornadoes are, of course, a notorious hazard in this part of the United States. In 2007, one of the largest tornadoes recorded completely destroyed the town of DeGolyer's birth, Greensburg, Kansas.

12. *MD,* 68.

13. Miner, *West of Wichita,* 215–17.

14. Ibid., 212.

15. Notes, n.d., box 24, folder 2435, ELDP; *HGP3,* 52–53; *MD,* 68–69.

16. Notes, n.d., box 24, folder 2435, ELDP; *HGP3,* 53; *MD,* 7.

17. *MD,* 70.

18. Notes, n.d., box 24, folder 2435, ELDP.

19. *MD,* 70.

20. Business card, Blue Point Chop House, n.d., box 25, folder 2468, ELDP.

21. "Pioneer Oklahoman of Six-Shooter Days Awarded Gold Medal," November 1939, box 24, folder 2432, ELDP.

22. *MD,* 73.

23. "Pioneer Oklahoman," ELDP; *MD,* 71.

24. "Holcomb has Stepped Out, Resigned from Superintendency of the City Schools, Vaught Chosen," *The Oklahoman,* March 2, 1902, 1. Vaught's later career is worth remark. Vaught served as president of the Chamber of Commerce of Oklahoma City, practiced law, and was appointed to the federal district court of western Oklahoma in 1928 by Calvin Coolidge. As judge, he presided over the trial of George "Machine Gun" Kelly in 1933. "Edgar S. Vaught, U.S. Judge, Dies of Heart Attack," *The Oklahoman,* December 6, 1959, 1.

25. Sweet, *HGP3,* 53.

26. Transcript, July 27, 1964, box 9, folder 188, LTP; *HGP1,* 53.

27. Ibid., 41–46; Kenny A. Franks, *The Rush Begins: A History of the Red Fork, Cleveland and Glenn Pool Oil Fields* (Oklahoma City: Oklahoma Heritage Foundation, 1984), 62–72.

28. Roy Gittinger, *The University of Oklahoma, 1892–1942* (Norman, Okla.: University of Oklahoma Press, 1942), 3; Eric G. Schroeder, "Good Timing, Solid Ability Keyed Local Man's Success," *DMN,* August 20, 1950.

29. Gittinger, *University of Oklahoma,* 28–29, 31; David W. Levy, *The University of Oklahoma: A History* (Norman, Okla.: University of Oklahoma Press, 2005), 67.

30. Charles N. Gould, *Covered Wagon Geologist* (Norman, Okla.: University of Oklahoma Press, 1959), 5, 8, 26, 31, 33, 39.

31. Ibid., 3–4.

32. Ibid., 47–48.

33. Ibid., 57–58, 61, 68, 70, 73–100.

34. George G. Huffman, *History of the School of Geology and Geophysics, The University of Oklahoma* (Norman, Okla.: University of Oklahoma Press, 1990), 1–2. For an extended examination of Gould's emphasis on field education, see Brian Frehner, *Finding Oil: The Nature of Petroleum Geology, 1859–1920* (Lincoln, Neb.: University of Nebraska Press, 2011), 112–17.

35. Huffman, *History of the School of Geology and Geophysics,* 2.

36. Levy, *University of Oklahoma,* 127.

37. "Professor Gould on Location of Oil," *Daily Ardmoreite,* September 17, 1911; University of Oklahoma, Transcript, July 27, 1964, box 9, folder 188, LTP. For

a general look at the OU geology program at this time: Huffman, *History of the School of Geology and Geophysics,* 67.

38. Levy, *The University of Oklahoma,* 140–44.

39. *The Mistletoe,* vol. 4 (Norman, Okla.: Junior Class of the University of Oklahoma, 1909); ELD to Homer DeGolyer, letter, October 23, 1916, box 34, folder 2939, ELDP; ELD and NGD, interview by Cleveland Amory, 29 pages, n.d., box 3, folder 15, LTP, 15–16; Levy, *University of Oklahoma,* 140–46.

40. Quote from Schroeder, "Good Timing, Solid Ability Keyed Local Man's Success"; *MD,* 32.

41. Quoted in *The Mistletoe,* vol. 2 (Norman, Okla.: Junior Class of the University of Oklahoma, 1907); *The Mistletoe,* vol. 3 (Norman, Okla.: Juniors of the University of Oklahoma, 1908); *The Mistletoe,* vol. 4 (Norman, Okla.: Junior Class of the University of Oklahoma, 1909); *MD,* 32.

42. *MD,* 33.

43. Quoted in ibid.

44. Quoted in ibid.

45. Ibid., 34.

46. Ibid., frontspiece, 4.

47. Huffman, *History of the School of Geology and Geophysics,* 1.

48. *MD,* 73.

49. N. H. Darton, "Department of the Interior, United States Geological Survey, Employment on Field Force," June 1, 1906, box 24, folder 2437, ELDP.

50. George E. Mowry, *The Era of Theodore Roosevelt, 1900–1912* (New York: Harper and Brothers, 1958), 57–58, 105; Mary C. Rabbitt, *Minerals, Lands, and Geology for the Common Defense and General Welfare,* vol. 2 (Washington, DC: United States Government Printing Office, 1980), 320–22.

51. Rabbitt, *Minerals, Lands, and Geology,* 329.

52. *MD,* 73–74.

53. N. H. Darton to ELD, November 17, 1906, box 24, folder 2437, ELDP.

54. Conversation with Mr. H. B. Fuqua, Fort Worth National Bank Building, June 21, 1967, box 3, folder 10, LTP.

55. Quoted in *MD,* 76–77. Notes on Talk with Mr. Heroy, 213 Dallas Hall, June 7, 1967, box 3, folder 11, LTP.

56. Spencer W. Robinson, ed., *Spindletop: Where Oil Became an Industry, Official Proceedings of the 50th Anniversary Program Commemorating the Discovery of the Spindletop Oil Field at Beaumont, Texas, January 10, 1901* (Beaumont, Texas: Spindletop 50th Anniversary Commission, 1951), 65.

57. Rabbitt, *Minerals, Lands, and Geology,* 303–04.

58. ELD, memorandum, "Summertime Employment by the U.S. Geological Survey, E. DeGolyer," n.d., box 25, folder 2468, ELDP.

59. Amory's interview with DeGolyer reports that the date was December 1908 and the location, Mound City, Montana. ELD and NGD, interview by Cleveland Amory, 34 pages, n.d., box 3, folder 15, LTP, 22–23. However, DeGolyer was in

Washington, DC, and not Montana, in the winter of 1908. It seems that Amory had difficulty keeping up with DeGolyer during these interviews. This makes it probable that the location was Miles City, Montana, during the summer of 1908, as suggested by Edwin Butcher Hopkins in *National Cyclopedia of American Biography*, vol. 30 (James T. White and Co., 1943); ELD, memorandum, "Summertime Employment by the U.S. Geological Survey, E. DeGolyer," n.d., box 25, folder 2468, ELDP; Carl D. Smith, "Department of the Interior, United States Geological Survey, Certificate of Employment," June 4, 1908, box 24, folder 2437, ELDP.

60. ELD and NGD, interview by Cleveland Amory, 34 pages, n.d., box 3, folder 15, LTP, 23.

61. Ibid., 24.

62. Ibid., 25.

63. Ibid., 26.

64. Ibid., 27.

65. E. G. Woodruff, "Topographic Maps for the Mining Engineer," *Bulletin of the American Institute of Mining Engineers,* no. 78 (1913): 1001.

66. Ibid., 1005.

67. Ibid., 1001.

68. Ibid., 1006–09.

69. ELD and NGD, interview by Cleveland Amory, 34 pages, n.d., box 3, folder 15, LTP, 27.

70. Carl D. Smith, "The Fort Berthold Indian Reservation Lignite Field, North Dakota," *Bulletin of the United States Geological Survey,* no. 381 (1910):30; Carl D. Smith, "The Fort Peck Indian Reservation Lignite Field, Montana," *Bulletin of the United States Geological Survey,* no. 381 (1910):40.

71. ELD and NGD, interview by Cleveland Amory, 34 pages, n.d., box 3, folder 15, LTP, 27–28; Willis T. Lee, "Coal Fields of Grand Mesa and the West Elk Mountains, Colorado," *Bulletin of the United States Geological Survey,* no. 510 (1912):13.

72. For treatment of the early rivalry between "practical" oil men and geologists, see Brian Frehner, *Finding Oil: The Nature of Petroleum Geology, 1859–1920* (Lincoln, Neb.: University of Nebraska Press, 2011), 81–102; *TOF,* 157.

73. *TOF,* 158; Frehner, *Finding Oil,* 13, 100–02.

74. *TOF,* 157.

75. Ibid.

76. Ibid., 61–62.

77. ELD, "The Geologist and the Petroleum Industry," *Bulletin of the American Petroleum Institute* 5, no. 69 (1924): 2.

78. *TOF,* 160–89.

79. Robinson, *Spindletop,* 65.

80. C. Willard Hayes and William Kennedy, "Oil Fields of the Texas-Louisiana Gulf Coastal Plain," *Bulletin of the United States Geological Survey,* no. 212 (1903).

81. Ibid., 72–74.

82. C. Willard Hayes, *Handbook for Field Geologists* (Washington, DC: Government Printing Office, 1908).

83. Ibid., 115.

84. Ibid.

85. *TOF,* 490–91.

86. Hayes, *Handbook for Field Geologists,* 115.

87. Ibid.

88. Alfred H. Brooks, "Memorial of Charles Willard Hayes," *Bulletin of the Geological Society of America* 28 (1916): 114–17; *MD,* 9–10.

89. *See* DeGolyer's account quoted in *MD,* 9. *See also* ELD and NGD, interview by Cleveland Amory, 34 pages, n.d., box 3, folder 15, LTP, 29.

90. Quoted in *MD,* 9–10.

### Chapter 2

1. ELD to Leonard M. Fanning, July 12, 1945, box 24, folder 2432, ELDP.

2. Present in some oil reservoirs, hydrogen sulfide gas is a toxic and potentially fatal hazard to workers.

3. ELD to C. Willard Hayes, letter, January 13, 1911, box 114, folder 5347, ELDP.

4. ELD and NGD, interview by Cleveland Amory, 34 pages, n.d., box 3, folder 15, LTP, 15.

5. ELD, report, "Potrero del Llano," July 1, 1910, box 114, folder 5347, ELDP, 3.

6. Ibid., 6–7.

7. See, for example, his interpretation of faulting near the axis of a surface anticline in ibid., 6.

8. ELD to Leonard M. Fanning, July 12, 1945, box 24, folder 2432, ELDP.

9. *ORM,* 25–35.

10. Desmond Young, *Member for Mexico: A Biography of Weetman Pearson, First Viscount Cowdray* (London: Cassell & Co. Ltd., 1966), 6, 10. Quoted in ibid., 41.

11. Ibid., 11–12, 46–48, 60–65.

12. Ibid., 83–93.

13. Ibid., 101–11.

14. Ibid., 123.

15. Ibid.

16. ELD and NGD, interview by Cleveland Amory, 34 pages, n.d., box 3, folder 15, LTP, 1.

17. ELD to Wallace E. Pratt, September 8, 1954, box 12, folder 1513, ELDP; ELD and NGD, interview by Cleveland Amory, 34 pages, n.d., box 3, folder 15, LTP, 2..

18. ELD, essay, n.d., box 24, folder 2437, ELDP.

19. ELD and NGD, interview by Cleveland Amory, 34 pages, n.d., box 3, folder 15, LTP, 2.

20. Ibid., 3.

21. Ibid.

22. *MD,* 11.

23. Quoted in ibid., 13.

24. ELD and NGD, interview by Cleveland Amory, 34 pages, n.d., box 3, folder 15, LTP, 3–4.

25. *ORM,* 59, 74–75, 257; ELD and NGD, interview by Cleveland Amory, 34 pages, n.d., box 3, folder 15, LTP, 4.

26. ELD, "Report on Hacienda Tierra Amarilla, State of Veracruz," 1910, box 114, folder 5347, ELDP.

27. ELD and NGD, interview by Cleveland Amory, 34 pages, n.d., box 3, folder 15, LTP, 5.

28. ELD, memorandum, "Instructions for Geologic and Topographic work of the Cia. Mex. de Petroleo, 'El Aguila,' S.A.," March 16, 1912, box 114, folder 5347, ELDP, 2.

29. ELD, "Report on Hacienda Tierra Amarilla, State of Veracruz," 1910, box 114, folder 5347, ELDP, 3.

30. Ibid.

31. ELD, memorandum, "Instructions for Geologic and Topographic work of the Cia. Mex. de Petroleo, 'El Aguila,' S.A.," March 16, 1912, box 114, folder 5347, ELDP, 5.

32. ELD to C. Willard Hayes, July 1, 1910, box 105, folder 5201, ELDP; ELD, report, "Isla del Toro: Reconnaisance," December 5, 1909, box 114, folder 5347, ELDP; ELD, report, "Potrero del Llano," July 1, 1910, box 114, folder 5347, ELDP; ELD, report, "Recommendations for Location #1 Tierra Amarilla," January 18, 1910, box 114, folder 5347, ELDP.

33. ELD, "Report on Hacienda Tierra Amarilla, State of Veracruz," 1910, box 114, folder 5347, ELDP, 4.

34. ELD, report, "Recommendations for Location #1 Tierra Amarilla," January 18, 1910, box 114, folder 5347, ELDP, 1; ELD, "Report on Hacienda Tierra Amarilla, State of Veracruz," 1910, box 114, folder 5347, ELDP, 6.

35. ELD, "Report on Hacienda Tierra Amarilla, State of Veracruz," 1910, box 114, folder 5347, ELDP, 10.

36. ELD, report, "The Oil Fields of Mexico, with Particular Reference to the Fields of The Tampico-Tuxpam Region," July 1, 1916, box 236, folder 1, ELDP, 357–58, 364; ELD and NGD, interview by Cleveland Amory, 34 pages, n.d., box 3, folder 15, LTP, 8.

37. *MD,* 31–32.

38. "Married—DeGolyer-Goodrich," *NT,* June 9, 1910; ELD and NGD, interview by Cleveland Amory, 34 pages, n.d., box 3, folder 15, LTP, 31; *MD,* 34.

39. ELD and NGD, interview by Cleveland Amory, 34 pages, n.d., box 3, folder 15, LTP, 30.

40. Ibid.

41. *MD,* 36.

42. ELD and NGD, interview by Cleveland Amory, 34 pages, n.d., box 3, folder 15, LTP, 32.

43. Ibid., 30.

44. *MD,* 37.

45. ELD and NGD, interview by Cleveland Amory, 34 pages, n.d., box 3, folder 15, LTP, 20.

46. Ibid.

47. Ibid., 33.

48. Ibid., 5.

49. For DeGolyer's analysis of surveyed properties, see, for example, ELD, report, "Estimate of Asphalt on Surface of Hacienda Cerro Viejo," October 3, 1910, box 114, folder 5347, ELDP; ELD, report, "Hacienda Alazan," July 15, 1910, box 114, folder 5347, ELDP; ELD, report, "Isla del Toro: Reconnaisance," December 5, 1909, box 114, folder 5347, ELDP; ELD, report, "Potrero del Llano," July 1, 1910, box 114, folder 5347, ELDP; ELD, report, "Recommendations for Location #1 Tierra Amarilla," January 18, 1910, box 114, folder 5347, ELDP; ELD, "Report on Cobos and Other Properties Adjacent to Juan Cassiano, San Antonio Chinampa," September 10, 1910, box 114, folder 5347, ELDP; ELD, "Report on Hacienda Tierra Amarilla, State of Veracruz," 1910, box 114, folder 5347, ELDP; ELD, "Report on the Los Naranjos Lease," September 15, 1910, box 114, folder 5347, ELDP; ELD, report, "Tierra Amarilla #2," March 18, 1910, box 114, folder 5347, ELDP. *ORM, 56–59; MD, 31; Young, Member for Mexico, 133.*

50. ELD and NGD, interview by Cleveland Amory, 34 pages, n.d., box 3, folder 15, LTP, 6.

51. ELD to C. Willard Hayes, July 1, 1910, box 105, folder 5201, ELDP, 2-A; ELD and NGD, interview by Cleveland Amory, 34 pages, n.d., box 3, folder 15, LTP, 4.

52. ELD to Leonard M. Fanning, July 12, 1945, box 24, folder 2432, ELDP.

53. ELD and NGD, interview by Cleveland Amory, 34 pages, n.d., box 3, folder 15, LTP, 7.

54. Ibid., 6. The crown block is the part of the oil derrick from which the cable that holds the drilling tools is suspended.

55. ELD, report, "The Oil Fields of Mexico, with Particular Reference to the Fields of The Tampico-Tuxpam Region," July 1, 1916, box 236, folder 1, ELDP, 394–95; ELD and NGD, interview by Cleveland Amory, 34 pages, n.d., box 3, folder 15, LTP, 7.

56. ELD and NGD, interview by Cleveland Amory, 34 pages, n.d., box 3, folder 15, LTP, 7.

57. ELD, memo, "Potrero del Llano," March 18, 1910, box 114, folder 5347, ELDP.

58. ELD, report, "The Oil Fields of Mexico, with Particular Reference to the Fields of The Tampico-Tuxpam Region," July 1, 1916, box 236, folder 1, ELDP, 395–96.

59. ELD to C. Willard Hayes, July 1, 1910, box 105, folder 5201, ELDP, 6.

60. Ibid.

61. Ibid., 10–12; ELD and NGD, interview by Cleveland Amory, 34 pages, n.d., box 3, folder 15, LTP, 8.

62. *MD,* 8.

63. ELD, report, "The Oil Fields of Mexico, with Particular Reference to the Fields of The Tampico-Tuxpam Region," July 1, 1916, box 236, folder 1, ELDP, 395.

64. Ibid., 396.

65. Ibid., 384–85; ELD and NGD, interview by Cleveland Amory, 34 pages, n.d., box 3, folder 15, LTP, 8.

66. ELD and NGD, interview by Cleveland Amory, 34 pages, n.d., box 3, folder 15, LTP, 10.

67. Ibid., 15.

68. ELD to C. Willard Hayes, letter, January 13, 1911, box 114, folder 5347, ELDP.

69. ELD and NGD, interview by Cleveland Amory, 34 pages, n.d., box 3, folder 15, LTP, 8–9.

70. Ibid., 9; John A. Spender, *Weetman Pearson, First Viscount Cowdray, 1856–1927* (New York: Arno Press, 1977), 182.

71. ELD and NGD, interview by Cleveland Amory, 34 pages, n.d., box 3, folder 15, LTP, 9.

72. Conversation with Mr. H. B. Fuqua, Fort Worth National Bank Building, June 21, 1967, box 3, folder 10, LTP; ELD and NGD, interview by Cleveland Amory, 34 pages, n.d., box 3, folder 15, LTP, 9, 18; Paul Garner, *British Lions and Mexican Eagles: Business, Politics, and Empire in the Career of Weetman Pearson in Mexico, 1889–1919* (Stanford, Cal.: Stanford University Press, 2011), 65–66, 71.

73. ELD and NGD, interview by Cleveland Amory, 34 pages, n.d., box 3, folder 15, LTP, 9–10.

74. Ibid.

75. Ibid.

76. Brown, *Oil and Revolution in Mexico,* 68; ELD and NGD, interview by Cleveland Amory, 34 pages, n.d., box 3, folder 15, LTP, 10–11.

77. ELD and NGD, interview by Cleveland Amory, 34 pages, n.d., box 3, folder 15, LTP, 10–11.

78. *ORM,* 68–69; *MD,* 44–47; Young, *Member for Mexico,* 133.

79. ELD and NGD, interview by Cleveland Amory, 34 pages, n.d., box 3, folder 15, LTP, 11–12; *MD,* 52.

80. *MD,* 33.

81. ELD, "The Metamorphism of the Coals of a Portion of the Anthracite and Crested Butte Quadrangles, Colorado," 1911, box 213, folder 30, ELDP; *MD,* 52.

82. ELD, biographical memorandum, "Everette Lee DeGolyer," n.d., box 24, folder 2437, ELDP; Willis T. Lee, "Coal Fields of Grand Mesa and the West Elk Mountains, Colorado," *BUSGS,* no. 510 (1912).

83. ELD to W. T. Lee, April 4, 1911, box 24, folder 2437, ELDP.

84. Lord Cowdray to ELD, March 13, 1911, box 24, folder 2437, ELDP.

85. *MD,* 34.

86. "Mexicans Not Ready For Self-Government," *NDT,* April 23, 1915.

87. Ibid.

88. "Society Notes," *DT,* April 20, 1915.

89. ELD and NGD, interview by Cleveland Amory, 34 pages, n.d., box 3, folder 15, LTP, 7.

90. *MD,* 58, 78–79.

91. Death certificate, 1912, box 214, folder 12, ELDP; *MD,* 78.

92. *MD,* 78, 80.

93. ELD, biographical memorandum, n.d., LTP; ELD, memorandum, "Instructions for Geologic and Topographic work of the Cia. Mex. de Petroleo, "El Aguila," S.A.," March 16, 1912, box 114, folder 5347, ELDP.

94. For reports based on DeGolyer's field work, see, for example, ELD, report, "Reconnaisance Geological Examination of Hacienda San Vicente and Environs, State of Coahuila," 1912, box 114, folder 5347, ELDP; ELD, "Report on Examinations of Lands of Ernest Dickert, San Mateo, S. L. P.," September 30, 1911, box 114, folder 5347, ELDP; ELD, "Report on Reconnaissance Geological Survey of the Hacienda Tlacolula, Canton of Tantoyuca, V. C.," January 16, 1912, box 114, folder 5347, ELDP; ELD, "Report on Salinas Caracol Oil Field," May 1, 1912, box 114, folder 5347, ELDP.

95. For reports based on the field work of other geologists or statistical analyses, see, for example, ELD, report, "Competitive Oil Production, Mexico," June 28, 1912, box 114, folder 5347, ELDP; ELD, report, "Lands in the Vicinity of Guerrero, San Luis Potosi, Hacienda Limon," December 5, 1911, box 114, folder 5347, ELDP; ELD, "Report on Companies and Holdings of John Hayes Hammond—Mestres—Consolidated Goldfields of South Africa, Ltd., Interests in Mexican Oil Fields," May 6, 1912, box 114, folder 5347, ELDP; ELD, "Report on Panuco Oil Field," June 12, 1912, box 114, folder 5347, ELDP; ELD, "Report on Storage Facilities of Various Competitive Oil Companies," May 3, 1912, box 114, folder 5347, ELDP; ELD, report, "Results of Petroleum Drilling in Tampico Region by S. Pearson & Son and Related Companies," October 4, 1913, box 114, folder 5347, ELDP.

96. *CMH,* 439–450, 472–74.

97. Paul Garner, *Porfirio Díaz* (Harlow, U.K.: Pearson Education, Ltd., 2001), 77–79; Alan Knight, *The Mexican Revolution: Porfirians, Liberals and Peasants,* vol. 1 (of 2) (Cambridge, U.K.: Cambridge University Press, 1986), 30–31, 36.

98. *CMH,* 475–83.

99. Garner, *Porfirio Díaz,* 222; Meyer, Sherman, and Deeds, *The Course of Mexican History,* 483–88.

100. *CMH,* 485–92. Quoted in ibid., 493.

101. Ibid., 499–510.

102. Young, *Member for Mexico,* 146.

103. *ORM,* 186.

104. Charles W. Hamilton, *Early Day Oil Tales of Mexico* (Houston, Texas: Gulf Publishing Company, 1966), 120.

105. Ibid.

106. Ibid., 123; *MD,* 91. The Norman Transcript reported the details a little differently: "During the fracas in Tampico Mr. DeGolyer got curious about what was going on, and stuck his head out a window. A bullet went through the crown of his hat, which was certainly getting pretty close to him." "DeGolyer Coming Home," *NT,* January 8, 1914.

107. ELD to Nell DeGolyer, telegram, December 13, 1913, box 1, folder 12, NGDP.

108. ELD to Nell DeGolyer, December 13, 1913, box 1, folder 12, NGDP.

109. Ibid.

110. ELD to Nell DeGolyer, December 27, 1913, box 1, folder 12, NGDP.

111. ELD, address, "History of the Petroleum Industry in Mexico," March 11, 1914, box 114, folder 5347, ELDP.

112. Ibid., 13.

113. Ibid. In the event, DeGolyer was overly optimistic. Production did increase in 1914, but less than he had predicted. *ORM,* 122.

114. Thomas Cresswell, "Mexican Oil Association," June 5, 1913, box 24, folder 2437, ELDP; ELD, address, "History of the Petroleum Industry in Mexico," March 11, 1914, box 114, folder 5347, ELDP.

115. *ORM,* 191.

116. *CMH,* 513.

117. Lon Tinkle, From Amory Interviews, n.d., box 3, folder 16, LTP, 2.

118. ELD, diary, 1914, box 207, folder 6, ELDP, 1.

119. Ibid.

120. Ibid; Lon Tinkle, From Amory Interviews, n.d., box 3, folder 16, LTP, 2.

121. "Statement of Facts Given to the People of the United States by 372 Tampico Refugees aboard the S.S. Esperanza," April 30, 1914, quoted in *ORM,* 194.

122. ELD, diary, 1914, box 207, folder 6, ELDP, 2.

123. *CMH,* 512–14.

124. ELD, diary, 1914, box 207, folder 6, ELDP, 3.

125. Ibid.

126. Quoted in *ORM,* 30.

127. ELD to K. C. Heald, letter, August 30, 1950, box 24, folder 2468, ELDP.

## Chapter 3

1. ELD, "What Is an Economic Geologist?," *EG* 19, no. 5 (1924):473.

2. Ibid.

3. ELD, biographical memorandum, n.d., LTP.

4. ELD to Blas E. Rodriguez, October 7, 1912, box 104, folder 5163, ELDP.

5. See, for example, ELD, "Memorandum re Aguila Company Leasehold in Northern Mexico," July 14, 1914, box 108, folder 5244, ELDP.

6. ELD, "Confidential Report Re—Furbero Field Conditions," February 23, 1912, box 114, folder 5347, ELDP, 5–6.

7. ELD to C. Willard Hayes, April 18, 1914, box 104, folder 5186, ELDP.

8. ELD, diary, 1914, box 207, folder 6, ELDP; Edwin B. Hopkins to ELD, July 19, 1914, box 6, folder 763, ELDP.

9. ELD, diary, 1914, box 207, folder 6, ELDP.

10. Ibid.

11. ELD, diary, 1914, box 205, folder 5, ELDP.

12. ELD to C. Willard Hayes, n.d., box 5, folder 0696, ELDP.

13. NGD, letter, June 7, 1914, box 1, folder 14, NGDP.

14. ELD, report, "Financial Position, Oil Fields of Mexico Company (After Re-organization)," July 4, 1914, box 114, folder 5347, ELDP; ELD, "Memo Re Oil Fields of Mexico Co.," June 26, 1914, box 114, folder 5347, ELDP; ELD, "Memorandum re Aguila Company Leasehold in Northern Mexico," July 14, 1914, box 108, folder 5244, ELDP; ELD, "Memorandum re Geological Work," July 17, 1914, box 108, folder 5244, ELDP; ELD, "Recision of Leases," July 20, 1914, box 108, folder 5244, ELDP; ELD, "Recommendations re Oil Fields of Mexico Work," July 21, 1914, box 108, folder 5244, ELDP.

15. *MD,* 98–99.

16. ELD, diary, 1914, box 207, folder 6, ELDP, 7.

17. Ibid.

18. Ibid., 7–8.

19. Ibid.

20. Ibid., 8.

21. Ibid.

22. Ibid., 8–9.

23. "Mrs. DeGolyer Home from England," *DT,* September 1, 1914; ELD to NGD, August 27, 1914, box 1, folder 13, NGDP; *MD,* 98.

24. ELD to NGD, August 27, 1914, box 1, folder 13, NGDP.

25. C. Willard Hayes to ELD, September 1, 1914, box 5, folder 0696, ELDP.

26. ELD to C. Willard Hayes, October 3, 1914, box 5, folder 0696, ELDP.

27. ELD to W. L. Gregory, October 23, 1914, box 5, folder 0627, ELDP.

28. C. Willard Hayes to ELD, September 1, 1914, box 5, folder 0696, ELDP.

29. ELD to W. L. Gregory, October 23, 1914, box 5, folder 0627, ELDP.

30. ELD to Charles W. Hamilton, February 20, 1915, box 5, folder 0668, ELDP.

31. ELD to C. Willard Hayes, April 2, 1915, box 5, folder 0696, ELDP.

32. Ibid.; Box 1, folder 15, NGDP.

33. ELD to A. C. Veatch, July 1, 1916, box 108, folder 5249, ELDP; ELD to J. B. Body, December 6, 1917, box 108, folder 5261, ELDP.

34. ELD to Charles W. Hamilton, May 4, 1915, box 5, folder 0668, ELDP.

35. ELD, report, "The Oil Fields of Mexico, with Particular Reference to the Fields of The Tampico-Tuxpam Region," July 1, 1916, box 236, folder 1, ELDP.

36. ELD to C. Willard Hayes, April 2, 1915, box 5, folder 0696, ELDP.

37. ELD to J. B. Body, November 17, 1915, box 24, folder 2438, ELDP.

38. Quoted in ELD, diary, 1916, box 205, folder 7, ELDP; *MD,* 105–06.

39. J. B. Body, memorandum, "Geological Department, Aguila Company," March 13, 1916, box 24, folder 2438, ELDP.

40. *MD,* 113–14.

41. Ibid., 117, 142.

42. ELD, diary, 1921, box 205, folder 12, ELDP; ELD, diary, 1916, box 205, folder 7, ELDP; ELD, diary, 1917, box 205, folder 8, ELDP; ELD, diary, 1922, box 205, folder 12A, ELDP; ELD to C. M. Wales, May 12, 1919, box 43, folder 3152A, ELDP.

43. ELD and NGD, interview by Cleveland Amory, 29 pages, n.d., box 3, folder 15, LTP, 20.

44. ELD, diary, 1923, box 205, folder 13, ELDP; ELD, diary, 1920, box 205, folder 11, ELDP; ELD, diary, 1919, box 205, folder 10, ELDP; ELD, diary, 1918, box 205, folder 9, ELDP; ELD, diary, 1921, box 205, folder 12, ELDP; ELD, diary, 1916, box 205, folder 7, ELDP; ELD, diary, 1917, box 205, folder 8, ELDP; ELD, diary, 1922, box 205, folder 12A, ELDP; ELD, diary, 1924, box 205, folder 14, ELDP.

45. ELD to C. Willard Hayes, December 20, 1914, box 5, folder 0696, ELDP.

46. ELD to Charles W. Hamilton, November 16, 1915, box 5, folder 0668, ELDP; ELD to Edwin B. Hopkins, April 4, 1917, box 6, folder 0763, ELDP; ELD to Edwin B. Hopkins, July 14, 1917, box 6, folder 0763, ELDP; ELD to Edwin B. Hopkins, January 21, 1915, box 6, folder 0763, ELDP; ELD, "Memorandum to Mr. Herbert J. Carr," July 14, 1917, box 6, folder 0763, ELDP.

47. ELD to A. W. McCoy, February 9, 1916, box 9, folder 1125, ELDP.

48. *MD,* 138–40.

49. ELD to Paul Weaver, June 24, 1916, box 15, folder 1970B, ELDP.

50. ELD to J. B. Body, June 24, 1916, box 108, folder 5261, ELDP.

51. ELD to J. B. Body, July 21, 1916, box 108, folder 5261, ELDP; ELD, report, "The Oil Fields of Mexico, with Particular Reference to the Fields of The Tampico-Tuxpam Region," July 1, 1916, box 236, folder 1, ELDP.

52. J. B. Body to ELD, August 1, 1916, box 108, folder 5261, ELDP.

53. ELD to A. C. Veatch, letter, November 22, 1916, box 24, folder 2438, ELDP; ELD to J. B. Body, letter, February 19, 1917, box 24, folder 2438, ELDP.

54. ELD to Herbert J. Carr, July 2, 1917, box 3, folder 0234, ELDP.

55. A. C. Veatch to ELD, August 31, 1917, box 3, folder 0234, ELDP.

56. J. B. Body to ELD, letter, August 24, 1917, box 24, folder 2438, ELDP.

57. ELD to Edwin B. Hopkins, August 29, 1918, box 6, folder 0763, ELDP; ELD to Edwin B. Hopkins, April 4, 1917, box 6, folder 0763, ELDP.

58. *MD,* 133–36.

59. ELD to Edwin B. Hopkins, September 21, 1917, box 6, folder 0763, ELDP.

60. ELD to Arthur H. Noble, April 29, 1918, box 10, folder 1328, ELDP.

61. ELD, diary, 1918, box 205, folder 9, ELDP.

62. ELD, diary, 1919, box 205, folder 10, ELDP; Desmond Young, *Member for*

*Mexico: A Biography of Weetman Pearson, First Viscount Cowdray* (London: Cassell & Co. Ltd., 1966), 189–90, 192–213.

63. ELD to NGD, March 6, 1919, box 1, folder 16, NGDP; ELD to NGD, January 19, 1919, box 1, folder 16, NGDP.

64. ELD to NGD, March 6, 1919, box 1, folder 16, NGDP.

65. ELD to Lord Cowdray, May 31, 1919, box 11, folder 1439, ELDP.

66. ELD to J. B. Body, March 31, 1919, box 108, folder 5261, ELDP.

67. "The First Quarter Century of Amerada Petroleum Corporation, 1919–1944," 1944, box 141, folder 5878H, ELDP.

68. Box 24, folder 2432, ELDP.

69. ELD to J. B. Body, June 7, 1919, box 108, folder 5261, ELDP.

70. J. B. Body to ELD, June 23, 1919, box 108, folder 5261, ELDP.

71. ELD to J. B. Body, July 24, 1919, box 108, folder 5261, ELDP.

72. ELD to Paul Weaver, August 18, 1920, box 15, folder 1970B, ELDP.

73. Edward Morrow, "Amerada Plays Them Close to the Chest," *Fortune,* January 1946.

74. Ibid.

75. A. C. Veatch to ELD, August 31, 1917, box 3, folder 0234, ELDP.

76. "The First Quarter Century of Amerada Petroleum Corporation, 1919–1944," 1944, box 141, folder 5878H, ELDP.

77. ELD, diary, 1923, box 205, folder 13, ELDP; ELD, diary, 1920, box 205, folder 11, ELDP; ELD, diary, 1921, box 205, folder 12, ELDP; ELD, diary, 1922, box 205, folder 12A, ELDP; ELD, diary, 1924, box 205, folder 14, ELDP.

78. "The First Quarter Century of Amerada Petroleum Corporation, 1919–1944," 1944, box 141, folder 5878H, ELDP; Morrow, "Amerada Plays Them Close to the Chest."

79. J. Elmer Thomas, "The Origin and Growth of the American Association of Petroleum Geologists," April 11, 1940, box 14, folder 1830, ELDP.

80. Quoted in Thomas C. Frick et al., eds., *Centennial History of the American Insitute of Mining, Metallurgical, and Petroleum Engineers, 1871–1970* (New York: The American Institute of Mining, Metallurgical, and Petroleum Engineers, 1971), 9.

81. "Rules," *Transactions of the American Institute of Mining and Metallurgical Engineers* 1 (1871–1873). Quoted in Edwin T. Layton Jr., *The Revolt of the Engineers: Social Responsibility and the American Engineering Profession* (Cleveland, Ohio: Press of Case Western Reserve University, 1971), 33.

82. Layton, *Revolt of the Engineers,* 34.

83. Ibid.

84. Ibid., 96.

85. Ibid., 100–01.

86. See, for example, ELD to A. C. Veatch, May 13, 1919, box 108, folder 5249, ELDP; ELD to Paul Weaver, May 13, 1919, box 15, folder 1970B, ELDP; ELD to R. H. Soper, May 13, 1919, box 13, folder 1740, ELDP.

87. ELD to American Institute of Mining and Metallurgical Engineers, May 20, 1921, box 38, folder 3070, ELDP.

88. ELD to Ralph Arnold, May 24, 1921, box 38, folder 3070, ELDP.

89. ELD to K. B. Nowels, April 14, 1924, box 38, folder 3065, ELDP; ELD, "Memorandum Re Organization of Petroleum Group in A. I. M. & M. E.," November 22, 1923, box 39, folder 3074, ELDP; ELD, "Organization of Petroleum Division," January 17, 1924, box 38, folder 3065, ELDP.

90. J. Elmer Thomas, "The Origin and Growth of the American Association of Petroleum Geologists," April 11, 1940, box 14, folder 1830, ELDP.

91. ELD, diary, 1916, box 205, folder 7, ELDP.

92. ELD, diary, 1917, box 205, folder 8, ELDP.

93. Box 24, folder 2432, ELDP.

94. J. Elmer Thomas, "The Origin and Growth of the American Association of Petroleum Geologists," April 11, 1940, box 14, folder 1830, ELDP.

95. W. E. Wrather, "Meeting of Research Committee, American Association of Petroleum Geologists," December 10, 1924, box 35, folder 3020, ELDP.

96. Box 24, folder 2432, ELDP.

97. ELD to W. T. Lee, April 4, 1911, box 24, folder 2437, ELDP.

98. ELD, "Petroleum Industry of the Tampico Region," *PR* 27, no. 535 (1912).

99. ELD, "The Mexican Petroleum Industry during 1912," *PR* 29, no. 592 (1913).

100. See, for example, ELD, "The Effect of Igneous Intrusions on the Accumulation of Oil in the Tampico-Tuxpam Region, Mexico," *EG* 10, no. 7 (1915); ELD, "The Furbero Oil Field, Mexico," *BAIME,* no. 105 (1915); ELD, "The Geology of Cuban Petroleum Deposits," *BAAPG* 2 (1918); ELD, "Oil in Southern Tamaulipas, Mexico," *BAIME,* no. 142 (1918); ELD, "Origin of the Cap Rock of the Gulf Coast Salt Domes," *EG* 13, no. 8 (1918); ELD, "The Significance of Certain Mexican Oil Field Temperatures," *EG* 13, no. 4 (1918); ELD, "A Simple Method of Taking Cores in Wells Being Drilled by the Rotary System," 1921, box 16, folder 2216, ELDP; ELD, "The Theory of Volcanic Origin of Salt Domes," *BAIME,* no. 137 (1918); ELD, "Zacamixtle Pool, Mexico," *BAAPG* 5, no. 1 (1921).

101. ELD to J. B. Body, August 7, 1916, box 108, folder 5261, ELDP.

102. J. B. Body to ELD, September 1, 1916, box 108, folder 5261, ELDP.

103. ELD to Donald C. Barton, October 30, 1920, box 1, folder 82, ELDP.

104. Ibid.

105. Ibid.

106. ELD to Donald C. Barton, March 3, 1923, box 1, folder 82, ELDP.

107. For granted requests, see, for example, ELD to Donald C. Barton, April 26, 1923, box 1, folder 82, ELDP; ELD to Sidney Powers, March 3, 1922, box 11, folder 1506, ELDP; ELD to Sidney Powers, June 16, 1922, box 11, folder 1506, ELDP; ELD to Sidney Powers, February 7, 1924, box 11, folder 1506, ELDP.

108. ELD to Donald C. Barton, March 3, 1923, box 1, folder 82, ELDP.

109. ELD to Sidney Powers, February 25, 1924, box 11, folder 1506, ELDP.

110. ELD to Donald C. Barton, March 3, 1923, box 1, folder 82, ELDP.

111. ELD to Donald C. Barton, December 18, 1923, box 1, folder 82, ELDP.

112. ELD to Donald C. Barton, December 3, 1920, box 1, folder 82, ELDP.

113. ELD, "Debt of Geology to the Petroleum Industry," *BAAPG* 5, no. 3 (1921):394.

114. Ibid., 395.

115. Ibid.

116. Ibid., 396–97.

117. Ibid., 398.

118. Ibid.

119. Ibid.

120. ELD, "Cooperation in Geology," *EG* 18, no. 1 (1923).

121. Ibid., 84.

122. Ibid., 84–85.

123. Ibid., 85–86.

124. Ibid., 86.

125. A. Rodger Denison et al., pamphlet, "AIME Honorary Membership Citation Given E. DeGolyer," February 1952, box 24, folder 2432, ELDP.

## Chapter 4

1. ELD, "Geophysical Methods in Economic Geology," *EG* 21, no. 3 (1926):294.

2. ELD to David White, September 19, 1924, box 88, folder 4867, ELDP.

3. Ibid.

4. Ibid.

5. ELD, "Discovery by Geophysical Methods of a New Salt Dome in the Gulf Coast," *Bulletin of the Geological Society of America* 36 (1925).

6. ELD, "Geophysical Methods in Economic Geology," *EG* 21, no. 3 (1926):294.

7. Ibid.

8. Ibid.

9. Ibid., 295.

10. Lewis L. Nettleton, "Salt Dome," in *McGraw-Hill Encyclopedia of the Geological Sciences,* ed. M. Charles Gilbert and George Klein (New York: McGraw Hill Book Company, 1988).

11. ELD, autobiographical essay, n.d., box 25, folder 2468, ELDP, 1.

12. Ibid., 2.

13. ELD, "Origin of the Cap Rock of the Gulf Coast Salt Domes," *EG* 13, no. 8 (1918); ELD, "The Theory of Volcanic Origin of Salt Domes," *BAIME,* no. 137 (1918).

14. ELD, autobiographical essay, n.d., box 25, folder 2468, ELDP, 4.

15. Ibid., 4–6.

16. *MD,* 140.

17. A general description of the early use of micropaleontology by the Humble Oil Company can be found in Henrietta Larson and Kenneth Wiggins Porter, *History of Humble Oil and Refining Company* (New York: Harper and Brothers, 1959), 115–16.

18. ELD, "The Divining Rod," *EG* 23, no. 4 (1928):461.

19. DeGolyer's early interest in the torsion balance is referred to in Donald C. Barton, "Geophysical Methods in the Gulf Coastal Plain," *BAAPG* 9, no. 3 (1925):670; ELD, manuscript, n.d., box 87, folder 4839, ELDP; ELD, "Use of the Eotvos Torsion Balance in Geologic Work," n.d., box 87, folder 4836, ELDP.

20. Raoul Vajk, "Baron Roland Eötvös," *Geophysics* 14, no. 1 (1949):6.

21. J. J. Jakosky, *Exploration Geophysics,* 2nd ed. (Los Angeles: Trija Publishing Company, 1950), 6–7; Vajk, "Baron Roland Eötvös," 6–8.

22. ELD, "Use of the Eotvos Torsion Balance in Geologic Work," n.d., box 87, folder 4836, ELDP.

23. Barton, "Geophysical Methods in the Gulf Coastal Plain," 670; ELD, manuscript, n.d., box 87, folder 4839, ELDP; ELD, "Use of the Eotvos Torsion Balance in Geologic Work," n.d., box 87, folder 4836, ELDP; *HGP3,* 117.

24. Eugene Wesley Shaw, "The Possibility of Using Gravity Anomalies in the Search for Salt-Dome Oil and Gas Pools," *Science* 46, no. 1197 (1917).

25. ELD to Sidney Paige, July 18, 1919, box 87, folder 4861, ELDP.

26. ELD, "Use of the Eotvos Torsion Balance in Geologic Work," n.d., box 87, folder 4836, ELDP; Vajk, "Baron Roland Eötvös," 9.

27. ELD to Thomas J. Ryder, July 15, 1921, box 87, folder 4861, ELDP; ELD, "Use of the Eotvos Torsion Balance in Geologic Work," n.d., box 87, folder 4836, ELDP.

28. Andrew Gilmour, "Dr. Donald C. Barton," *Geophysics* 4, no. 4 (1939):235.

29. Barton, "Geophysical Methods in the Gulf Coastal Plain," 670; James A. Clark, *The Chronological History of the Petroleum and Natural Gas Industries* (Houston, Texas: Clark Book Co., 1963), 135; Gilmour, "Dr. Donald C. Barton," 235; *MD,* 159. For European reports, see, for example, Donald C. Barton to ELD, May 13, 1922; May 20 1922; May 29, 1922, box 87, folder 4861, ELDP.

30. C. Willard Hayes and William Kennedy, "Oil Fields of the Texas-Louisiana Gulf Coastal Plain," *BUSGS,* no. 212 (1903).

31. Donald C. Barton, "E.G.M. Survey of the Spindletop Salt Dome," April 12, 1923, box 91, folder 4906, ELDP, 2.

32. Ibid., 1.

33. Clark, *The Chronological History of the Petroleum and Natural Gas Industries,* 135.

34. Donald C. Barton, "E.G.M. Survey of the Spindletop Salt Dome," April 12, 1923, box 91, folder 4906, ELDP, 3.

35. Ibid.

36. Ibid., 2.

37. Donald C. Barton, "Preliminary Report of Nash Prospect," February 26, 1924, box 93, folder 4937, ELDP, 1.

38. Ibid., 2.

39. *HGP3,* 47.

40. Donald C. Barton, "Report: V.I.M. Survey No. 1, Blue Ridge Salt Dome, Fort Bend County, Texas," May 22, 1924, box 93, folder 4937, ELDP.

41. Charles C. Bates, Thomas F. Gaskell, and Robert B. Rice, *Geophysics in the Affairs of Man: A Personalized History of Exploration Geophysics and its Allied Sciences of Seismology and Oceanography* (Oxford: Pergamon Press, 1982), 3–11.

42. Ibid., 10–11; *HGP3*, 107.

43. Gerhard Keppner, "Ludger Mintrop," *The Leading Edge* 10, no. 9 (1991):22; *HGP3*, 106.

44. Keppner, "Ludger Mintrop," 22; *HGP3*, 106.

45. Keppner, "Ludger Mintrop," 22; *HGP3*, 107.

46. P. C. A. Stewart to Andrew Gilmour, August 19, 1922, box 87, folder 4861, ELDP.

47. ELD to J. B. Body, March 13, 1923, box 88, folder 4867, ELDP; *TOF,* 504. Quote from ELD, manuscript, n.d., box 87, folder 4839, ELDP.

48. Quoted in Keppner, "Ludger Mintrop," 24.

49. ELD, manuscript, n.d., box 87, folder 4839, ELDP.

50. Ibid.

51. J. C. Karcher, *The Reflection Seismograph: Its Invention and Use in the Discovery of Oil and Gas Fields* (New York: American Institute of Physics, 1974), 1–3. Quote from ibid., 3.

52. Ibid., 5–12.

53. Ibid., 12–13.

54. Ibid., 13–16.

55. Ibid., 17–19.

56. Ibid., 19–21.

57. Ibid., 21.

58. Ibid., 22–25.

59. Ibid., 24–27.

60. Elliot Sweet to ELD, May 15, 1932, box 24, folder 2432, ELDP, 123. Quote from Karcher, *The Reflection Seismograph,* 27–28.

61. Karcher, *The Reflection Seismograph,* 28; *HGP3,* 123–24.

62. David F. Noble, *America by Design: Science, Technology, and the Rise of Corporate Capitalism* (New York: Alfred A. Knopf, 1977), 112; *TOF,* 157–60, 166, 188.

63. ELD, biographical memorandum, "Everette Lee DeGolyer," n.d., box 24, folder 2437, ELDP; *HGP3,* 124, 146.

64. *HGP1,* 103, 302.

65. ELD, "The Development of the Art of Prospecting" (paper presented at the Cyrus Fogg Brackett Lecture, Princeton, New Jersey, December 12, 1940), 35; *TOF,* 510.

66. *HGP1,* 119–120.

67. Keppner, "Ludger Mintrop," 27; *HGP3,* 109.

68. *Twentieth Century Petroleum Statistics, 1950* (Dallas, Texas: DeGolyer and MacNaughton, 1950), 49; Bates, Gaskell, and Rice, *Geophysics in the Affairs of Man,* 293; *HGP3,* 229–31.

69. Mody C. Boatright, *Folklore of the Oil Industry* (Dallas: Southern Methodist University Press, 1963), 34–45; Harold F. Williamson and Arnold R. Daum, *The American Petroleum Industry: The Age of Illumination, 1859–1899,* vol. 1 (Evanston, Ill.: Northwestern University Press, 1959), 90–91.

70. ELD to Edwin B. Hopkins, July 28, 1926, box 88, folder 4867, ELDP; Edwin B. Hopkins to ELD, July 24, 1926, box 88, folder 4867, ELDP.

71. Emphasis original. Clarence V. Elliott to ELD, July 7, 1945, box 86, folder 4824, ELDP.

72. ELD to Clarence V. Elliott, July 17, 1945, box 86, folder 4824, ELDP.

73. ELD to Sidney Powers, January 31, 1930, box 88, folder 4867, ELDP.

74. Wallace E. Pratt, "Memorial to Chester Wesley Washburne, 1883–1971," in *Memorials: The Geological Society of America,* vol. 3 (Boulder, Colorado: The Geological Society of America, 1974).

75. Chester W. Washburne, Memorandum, May 10, 1935, box 86, folder 4830, ELDP.

76. Ibid.

77. Ibid.

78. Ibid.

79. Emphasis original. W. R. Calvert to ELD, June 10, 1935, box 87, folder 4837, ELDP.

80. ELD to J. C. Karcher, telegram, July 18, 1935, box 86, folder 4830, ELDP.

81. W. R. Calvert to ELD, July 28, 1935, box 87, folder 4837, ELDP.

82. ELD to J. C. Karcher, August 2, 1935, box 87, folder 4837, ELDP.

83. Ibid.

84. J. C. Karcher to ELD, August 17, 1935, box 87, folder 4837, ELDP.

85. Ibid.

86. ELD to W. R. Calvert, March 14, 1936, box 86, folder 4830, ELDP.

87. Ibid.

88. ELD to J. B. Body, March 13, 1923, box 88, folder 4867, ELDP.

89. ELD, "The Development of the Art of Prospecting" (paper presented at the Cyrus Fogg Brackett Lecture, Princeton, New Jersey, December 12, 1940), 28–29.

90. ELD, address, "The Role of the Technician in International Management," March 14, 1952, box 25, folder 2461A, ELDP.

91. Ibid.

92. Ibid.

93. Ibid.

94. See, for example, Lewis W. MacNaughton, "E. L. DeGolyer, Father of Applied Geophysics," *Science* 125 (1957). Time magazine described him as the "father of geophysical exploration" in "Well Chosen Words," *Time,* April 3, 1944. John Murrell referred to him simply as the "father of geophysics" in John H. Murrell, *Science—Skill—Service: The Story of DeGolyer and MacNaughton* (New York: Newcomen Society in North America, 1964), 13.

## Chapter 5

1. ELD to Arthur H. Bunker, February 6, 1934, box 2, folder 164A, ELDP.

2. ELD to Pomeroy and Company Case, September 20, 1934, box 148, folder 5964, ELDP; Bishops' Service Inc., memorandum, n.d., box 144, folder 5940A, ELDP.

3. F. A. Judson, "Felmont Corporation," August 16, 1937, box 148, folder 5964, ELDP.

4. ELD to Henry R. Johnston, April 26, 1939, box 148, folder 5964, ELDP.

5. Ibid.

6. Ibid.

7. Harold F. Williamson et al., *The American Petroleum Industry: The Age of Energy, 1899–1959,* vol. 2 (Evanston, Ill.: Northwestern University Press, 1963), 336.

8. ELD to Charles W. Wrightsman, July 1, 1929, box 16, folder 2040, ELDP.

9. James A. Clark, *Three Stars for the Colonel: The Biography of Ernest O. Thompson* (New York: Random House, 1954), 3–15.

10. Diana Davids Olien and Roger M. Olien, *Oil in Texas: The Gusher Age, 1895–1945* (Austin, Texas: University of Texas Press, 2002), 167–71, 180; *TP,* 246–47.

11. Kenny A. Franks, *The Oklahoma Petroleum Industry* (Norman, Okla.: The University of Oklahoma Press, 1980), 162–68; Diana Davids Olien and Roger M. Olien, *Oil in Texas: The Gusher Age, 1895–1945* (Austin, Texas: University of Texas Press, 2002), 185–89.

12. ELD to Robert D. Goodrich, December 12, 1929, box 5, folder 0599, ELDP.

13. ELD, federal income tax form 1040, 1929, box 181, folder 18, ELDP.

14. ELD, federal income tax form 1040, 1931, box 181, folder 20, ELDP; ELD, federal income tax form 1040, 1930, box 181, folder 19, ELDP.

15. Edward Morrow, "Amerada Plays Them Close to the Chest," *Fortune,* January 1946.

16. Ibid.

17. Ibid.; *HGP3,* 145.

18. *HGP3,* 145.

19. J. C. Karcher to Lon Tinkle, June 15, 1967, box 12, folder 112, LTP.

20. *HGP3,* 146.

21. Ibid.

22. Ibid.

23. Nell DeGolyer's mother was a Womens' Christian Temperance Union adherent and generally "stingy" with cocktails. Everette DeGolyer may have been less restrained in the absence of his wife. Overall, he is remembered in the family as being a moderate rather than heavy drinker. Peter Flagg Maxson to Houston Mount, August 17, 2013.

24. *HGP3,* 146.

25. Karcher refers to this meeting and gives the date of December 1929: J. C. Karcher to Lon Tinkle, June 15, 1967, box 12, folder 112, LTP.

26. "Dr. E. E. Rosaire, 62, Dies After Heart Attack," *DMN,* September 22, 1959;

J. C. Karcher to Lon Tinkle, June 15, 1967, box 12, folder 112, Lon Tinkle Collection, DeGolyer Library, Southern Methodist University; *HGP3,* 147; Lon Tinkle, "Gene McDermott: 'Universal Man,'" *DMN,* September 2, 1973.

27. ELD to Amerada Petroleum Corporation Board of Directors, Amerada Refining Corporation, Geopohysical Research Corporation, Esperanza Petroleum Corporation, Amerada Petroleum Corporation of California, October 3, 1932, box 32, folder 2906, ELDP.

28. "Wall Street Briefs," *DMN,* October 4, 1932.

29. ELD to Clive Pearson, telegram, October 25, 1932, box 32, folder 2906, ELDP.

30. Caleb Pirtle, III, *Engineering the World: Stories from the First 75 Years of Texas Instruments* (Dallas: Southern Methodist University Press, 2005), 1.

31. ELD, federal income tax form 1040, 1941, box 184, folder 5, ELDP. Stanolind later became Amoco Corporation, then following a merger in 1998, BP Amoco. "Federal Regulators Approve British Petroleum Purchase of Amoco," *NYT,* December 31, 1998.

32. "Option Taken On Big Dallas Oil Company," *DMN,* September 29, 1941; Pirtle, *Engineering the World,* 13; Robertson, *The ABCs of De,* 36.

33. "Texas Instruments, Inc.," in *International Directory of Company Histories,* vol. 46 (St. James Press, 2002).

34. Brent Filson, *Case & Son: The Seventy-Five Year Saga of Case, Pomeroy & Company* (Lyme, Conn.: Greenwich Publishing Group, Inc., 1992), 47, 93.

35. Ibid., 48.

36. *MD,* 228–30.

37. Filson, *Case & Son,* 48.

38. Charles J. Deegan and Lewis W. MacNaughton, "E. DeGolyer, Honorary Member," *Bulletin of the American Association of Petroleum Geologists* 29, no. 3 (1945):397.

39. William L. Horner, "Core Laboratories, Inc., Field Service Brochure, Preliminary Text Draft," June 1, 1937, box 145, folder 5941, ELDP.

40. Filson, *Case & Son,* 48.

41. Deegan and MacNaughton, "E. DeGolyer, Honorary Member," 397.

42. ELD to R. C. Stewart, July 7, 1938, box 145, folder 5941, ELDP.

43. Filson, *Case & Son,* 102. Hadley Case was now in charge following the death of his father in 1937: ibid., 68.

44. ELD to Henry R. Johnston, June 12, 1939, box 145, folder 5941, ELDP.

45. ELD to Adrian Moore, October 30, 1924, box 168, folder 6124B, ELDP.

46. "Alamo Royalties Corporation," October 29, 1925, box 168, folder 6124B, ELDP; ELD to L. DeWitt Wolfe, December 22, 1924, box 168, folder 6124B, ELDP.

47. ELD to J. B. Body, February 19, 1926, box 168, folder 6124B, ELDP.

48. ELD, federal income tax form 1040, 1941, box 184, folder 5, ELDP.

49. Alamo Royalties Corporation described as a small company in ELD to Frank VanSant, January 12, 1940, box 168, folder 6124B, ELDP.

50. David Donoghue, "Federal Royalties Company, Inc.," December 31, 1934, box 147, folder 5954C, ELDP. In 1950, DeGolyer would sell Federal Royalties Company shares for $174,616 at a gain of $164,316. ELD, federal income tax form 1040, 1950, box 185, folder 19, ELDP.

51. Phil F. Martyn, "Evaluation Report: Atlatl Royalty Corporation," December 1, 1946, box 144, folder 5934, ELDP, 2–4.

52. Ibid., 4.

53. ELD to Henry R. Johnston, April 26, 1939, box 148, folder 5964, ELDP. Felmont was associated with yet another similar venture, Essex Royalty Corporation, founded in 1935. Essex took its name from DeGolyer and Walter Case's residences in New Jersey's Essex County. Filson, *Case & Son,* 97.

54. "Atlatl Royalty Sold," *NYT,* February 18, 1951; "Oil Royalty Firm Brings $7,500,000," *DMN,* February 17, 1951; Phil F. Martyn, "Evaluation Report: Atlatl Royalty Corporation," December 1, 1946, box 144, folder 5934, ELDP, 3.

55. Box 140, folder 5863, ELDP.

56. "South Shore Oil Lands, Ltd.," March 5, 1931, box 168, folder 6125A, ELDP.

57. For an account of the practice of geology as a profession during these years: *TOF,* 157–60.

58. "Handsome Home Bought by Jersey Oil Man," *DMN,* March 15, 1936.

59. NGD to ELD, January 3, 1937, box 1, folder 23, NGDP.

60. Ibid..

61. "Handsome Home Bought by Jersey Oil Man," *DMN,* March 15, 1936.

62. "Dallas Oilman Takes PRC Job," August 23, 1943, box 56, folder 3535, ELDP; "Dallas Oilman, Engineer Named to Coordinating Post," July, n.d., box 56, folder 3535, ELDP.

63. "Memorandum of Telephone Conversation with Mr. B. P. Manning," February 29, 1940, box 41, folder 3102, ELDP; *ABCD,* 12.

64. ELD to Ben P. Manning, March 10, 1948, box 41, folder 3102, ELDP; B. P. Manning to Rad Pike, March 15, 1938, box 11, folder 1477, ELDP.

65. The planned pool was never constructed. Peter Flagg Maxson to Houston Mount, August 18, 2013.

66. "Cool Corridors to Connect Units of DeGolyer Mansion on White Rock Lake," *DMN,* July 16, 1939.

67. "Huge Home on Lake Front Nearly Ready," February 1940, box 33, folder 2924A, ELDP; ELD to Hawley Kerr, December 7, 1939, box 7, folder 0925A, ELDP.

68. "DeGolyer Sisters Entertained with Dinner and Dance," *DMN,* March 13, 1937; "DeGolyer Sisters Named Honorees at Friday Party," *DMN,* May 15, 1937; "Dorothy DeGolyer to Become Bride at June Ceremony," *DMN,* January 16, 1937; ibid; "John Sherman Maxson Marries Miss DeGolyer," *DMN,* July 3, 1937; "Miss DeGolyer Engaged to Wed," *NYT,* January 17, 1937; "Miss Dorothy Margaret DeGolyer and David Perry Stephenson Wed," *DMN,* June 3, 1937; "Six Local Gridders Due to Be Regulars On Longhorn Eleven," *DMN,* May 20, 1934; "Stephenson-

DeGolyer," *NYT,* January 3, 1937; "Virginia DeGolyer's Betrothal to Jack Maxson Announced," *DMN,* April 22, 1937. See also Peter Flagg Maxson, "The DeGolyer Children," in *Talks to the DeGolyer Estate Docents, 1990s to Present* (Dallas, Texas, 2011).

69. Margaret Milam, "Forthcoming Wedding of Cecilia DeGolyer and George McGhee Revealed at Reception," *DMN,* October 9, 1938. For an overview of some major foreign policy decisions in which McGhee was involved: *TP.* McGhee also published an autobiography: George C. McGhee, *I Did It This Way: From Texas and Oil to Oxford, Diplomacy, and Corporate Boards* (Danbury, Conn.: Rutledge Books, Inc., 2001).

70. "Mrs. N. K. DeGolyer Dies at Home of Son," *DMN,* September 1, 1938; Peter Flagg Maxson, "The DeGolyers and Goodriches," in *Talks to the DeGolyer Estate Docents, 1990s to Present* (Dallas, Texas, 2011).

71. "MacNaughton, Lewis Winslow," in *National Cyclopedia of American Biography,* vol. 55 (Clifton, N.J.: James T. White and Co., 1974); Eric G. Schroeder, "Geology Provides Pathway for Oilman's Success Story," *DMN,* October 9, 1949; *MD,* 224–25. For conspiratorial speculation: "Transcript of Testimony at Afternoon Session of Acheson's Second Day Before Inquiry," *NYT,* June 4, 1951.

72. "MacNaughton, Lewis Winslow," in *National Cyclopedia of American Biography,* vol. 55 (Clifton, N.J.: James T. White and Co., 1974); Eric G. Schroeder, "Geology Provides Pathway for Oilman's Success Story," *DMN,* October 9, 1949; *MD,* 224–25.

73. ELD to Lewis W. MacNaughton, October 10, 1936, box 9, folder 1162, ELDP.

74. Ibid.

75. *MD,* 224.

76. For an account of the practice of geology as a profession during these years, see *TOF,* 157–60.

77. For an overviews of early attempts to deal with the crisis, see *USOP,* 112–27; *O&I,* 185–208.

78. E. O. Thompson, the powerful chairman of the Texas Railroad Commission, justified his support for prorationing, stating, "I believe the oil industry should be regulated to the extent necessary to prevent physical waste and that whenever, in the prevention of waste, it is necessary to limit production, the production should, as an incident to fair play, be prorated. Regulations should not go beyond this." Ernest O. Thompson, "An Administrator's Views on Proration," *O&GJ,* February 23, 1939.

79. For discussion of maximum efficiency rate: Edward W. Constant, II, "Cause or Consequence: Science, Technology, and Regulatory Change in the Oil Business in Texas, 1930–1975," *Technology and Culture* 30, no. 2 (1989):433; *O&I,* 235–236; *TOF,* 472–74; Carl E. Reistle Jr., "Reservoir Engineering," in *History of Petroleum Engineering* (Dallas, Texas: American Petroleum Institute, 1961). For optimum rate of production: Joseph E. Pogue, "Principles of Allocation in Conservation of Oil," *O&GJ,* December 12, 1940.

80. John H. Murrell, *Science—Skill—Service: The Story of DeGolyer and Mac-Naughton* (New York: Newcomen Society in North America, 1964), 15.

81. Ibid., 12, 15.

82. "MacNaughton, Lewis Winslow," in *National Cyclopedia of American Biography,* vol. 55 (Clifton, N.J.: James T. White and Co., 1974); Murrell, *Science—Skill—Service,* 12; *MD,* 225–26.

83. Ralph Arnold to ELD, October 14, 1918, box 50, folder 3402, ELDP; ELD to Thomas J. Ryder, October 30, 1918, box 50, folder 3402, ELDP.

84. Thomas J. Ryder to J. B. Body, telegram, October 11, 1918, box 50, folder 3402, ELDP.

85. Ralph Arnold to ELD, October 14, 1918, box 50, folder 3402, ELDP; ELD to Thomas J. Ryder, October 30, 1918, box 50, folder 3402, ELDP.

86. Ralph Arnold to ELD, October 17, 1918, box 50, folder 3402, ELDP. For a detailed account of the pandemic in the Unites States, see Alfred W. Crosby Jr., *Epidemic and Peace, 1918* (Westport, Connecticut: Greenwood Press, 1976).

87. ELD to Ralph Arnold, December 5, 1918, box 50, folder 3402, ELDP.

88. ELD to Ralph Arnold, February 3, 1919, box 50, folder 3402, ELDP.

89. Ibid. Despite Arnold's obvious frustration with DeGolyer's hesitance to conjure a solution, Arnold himself had admitted that estimating the longevity of oil wells was uncertain business: Ralph Arnold, "Conservation of the Oil and Gas Resources of the Americas, Part I," *EG* 11, no. 3 (1916):222. DeGolyer's associate Chester Washburne put probable error in such estimates at a less than assuring 50 percent: Chester W. Washburne, "The Estimation of Oil Reserves," *BAIME* 98 (1915):469. Another geologist who was willing to develop his own production curve admitted that such estimates were "necessarily inaccurate." Robert W. Pack, "The Estimation of Petroleum Reserves," *Metallurgical and Chemical Engineering* 17, no. 5 (1917):227.

90. ELD to Earle Oliver, January 13, 1925, box 10, folder 1365, ELDP.

91. Ibid.

92. ELD, "On the Estimating of Petroleum Reserves," *EG* 17, no. 1 (1922):44.

93. Warren Sinsheimer, correspondence, box 13, folder 1715, ELDP.

94. Murrell, *Science—Skill—Service,* 19.

95. Ibid., 9.

96. "Brazil Sees Gains in Oil, 'Czar' Says," *DMN,* November 11, 1949; Jay Hall, "Dallas Partnership Does Big Business," *DMN,* March 20, 1949; Eric G. Schroeder, "Geology Provides Pathway For Oilman's Success Story," *DMN,* October 9, 1949.

## Chapter 6

1. ELD, address, "Science: A Method, Not a Field," May 31, 1948, box 21, folder 2362, ELDP.

2. ELD, n.d., box 3, folder 17, Lon Tinkle Collection, Southern Methodist University.

3. Hal P. Bybee to ELD, August 11, 1938, box 73, folder 4343, ELDP.

4. ELD to Hal P. Bybee, February 3, 1939, box 73, folder 4343, ELDP.

5. "Dallas Man Made U. of T. Professor," *DMN,* November 12, 1939; "Dallasite Gets Distinguished Professorship," November 11, 1939, box 73, folder 4343, ELDP; Leo C. Haynes to ELD, November 7, 1939, box 73, folder 4343, ELDP.

6. J. C. Karcher to Lon Tinkle, June 15, 1967, box 12, folder 112, Lon Tinkle Collection, DeGolyer Library, Southern Methodist University.

7. ELD, address, "Science: A Method, Not a Field," May 31, 1948, box 21, folder 2362, ELDP.

8. "Oklahoma University News," *The Weekly Times-Journal,* October 25, 1907.

9. ELD, "The Furbero Oil Field, Mexico," *BAIME,* no. 105 (1915).

10. ELD, "The Effect of Igneous Intrusions on the Accumulation of Oil in the Tampico-Tuxpam Region, Mexico," *EG* 10, no. 7 (1915); ELD, "The Geology of Cuban Petroleum Deposits," *BAAPG* 2 (1918).

11. ELD, "The Theory of Volcanic Origin of Salt Domes," *BAIME,* no. 137 (1918).

12. ELD, "The Significance of Certain Mexican Oil Field Temperatures," *EG* 13, no. 4 (1918).

13. ELD, "Proposed Book in Occurrence of Petroleum," March 5, 1918, box 23, folder 2403, ELDP.

14. See, for example, ELD, "Discovery of Potash Salts and Fossil Algae in Texas Salt Dome," *BAAPG* 9, no. 2 (1925); ELD, "Occurrence of Vanadium and Nickel in Petroleum," *EG* 19, no. 6 (1924); ELD, "Origin of North American Salt Domes," *BAAPG* 9, no. 5 (1925); ELD, "Origin of the Cap Rock of the Gulf Coast Salt Domes," *EG* 13, no. 8 (1918); ELD, "The West Point, Texas, Salt Dome, Freestone County," November–December 1919, box 16, folder 2215, ELDP; ELD, "Zacamixtle Pool, Mexico," *BAAPG* 5, no. 1 (1921).

15. ELD, "The Application of Seismic Methods to Submarine Geology," *Transactions of the American Geophysical Union* (1932); ELD, "Choice of Geophysical Methods in Prospecting for Oil Deposits," *TAIME* (1932); ELD, "Geophysics, A New Tool for the Geologist," November 26, 1930, box 17, folder 2263, ELDP; ELD, "A Simple Method of Taking Cores in Wells Being Drilled by the Rotary System," 1921, box 16, folder 2216, ELDP.

16. See, for example, ELD, "History and Status of Petroleum Production," September 1936, box 17, folder 2277, ELDP; ELD, "The Mexican Petroleum Industry during 1912," *PR* 29, no. 592 (1913); ELD, "Mexico as a Source of Petroleum and Its Products," 1919, box 16, folder 2214, ELDP; ELD, "Naval Oil Reserves," *Mining and Metallurgy* 5, no. 209 (1924); ELD, "The Petroleum Industry of Mexico," 1918, box 16, folder 2210, ELDP; ELD, "Petroleum Industry of the Tampico Region," *PR* 27, no. 535 (1912); ELD, "Petroleum Resources of the World," *EG* 19, no. 2 (1924); ELD, "Production of Petroleum in Mexico during 1922," *TAIME,* no. 1241-P (1923).

17. See, for example, ELD, "Cooperation in Geology," *EG* 18, no. 1 (1923); ELD, "Debt of Geology to the Petroleum Industry," *BAAPG* 5, no. 3 (1921); ELD, "The Geologist and the Petroleum Industry," *BAPI* 5, no. 69 (1924); ELD, "Oil Finding," 1925, box 16, folder 2247C, ELDP; ELD, "On the Estimating of Petroleum Re-

serves," *EG* 17, no. 1 (1922); ELD, "The Seductive Influence of the Closed Contour," *EG* 23, no. 6 (1928); ELD, "State Geological Surveys and *EG*," 1925, box 16, folder 2245, ELDP; ELD, "What Is an Economic Geologist?," *EG* 19, no. 5 (1924).

18. Vannevar Bush to ELD, November 2, 1927, box 17, folder 2261, ELDP.

19. ELD, "Our Mineral Virtues," March 15, 1929, box 17, folder 2261, ELDP.

20. This is discussed in greater detail in the earlier chapter titled "Technologist." ELD, "The Development of the Art of Prospecting" (paper presented at the Cyrus Fogg Brackett Lecture, Princeton, New Jersey, December 12, 1940); Princeton University, Cyrus Fogg Brackett Lecturer, certificate of appreciation December 12, 1939, box 227X, folder 9, ELDP.

21. ELD to C. Willard Hayes, April 2, 1915, box 5, folder 0696, ELDP.

22. ELD to Charles W. Hamilton, May 4, 1915, box 5, folder 0668, ELDP.

23. ELD, "The Mines of Laurium," June 14, 1947, box 21, folder 2349, ELDP; ELD, "Science: A Method, Not a Field," May 31, 1948, box 21, folder 2362, ELDP.

24. Various diplomas, box 227X, folder 9, ELDP.

25. Note, n.d., box 24, folder 2432, ELDP.

26. Frank W. Chappell to ELD, October 9, 1939, box 3, folder 0223, ELDP; ELD to Hawley Kerr, December 7, 1939, box 7, folder 0925A, ELDP.

27. *MD*, 230–31.

28. Box 214, folder 13, ELDP, Southern Methodist University.

29. ELD to Hawley Kerr, December 7, 1939, box 7, folder 0925A, ELDP.

30. ELD to Sumner Pike, January 27, 1940, quoted in Herbert Robertson, *The ABCs of De: A Primer on Everette DeGolyer Sr., 1886–1956* (Dallas: DeGolyer Library, 2007), 181.

31. *MD*, 231, 236.

32. ELD to Sumner Pike, January 27, 1940, quoted in Robertson, *The ABCs of De*, 181.

33. ELD, "Severinus Up-To-Date," March 18, 1940, box 18, folder 2285, ELDP.

34. ELD, "The Engineer in the Petroleum Industry," April 2, 1940, box 18, folder 2286, ELDP.

35. ELD, "Oil in the Near East," May 6, 1940, box 18, folder 2288, ELDP.

36. ELD to Walter W. Stewart, September 27, 1940, box 13, folder 1765, ELDP.

37. Ibid.

38. Ibid.; Box 24, folder 2432, ELDP.

39. See, for example, ELD, "Future Position of Petroleum Geology in the Oil Industry," *BAAPG* 24, no. 8 (1940), which explores themes developed in ELD, "Severinus Up-To-Date," March 18, 1940, box 18, folder 2285, ELDP.

40. See, for example, ELD, "Drilling Requirements . . . Before and After V-Day," *Drilling Contractor* 1, no. 1 (1944); ELD, "Oil for Peace or War," *SR* 30, no. 1 (1944); ELD, "Petroleum Exploration and Development in Wartime," *Mining and Metallurgy* 24, no. 436 (1943); ELD, "We Will Want More Wells," *The Guiberson Guidon* 2, no. 2 (1945).

41. See, for example, ELD, "Avoidable Waste," *Oil Conservation News* 2, no. 3 (1949); ELD, "Conservation of Oil and Gas," *American Bar Association Journal* 35, no. 3 (1949); ELD, "Natural-Gas Reserves," *Oil and Gas Journal,* May 4, 1946; ELD, "Oil and Geologists," *SRL,* January 20, 1951; ELD, "Oil Exploration in the Middle East," *The Mines Magazine,* November 1946; ELD, "On the Estimation of Undiscovered Oil Reserves," *JPT* (1951); ELD, "Our Mineral Resources," *The Mines Magazine,* March 1948.

42. Andrew Dickson White, *A History of the Warfare of Science with Theology in Christendom* (1st ed., 1896) (New York: D. Appleton and Company, 1930).

43. ELD, diary, 1922, box 205, folder 12A, ELDP.

44. ELD, "E. DeGolyer Picks Ten Unusual Books He Would Have Most Hated to Miss; He Writes a Description of Them," January 6, 1945, box 19, folder 2322, ELDP.

45. Ibid.

46. He also offered as supporting evidence the presence of "the sixty-four dollar dictionary of the University of Chicago Press" in city bookstores. ELD to Lobdell, January 18, 1947, box 8, folder 1052, ELDP.

47. White, *History of the Warfare of Science,* v–xii.

48. "A History of the Warfare of Science with Theology in Christendom," *American Historical Review* 2, no. 1 (1896):108.

49. ELD to F. E. Wellings, August 6, 1945, box 15, folder 1982, ELDP.

50. ELD, address, "Science: A Method, Not a Field," May 31, 1948, box 21, folder 2362, ELDP.

51. ELD, address, "History of the Petroleum Industry in Mexico," March 11, 1914, box 114, folder 5347, ELDP.

52. ELD, "The Oil Industry of Mexico: An Historical Sketch," *PR* 30, no. 613 (1914).

53. A. Rodger Denison et al., pamphlet, "AIME Honorary Membership Citation Given E. DeGolyer," February 1952, box 24, folder 2432, ELDP; *MD,* 120.

54. Paul McPharlin, "Carl Hertzog, Printer, The Peripatetic Press: Manifestations of Southwestiana," *Publishers' Weekly,* July 3, 1948.

55. Frank Hamilton Cushing, *My Adventures in Zuñi* (Santa Fe, New Mexico: Peripatetic Press, 1941); ELD, "The Antiquity of the Oil Industry," 1947, box 20, folder 2344, ELDP; ELD, *The Journey of Three Englishmen Across Texas in 1568* (El Paso, Texas: Peripatetic Press, 1947); ELD, "Zuni and Cushing," in *My Adventures in Zuni* (Santa Fe: Peripatetic Press, 1941); Paul McPharlin, "Carl Hertzog, Printer, The Peripatetic Press: Manifestations of Southwestiana," *Publishers' Weekly,* July 3, 1948.

56. Norman Cousins, December 14, 1942, box 74, folder 4371, ELDP; ELD, statement, January 28, 1944, box 74, folder 4371, ELDP.

57. Notes on Talk with Mr. Heroy, 213 Dallas Hall, June 7, 1967, box 3, folder 11, LTP.

58. ELD to Norman Cousins, January 15, 1946, box 74, folder 4372, ELDP.

59. "Saturday Review of Recordings," September 1947, box 74, folder 4372, ELDP.

60. ELD, "Out of a Bottomless Well?," *SRL,* June 17, 1944.

61. "Twelve Travelers," *SRL,* June 21, 1947; ELD to Norman Cousins, March 3, 1947, box 74, folder 4372, ELDP.

62. Norman Cousins to ELD, March 22, 1947, box 74, folder 4372, ELDP.

63. "My Current Reading: Sumner T. Pike," *SRL,* June 12, 1948.

64. ELD to Norman Cousins, June 25, 1948, box 74, folder 4373, ELDP.

65. Dillon Anderson, "Summer on the Water," *SRL,* May 29, 1948.

66. Dillon Anderson, *I and Claudie* (Boston: Little, Brown, 1951).

67. ELD to Norman Cousins, September 14, 1951, box 74, folder 4376, ELDP.

68. Ibid.

69. John T. Winterich, "I and Claudie," *SRL,* November 3, 1951. Reviews in other publications were also somewhat positive. *Kirkus,* July 15, 1951; *New York Herald Tribune Book Review,* November 18, 1951. A reviewer writing in the New York Times was the least impressed: "The author's free-hand style is always refreshing; but his descriptive power is never quite strong enough to blend his stereotyped ingredients into anything but a rather pleasant adult comic book—however successful the best of them may be." *New York Times,* November 18, 1951.

70. Ray Pierre, "The Big Play," *SRL,* November 24, 1951. Interestingly, reviews appearing in other publications were more positive. *New York Herald Tribune Book Review,* September 23, 1951; *New York Times,* October 7, 1951.

71. Norman Cousins, "Foreword," in *MD,* xv.

72. See, for example, ELD, *BAIME* 136 (1918); ELD, *BAIME* 108 (1915).

73. ELD, "The Divining Rod," *EG* 23, no. 4 (1928).

74. ELD, "Story of the Golden Flood," *SRL,* April 18, 1942.

75. ELD, "California's Golden Age," *SRL,* June 19, 1943; ELD, "From Nomads to Farmers," *SRL,* March 3, 1945; ELD, "New Mexicana," *SRL,* May 16, 1942; ELD, "A Virginian in Texas," *SRL,* August 8, 1942.

76. ELD, "Ickes Chronicles Amiably His Hate-Provoking Career," *DMN,* May 23, 1943.

77. See, for example, ELD, "Authoritative Volume Surveys Indian Working of Silver," *DMN,* December 24, 1944; ELD, "Best Books on Mexico," *DMN,* June 1, 1947; ELD, "Biographer Marquis James Recalls Oklahoma Boyhood," *DMN,* September 16, 1945; ELD, "Dallas Museum of Fine Arts Publishes Work by Medellin," *DMN,* September 28, 1947; ELD, "Impressive Novel Dramatizes Problems of Modern Mexico," *DMN,* September 23, 1945; ELD, "Pictorial Panorama Of Early Oil History," *DMN,* October 17, 1948; ELD, "Search for the Seven Cities of Cibola," *DMN,* December 4, 1949.

78. See, for example, ELD, "DeGolyer Examines Mexican Background of Our Culture," *DTH,* October 7, 1945; ELD, "E. L. DeGolyer Discusses New Anglo-Mexican Novel of 1812," *DTH,* September 17, 1944.

79. ELD, "California Here We Come," *SR* 31, no. 2 (1946); ELD, "Paul Bunyan of Oil Fields," *SR* 31, no. 4 (1946).

80. Lon Tinkle, "Many-Sided DeGolyer Career Heaped With Diverse Honors," *DMN,* November 20, 1949.

81. "Bennet Cerf in City Sharing Latest Joke," *DMN,* February 6, 1947; Fairfax Nisbit, "'Cafe Society' Carries on In New Beanery," *DMN,* March 30, 1949.

82. *HGP3,* 53.

83. Suzan Napier, "The History of the Everette DeGolyer Book Collections" (Unpublished Thesis, Southern Methodist University, 1967), 3–4.

84. Ibid., 6.

85. Ibid., 16, 19.

86. Ibid., 18, 22, 29, 32.

87. Ibid., 24.

88. ELD to James F. Drake, June 18, 1947, box 66, folder 4023, ELDP.

89. Napier, "The History of the Everette DeGolyer Book Collections," 5, 50.

90. Ibid., 63.

91. On his death, DeGolyer's private library was placed in the hands of a foundation, with its final destination still indeterminate. In the meantime, Southern Methodist University held the books on loan. In 1973, the foundation made the loan officially permanent. "DeGolyer Library Given to SMU," *DMN,* September 8, 1973; *MD,* 377–79.

92. ELD and NGD, interview by Cleveland Amory, 29 pages, n.d., box 3, folder 15, LTP, 20.

93. Willilam G. Robbins, *Colony and Empire: The Capitalist Transformation of the American West* (Lawrence, Kansas: University of Kansas Press, 1994).

94. Diana Davids Olien and Roger M. Olien, *Oil in Texas: The Gusher Age, 1895–1945* (Austin, Texas: University of Texas Press, 2002), 21–23.

95. "Chili Connoisseurs Ready for Contest," *DMN,* September 14, 1952; ELD, "Chile Con Carne," 1948, box 22, folder 2374, ELDP; ELD to F. E. Wellings, December 18, 1950, box 15, folder 1982, ELDP; ELD to Gebhardt Chili Company, October 26, 1946, box 5, folder 0558, ELDP; ELD to Herbert Gambrell, August 30, 1952, box 5, folder 0539, ELDP; ELD to Olin Culberson, June 5, 1944, box 3, folder 0285, ELDP; Herbert Gambrell to ELD, August 27, 1952, box 5, folder 0539, ELDP; Dick West, "In Recognition of Chilecrats," *DMN,* October 4, 1952.

96. "Mexicans Not Ready For Self-Government," *NDT,* April 23, 1915.

97. Ibid.

98. ELD, address, "Science: A Method, Not a Field," May 31, 1948, box 21, folder 2362, ELDP.

99. ELD, "The New Frontiers," May 15, 1925, box 16, folder 2247B, ELDP.

100. Ibid.

101. Ibid.

## Chapter 7

1. ELD, "Conservation," October 16, 1941, box 44, folder 3195, ELDP, 2.
2. Reprinted in Fritz L. Aurin, "The Geologist in the War," *O&GJ,* April 8, 1943.
3. Ibid., 37.
4. Ibid.
5. Ibid., 66.
6. For a contemporary account of the relationship between petroleum engineering and the regulation, see M. L. Haider, "Constitutionality of Conservation Laws Supported by Engineering Principles," *O&GJ,* October 14, 1937. For a description of the important, if not exclusive, role of petroleum engineering in shaping petroleum regulation, see Edward W. Constant, II, "Cause or Consequence: Science, Technology, and Regulatory Change in the Oil Business in Texas, 1930–1975," *Technology and Culture* 30, no. 2 (1989).
7. For an overview of shifting attitudes in industry toward regulation, see *O&I.*
8. George Otis Smith to ELD, telegram, March 30, 1917, box 50, folder 3401, ELDP.
9. ELD to George Otis Smith, telegram, April 3, 1917, box 50, folder 3401, ELDP.
10. Major Ralph H. Van Deman to ELD, April 7, 1917, box 50, folder 3401, ELDP.
11. Jonathan C. Brown, *Oil and Revolution in Mexico* (Berkeley, California: University of California Press, 1993), 122.
12. *TP,* 167–73.
13. For an overview of border violence during this period: Benjamin Johnson, *Revolution in Texas: How a Forgotten Rebellion and its Bloody Suppression Turned Mexicans into Americans* (New Haven, Conn.: Yale University Press, 2003).
14. Arthur S. Link, *Woodrow Wilson and the Progressive Era, 1900–1917* (New York: Harper and Brothers, 1954), 271–73.
15. Ralph E. Weber, ed., *The Final Memoranda: Major General Ralph H. Van Deman, USA Ret., 1865–1952, Father of U.S. Military Intelligence* (Wilmington, Del.: Scholarly Resources, 1988).
16. Major Ralph H. Van Deman to ELD, April 7, 1917, box 50, folder 3401, ELDP.
17. Ibid.
18. ELD to Edward M. Fickett, January 22, 1925, box 50, folder 3401, ELDP; G. L. McEntee to ELD, May 7, 1925, box 50, folder 3401, ELDP.
19. "War Geology," *Scientific American Supplement,* October 23, 1915.
20. Ralph Arnold to ELD, October 14, 1918, box 50, folder 3402, ELDP; ELD to Ralph Arnold, February 17, 1919, box 50, folder 3402, ELDP.
21. Leonard M. Fanning, "Conservation Board Creation Epochal," *O&GJ,* January 29, 1925; *USOP,* 29–43, 84–85; *O&I,* 157.
22. Henry L. Doherty, "Doherty Answers Committee of Eleven," *O&GJ,* January 7, 1926; Leonard M. Fanning, "Conservation Board Creation Epochal," *O&GJ,* January 29, 1925; *USOP,* 82–85; *O&I,* 154–58.

23. Hubert Work to ELD, January 10, 1925, box 50, folder 3405, ELDP.

24. "Secretary Work Chosen Chairman, Asks Oil Men for Suggestions," *O&GJ*, January 15, 1925; Leonard M. Fanning, "Conservation Board Creation Epochal," *O&GJ*, January 29, 1925.

25. ELD to Hubert Work, April 24, 1925, box 50, folder 3405, ELDP, 1–2.

26. Ibid., 9.

27. Ibid., 3–4.

28. Ibid., 8.

29. Ibid., 5.

30. C. E. Kern, "Federal Oil Board's First Report," *O&GJ*, September 9, 1926.

31. ELD to Charles W. Wrightsman, July 1, 1929, box 16, folder 2040, ELDP.

32. *Twentieth Century Petroleum Statistics, 1946* (Dallas, Texas: DeGolyer and MacNaughton, 1946), 21; *TP*, 220–28.

33. *Twentieth Century Petroleum Statistics, 1946* (Dallas, Texas: DeGolyer and MacNaughton, 1946), 21; Diana Davids Olien and Roger M. Olien, *Oil in Texas: The Gusher Age, 1895–1945* (Austin: University of Texas Press, 2002), 183; *O&I*, 185–86; Earl Oliver, "Changes Needed in Oil Ownership Law," *O&GJ*, July 23, 1931; *TP*, 244–47.

34. Kenny A. Franks, *The Oklahoma Petroleum Industry* (Norman, Okla.: The University of Oklahoma Press, 1980), 139–50; Olien and Olien, *Oil in Texas*, 185–88; *TP*, 251.

35. Franks, *Oklahoma Petroleum Industry*, 139–50; Olien and Olien, *Oil in Texas*, 182–83; *O&I*, 189, 205.

36. *USOP*, 98–111.

37. David M. Kennedy, *Freedom From Fear: The American People in Depression and War, 1929–1945* (New York: Oxford University Press, 1999), 202–04.

38. *A Handbook of N.R.A. Laws, Regulations, Codes* (Washington, DC: Federal Codes, Inc., 1933), 11; David M. Kennedy, *Freedom From Fear: The American People in Depression and War, 1929–1945* (New York: Oxford University Press, 1999), 177–80; *USOP*, 98–111.

39. *O&I*, 196.

40. Ibid., 195–98.

41. Ibid., 197–98.

42. "Petroleum Industry Code is Ready for Presentation," *DMN*, July 4, 1933; "Price Fixing by President Part of New Oil Code," *DMN*, June 18, 1933; Donald R. Brand, "Corporatism, the NRA and the Oil Industry," *Political Science Quarterly* 98, no. 1 (1983):113–14.

43. Hugh S. Johnson, *The Blue Eagle from Egg to Earth* (Garden City, New York: Doubleday, Doran and Company, Inc., 1935), 247.

44. "A Workable Oil Plan," *Tulsa Tribune*, July 17, 1933.

45. Others who derided the logic of price controls included, among others, Judge C. B. Ames of Texaco, C. C. Herndon of Skelly Oil Company, and R. G. A. Van dear Woude of Shell Petroleum Corporation. Donald R. Brand,

"Corporatism, the NRA and the Oil Industry," *Political Science Quarterly* 98, no. 1 (1983):113–14.

46. Johnson, *The Blue Eagle,* 181.

47. ELD and Joseph E. Pogue, "A Suggested Code of Fair Competition for the Petroleum Industry," 1933, box 75, folder 4388, ELDP.

48. William S. Powell, ed., *Dictionary of North Carolina Biography,* vol. 5 (Chapel Hill, N.C.: University of North Carolina Press, 1994), 106–07.

49. ELD to K. R. Simpson, July 22, 1933, box 75, folder 4388, ELDP.

50. American Petroleum Institute, "Code of Fair Competition for the Petroleum Industry as Submitted to the Administrator," July 13, 1933, box 75, folder 4388, ELDP, 5–6.

51. ELD and Joseph E. Pogue, "A Suggested Code of Fair Competition for the Petroleum Industry," 1933, box 75, folder 4388, ELDP, 4–6. Although DeGolyer and Pogue's suggested code included federally mandated planning for new reservoirs, DeGolyer denied that these provisions meant compulsory unitization. John B. Elliott to K. M. Simpson, July 30, 1933, box 76, folder 4415, ELDP.

52. *USOP,* 139.

53. "Code of Fair Competition for the Petroleum Industry," in *A Handbook of N.R.A. Laws, Regulations, Codes* (Washington, DC: Federal Codes, Inc., 1933), 242; "Ickes Calls on the President," *New York Times,* August 17, 1933; *USOP,* 140–41.

54. ELD to K. M. Simpson, July 31, 1933, box 75, folder 4400, ELDP.

55. Simpson to Hugh Johnson, August 11, 1933, box 75, folder 4396, ELDP.

56. ELD and Joseph E. Pogue to Hugh Johnson, telegram, August 24, 1933, box 75, folder 4398, ELDP.

57. ELD and Joseph E. Pogue, "Explanation of Schedules 1 & 2, Group Investigation, Crude Oil," October 9, 1933, box 75, folder 4396, ELDP.

58. *USOP,* 140–42.

59. ELD to J. B. Body, November 1, 1934, box 2, folder 128, ELDP.

60. Kennedy, *Freedom From Fear,* 182–88, 328; Hugh D. Mallon, "Petroleum Code and P.A.B. Knocked Out by Supreme Court," *O&GJ,* May 30, 1935.

61. "Oilmen Favor Self-Control for Industry," *DMN,* November 13, 1935.

62. William R. Childs, *The Texas Railroad Commission: Understanding Regulation in America to the Mid-Twentieth Century* (College Station, Texas, 2005), 209–24.

63. ELD to Ernest O. Thompson, January 13, 1939, box 14, folder 1833, ELDP.

64. "Thompson Tells Of Commission's Oil Field Work," *DMN,* July 10, 1936; Clarence E. Linz to ELD, June 17, 1936, box 14, folder 1833, ELDP.

65. ELD to Ernest O. Thompson, January 13, 1939, box 14, folder 1833, ELDP.

66. *MD,* 217.

67. Hugh D. Mallon, "Ickes Again Threatens to Declare Petroleum Industry Public Utility," *O&GJ,* December 27, 1934.

68. ELD, "Stabilization," n.d., box 25, folder 2448, ELDP; Blakely M. Murphy, ed., *Conservation of Oil and Gas, A Legal History, 1948* (Chicago: American Bar

Association, 1949), 558–59; Ernest O. Thompson to ELD, July 30, 1938, box 14, folder 1833, ELDP; Ernest O. Thompson to ELD, August 6, 1948, box 14, folder 1833, ELDP.

69. *O&I*, 182.

70. "Collected correspondence," box 159, folder 6072, ELDP; ELD to Earl Oliver, February 26, 1935, box 39, folder 3075, ELDP; ELD, "Waste in Production," n.d., box 24, folder 2447, ELDP.

71. *USOP*, 148–49.

72. Quoted in Murphy, *Conservation of Oil and Gas,* 569.

73. "Interstate Compact Commission Lays Groundwork for Uniform Laws," *O&GJ*, December 19, 1935.

74. Hugh D. Mallon, "Congress Ratifies Interstate Compact; Oil Bills Off Until Next Season," *O&GJ*, August 29, 1935; Murphy, *Conservation of Oil and Gas,* 570; Andrew M. Rowley, "Oil State Governors Meet Sept. 12 to Form Interstate Compact Commission," *O&GJ*, August 29, 1935.

75. "Transcript of Proceedings of the Interstate Oil Compact Commission," April 29–30, 1938, box 45, folder 3208, ELDP, 47.

76. Ibid., 51.

77. "Transcript of Proceedings of the Interstate Oil Compact Commission," July 19–20, 1939, box 45, folder 3207, ELDP, 1.

78. Ibid., 35–36.

79. Ibid., 37.

80. Murphy, *Conservation of Oil and Gas,* 582.

81. Leon C. Phillips to ELD, November 8, 1940, box 45, folder 3201, ELDP.

82. "Meeting of the Engineering Committee of the Interstate Oil Compact," January 3, 1941, box 45, folder 3202, ELDP, 53.

83. Ibid.

84. Ibid., 13.

85. *O&I*, 185.

86. "Transcript of Proceedings of the Regular Quarterly Meeting of the Interstate Oil Compact Commission," April 14, 1941, box 45, folder 3204, ELDP, 25.

87. Ibid. Emphasis added.

88. "Local Oilmen to Attend Washington Oil Parley," *DMN*, June 18, 1941.

89. Harold Ickes to ELD, telegram, June 14, 1941, box 56, folder 3535, ELDP.

90. "Purl Charges Oil Men Help Republicans," *DMN*, November 4, 1940; "Texans Put $53,373 Into Wilkie Race," *DMN*, November 17, 1940.

91. *O&I*, 227.

92. *USOP*, 159–60; *O&I*, 228.

93. ELD to Harold Ickes, telegram, June 14, 1941, box 56, folder 3535, ELDP.

94. ELD, "Memorandum Regarding War Employment," March 4, 1947, box 56, folder 3535, ELDP.

95. *HPAW*, 302.

96. Ibid.

97. ELD, "Petroleum Exploration and Development in Wartime," *O&GJ,* February 25, 1943; ELD, "Still Hunting for Oil," *New York Times,* October 3, 1943.

98. "Transcript of Proceedings of the Regular Quarterly Meeting of the Interstate Oil Compact Commission," April 14, 1941, box 45, folder 3204, ELDP, 25.

99. ELD, "Memorandum for Mr. Ralph K. Davies," September 12, 1941, box 56, folder 3538, ELDP.

100. "Production Director for OPC to Address Oil Compact Meeting," *DMN,* October 8, 1941; "Resolutions Passed," *DMN,* October 17, 1941; "Transcript of Proceedings of the Regular Quarterly Meeting of the Interstate Oil Compact Commission," October 16, 1941, box 45, folder 3204, ELDP, 19.

101. "Transcript of Proceedings of the Regular Quarterly Meeting of the Interstate Oil Compact Commission," April 14, 1941, box 45, folder 3204, ELDP, 25.

102. Ibid., 20.

103. ELD, "Petroleum Exploration and Development in Wartime," *O&GJ,* February 25, 1943.

104. ELD, "Memorandum for Mr. Ralph K. Davies," August 20, 1941, box 56, folder 3538, ELDP; *HPAW,* 178–79; *USOP,* 167–68.

105. *O&I,* 235–38.

106. ELD, "Memorandum Draft," n.d., box 57, folder 3561, ELDP.

107. "Texans Plead for Increase In Oil Prices," *DMN,* April 16, 1943; ELD, "Memorandum for Mr. Davies," February 27, 1943, box 51, folder 3423, ELDP; *O&I,* 245.

108. ELD, "Memorandum for Mr. Ralph K. Davies," August 24, 1941, box 56, folder 3538, ELDP.

109. Ibid.

110. Harry F. Simons, "East Texas' Future Directly Related To Return of Water to Woodbine Sand," *O&GJ,* January 28, 1943.

111. ELD, "Memorandum for Mr. Ralph K. Davies," August 24, 1941, box 56, folder 3538, ELDP; Harry F. Simons, "East Texas' Future Directly Related To Return of Water to Woodbine Sand," *O&GJ,* January 28, 1943.

112. ELD, "Memorandum for Mr. Ralph K. Davies," December 11, 1941, box 56, folder 3538, ELDP; Harry F. Simons, "East Texas Salt-Water-Disposal Project May Set Pattern for Future," *O&GJ,* February 4, 1943.

113. ELD, "Memorandum for Mr. Ralph K. Davies," December 11, 1941, box 56, folder 3538, ELDP, 1–2.

114. Ibid., 2–3.

115. Ibid., 4.

116. Ibid.

117. "Plans Mapped Here for Etex Salt Disposal," *DMN,* December 11, 1941.

118. Ibid; *HPAW,* 189.

119. ELD, "Memorandum for Mr. Ralph K. Davies," October 14, 1941, box 56, folder 3538, ELDP.

120. ELD, "Memorandum for Mr. Ralph K. Davies," August 15, 1941, box 56, folder 3538, ELDP.

121. "Data on Existing and Available Reserves in Southwest Gathered by Committees," March 22, 1942, box 50, folder 3411, ELDP; ELD to Ralph K. Davies, March 17, 1942, box 56, folder 3538, ELDP; ELD, "Memorandum to Production Committee," February 25, 1942, box 50, folder 3411, ELDP.

122. ELD to Ralph K. Davies, March 17, 1942, box 56, folder 3538, ELDP, 3–4.

123. Ibid.

124. ELD to Ralph K. Davies, March 17, 1942, box 56, folder 3538, ELDP, 1, 4.

125. Ralph K. Davies to ELD, March 23, 1942, box 56, folder 3538, ELDP; ELD, "Memorandum for District Directors in Charge," December 26, 1942, box 53, folder 3473, ELDP.

126. "Texas, OPC Row Nears Settlement," *DMN,* June 19, 1942.

127. "DeGolyer Made Deputy Oil Co-ordinator," *DMN,* June 19, 1942.

128. Ibid.

129. Ibid.

130. ELD, "Memorandum Regarding War Employment," March 4, 1947, box 56, folder 3535, ELDP; Frey and Ide, *History of the Petroleum Administration for War,* 27–28, 301.

131. ELD to Carl A. Young, July 7, 1942, box 53, folder 3473, ELDP.

132. *USOP,* 165–67.

133. ELD, "Memorandum for Mr. Davies," October 22, 1942, box 53, folder 3473, ELDP.

134. Ibid..

135. ELD, "Memorandum for Mr. Davies," October 23, 1942, box 53, folder 3473, ELDP; Murphy, *Conservation of Oil and Gas,* 122, 571.

136. ELD, "Memorandum for Mr. Davies," December 14, 1942, box 53, folder 3472, ELDP.

137. ELD, "Unitization Plans," January 21, 1943, box 53, folder 3472, ELDP.

138. Harold Ickes, "The Harold Ickes Diaries, 1933–1951," (Library of Congress Photoduplication Service, Washington, DC), 7663.

139. Frank I. Brinegar to ELD, January 2, 1945, box 2, folder 147, ELDP; ELD to Wilber Judson, December 19, 1944, box 7, folder 0884, ELDP; Friedrich von Hayek, *The Road to Serfdom* (Chicago, Ill.: University of Chicago Press, 1944); Harry I. Maxson to ELD, December 26, 1944, box 9, folder 1198, ELDP.

140. ELD to Ralph K. Davies, March 15, 1943, box 56, folder 3535, ELDP.

141. Harold Ickes to ELD, April 22, 1943, box 56, folder 3535, ELDP.

142. ELD to Ralph K. Davies, July 19, 1943, box 56, folder 3535, ELDP.

143. Ibid.

144. Frey and Ide, *History of the Petroleum Administration for War,* 276; *USOP,* 172–73.

145. "Dallas Oilman Takes PRC Job," *DMN,* August 24, 1943; "Ickes and De-Golyer will Head Petroleum Reserve Corporation," *O&GJ,* August 26, 1943.

146. "Ickes and DeGolyer will Head Petroleum Reserve Corporation," *O&GJ*, August 26, 1943.

147. Ibid.

## Chapter 8

1. ELD, "Control of Oil as an Instrument of Post-War Security," April 19, 1943, box 56, folder 3537, ELDP, 5.

2. ELD, "Report No. 36, Week Ending April 3, 1943," April 5, 1943, box 53, folder 3470, ELDP.

3. ELD, "Report No. 39, Week Ending April 24, 1943," April 26, 1943, box 53, folder 3470, ELDP.

4. Quoted in James Allen Smith, *Brookings at Seventy-Five* (Washington, DC: The Brookings Institution, 1991), 25.

5. For histories of the Brookings Institution: Donald T. Critchlow, *The Brookings Institution, 1916–1952* (DeKalb: Northern Illinois University Press, 1985); James Allen Smith, *Brookings at Seventy-Five* (Washington, DC: The Brookings Institution, 1991).

6. ELD, "Control of Oil as an Instrument of Post-War Security," April 19, 1943, box 56, folder 3537, ELDP, 5.

7. Ibid.

8. Ibid.

9. Ibid., 5–6. At this point, DeGolyer seems to have been concerned about a resurgent Germany or Japan rather than the cobelligerent Soviet Union, which would, of course, become the actual nemesis of the United States in the postwar years. See ibid., 1.

10. Ibid., 7; *O&I*, 132–33.

11. Major Ralph H. Van Deman to ELD, April 7, 1917, box 50, folder 3401, ELDP.

12. *CMH*, 582–83, 608.

13. Ibid., 608.

14. For a brief overview of the needs and challenges faced by the Mexican petroleum industry during this period: Antonio J. Bermúdez, *The Mexican National Petroleum Industry: A Case Study in Nationalization* (Stanford, Cal.: Institute of Hispanic American and Luso-Brazilian Studies, Stanford University, 1963), 61–63.

15. *PPPP*, 26.

16. Ibid., 27.

17. "Paraphrase of Telegram to Mexico City," August 20, 1942, box 59, folder 3657, ELDP.

18. ELD, "Memorandum for Mr. Ralph K. Davies," October 27, 1942, box 51, folder 3431, ELDP.

19. "Paraphrase of Telegram to Mexico City," August 20, 1942, box 59, folder 3657, ELDP, 3.

20. Ibid., 2.

21. "Paraphrase of Telegram to American Embassy, Mexico City," August 22, 1942, box 59, folder 3657, ELDP.

22. ELD, "Memorandum for Miss Fleming," August 17, 1942, box 53, folder 3473, ELDP; ELD, "Report No. 4, Week Ending August 22, 1942," October 12, 1942, box 53, folder 3473, ELDP; ELD, "Report No. 5, Week Ending August 29, 1942," 1942, box 53, folder 3473, ELDP.

23. ELD, "Report No. 5, Week Ending August 29, 1942," 1942, box 53, folder 3473, ELDP.

24. Ibid; ELD, "Report No. 6, Week Ending September 5, 1942," 1942, box 53, folder 3473, ELDP; ELD, "Report No. 7, Week Ending September 12, 1942," 1942, box 53, folder 3473, ELDP; ELD, "Report No. 8, Week Ending September 19, 1942," 1942, box 54, folder 3473, ELDP; NGD to ELD, August 24, 1942, box 59, folder 3657, ELDP.

25. ELD, "Report No. 9, Week Ending September 26, 1942," 1942, box 53, folder 3473, ELDP.

26. ELD, "Memorandum for Mr. Ralph K. Davies," October 27, 1942, box 51, folder 3431, ELDP.

27. Ibid; ELD, "Report No. 10, Week Ending October 3, 1942," 1942, box 53, folder 3473, ELDP; ELD, "Report No. 11, Week Ending October 10, 1942," 1942, box 53, folder 3473, ELDP.

28. ELD, "Memorandum for Mr. Ralph K. Davies," October 27, 1942, box 51, folder 3431, ELDP.

29. Ironically, in the case of Mexico, maximizing ultimate production meant slowing the rate of production in its major oilfield at Poza Rica.

30. Efrin Buenrostro to ELD, November 7, 1942, box 59, folder 3657, ELDP.

31. For an account of wartime efforts by the Mexican government to secure the loan: *PPPP,* 81–85.

32. For DeGolyer's involvement in the negotiations, see, for example, "Memorandum of Meeting with Representatives of Petroleos Mexicanos," May 28, 1943, box 59, folder 3657, ELDP; "Memorandum of Meeting with Representatives of Petroleos Mexicanos," June 4, 1943, box 59, folder 3657, ELDP; ELD, "Memorandum for Mr. Davies," May 26, 1943, box 59, folder 3657, ELDP. For the resolution of the high octane plant controversy: Clayton R. Koppes, "The Good Neighbor Policy and the Nationalization of Mexican Oil," *Journal of American History* 69 (1982):78; *PPPP,* 29–31. Tinkle mistakenly concludes that the plant was not constructed: *MD,* 279. DeGolyer's battle to obtain US aid to restructure the Mexican oil industry did not end with the war. Subsequently hired as a technical adviser by PEMEX, he repeatedly conferred with Mexican officials and American politicians as Mexico sought to secure a loan to develop an aggressive exploration program. Although some American independent oil companies were ultimately brought in as contractors to develop Mexican fields, the search for a US government oil loan proved elusive, sabotaged by the major oil corporations and

their allies in the State Department. For DeGolyer's activities in this regard, see Barry Bishop, "DeGolyer Consults With Pemex Chiefs," *DMN*, January 9, 1949; Barry Bishop, "DeGolyer Report Will Guide Efforts to Hike Mexican Oil," *DMN*, August 24, 1948; Barry Bishop, "Mexico Plans Speedy Development of Oil," *DMN*, December 12, 1948; Barry Bishop, "Mexico Signs New Contracts For Geophysical Operations," *DMN*, January 22, 1950. For an account of US policy regarding American petroleum companies in Mexico and the Mexican government's quest for an oil loan from 1946 to 1950, see *PPPP, 136–52*.

33. *TP,* 147.

34. Ibid., 280–83.

35. Ibid., 289–300.

36. Ibid., 300.

37. Ibid., 301.

38. Ibid., 393.

39. Ibid., 394–97.

40. *HPAW,* 276; *USOP,* 172–73; *TP,* 397–98.

41. *TP,* 398.

42. Harold Ickes, "The Harold Ickes Diaries, 1933–1951," (Library of Congress Photoduplication Service, Washington, DC), 8064.

43. ELD, "Memorandum Regarding War Employment," March 4, 1947, box 56, folder 3535, ELDP.

44. ELD, "Oil in the Near East," May 6, 1940, box 18, folder 2288, ELDP.

45. Ickes, "The Harold Ickes Diaries, 1933–1951," 5790, 7610.

46. Ibid., 8125.

47. Henry D. Ralph, "Government Ownership May Become Part of U.S. World Petroleum Policy," *O&GJ,* October 14, 1943; Henry D. Ralph, "Suspicion Over Objectives of P.R.C. May Force Disclosure of Foreign-Oil Policy," *O&GJ,* October 21, 1943.

48. *USFOP,* 142–45; *TP,* 398–99.

49. Quoted in "U.S. Dealing Itself a Hand in the Game for Arabian Oil," *Newsweek,* November 1, 1943.

50. "Dallas Oilmen Named by PAW to Assist PRC," *DMN,* October 13, 1943; "U.S. Dealing Itself a Hand in the Game for Arabian Oil," *Newsweek,* November 1, 1943. For details on Wrather, see "Bill Wrather Garners Honors in Oil Geology He Helped to Found," *O&GJ,* February 3, 1949; "Dallas Oilmen Named by PAW To Assist PRC," *DMN,* October 13, 1943; Eric G. Schroeder, "Long Pull Gains National Fame for Dallas Geologist," *DMN,* October 23, 1949. Dillon Anderson, a lawyer with the Houston firm of Baker Botts, would go on to serve in the Eisenhower Administration as national security advisor.

51. ELD to NGD, November 7, 1943, box 1, folder 27, NGDP.

52. "Forward Programme, American Party," December 11, 1943, box 52, folder 3459, ELDP. Fortas, who was, after all, a lawyer, would eventually rise to the rank of associate justice of the US Supreme Court during the Johnson administra-

tion. In 1968, Congress would once more famously foil his ambitions when the Senate blocked his nomination as chief justice.

53. ELD to NGD, November 10, 1943, box 1, folder 27, NGDP.

54. Ibid.

55. Ibid.

56. ELD to NGD, November 14, 1943, box 1, folder 27, NGDP; ELD to NGD, November 16, 1943, box 1, folder 27, NGDP; ELD to NGD, November 20, 1943, box 1, folder 27, NGDP; ELD to NGD, November 23, 1943, box 1, folder 27, NGDP.

57. Now the United Arab Emirates.

58. ELD, "Preliminary Report of the Technical Oil Mission to the Middle East," *BAAPG* 28, no. 7 (1944):921.

59. Dillon Anderson, "My Own Version of My Service in the Army in World War II," in *Baker, Botts in World War II: A Collection of Narrative Accounts of Their Service Experiences Written by Men of the Law Firm of Baker, Botts, Andrews & Wharton* (Houston, Texas: North River Press, 1947), 14.

60. Ibid., 15.

61. Ibid.

62. Ibid.

63. Ibid., 16.

64. Ibid., 15–16.

65. Ibid., 17.

66. Ibid., 18–20.

67. Ibid., 21.

68. "American Petroleum Mission: Provisional Itinerary," 1943, box 52, folder 3459, ELDP.

69. "Substance of Telegram from Department of State to Legation at Cairo," December 31, 1943, box 52, folder 3459, ELDP.

70. Ibid.

71. Quoted at *TP,* 397.

72. Ickes, "The Harold Ickes Diaries, 1933–1951," 8302–05, 8368.

73. ELD to Dillon Anderson, May 24, 1945, box 1, folder 32, ELDP. For an account of conflict within the Roosevelt administration over the Petroleum Reserves Corporation, see *USFOP,* 142–54.

74. "Dallas Expert Surveys Oil in Persian Gulf," *DMN,* February 6, 1944.

75. ELD, "Preliminary Report of the Technical Oil Mission to the Middle East," *BAAPG* 28, no. 7 (1944):919.

76. ELD, notes, 1943, box 56, folder 3532, ELDP.

77. Ickes, "The Harold Ickes Diaries, 1933–1951," 8717.

78. "Immediate Development of Oil Supplies in Middle East Recommended by DeGolyer," March 14, 1944, box 52, folder 3459, ELDP.

79. *TP,* 399.

80. For a summary of industry positions on the pipleline project, see *USFOP,* 148–49.

81. Quoted in *TP,* 399.

82. "Pew Denounces Arabian Oil Line Scheme as Extravagant, Dangerous Undertaking," *DMN,* March 25, 1944.

83. Ibid.

84. Ibid.

85. "Well Chosen Words," *Time,* April 3, 1944.

86. Ibid.

87. Ibid.

88. Ibid.

89. Ibid., 77.

90. ELD to Dillon Anderson, August 21, 1944, box 1, folder 32, ELDP.

91. Quoted in *TP,* 399.

92. Ibid.

93. Christopher James Castaneda and Joseph A. Pratt, *From Texas to the East: A Strategic History of Texas Eastern Corporation* (College Station, Texas: Texas A&M University Press, 1993), 15–24, 32–33.

94. Ibid., 36–53.

95. "The 'Inch' Lines," *NYT,* February 16, 1947; "A Milestone in Achievement," *The Inch* 17, no. 1 (1967); Christopher James Castaneda and Joseph A. Pratt, *From Texas to the East : A Strategic History of Texas Eastern Corporation* (College Station, Texas: Texas A&M University Press, 1993), 52–53.

96. ELD, "The Job Ahead," *DTH,* September 20, 1945.

97. Ibid.

98. ELD, "The Mines of Laurium," June 14, 1947, box 21, folder 2349, ELDP.

99. Ibid.

100. W. G. Greenman to ELD, April 26, 1946, box 61, folder 3693, ELDP.

101. W. G. Greenman to DeGolyer and MacNaughton, April 26, 1946, box 61, folder 3693, ELDP.

102. Ibid.

103. ELD to W. G. Greenman, May 6, 1946, box 61, folder 3693, ELDP.

104. DeGolyer and MacNaughton to W. G. Greenman, April 19, 1947, box 61, folder 3693, ELDP.

105. Quoted in *TP,* 407.

106. Quote from ELD to J. A. Krug, telegram, June 18, 1946, box 59, folder 3651, ELDP; J. A. Krug to ELD, telegram, June 18, 1946, box 59, folder 3651, ELDP; *EPA,* 37–38.

107. "National Petroleum Council, Minutes of Meeting," July 25, 1950, box 59, folder 3651, ELDP, 5.

108. *EPA,* 38.

109. Quote from Joseph E. Pogue, "To the Members of the Temporary Statistical Advisory Committee of the National Petroleum Council," February 24, 1947, box 59, folder 3654, ELDP. ELD to Joseph E. Pogue, February 21, 1947, box 59, folder 3654, ELDP.

110. Quote from *EPA*, 39.

111. ELD to Walter S. Hallanan, telegram, May 20, 1947, box 59, folder 3653, ELDP.

112. "Oil and Gas Aides Named," *NYT*, June 5, 1947; ELD to J. A. Krug, June 2, 1947, box 54, folder 3496, ELDP.

113. Military Petroleum Advisory Committee, minutes, "M.P.A.C. 1st Meeting," July 9, 1947, box 55, folder 3504, ELDP; J. A. Krug to ELD, May 27, 1947, box 54, folder 3496, ELDP.

114. ELD to Colonel O. F. Kotick, June 2, 1947, box 54, folder 3496, ELDP.

115. ELD to Robert E. Friedman, June 2, 1947, box 54, folder 3496, ELDP.

116. See, for example, Military Petroleum Advisory Committee, minutes, "M.P.A.C. 3rd Meeting," January 23, 1948, box 55, folder 3504, ELDP; Military Petroleum Advisory Committee, minutes, "M.P.A.C. 4th Meeting," April 7, 8, and 9, 1948, box 55, folder 3504, ELDP.

117. For absences, see, for example, Military Petroleum Advisory Committee, minutes, "M.P.A.C. 2nd Meeting," October 8, 1947, box 55, folder 3504, ELDP; Military Petroleum Advisory Committee, "M.P.A.C. 5th Meeting," June 2, 1948, box 55, folder 3504, ELDP. For meetings with Murrel as designated alternate, see, for example, Military Petroleum Advisory Board, minutes, "M.P.A.B. 10th Meeting," July 27, 1949, box 55, folder 3504, ELDP; Military Petroleum Advisory Committee, minutes, "M.P.A.C. 6th Meeting," July 27 and 28, 1948, box 55, folder 3504, ELDP.

118. "Pike, Sumner T(ucker)," in *Current Biography, 1947*, ed. Anna Rothe (New York: H. W. Wilson Company, 1948).

119. Sumner Pike to ELD, March 24, 1947, box 11, folder 1477, ELDP.

120. Ibid.

121. Ibid.

122. ELD to Sumner Pike, April 4, 1947, box 11, folder 1477, ELDP.

123. David E. Lilienthal to ELD, October 13, 1947, box 53, folder 3481, ELDP.

124. Box 54, folders 3481–82, ELDP.

125. Richard G. Hewlett and Francis Duncan, *Atomic Shield: A History of the United States Atomic Energy Commission*, vol. 2 (University Park, Pennsylvania: The Pennsylvania State University Press, 1969), 147–49, 172–74, 551–52.

126. Robert H. S. Eakens to ELD, August 22, 1947, box 61, folder 3682, ELDP.

127. ELD to Robert H. S. Eakens, August 29, 1947, box 61, folder 3682, ELDP.

128. Special Subcommittee on Petroleum of the Committee on Armed Services, *Petroleum for National Defense*, 2d sess., 1948.

129. Valentine B. Deale to ELD, January 16, 1948, box 60, folder 3676, ELDP.

130. Special Subcommittee on Petroleum of the Committee on Armed Services, *Petroleum for National Defense*, 2d sess., 1948, 3.

131. Ibid., 19.

132. Ibid., 357–64.

133. Ibid., 365–66.

134. Ibid., 371.

135. Ibid.

136. Ibid.

137. Ibid.

138. "Want Tank Farms For Oil for Navy: Engineers Favor Storing Country's Reserves Above Ground Near Transportation Lines," *NYT,* May 18, 1924.

139. "Local Oilmen to Assist With Goverment Study," *DMN,* September 13, 1946.

140. Special Subcommittee on Petroleum of the Committee on Armed Services, *Petroleum for National Defense,* 2d sess., 1948, 371–72.

141. Ibid., 368.

142. Ibid., 382.

143. Ibid.

144. Ibid.

145. Ibid.

146. "Oilmen Criticize DeGolyer's Speech," *Kilgore News Herald,* March 23, 1948.

147. Ibid.

148. "Oil Import Plan Termed Fantastic," 1948, box 21, folder 2358, ELDP.

149. "Oilmen Criticize DeGolyer's Speech," *Kilgore News Herald,* March 23, 1948.

150. *TP,* 410.

151. *USOP,* 206; *TP,* 538.

## Chapter 9

1. ELD to Becky Jones, April 2, 1948, box 7, folder 0878, ELDP.

2. Carey Croneis, "E. DeGolyer, Sidney Powers Memorial Medalist," *Bulletin of the American Association of Petroleum Geologists* 34, no. 5 (1950).

3. "City Awaits Major Talk By Acheson," *DMN,* June 13, 1950; "Unofficial Visit Paid By Sardar," *DMN,* May 11, 1951; Warren Leslie, "Irresponsible Forces In Government Rapped," *DMN,* June 14, 1950; Frank X. Tolbert, "Son of Ibn Saud Slips into Dallas," *DMN,* December 10, 1951.

4. ELD to Dillon Anderson, May 31, 1949, box 1, folder 32, ELDP. Tragically, Ev's bride would pass away a little more than a year later, a victim of melanoma "Mrs. Peggy Dee Bride Of E. L. DeGolyer Jr.," *DMN,* May 29, 1949; "Rites Set at 4 P.M. Tuesday For Mrs. E. L. DeGolyer Jr.," *DMN,* September 26, 1950; Peter Flagg Maxson, "The DeGolyer Children," in *Talks to the DeGolyer Estate Docents, 1990s to Present* (Dallas, 1989), 5. He would remarry in 1952. "Helen Warren Weds Everett DeGolyer Jr.," *DMN,* January 20, 1952.

5. *MD,* 319–20.

6. Ibid., 320–21.

7. Ibid., 321.

8. Ruth S. Castleman to Paul H. Giddens, September 27, 1949, box 5, folder 0573, ELDP.

9. ELD to Wallace E. Pratt, October 20, 1949, box 12, folder 1513, ELDP.

10. *MD,* 324.

11. ELD to Alexander Deussen, December 16, 1949, box 3, folder 0332, ELDP; ELD to James M. Hewgley, May 2, 1950, box 6, folder 0727, ELDP; ELD to Merle Buttram, June 13, 1950, box 2, folder 171, ELDP.

12. ELD to F. E. Wellings, March 8, 1954, box 15, folder 1982, ELDP; ELD to Grayson Kirk, October 2, 1952, box 7, folder 0939, ELDP.

13. ELD to Paul Paine, March 23, 1951, box 10, folder 1408, ELDP.

14. ELD to Carl Hertzog, April 6, 1951, box 6, folder 0722, ELDP; ELD to Paul Paine, March 23, 1951, box 10, folder 1408, ELDP.

15. Ruth S. Castleman to Bernard H. Lasky, March 23, 1951, box 7, folder 1003, ELDP; ELD to G. L. Cross, April 13, 1951, box 3, folder 0280, ELDP; ELD to Jesse C. Johnson, March 26, 1951, box 54, folder 3482, ELDP.

16. ELD to John M. Lovejoy, April 16, 1951, box 8, folder 1068, ELDP.

17. ELD to F. E. Wellings, March 8, 1954, box 15, folder 1982, ELDP; ELD to Grayson Kirk, October 2, 1952, box 7, folder 0939, ELDP.

18. "Aplastic Anemia," in *International Dictionary of Medicine and Biology,* ed. Sidney I. Landau, vol. 1 (New York: Wiley and Sons, 1986).

19. ELD to A. E. Chambers, January 7, 1952, box 3, folder 0215, ELDP; ELD to Wallace E. Pratt, January 22, 1952, box 12, folder 1513, ELDP.

20. ELD to Cleveland Amory, February 14, 1955, box 1, folder 31, ELDP.

21. ELD to Helmut de Terra, July 23, 1953, box 5, folder 0707, ELDP.

22. Interview with Dr. Jeffrey Hesse, November 7, 2007.

23. ELD to Cleveland Amory, February 14, 1955, box 1, folder 31, ELDP.

24. ELD to John H. Murrell, telegram, February 24, 1955, box 10, folder 1290, ELDP.

25. ELD to Wallace E. Pratt, March 28, 1955, box 12, folder 1513, ELDP.

26. Dorothy E. Pitts to L. A. Wainwright, December 1, 1954, box 24, folder 2432, ELDP.

27. News release, "E. L. DeGolyer Elected to Dresser Industries Board," July 8, 1954, box 24, folder 2432, ELDP.

28. ELD to Neil Mallon, November 16, 1956, box 146, folder 5948A, ELDP.

29. Letter to the Valdebro Participants, July 16, 1953, box 165, folder 6, ELDP.

30. "Dallas Firm Organized for Exploration Works," *DMN,* July 6, 1955; "New Dallas Uranium Corporation Formed," *DTH,* July 7, 1955.

31. See, for example, ELD to W. H. Wildes, April 3, 1956, box 165, folder 6088C, ELDP.

32. ELD to Walter S. Hallanan, August 27, 1954, box 60, folder 3662, ELDP.

33. ELD to L. F. McCollum, April 18, 1955, box 60, folder 3662, ELDP; ELD to L. F. McCollum, December 1, 1954, box 60, folder 3662, ELDP.

34. ELD to Oscar L. Chapman, July 30, 1951, box 54, folder 3496B, ELDP.

35. ELD to W. Stuart Symington, December 28, 1950, box 14, folder 1801, ELDP.

36. "DeGolyer Wins Advisory Post," *DMN,* December 19, 1950; "Will We Lose Our 'Secret Weapon,'" *U.S. News and World Report,* March 9, 1951.

37. ELD to Robert R. Shrock, May 12, 1952, box 54, folder 3482, ELDP.

38. ELD to Wallace E. Pratt, January 29, 1954, box 12, folder 1513, ELDP.

39. ELD to E. L. Ferullo, May 28, 1955, box 54, folder 3484, ELDP.

40. ELD to Jesse C. Johnson, May 31, 1955, box 54, folder 3484, ELDP.

41. "Agenda for Special Meeting of Stockholders of General Minerals Corporation," July 8, 1955, box 149, folder 5972C, ELDP; "Dallas Firm Organized for Exploration Works," *DMN,* July 6, 1955; "New Dallas Uranium Corporation Formed," *DTH,* July 7, 1955.

42. ELD to Alfred D. Lindley, April 29, 1948, box 48, folder 3285, ELDP; ELD to E. R. Brown, August 15, 1940, box 48, folder 3285, ELDP; ELD to Harry I. Maxson, October 1, 1940, box 48, folder 3285, ELDP; ELD to Jake L. Hamon, July 13, 1953, box 5, folder 0669, ELDP; ELD to Jake L. Hamon, October 2, 1952, box 5, folder 0669, ELDP; ELD to Samuel Dolbear, September 26, 1928, box 12, folder 1559, ELDP; ELD to W. J. Morris, July 30, 1940, box 48, folder 3285, ELDP; John M. Lovejoy to ELD, September 16, 1932, box 8, folder 1068, ELDP; John M. Lovejoy to ELD, September 30, 1932, box 8, folder 1068, ELDP.

43. "Purl Charges Oil Men Help Republicans," *DMN,* November 4, 1940; "Texans Put $53,373 Into Wilkie Race," *DMN,* November 17, 1940; ELD to Harry I. Maxson, October 1, 1940, box 48, folder 3285, ELDP.

44. ELD, address, "Spindletop: 1901–1951," 1951, box 22, folder 2384, ELDP.

45. "Declaration of Freedom," 1951, box 43, folder 3159, ELDP.

46. ELD to Norman Cousins, July 8, 1953, box 75, folder 4379, ELDP.

47. ELD to Cleora Clanton, March 2, 1953, box 42, folder 3138, ELDP.

48. Critical of McCarthy: ELD to Henry Regnery, December 8, 1953, box 75, folder 4379, ELDP. Critical of McCarthy opponents: ibid; ELD to Norman Cousins, October 23, 1953, box 75, folder 4379, ELDP; ELD to Norman Cousins, April 8, 1954, box 75, folder 4380, ELDP. "I am not pro-McCarthy nor anti-McCarthy." Ibid.

49. William F. Buckley Sr. to ELD, January 5, 1952, box 2, folder 159, ELDP; William F. Buckley Sr. to ELD, January 20, 1952, box 2, folder 159, ELDP; ELD to William F. Buckley Sr., January 29, 1952, box 2, folder 159, ELDP.

50. ELD to William F. Buckley Jr., August 25, 1955, box 2, folder 159, ELDP.

51. "Soviets Play Chess Game, Editor Says," *DMN,* June 5, 1953.

52. Norman Cousins, "Foreword," in *MD,* xv–xvi.

53. ELD to Cleora Clanton, March 2, 1953, box 42, folder 3138, ELDP.

54. Carey Croneis to Dwight D. Eisenhower, November 20, 1952, box 3, folder 0275, ELDP.

55. Ibid.

56. Dwight D. Eisenhower to Carey Croneis, November 25, 1952, box 3, folder 0275, ELDP.

57. ELD to Carey Croneis, December 2, 1952, box 3, folder 0275, ELDP.

58. ELD to Sumner Pike, May 17, 1951, box 11, folder 1477, ELDP.

59. Ibid.

60. DeGolyer turned to the familiar subject of petroleum exploration in ELD, "Development of the Art of Oil Prospecting in the Gulf Coast of Louisiana and Texas " *Texas Parade,* December 1950. He treated a more technical subject in ELD, "On the Estimation of Undiscovered Oil Reserves," *JPT* (1951). He reviewed an oil book by his old friend Wallace Pratt in ELD, "Oil and Geologists," *SRL,* January 20, 1951. He also produced an introduction to oil in the Soviet Union at a time when the Red Scare was in full reign with ELD, "Introduction," in *Oil in the Soviet Union,* ed. Heinrich Hassman (Princeton, N. J.: Princeton University Press, 1953). Also related to petroleum was a short piece on salt domes ELD, "Salt Domes," 1953, box 22, folder 2392, ELDP. Related to the petroleum industry was another review of a book on the natural gas industry ELD, "Economics of Natural Gas in Texas," July 1, 1953, box 23, folder 2411, ELDP. Book reviews on "science" included ELD, "Down with Trial and Error!," *SRL,* April 8, 1950. DeGolyer reviewed the state of cultural literacy among scientists in ELD, "More Poetry and Less Physics?," *The Shamrock* 2, no. 3 (1952).

61. One notable article came a little after his eye surgery and explored the history of the Coronado Expedition. ELD, "Coronado's Northern Exploration," *Southwest Review* 35, no. 2 (1950). He reviewed a "Texas" novel by his friend Dillon Anderson in ELD, "Of Two Picaroons Across Texas: Anderson's Exhuberant Narrative," *DMN,* September 30, 1951. He also reviewed *Billy the Kid: The Bibliography of the Legend* in the *Saturday Review* ELD, "Billy the Kid," *SRL,* June 27, 1953.

62. ELD to E. B. Swanson, February 25, 1954, box 14, folder 1793, ELDP.

63. ELD to G. L. Cross, December 16, 1949, box 3, folder 0280, ELDP.

64. ELD to Savoie Lottinville, December 2, 1952, box 8, folder 1067B, ELDP. DeGolyer's interest in creating a Western classics series was prefigured in discussions with Carl Hertzog held in 1948. Carl Hertzog, "Siringo Rides Again in New Item," *DMN,* July 2, 1950.

65. ELD to Savoie Lottinville, December 2, 1952, box 8, folder 1067B, ELDP; A. S. Mercer, *The Banditti of the Plains: The Cattlemen's Invasion of Wyoming in 1892* (Norman, Okla.: University of Oklahoma Press, 1954).

66. ELD to Savoie Lottinville, November 2, 1954, box 8, folder 1067C, ELDP; ELD to Savoie Lottinville, March 2, 1953, box 8, folder 1067C, ELDP; ELD to Savoie Lottinville, January 7, 1954, box 8, folder 1067C, ELDP; ELD to Savoie Lottinville, July 19, 1954, box 8, folder 1067C, ELDP; ELD to Savoie Lottinville, January 5, 1953, box 8, folder 1067C, ELDP.

67. ELD to Savoie Lottinville, March 2, 1953, box 8, folder 1067C, ELDP; Thomas Josiah Dimsdale, *The Vigilantes of Montana* (Norman, Okla.: University of Oklahoma Press, 1953).

68. ELD to Francis P. Farquhar, January 31, 1955, box 4, folder 0441, ELDP; ELD to Savoie Lottinville, March 2, 1953, box 8, folder 1067C, ELDP.

69. ELD to Francis P. Farquhar, January 31, 1955, box 4, folder 0441, ELDP; Lewis Hector Garrard, *Wah-To-Yah and the Taos Trail* (Norman, Okla.: University

of Oklahoma Press, 1955); Pat Floyd Garrett, *Authentic Life of Billy, the Kid* (Norman, Okla.: University of Oklahoma Press, 1954).

70. ELD to Francis P. Farquhar, January 31, 1955, box 4, folder 0441, ELDP.

71. ELD to Norman Cousins, January 27, 1955, box 75, folder 4380, ELDP.

72. ELD to Norman Cousins, January 6 ,1955, box 75, folder 4380, ELDP.

73. Suzan Napier, "The History of the Everette DeGolyer Book Collections" (Unpublished Thesis, Southern Methodist University, 1967), 28.

74. Ibid., 29.

75. ELD to Savoie Lottinville, February 7, 1950, box 72, folder 4329, ELDP.

76. "DeGolyer to Display Noted Scientific Books," *DTH,* May 8, 1950; Suzan Napier, "The History of the Everette DeGolyer Book Collections" (Unpublished Thesis, Southern Methodist University, 1967), 29–30.

77. ELD to Herbert Reichner, March 21, 1950, box 69, folder 4180, ELDP.

78. ELD to G. L. Cross, May 13, 1950, box 3, folder 0280, ELDP.

79. Savoie Lottinville to ELD, May 31, 1950, box 72, folder 4329, ELDP.

80. Suzan Napier, "The History of the Everette DeGolyer Book Collections" (Unpublished Thesis, Southern Methodist University, 1967), 30–31.

81. Ibid., 31.

82. ELD to G. L. Cross, April 13, 1951, box 3, folder 0280, ELDP; ELD to Savoie Lottinville, May 16, 1951, box 8, folder 1067B, ELDP; Suzan Napier, "The History of the Everette DeGolyer Book Collections" (Unpublished Thesis, Southern Methodist University, 1967), 33.

83. ELD to Wallace E. Pratt, October 26, 1951, box 12, folder 1513, ELDP.

84. ELD to Charles Walter Hamilton, December 29, 1952, box 5, folder 0668, ELDP.

85. ELD to Madeline Stanton, July 13, 1953, box 13, folder 1748, ELDP.

86. ELD to G. L. Cross, November 3, 1954, box 3, folder 0280, ELDP.

87. ELD to G. L. Cross, January 28, 1955, box 3, folder 0280, ELDP.

88. Arthur McAnally to G. L. Cross, March 15, 1955, box 3, folder 0280, ELDP.

89. ELD to G. L. Cross, March 23, 1955, box 3, folder 0280, ELDP.

90. "3 Join Smithsonian," *NYT,* April 8, 1956; "DeGolyer Given Smithsonian Post," *DMN,* May 11, 1956; ELD to Leonard Carmichael, April 16, 1956, box 48, folder 3301, ELDP.

91. *MD,* 370.

92. Telephone Conversation with Miss Dorothy Pitts, June 16, 1967, box 3, folder 12, LTP.

93. Notes of Interview with Ev DeGolyer, June 8, 1967, box 3, folder 13, LTP.

94. Telephone Conversation with Miss Dorothy Pitts, June 16, 1967, box 3, folder 12, LTP.

95. Ibid.

96. "Top Oil Geologist A Suicide in Texas," *NYT,* December 15, 1956.

97. Telephone Conversation with Miss Dorothy Pitts, June 16, 1967, box 3, folder 12, Lon Tinkle Collection, Southern Methodist University; *MD,* 372–73.

98. Quoted in *MD,* 373.

99. Notes of Interview with Ev DeGolyer, June 8, 1967, box 3, folder 13, LTP.

## Epilogue

1. ELD, "More Poetry and Less Physics?," *The Shamrock* 2, no. 3 (1952).

2. "Everett Lee DeGolyer," *DMN,* December 16, 1956.

3. "Top Oil Geologist A Suicide in Texas," *NYT,* December 15, 1956.

4. "DeGolyer: An Oil Legend," *O&GJ,* December 24, 1956.

5. "In Memoriam: E. DeGolyer," *Petroleum Engineer* 29, no. 1 (1957).

6. Ibid.

7. Carl C. Branson, "E. L. DeGolyer, 1886–1956," *Oklahoma Geology Notes* 17, no. 2 (1957).

8. Author's translation. Manuel Alvarez Jr., "Everette L. DeGolyer," *Boletín de la Asociación Mexicana de Geólogos Petroleros* 9, no. 3–4 (1957):273, 280.

9. J. C. Karcher, "Memorial: Everette Lee DeGolyer," *Geophysics* 22, no. 2 (1957).

10. Emphasis added. Lewis W. MacNaughton, "E. L. DeGolyer, Father of Applied Geophysics," *Science* 125, no. 3243 (1957):339.

11. Ibid., 338. For some references to DeGolyer as the "father of geophysical research": Edward Morrow, "Amerada Plays Them Close to the Chest," *Fortune,* January 1946. As the "father of geophysical exploration": "Well Chosen Words," *Time,* April 3, 1944. These claims were a bit of an overstatement and decidedly unfair to the geophysicists that worked with DeGolyer. This is particularly true for J. C. Karcher and it is significant that he did not include such a "fatherly" reference in his own memorial to DeGolyer.

12. Isaiah Berlin, *The Hedgehog and the Fox: An Essay on Tolstoy's View of History* (New York: Simon and Schuster, 1953), 1.

# Index

AAPG. *See* American Association of Petroleum Geologists
Acheson, Dean, 243–44
AEC. *See* Atomic Energy Commission
Águilar, Cándido, 64
AIME. *See* American Institute of Mining and Metallurgical Engineers
Alabama Exploration Syndicate, 81
Alamo Royalties Corporation, 138–39
Alaska, 6, 150
Álvarez, Jr., Manuel, 264
Amerada Petroleum Corporation, 93, 105, 133–35, 138, 143–44, 185, 233; "Amerada Tree,"121; early success, 87; founding, 85; gravimetric prospecting, 111, 113; seismic prospecting, 117–18; struggle over GRC, 132–33, 135, 290n23
American Association of Petroleum Geologists (AAPG), 71, 90–91, 94, 155, 174
American Friends' Service Committee, 252
American Geological Institute, 253
American Institute of Mining and Metallurgical Engineers (AIME), 71, 88–91
American Petroleum Institute, 183–84
Anahuac Piquant Pepper Company, 141
Anderson, Dillon, 163, 222–23, 226, 230, 298n69
Anglo-Persian Oil Company, 217–19
anticlines, 28–29, 33, 101–102, 115
Army-Navy Petroleum Board, 232, 235
Arnold, Ralph, 147–49, 294n89
Atlantic Richfield Company, 6
Atlatl Royalty Corporation, 139, 141

Atomic Energy Commission (AEC), 236–37, 250
Aurin, Fritz, 174
Avila Camacho, Manuel, 211–12

Baghdad, Iraq, 224–25
Bahrain, 217–18, 221, 225
Barton, Donald C., 93–94, 105–108, 110–111, 113, 117
Belt, Ben, 73
Big Inch and Little Inch Pipelines, 230–231
Blue Point Chop House, 14–15
Body, John B., 41, 78–79, 81–82, 85, 92–93, 104–105, 138, 185
Borglum, Gutzon, 1
Borglum, Solon, 1–2
Boyd, David Ross, 16
Bozell, Harold, 117
Bradford oilfield, 137
Branson, Carl, 263
Brazil, 139, 150
British Petroleum. *See* Anglo-Persian Oil Company
Brookings Institution, 208–209
Brooks, Overton, 240
Buckley Jr., William F., 252
Buenrostro, Efrin 213
Bunker, Arthur H., 129
Burnet (Mexican Eagle employee), 44
Bush, Vannevar, 155
Bybee, Hal P., 152
Byrnes, James, 233

Cairo Conference, 223
Calder, William, 44
California-Arabian Standard Oil Company (Casoc), 218–21, 227

Calvert, W. R., 123–25
Canada, 140
Cárdenas, Lázaro, 211
Carmody, Lester, 124–25
Carr, Herbert, 81, 138
Carranza, Venustiano, 63–64
Case, Hadley, 137–38
Case, Pomeroy & Company, 129, 137, 236
Case, Walter, 137–38, 292n53
Casoc. *See* California-Arabian Standard Oil Company
Cerf, Bennett, 165
*chapapotes* (see also oil seep), 39, 47
Christiana Oil Corporation, 249
Cities Service Oil Company, 149
Cold War, 7, 9, 232–37, 251–52, 266, 306n9
Cole, William S., 238
Colombia, 150
Colorado School of Mines, 153, 156, 172
Compton, Arthur Holley, 258
conservation and regulation, 9, 188; changing views of industry leaders, 176; Connally Hot Oil Act, 186, 193; DeGolyer's views, 179–81, 190–195, 203–204, 206, 239–40, 242; East Texas Salt Water Disposal Company, 197–98; effect of oil import quotas, 242; Federal Oil Conservation Board, 179–80, 190; federal regulation, 6, 13, 145, 147, 155, 175–76, 180–186, 188–89, 193–94, 199, 206, 211, 231; Henry Doherty, 179; impact of East Texas field, 181; Interstate Oil Compact Commission, 174, 188–96, 204, 206; and martial law, 181; maximum efficient rate, 145–46, 195; meaning of conservation in wartime, 193–94, 199, 206; Mexican Technical Mission, 215; National Recovery Administration, 182–86, 188, 192, 206, 208; Office of the Petroleum Coordinator, 193–95, 197–98; Oklahoma Corporation Commission, 181; Order M-68, 195; Petroleum Administration for War, 203–204; price controls, 175, 184–85, 192, 301n45; prorationing, 145–47, 182, 186–88, 194, 293n78; and scientists, 9, 175, 195, 206, 266; Texas Railroad Commission (TRC), 181–82, 186–87, 198, 201–202; United States Geological Survey, 23; unitization, 179–81, 191–92, 196, 203–204
Coolidge, Calvin, 179
Core Laboratories, Inc., 130, 137–39, 141, 144
core sampling. *See* exploration methods, core sampling
Coronado Corporation, 135–36
Cousins, Norman, 163–64, 251–52, 256
Cowdray, W. D. Pearson, Lord, 36, 40, 58–59, 70, 74, 79, 85–87; on the ability to say no, 84; close relationship with Porfirio Díaz, 64; construction of Grand Canal, 41; and construction of Hudson River tunnel, 40; and construction of Minatitlán refinery, 52; death, 129; decisions regarding Potrero del Llano well, 55; decision to enter business in United States, 84; early career, 40–41; and evacuation of Mexican Eagle employees, 73; and founding of Amerada, 85; and founding of Mexican Eagle Oil, 42; and Isthmus of Tehuantepec railroad, 41; negotiations with DeGolyer over employment, 74–77; and origins of DeGolyer book collection, 166; and Peláez family, 46; raised to the peerage, 56; regard for DeGolyer, 58–59; and reluctance to enter business in United States, 81–82, 84; use of political connections in Mexico, 57

Croneis, Carey, 253–54
Cross, G. L., 257–59
Cuba, 67, 73, 78, 155
Cullinan, Ralph, 51
Cushing, Frank Hamilton, 162

Dallas, Texas, 142, 159, 168–69, 186, 229, 235, 260; Dallas Arboretum, 2; *Dallas Morning News,* 8, 141, 165, 202, 263; *Dallas Times-Herald,* 160, 165, 231; DeGolyer relocation to, 140–141; *El Rancho Encinal* residence, 2, 142, 157, 169–70, 246, 257; events sponsored by DeGolyer, 252; and founding of DeGolyer and MacNaughton, 143–44; suggested move of Conservation Division to, 199; visiting dignitaries and DeGolyer home, 243–44
Darton, N. H., 22–23
Davies, Ralph K., 194, 197–98, 200–201, 204–205, 208, 212, 215, 234
Davis, John Allen, 28
Day, David T., 36
Deale, Valentine, 238
De Golier, Jacques, 11
DeGolyer, Anthony, 11
DeGolyer, Cecilia Jeanne, 80, 142
DeGolyer, Dorothy Margaret, 80, 142
DeGolyer, Edith Christine, 13
DeGolyer, Everette Lee: ancestry, 11–12; attempt to reconcile science with business, 70–72, 87–97; book collecting, 166–68, 256–59, 299n91; book reviews, 102, 164–66; childhood, 12–13; children, 61, 68, 76, 80, 142–43, 163, 245, 261; commencement speeches, 19, 152–53, 156, 172, 232, 245; and company secrets, 50–51, 92–95, 98–99; congressional hearings, 237–41, 245, 249; courtship, 20–21; death and public reaction, 260–265; and the Depression, 131; and doodlebugs, 122–26; education, 15–16, 19–20, 59–60; *El Rancho Encinal,* 2, 141–42, 157, 169–70, 246, 257; encouragement of Cowdray investment in U.S., 81–83; entrepreneurial activities, 82–83, 121, 129–31, 134–41, 144–47, 151, 230–31, 249–50; family life, 49–50, 61, 68, 76, 79–80, 140–43, 163, 245; family life in Mexico, 49–50, 61; fascination with Mexico and U.S. Southwest, 141, 152, 161–62, 168–71; "father of applied geophysics," 127, 265, 317n11; "father of geophysical exploration," 127, 317n11; "father of geophysics," 127, 317n11; and founding of Amerada, 84–85; geological work in Cuba, 67, 73, 78, 155; geological work in Mexico, 45–48, 52, 101; and geophysical exploration, 98–100, 102–108, 110–11, 113, 117–19, *120,* 121–22, 126–28, 133–35; government service (non-wartime), 183–86, 188–95, 232–37, 249–50; government service (wartime), 195–96, 199–205, 208–28; health problems, 243, 245–48, 250, 254, 258, 260; honorary degrees, 156–57; increasing managerial duties with Mexican Eagle, 72, 79; involvement with publishing presses, 162, 255–56; location of Potrero del Llano No. 4, 54–55; and luck, 2–3, 39, 55, 58, 129, 151; and Mexican Revolution, 64–65, 67–68, 281n106; Mexican sympathies, 60; Mexican Technical Mission, 211–17, 307n32; in Mexico, 42–61, 64–68, 213–16; Middle East Technical Mission, 221–27; negotiations over job with Cowdray, 74–77; oil import views 240–42; at outbreak of World War I, 76; philanthropy, 167, 254, 257–59; political views, 187, 192, 204–205, 250–53; and Potrero del Llano oilfield, 38–39, 53–58; and

DeGolyer, Everette Lee (*cont.*)
  professional associations, 71, 88–91,
  94, 155, 174; as professor, 152–53,
  157, 159; relocation to Dallas, 140–41
  relocation to Montclair, New Jersey,
  79–80; and reserve estimation,
  147–49, 199–200, 241, 294n89; and
  salt domes, 100–101; scholarship
  (scientific-industrial), 65–66, 77–78,
  81, 90, 92–96, 99, 154–57, 159, 254;
  and strategic oil reserve views,
  239–40; strategic thought on national petroleum policy, 208–11,
  229–30, 232, 239–42; and struggle
  over GRC, 132–33, 135, 290n23; and
  USGS, 22–28, 31; views on conservation and regulation, 179–81, 190–95,
  203–206, 229–30, 232, 239–42; views
  on PRC pipeline project, 229–30;
  wedding, 48
DeGolyer, Everett Lee, Jr., 80, 143, 163,
  245, 261
DeGolyer, Homer, 13, 20
DeGolyer, Jacob, 11
DeGolyer, John, 11–14, 142
DeGolyer, Narcissus Kagy Huddle,
  11–13, 142
DeGolyer, Nell Goodrich, 48, 61, 79, 101,
  111–12, 117, 245, 261
DeGolyer, Nell Virginia, 61, 68, 76, 142
DeGolyer and MacNaughton, 6, 130,
  138, 143–45, 147, 150, 195, 232–34, 241,
  249, 260
Denison, Rodger, 97
Department of Defense, 233
Department of State, 212–13, 221–22,
  225–26, 237
Department of the Interior, Oil and
  Gas Division, 234–35
Department of the Treasury, 147, 199
Department of War, 222, 233
Depression, 130–31, 135, 139, 145, 153,
  168, 176, 181–82, 186, 236, 265

Dhahran, Saudi Arabia, 225
Díaz, Porfirio, 39–41, 62–64, 66
Doheny, Edward L., 38–40, 68
Doherty, Henry, 179, 190–192
doodlebug. *See* exploration methods,
  doodlebugs
Dos Bocas oilfield, 42, 44
Douglas, Lewis W., 246
Dresser Industries, 249

Eakens, Robert, 237
Earle, Captain Ralph T., 66
East Texas oilfield, 5, 130, 145, 181,
  196–99, 241
East Texas Salt Water Disposal
  Company, 198
Ecuador, 150
Edison, Thomas, 7
Egypt, 223
Eisenhower, Dwight D., 7, 242, 251,
  253–54
El Águila Oil Company (Compañía
  Mexicana de Petróleo El Aguila).
  *See* Mexican Eagle Oil Company
El Ébano oilfield, 40
Elk Hills Naval Petroleum Reserve, 239
*El Rancho Encinal,* 2, 141–42, 157, 169–
  70, 246, 257
Empire Gas and Fuel Company, 105
Eötvös, Roland, Baron, 103–104, 127
Essex Royalty Corporation, 292n53
exploration methods (*see also* geo-
  physical exploration): core sam-
  pling, 137–38, 225; doodlebugs, 122–
  26; micropaleontology, 51, 286n17;
  oil seep, 4, 32–33, 39, 41, 47, 50, 54, 69,
  126; rock outcrops, 33, 35, 47–48, 116;
  topographic maps, 28–33, 46–48, 54,
  58, 77, 102, 107, 116, 126, 177–78

Fanning, Leonard M., 38
Federal Oil Conservation Board
  (FOCB), 179–80, 190

Federal Royalties Company, 121, 129–31, 135–41, 144, 151, 250

Felicitos, Don, 52, 58

Felmont Corporation, 129–30, 137, 139, 141, 292n53

First National Bank of Dallas, 248

FOCB. *See* Federal Oil Conservation Board

Forrestal, James, 233–34, 238–39

Fortas, Abe, 222

Fort Worth, Texas, 174, 195

Francis, Charles, 244

Fuqua, H. B., 24, 56

Furbero oilfield, 55, 154

Galveston, Texas, 67, 73–74

General Minerals Corporation, 250

Geological Engineering Company, 115–16

geological phenomena: anticlines, 28–29, 33, 101–2, 115; oil seep, 4, 32–33, 39, 41, 47, 50, 54, 69, 126; salt domes, 4–5, 93–94, 98–108, 110–113, 115, 119, 148, 155

Geological Society of America, 98–99

geologists. *See* scientists

geology, 3–10, 16–20, 95, 100, 118; and business, 8, 94–96, 174, 265; and C. W. Hayes, 26; DeGolyer's scholarly interest in, 156–59; early limitations of, 34–35, 39, 69; early skepticism of, 3, 8, 32, 34, 68, 161, 174; and goverment, 175; and government, 174, 178, 184, 197, 206, 220; and professional associations, 88–90; rising importance, 3, 5–8, 140; and salt domes, 100–102; and topographic analysis, 32–34

geophysical exploration, 1, 3, 6, 9, 98–99, 118–19, 121, 127–28, 133–35, 138, 161, 215, 263; gravimetric (torsion balance), 103–10, 112–13, 122; gravimetric methods (torsion bal-

ance and gravimeter), 98, 103–104, 106–107, *109,* 111, 118, 127; magnetic, 108–109; reflection seismology, 114–17, 119, 121–22, 135; refraction seismology, 108–13, 116–17, 119–22, 135; seismology, 6, 105, 108–12, 114–16, 118–19, 133–34, 136

Geophysical Research Corporation (GRC), 113, 117–21, 131–35, 143; struggle over direction of company, 132–33, 135, 290n23

Geophysical Service Incorporated (GSI), 121, 130–131, 135–36 *136,* 138–41, 144, 151

geophysicists. *See* scientists

George Washington University, 27

Gerken, Archbishop Rudolph Aloysius, 189

Glenn Pool oilfield, 16

Goodrich, Emma Hatton, 59

Goodrich, Robert, 131

Gould, Charles Newton, 16–20, 22, 154

government: Army-Navy Petroleum Board, 232, 235; Atomic Energy Commission (AEC), 236–37, 250; congressional hearings, 208, 231, 237, 239–40, 245, 249; Department of Defense, 233; Department of State, 212–13, 221–22, 225–26, 237; Department of the Interior, Oil and Gas Division, 234–35; Department of the Treasury, 147, 199; Department of War, 222, 233; Internal Revenue Bureau (IRB), 147–49, 178; Interstate Oil Compact Commission (IOCC), 174, 188–96, 204, 206; National Petroleum Council, Statistical Advisory Committee, 234; National Recovery Administration (NRA), 182–88, 192, 206, 208; Office of Price Administration (OPA), 196, 203, 236; Office of Production Management, 198; Office of the Petroleum

government (*cont.*)
 Coordinator (OPC), 192–93, 197–203, 212–13, 217; Oklahoma Corporation Commission, 181; Petroleum Administration for War (PAW), 165, 176, 201, 203–206, 208, 220, 231, 234; Petroleum Industry War Council, 234; Raw Materials Advisory Committee, 236, 250; Reclamation Service, 27; Scientific Manpower Advisory Committee (SMAC), 250, 253; Texas Railroad Commission (TRC), 181–82, 186–87, 198, 201–202; United States Fuel Administration, 175, 178, 210; United States Geological Survey (USGS), 5, 22, 30–31, 34, 43, 59–60, 73–74, 98, 175–76, 184, 221–22; United States Geological Survey (USGS), DeGolyer's work for, 22–24, 26–28, 31–32; United States Geological Survey (USGS), early history, 23; United States Supreme Court, 186; War Production Board (WPB), 203, 213
GRC. *See* Geophysical Research Corporation
Great Depression, 130–131, 176, 181–82, 186, 230
Great Plains Development Company, 249
Green, Cecil, 136
Greenman, W. G., 232–33
Greensburg, Kansas, 11–12, 113, 272n11 (chap. 1)
GSI. *See* Geophysical Service Incorporated
Gulf Coast (United States), 4, 36, 44, 74, 93, 98, 100, 105, 113, 119, 178
Gulf Oil Company, 111
Gustafson, John K., 236–37

Hamilton, Charles W., 65, 81, 83, 156, 259

Harding, Warren G., 178
Hayek, Friedrich von, 204
Hayes, C. Willard, *43,* 61, 67, 72–73, 75, 77–78, 100, 156; death, 79; *Handbook for Field Geologists,* 34–36; hired by Cowdray, 36; and hiring of DeGolyer, 37; and Mexican Oil Association, 66; and petroleum geology, 34–36; and Potrero del Llano field, 38, 54–55; and Spindletop, 5, 34; and the United States Geological Survey, 24, 26
Henderson, Leon, 236
Herschel, John, 103
Hertzog, Carl, 162–63
Hess, Julius, 44
Higgins, Patillo, 4–5
Hippolyto (Mexican guide), 45
Hobart, Oklahoma, 13–16
Holmes, Frank, 217
Holmes, Oliver W., 252
Hoover, Herbert, 182, 251
Hopkins, Edwin B., 27–28, 30–31, 36, 43–45, 67, 73–74, 81, 83
Horcones hacienda, 52, 58
Horner, William, "Jack," 137–38
Huerta, Victoriano, 63–64, 66–68
Humble Oil and Refining Company of Houston, 143
Hunt, T. Sterry, 33
Hydrocarbon Man, 7

Ickes, Harold L., 165, 183–85, 187–88, 192–93, 196–97, 201–205, 207, 212, 219–21, 225–29, 233
Internal Revenue Bureau (IRB), 147–49, 178
Interstate Oil Compact Commission (IOCC), 174, 188–96, 204, 206
IOCC. *See* Interstate Oil Compact Commission
Iran, 223
Iraq, 223–24
IRB. *See* Internal Revenue Bureau

Isthmus of Tehuantepec oilfield, 41, 92, 100, 215

Ixhuatlán oilfield, 100

Jacobsen, Alfred, 132–34
Jeffries, Geoffrey, 53
Johnson, Hugh, 184–85, 208
Johnson, Lyndon B., 239–40
Johnston, Henry, 129, 137
Joiner, "Dad" (oilman), 130
Jones, Becky, 243
Jonsson, Erik, 136
Joplin, Missouri, 12–13
Juan Casiano oilfield, 38

Kansas, 10–14, 17–18, 83, 113, 141, 169, 188
Kappa Alpha fraternity, 20
Karcher, John Clarence, 113–19, 121, 124–25, 127, 131, 133–36, 153, 264
Kennedy, William, 4
Kenyon, Luis, 45
Kirkuk, Iraq, 224
Korean War, 252
Krug, J. A. 234
Kuwait, 209, 217–18, 223, 225, 228

Landa y Escandón, Guillermo de, 56
Laramie, Wyoming, 23
Laredo, Texas, 41–42
Lea, Tom, 162
Leavell, John H., 222, 225
LeBarron, Lou, 38
Lee, Willis T., 32
Lewis, James, 137–38
Lloyd George, David, 40
London, 73–74, 76, 81–82, 84, 104, 166, 177, 246
Los Angeles, California, 39
Lottinville, Savoie, 255–58
Louisiana, 4, 73, 83, 101, 140, 148, 240
Louisiana Land and Exploration Company, 248

Lucas, Captain Anthony, 3–5, 271n2
Ludendorff, Erich, 110

MacKay, Douglas, 253
MacLeish, Archibald, 251
MacNaughton, Lewis Winslow, 143–45, 149–51, 261, 264–65
Madero, Francisco I., 62–63
Mahmud, Sardar Shah, 243
Mallet, Robert, 108–109
Manning, B. P., 141
Marland, Ernest W., 188
Marland Oil Company, 116
Massachusetts Institute of Technology, 155
Maud, Oklahoma, 121
Maxson, John, "Jack," 142
Mayo, Henry T., 66
Mazza, Renato, 264
McCoy, A. W., 81
McDermott, Eugene, 119, 134–36
McGhee, George C., 142, 147, 244
McKinley, William, 23
McMurray, Elizabeth Ann, 162, 165
Messersmith, Ambassador George S., 213–14
Mexican Eagle Oil Company, 36, 39, 46, 60, 79, 81, 103, 153, 161, 215; and Alfred Jacobsen, 132; company secrets, 50–51; concessions, 42; DeGolyer as Chief Geologist of, 61; DeGolyer reports on non-geological issues, 74; DeGolyer's attempted resignation, 85; DeGolyer's encounter with salt domes, 100; Dos Bocas field, 42; Foreign Department, 82; and Guillermo de Landa y Escandón, 56; hiring of staff geologists, 145; interdepartmental disputes, 72; and Isthmus of Tehuantepec, 92; leasing practices in Mexico, 51–52; Legal Department, 72; and the Mexican Revolution, 64;

Mexican Eagle Oil Company, (*cont.*)
Minatitlán refinery, 52, 58; New York
office, 81; *Oil Fields of Mexico* report,
77–78; and Peláez family, 46; Potrero
del Llano field, 38, 53, 55, 57; sale
to Royal Dutch Shell, 84; Seismos
survey for, 111; Tampico office, 43,
61, 74; Tierra Amarilla field, 48
Mexican Petroleum Company, 38, 40
Mexican Technical Mission, 211–17,
307n32
Mexico, 36–37, 48, 58–59, 61, 65, 69–70,
78–81, 83–85, 90, 92, 154–55, 161, 207,
209, 211; and Alfred Jacobsen, 132;
birth of Mexican oil industry, 39–40;
and Cowdray's early years, 40–42;
and DeGolyer and MacNaughton
consulting for, 150; DeGolyers'
family life in, 49–50, 61; DeGolyer's
fascination with, 153, 161, 165,
167–68, 170–171, 257; and DeGolyer's
impressions of, 43–44, 60; and
DeGolyer's *Oil Fields of Mexico*
report, 78; and DeGolyer's transition
to executive after departure, 72; Dos
Bocas oilfield, 42, 44; Furbero oilfield, 55, 154; and "Good Neighbor"
policy, 211; Horcones hacienda, 52,
58; Isthmus of Tehuantepec oilfield,
41, 92, 100, 215; Ixhuatlán oilfield,
100; Juan Casiano oilfield, 38; and
Mexican Revolution, 62–64, 66–68,
77, 171, 211; and Mexican Technical
Mission, 211–17, 307n32; nationalization of oil industry, 211; and Porfirio
Díaz, 39–41, 62–64, 66; Potrero del
Llano oilfield, 38–39, 53–59, 70, 211;
Poza Rica oilfield, 214–15; require-
ments of field geology in, 45; salt
domes, 100; and Tampico Flag
Incident, 66–67; Tierra Amarilla
oilfield, 45–48, 53; and United States
occupation of Veracruz, 67–68; and
World War I, 176–77; and World
War II, 211–13, 215
Mexico City, Mexico, 51, 56, 58, 61,
67–68, 132, 171, 213–16
México, Universidad Nacional
Autónoma de, 157
Mid-Continent Oil and Gas
Association, 187
Mid-Continent oilfields, 74, 81
Middle East, 150, 157, 217–27, 230, 233,
241–42, 266
Middle East, Technical Mission
Miles City, Montana, 27
Military Petroleum Advisory Board,
235, 250
Military Petroleum Advisory
Committee (MPAC), 235
Mintrop, Ludger, 109–16, 119–21, 127, 135
Mishaal (Saudi Prince), 243
Missouri, 10, 12–15, 102, 141, 157, 169
Mobil. *See* Socony-Vacuum
Montana, 27, 256
Montclair, New Jersey, 80–81, 140
Moore, Adrian, 138
Mori (Japanese naval officer), 68
Murray, William H. "Alfalfa Bill," 181
Murrell, John H., 150, 216, 221, 235

Nash Dome, Texas, 107–109
Natchez, Mississippi, 162
National Industrial Recovery Act. *See*
United States Government, National
Recovery Administration (NRA)
National Petroleum Council (NPC),
234–35, 250; Committee on Military
and Government Petroleum
Requirements, 235; Committee on
Productive Petroleum Capacity,
250; Government Petroleum
Requirements Committee, 235;
Statistical Advisory Committee, 234
National Recovery Administration
(NRA), 182–88, 192, 206, 208

*National Review,* 252
*National Weekly. See National Review*
Naval Petroleum Reserves, 232, 239
Nebraska, 18
New Jersey, 79–81, 137, 140–143, 166
New Mexico, 162, 189
New York, 80, 168–69
*New York Times,* 231, 263
Nicaragua, 26
Niebuhr, Reinhold, 251
Nock, Robert, 118
Norman, Oklahoma, 16, 19, 22, 42, 48, 59, 61, 80, 90, 257
North Carolina, 4
North Dakota, 27
NPC. *See* National Petroleum Council
NRA. *See* National Recovery Administration

Office of Price Administration (OPA), 196, 203, 236
Office of Production Management, 198
Office of the Petroleum Coordinator (OPC), 192–93, 197–203, 212–13, 217
Ohern, D. W., 115
Ohio, 4, 11, 17
Oil and Gas Journal, 207, 221, 263
Oil Code. *See* National Recovery Administration (NRA)
oil imports, 240–42
oil seep, 4, 32–33
Oklahoma, 14–22, 77, 80–82, 87, 113, 131, 140–141, 166, 188, 257; DeGolyer's early years, 10, 13–18, 21–22, 28; geophysical prospecting, 116, 121; martial law, 131, 181; oilfields, 16, 74, 81–82; Tonkawa field, 87
Oklahoma, University of, 19, 24, 90, 113, 115, 152, 259; DeGolyer commencement address, 156, 245; DeGolyer History of Science program, 167, 245, 257–59; DeGolyer's

education, 16, 19–21, 32, 58–60, 154; DeGolyer's graduation, 60
Oklahoma Corporation Commission, 181
OPA. *See* Office of Price Administration
OPC. *See* Office of the Petroleum Coordinator
Orchard Dome, Texas, 112, 120
Order M-68, 195
Osage Reservation, Oklahoma, 82, 87

Palestine, 223–24
Parker, Edward W., 5
Pauley, Edwin, 212, 216
PAW. *See* Petroleum Administration for War
Pearl Harbor attack, 159, 176, 193, 199, 203, 211
Pearson, Clive, 135
Pearson, Weetman. *See* Cowdray, W. D. Pearson, Lord
Peláez, Alfredo, 46
Peláez, Ignacio, 46
Peláez, Manuel, 46
PEMEX. *See* Petróleos Mexicanos
Pennsylvania, 3, 122; Bradford oilfield, 137
Peripatetic Press, 162
Persian Gulf, 224–26
Peru, 150
Pete Rec. *See* Petroleum Reclamation Corporation
Petróleos Mexicanos (PEMEX), 213, 215
Petroleum Administration for War (PAW), 165, 176, 201, 203–206, 208, 220, 231, 234
petroleum geology. *See* geology
Petroleum Industry War Council, 234
Petroleum Reclamation Corporation, 137
Petroleum Reserves Corporation (PRC), 207, 219–21, 225, 227–28, 249; Middle

Petroleum Reserves Corporation (*cont.*)
East pipeline project, 228–30; Middle
East Technical Mission, 221–27
Pew, J. Edgar, 229–30
Phillips, William Battle, 5
Pike, Sumner, 163, 236
Poe, E. Holley, 228, 231
Pogue, Joseph, 184–85, 189, 234
Pompton Plains, New Jersey, 142
Ponca City, Oklahoma, 116, 188
Porter, Earle, 83
Porter, H. J., 240–41
Porter, Phil, 261
Potrero del Llano oilfield, 38–39, 53–59,
70, 211
Poza Rica oilfield, 214–15
Pratt, Wallace, 143, 163, 246, 248, 250,
259
PRC. *See* Petroleum Reserves
Corporation
Princeton University, 156–57, 159
Prior, Ralph J., 163
prorationing. *See* regulation, pro-
rationing
prospecting. *See* exploration methods
*Prospector, The,* 1–2, 2
Prudhoe Bay, Alaska, 6–7

Qatar, 223

Rainey, Homer P., 167
Raw Materials Advisory Committee,
236, 250
Raymond, Rossiter W., 88
Reclamation Service, 27
regulation. *See* conservation and
regulation
Republican Party, 251, 253
Republic Natural Gas Company, 163,
249
Rice University, 257
Rockefeller, John D., 9, 40
Roller, Duane, 258

Roosevelt, Franklin D., 184, 188, 203,
207, 211–12, 223
Roosevelt, Theodore, 23
Rosaire, E. E., 119, 134
Royal Dutch Shell, 84, 104, 132, 185
Rycade Corporation, 118, 143
Ryder, Thomas J., 51, 81, 104–105, 138,
148

Sachs, Alexander, 189
salt domes, 4–5, 93–94, 98–108, 100–101,
110–112, 119, 148, 155
San Francisco, California, 221
Santa Anna, Antonio López de, 161,
170–171
Santa Fe, New Mexico, 162, 189
Saturday Review of Literature, 162–65,
245, 249, 256; Saturday Review of
Recordings, 163
Saudi Arabia, 207, 209, 218–19, 221, 223,
228
Scientific Manpower Advisory
Committee (SMAC), 250, 253
Scientists: and business, 8, 70–72, 87–
97, 174, 265; and conservation, 9, 175,
195, 206, 266
seismic exploration. *See* geophysical
exploration
Seismos Institute, 110–113, 116, 119–20
Shell Oil Company. *See* Royal Dutch
Shell
Simpson, K., 185
SMAC. *See* Scientific Manpower
Advisory Committee
Smith, Carl D., 27–28, 31
Smith, George Otis, 176
Smithsonian Institution, 260
Socal. *See* Standard Oil of California
Society of Economic Geophysicists.
*See* Society of Exploration
Geophysicists
Society of Exploration Geophysicists,
8, 119–20

Socony-Vacuum, 185, 221
Southern Methodist University, 157, 165, 257–58, 299n91
Southern Pacific Railroad, 33, 248
Southwestern Association of Petroleum Geologists. *See* American Association of Petroleum Geologists (AAPG)
Southwestern College, 18
Soviet Union. *See* Union of Soviet Socialist Republics
Spindletop oilfield, 3–8, 16, 34, 100, 105–107, 169, 251
Standard Oil Company of Indiana, 135–36, 185
Standard Oil of California (*see also* California-Arabian Standard Oil Company), 217, 219
Standard Oil of New Jersey, 33, 185, 221
Standard Oil of Venezuela, 143
Stassen, Harold, 251
Stephenson, David Perry, 142
Sterling, Ross, 181
Stewart, P. C. A., 103–104
Stewart, Walter, 159
Sun Oil Company, 229
Suss, Ferdinand, 104–105

Tampico, Mexico, 44, 49, 53, 56–57, 71, 77, 79, 90, 123, 141, 177; DeGolyer's impressions of, 42–43; Mexican Revolution, 64–66, 161; Mexican Technical Mission, 214; Tampico flag incident, 66–67
Taylor, Charles H., 90
Teapot Dome scandal, 39, 179
Texaco, 185, 219
Texas, 74, 80–81, 83, 91, 137, 148, 168–69, 174, 192, 200, 241; DeGolyer relocaiton to, 142; DeGolyer relocation to, 140–141; DeGolyer's arrival in Galveston, 73; East Texas oilfield, 130, 145, 181, 197–98, 241; geophysical prospecting, 98, 105; martial law, 131, 181; oil regulation, 182, 186–87; salt domes, 101; Spindletop oilfield, 3–8, 16, 34, 100, 105–107, 169, 251
Texas Eastern Transmission Corporation, 230–231, 242, 244, 249; Big Inch and Little Inch Pipelines, 230–231
Texas Independent Producers and Royalty Owners Association (TIPROA), 240
Texas Railroad Commission (TRC), 181–82, 186–87, 198, 201–202
Texas, University of, 5, 115, 151–53, 155, 157, 159, 167, 220
Thomas, Elmer, 90
Thompson, Ernest O., 186–87, 189, 192, 196, 201–202, 293n78
Thornburg, Max, 212
Tierra Amarilla oilfield, 45–48, 53
Tinkle, Lon, ix-x, 165
TIPROA. *See* Texas Independent Producers and Royalty Owners Association
Tonkawa oilfield, 87
topographic maps, 28–33, 46–48, 54, 58, 77, 102, 107, 116, 126, 177–78
TRC. *See* Texas Railroad Commission
Trinity College (Hartford, Connecticut), 156–57, 232
Truman, Harry S., 244
Tulane University, 157
*Tulsa Tribune,* 183
Tuxpan, Mexico, 44, 49–50, 53, 55, 61, 214

Udden, Anton, 115
Union of Soviet Socialist Republics, 232–33, 241, 250
Union Oil Company, 33, 118
United States Geological Survey (USGS), 5, 22, 30–31, 34, 43, 59–60,

United States Geological Survey (*cont.*) 73–74, 98, 175–76, 184, 221–22; DeGolyer's work for, 22–24, 26–28, 31–32; early history, 23
United States Supreme Court, 186
unitization, 179–81, 191–92, 196, 203–204
USGS. *See* United States Geological Survey

Valdebro, 249
Van Deman, Ralph H., 177
Varnell, Tom, 14
Vaught, Edgar S., 15, 273n24
Veatch, A. C., 84
Venezuela, 150, 209
Veracruz, Mexico, 41–42, 59, 66–68, 70, 74, 80, 177
Villa, Francisco "Pancho," 63, 77

Walcott, Charles D., 23
War Production Board (WPB), 203, 213
Washburne, Chester W., 43, 123–24

Washington, D.C., 9, 42, 73, 116, 176, 235–36, 261; DeGolyer's USGS work in, 28, 31–32; DeGolyer's World War II service in, 193, 199, 205, 215
Washington University, 105, 157
Weaver, Paul, 79, 81, 100–101
White, I. C., 33
White, David, 98
Wiechert, Emil, 110
Willkie, Wendell, 192, 251
Wilson, Woodrow, 66–67, 177–78, 211
Woodruff, Elmer Grant, 24, 28–31, 33, 154
Wooster, L.C., 18
World War I, 75–76, 84, 175–78, 193, 199, 205, 209, 211, 217, 266
World War II, 159, 162, 175–76, 186, 192–93, 199, 203–206, 211, 216, 218, 230, 266
WPB. *See* War Production Board
Wrather, W. E., 221

Zapata, Emiliano, 63
Zaragoza (Mexican general), 66